Yesterday's Enemy

ÅFGHÅN INTERIM GOVERNMENT
Public Health Ministry

The Health Ministry of the Afghan Interim Government wishes to show its appreciation to Dr. Rupert Chetwynd for contribution of Medical Aid to the Afghan people in their time of greatest need.

N. Mujaddidi

Dr. Najibullah Mujaddidi

First Deputy Minister of

Public Health, AIG.

دولت اسلامی افغانستان

وزارت صحت عامه

وزارت صحت عامه حکومت اسلامی افغانستان
مراتب امتنان خود را به تشبیت
سهیم نمودنهای طبی که به مردم افغانستان نموده اند ابراز
می دارد.

S. F. Rabbani

دوکتور سید فضل الربانی

رئیس طب معالجوی وزارت صحت عامه

Rupert Chetwynd

Yesterday's Enemy

FREEDOM FIGHTERS
OR TERRORISTS?

Rupert Chetwynd

IMPALA

Published by
Impala
(International Media Publication and Literary Associates) Ltd
Registered Office:
c/o Davenport Lyons
30 Old Burlington Street
London W1S 3NL

Edited by Ray Keene, O.B.E. of *The Times*
Photography Peter Stiles and Adam Pensotti
Design Patrick Smith

Der Spiegel 44, 1988 article © Der Spiegel 1988,
translated by Dr John Sugden, formerly St Johns College, Cambridge

Photograph on page 64 © Gerhard Stromberg 2005
Photographs on pages 67, 91, 101, 130, 135, 155, 158, 187, 192, 194,
196, 269 © Peter Stiles FRCS 2005
Photograph on page 151 © Rupert Chetwynd 2005
Photograph on page 153 © Dittmar Hack 2005
Photograph on page 302 © Melissa Gibbs 2005
Photograph on page 453 © Duke of Valderano 2005

IMPALA logo design by Barry Martin © Impala 2005

First published April 2005
Reprinted with corrections May 2005

ISBN 0 9549943 0 2 Paperback
ISBN 0 9549943 1 0 Hardback

To Robert,
The Most Hon., The Most Noble The Marquess of Salisbury PC DL,
Chairman, Afghan Support Committee,
Chairman, AfghanAid,
who first introduced me to Afghanistan,

and to
Peter Stiles Esq., Fellow of The Royal College of Surgeons,
Committee member, Sandy Gall Afghanistan Committee,
Committee member and Trustee, *Afghanconnection*
(Dr Sarah Fane's charity), who made my
exposure so thoroughly worthwhile.

Contents

Part 1 - Foreign Bodies

Part 2 - The Enemy Within

Part 3 - A Conspiracy of Silence

Introduction
by Sandy Gall

Rupert Chetwynd is a man of many parts: soldier, advertising maestro who once had hundreds of minions at his beck and call, *paterfamilias*, clubman and traveller extraordinary who, rather late in life, decided to take Afghanistan under his wing. That is only a brief and inevitably inadequate thumb-nail sketch. For example, under 'soldier' read Grenadier, Guards Parachute Pathfinder Company, and member of 'The Regiment', the insider's appellation for 21 Special Air Service, better known as the SAS. Those activities in themselves would seem to be quite enough to be going on with, never mind all the other antics he has got up to, and continues to get up to. Digging deeper you come across a variety of *persona* such as stockbroker with De Zoete & Gorton, Butlin's Camp Manager, carbon paper salesman and then, rocketing up the charts, consultant to Boeing.

Rupert grew up with a weight on his shoulders: the legacy of the First World War, which had wiped out the cream of British manhood. In an attempt to replace this lost generation, he says, he was originally destined for the Royal Naval College at Dartmouth - his great-grandfather and grandfather were both sailors, the latter inventing the non-magnetic compass and providing Erskine Childers with the model for Carruthers, the hero of *The Riddle in the Sands*, the first spy thriller. Rupert remembers staying with the Childers family* in Dublin, one consquence being his induction later into the secret world of Carruthers. in between he found time to travel to Moscow, Warsaw, Canton, Hanoi and of course Afghanistan.

It was in 1984 that he first put on his walking boots to visit the Hindu Kush. His motivation was as always *wanderlust* but also charitable. Then in 2000 he joined some other old warriors taking money, medicines and moral support from Badakhstan, in the wild north-east of Afghanistan, over the Anjuman Pass to Rokha in the Panjsher Valley. In 2003 he rose at 5 every morning and was first off on a sponsored walk for Sandy Gall's Afghanistan Appeal. And now, in *Yesterday's Enemy*, he takes us into the wilderness of Afghanistan at war, in true Carruthers style.

Erskine Childers II, the 'Son of the Riddle' went on to become the first Anglo-Irish President of Eire.

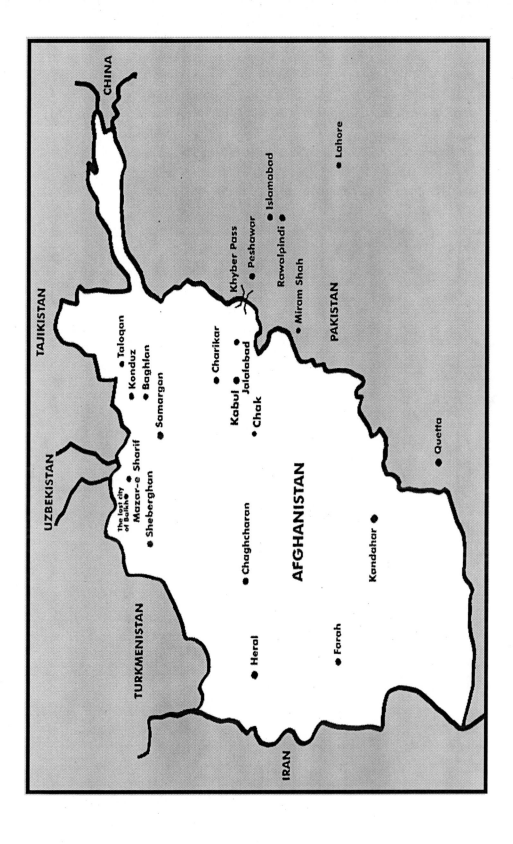

List of Illustrations

Acknowledgements

Twenty years ago now, the late Norman Reddaway, of The Foreign & Commonwealth Office, invited me along to address The Romilly Street Club over a sandwich lunch at The Athenaeum. The subject was to be Afghanistan and Peter Stiles kindly agreed to bring along a carousel of his colour slides. The audience was made up mostly of top civil servants plus my wife. All seemed wholly unmoved. However we learned later that the Secretary, a Mr Terry Price I recall, had minuted that mine had been the most stimulating address since Alcock & Brown. One could only wonder what had intervened, besides WWII. Norman added that there was the promise of a good book in the making... Up until then, the only consistent writing I had done was regular monthly reports for The Boeing Company in Seattle. The subject was defined as geo-political overview, which translates as best-guessing the future, with, in Boeing's case a twenty year view! Consequently, the first draft of this book was written as a matter of record, very much as the events unfolded. I should perhaps disclose that both my mother and brother were established authors and had often told me "to get on with it!" Indeed my mother's ghost still haunts my bedside to chide me...

The next good fairy however, was David Malouf, who kindly showed me how to begin the book. He told me it was often the trickiest part, requiring as many as ten attempts. "Why not begin with the bl--dy bank manager?" he advised. So I did.

Roger Schlesinger came next. A life-long friend and brother of John, who was already a most experienced publisher, Indeed he had published a number of my wife's children's books. Roger has given me more encouragement and more of his time than anybody else. Imagine the patience in coping with an initial half million words! Not only did he enable me to reduce these to 186,000, without bloodshed, but it was he who counselled that no publisher was going to look at the book until I could prove the allegations made.

I have been blessed with unlimited access to prime source material. Firstly the reports of the Royal Surrey County Hospital, Guildford Medical Team members were freely circulated. Next, Dr Sarah Fane entrusted her elective year report to Peter Stiles and myself. There could not be a fresher or more vivid description of Dr Ruth Coggan and the William Penell Memorial Hospital scene at Bannu.

I am also, as with so much else, deeply indebted to my old commanding officer of more than fifty years ago, Brigadier Peter Stewart-Richardson MBE for allowing me to make extensive use of his eye-witness accounts of momentous events I did not see for myself. Likewise, I must thank his friend Lt.Col Brian Rae, OBE for permission to plagiarise extracts from his excellent account "Return to Kabul".

Above all, it was David C. Isbey of Freedom House whose book "War in a Distant Country" that helped to confirm what little I thought I understood of a complex subject, plus a whole lot more that I had patently failed to grasp. John Fullerton also wrote a masterly book in the early stages after the arrival of the Russians, which was an invaluable help. However, the real heavyweights remain Olivier Roy and Louis Dupree.

Photographs matter and I have been most fortunate in having a free run of Dominique Vergos's collection of 15,000 slides, Karla Schefter's more modest but outstanding collection of 2,000 colour slides and more germane to this story, Peter Stiles's vast collection. Photographs are invaluable memory triggers.

Special thanks are due to the late Charles Berges of Vermont, a sophisticated American who joined up with our team at an early stage to offer his most welcome physiotherapy skills. He subsequently offered to undertake a number of research assignments on my behalf in the USA. A published historian himself, he wrote continuously to badger and encourage me "to get on with it".

Of course there have been knockers too. There are said to be too many proper and place names for the average reader. I cannot help that, Try "War & Peace"! There, the names even change by the chapter. After all, it is only the convenience of fiction that allows characters to appear, disappear and reappear at the author's whim. Real life is not like that. It is not a game of consequences, or, at least, not in my experience.

Prominent among the proof-readers have been Juliet Peck and Peter Stiles. Never much good at taking criticism, I have to admit that all their suggestions, modifications and amendments were entirely valid and have been effected without too much "doctoring"- my euphemism for castrating the beast. Others, to whom the whole text was submitted for comment, sometimes surprised me with their brevity. Colin C Mitchell: " It is both witty and informative". Brigadier Peter Stewart-Richardson: "It is your duty to see this thing through to the end, and you are not to let *me* down!" Special thanks are also due to Edmund Launert and his wife Jean for their painstaking translation of the German Court Proceedings.

It would be an act of gross ingratitude if I were not to close in thanking my wife, Luciana Arrighi for affording me board, lodging and all the time in the world to isolate myself in order to undertake such a mammoth task. Unless, it also happened, at the time, to be a most convenient way to be rid of me!

R.C., Paris, 2005

Dramatis Personae

Germans in Afghanistan

Dr Reinhard and Annette Erös
Dr Victor Freigang
Nurse Karla Schefter
Peter Forster - works for UN

Saints

Juliet Crawley Vergos Peck
Ruth Coggan OBE
Mary Macmakin
Dr Sarah Fane

Whistle Blowers

Kate Straub at Chak
Leotard Bleifrei - codename for Chetwynd's mole in German Foreign Ministry,
Bonn

German Afghanistan Committee and related organisations

Denny Hundeshagen
Dietrich, Andrea and Willi Kantel
Andrea Hörst
Kakojan Niazi
Ahmed Jan
Rashid brothers
Dr Nassery
Maria Mueller
Thomas Gaida

Political and Intelligence Contacts

18th Duke of Valderano *aka* Ronnie Waring
Jurgen Todenhofer
Michael Sagurna

Guildford Surgical Team and their supporters

Peter Stiles
Rupert Chetwynd (admin)
Brigadier General P.N.J. ""Scrubber"" Stewart-Richardson MBE (admin)
Anwar Chaudhri
John Stoneham
Frank Schweitzer
Tony Bray
Robin Jago
Charles Berges, Esq., (attached American physiotherapist)

Journalists

Sandy Gall, C.B.E.
Dittmar Hack
Christoph Hörstel

Pakistani and Afghan officials and doctors

Pir Mohammed, Security in Charge
Abdul Haq, friend of Mrs Thatcher
Abdul Haq - a guide
Zia-ul-Haq, the President of Pakistan
Dr Abdul Satar Paktiss - initially successful but had his equipment looted
Ali Jan - local official i/c transport
Tariq Mahmood, "TM" Brigadier i/c Pakistani Special Forces

Mujahedeen

Engineer Gulbuddin Hekmatyar - a particularly nasty specimen given to rocketing his own side - leader of Hesbe-i-Islami faction - now alive and well and living in tribal areas.

Jalaluddin Haqqanni - his men provided an escort for the team in hazardous areas, subsequently enrolled as mainstay team member, Al Quaida

Ahmed Shah Masoud - Afghanistans most renowned guerilla leader. He was martyred two days before 9/11. Our wake-up call. The Lion of the Panjshir.

Supportive Brits

Sir Nicholas Barrington, High Commissioner Pakistan
Sir Oliver Forster, formerly High Commissioner Pakistan,
Director of London-based Afghanistan Support Committee
Sarah Forster
Colonel Colin Mitchell, founder of HALO (Hazardous Areas Logistical
Organisation), possibly the world's leading mine clearing organisation.
Charles Douglas-Home, Editor of *The Times*

Doctors

Dr Kermit Veggeberg, Director of Orthopaedics Overseas
- USA charity operating world-wide
Dr Markus Thonius, ICRC
Dr Chris Giannou, ICRC

Men at Afghan Surgical
Dr Sayed Iftikhar Hussain
Dr Faisal Rabbani
Firdos Khan

President of Afghanistan on Russian withdrawal, and afterwards for two years

President Najibullah

President of Afghanistan thereafter

Dr Burnuhuddin Rabbani - he disastrously clung onto power beyond his term.

Innocent American bystanders with access to huge funding - approached at various times by German Afghanistan Committee

Dr Alan Sabroski
General Milner Roberts
Anne Hurd
Phyllis Oakley
Antony L. Campaigne
Ms. Millikan - her request for detailed info from the German Afghanistan
Committee probably led directly to the writing of the "Potemkin" hospitals
brochure.

Glossary

Afghani the currency, *not* the people, who are Afghans

Afghanwali code of conduct for Afghans

Baksheesh backhander, bribe

BCE Before Current Era

burqa ladies' head-to-toe purdah garment

buzkashi an Afghan game occasionally played by Pathans, the ball and sticks replacing the headless goat and lead-lined whips of the Tadjiks and Uzbeks.

caravanserai overnight enclosure where caravan trains could put up for security

CE Current Era

chaff window, anti ground-to-air missile measure

chaikhana teahouse with meals and accommodation often available

Chak-e-Wardak DAK "Potemkin" hospital

chapan national costume

chapli extra stout sandals, often made of old car tyre sections

charpayee wooden frame bed with legs and string lattice stretched overall *charpoy*

chawdor ladies headscarf

chowkidar gatekeeper, usually armed

DAF/GAF Deutsche Afghanistan Foundation, German Afghanistan Foundation

DAK/GAC Deutsches Afghanistan Komitee, German Afghanistan Committee

DM Deutsch Mark

dobi-wala laundryman - derived from family name of British India Army operators

dupattas hair decoration

Eid -ul- Adha Muslim festival marking end of the Pilgrimage to Mecca

faranghi, ferenghi foreigner

Grand Multip woman with four or more previous pregnancies and deliveries

Haji someone who has made the pilgrimage to Mecca

jellaba kaftan, cloak

Jihad Holy War / common cause

KHAD Kabul, Russian regime established, Afghan secret service

lhassi yoghurt drink (Arabic)

Loya Jirga national assembly.

majlis open assembly of village elders

muerta a mafia-like oath of silence

mujahedeen Holy Warrior

MT metric tonnes, or at times, Mechanical Transport

naswar supposedly mild (green) narcotic pouched in cheek, rots gums

pakool hat made famous by Ahmed Shah Massoud

paramedics in Afghan context, barefoot doctors

Parachinar "parrots beak" place name, resembling such on map

Pashtu language of Pashtuns (British: Pathans) of Afghanistan and North West Frontier Province Pakistan

Pashtunwali, pachtunwali code of conduct for Pashtuns.

patoo all purpose blanket

Pol-e-Charkhi notorious prison outside Kabul

Pye Dog ownerless half-wild mongrel dog, common around Asian villages.

qasaki traditional Afghan guerilla warfare hit-and-run tactic

Sadda DAK "Potemkin" hospital

serai shortened version of caravanserai; especially along "Silk Route" staging posts

shaheed holy martyr, who perforce died in battle

sharia law literal interpretation of Koranic stricture

shalwar kamees pyjama like apparel, ideal for heat and dust

shora, shura, shoora assembly, council

souk market

sura any of the chapters from the Koran

tonga, tonka horse drawn buggy

trishaw motor cycle engined two seater taxi, plus driver

tut, toot dried mulberrries, a winter standby which generates a lot of energy

wadi valley or cut

"Worry"beads prayer or rosary beads

Chronology and Key Dates

4th century BCE Alexander the Great conquers Afghanistan

632 CE Muhammad the Prophet dies and tide of Islamic conquest begins

7th century Afghanistan converts to Islam

1219 Genghis Khan conquers Afghanistan

1838-1842 First British v Afghan War

1878-80 Second Afghan War

1919 Third Afghan War

1979 December Russians invade Afghanistan on Christmas Eve

1979 onwards - Six million refugees created. Up to 15 million land mines sown. Mujahedeen Freedom Fighters oppose Red Army with weapons supplied by USA. Very many pro-Afghan charities set up world wide.

German Afghanistan Committee GAC is amongst these - genesis 1982 in Bonn; originally constituted as Bonn Afghanistan Committee

1984-1985 German Afghanistan Committee - whilst maintaining an outward show of great activity on the Afghanistan charitable front- secretly begins to milk the German public, siphoning off charitable donations for its own purposes.

British guerilla warfare and anti terror specialist the Duke of Valderano advocates use of Stinger missiles against Russian aircraft and helicopters in Afghan war. He facilitates access (from 1984) to these via his *protégé* Kakokan Niazi. The Stingers turn out to be the key weapon in the defeat of the Russian army. However, 194 missiles, unaccounted for and unused are believed to be still (2004) in the hands of radical Islamic militia groups.

1985 Rupert Chetwynd and Guildford Surgical Team first travel to Pakistan to help the war wounded on a voluntary basis

1986 Maria Müller addresses Bundestag / German Parliament on behalf of German Afghanistan Committee - high point of public reputation in Germany of GAC.

1988 German Afghanistan Committee makes contact with USA sponsors - Creation of deluxe *Potemkin Hospitals* brochure by GAC, as a result of which millions of dollars flow in from American sources

British team offer to assist efforts of GAC having no idea as yet that they are a front for criminal activities

Der Spiegel article appears in German attacking GAC. This article is reprinted in full as an Appendix to this book.

1989 February 15th Russians withdraw from Afghanistan.

1989 Pro-communist regime of President Najibullah remains in power in Kabul. Berlin wall demolished.

1989-1991 Guildford surgeons attempt to expand their efforts into Afghanistan. Efforts made in specific areas by German Afghanistan Committee to discourage British team from inspecting their much vaunted 'model hospital' at Chak.

1991 USSR collapses and ceases to exist.

1992 Najibullah pro-Russia regime in Kabul overthrown by Mujahedeen freedom fighters.

1992-1996 Civil war in Afghanistan.

1992 October Brigadier Peter Stewart-Richardson visits Chak.

1992 Kate Straub, a British charity volunteer under the protection of the Brigadier, discovers conspiracy to defraud funds and smuggle heroin and trade in arms by the GAC during a visit by GAC CEO Denny Hundeshagen to Chak.

Serious falling out between GAC and their local accomplices the Rashid brothers.

1993 German Committee dissolves amidst a flurry of suppressed lawsuits.

1994 Rupert Chetwynd's subsequent investigations in Bonn and Hamburg provide firm evidence of the nefarious activities of the GAC. Chetwynd discovers clear links between GAC and Kakokan Niazi.

Chetwynd confronts the 18th Duke of Valderano; poses direct questions re arms dealing and heroin running in relation to GAC and Kajokan Niazi.

1996 Fanatical Islamic Fundamentalists, the Taliban, seize control in Kabul.

2001 Al Quaida terrorist attack on Twin Towers inspired by Osama bin Laden based in Afghanistan and nourished by the Taliban.

2002 USA invades Afghanistan and overthrows Taliban.

2003 USA invades Iraq and overthrows Saddam Hussain.

2004 Al Quaida Bombing in Madrid.

Osama bin Laden targets become the most popular in Las Vegas shooting galleries, overtaking Saddam Hussain.

2004 July Washington Congressional Report outlines numerous failings in war against Islamic terrorism.

2004 August *Sunday Times* newspaper, London directly accuses Tony Blair's British government of allowing cheap Afghan heroin to 'flood into Britain' for political reasons.

2005 April Frontline Club, London - launch of *Yesterday's Enemy*.

Remember that the happiness of his humble home, remember that the sanctity of life in the hill villages of Afghanistan, among the winter snows, is as inviolable in the eyes of Almighty God as can be in your own!

William Ewart Gladstone (1809-1898)
British Liberal Statesman and four times Prime Minister

One Afghan on a donkey is worth four Russians in a tank.

General Alexander Lebed,
Commander of the Russian force which invaded Afghanistan

You will see - not a soul will reach here from Kabul except one man, who will come to tell us the rest are destroyed.

Colonel Dennie 13th Light Infantry,
writing in 1841 of the British occupation of Kabul
in the First Afghan War

The greatest disaster and disgrace which our arms ever suffered, shaking this Empire to its very foundation, lowering the prestige of British invincibility, elevating the hopes of our enemies and loading the finances of the state with 30 millions of debt.

Viscount Hardinge of Lahore,
Governor General of India,
July 24, 1847, on the First war
between Afghanistan and the British Empire.

Prince Grigori Alexandrovich Potemkin was the favourite and lover of the Russian Empress Catherine the Great. In 1787 the Empress made a royal tour of the recently conquered southern regions of the Russian Empire, now under the control of the Prince. From this time dates the story that he lined her route with staged villages, featuring hired villagers, beaming with health, happiness and loyalty to the Empire. Since then such bogus artifices have gone by the name *Potemkin Villages.*

Preface

One of the early lessons of the war launched by the USSR against Afghanistan in 1979, or indeed any Afghan war, was that things were rarely what they seemed to be and hardly ever what they were said to be. Even the border lines wandered between 'tribal areas' buffer states and the vagaries of transhumance. For the Pakistani Government, the massive programme of humanitarian aid (US $5 billion ex-Saudi and USA) to the world's largest ever refugee population (5 million) was their most legitimate source of hard currency earnings - said to be second only to heroin. It didn't take Rudyard Kipling's master spy and super observer 'Kim' to recognise that the self-same army lorries used to transport all that refugee aid and military hardware on the back haul up the Grand Trunk Road were busy shipping 'tribal areas' heroin out through the Karachi docks. Supposedly empty, they were the only vehicles exempted from the innumerable high profile Drugs Enforcement Agency (DEA) road blocks. Then, the American Government was not so much engaged in helping the Afghans (no money, no votes) as punishing the Russians.

This is a first-hand account of how an altruistic British medical mission, with no hidden agenda, accidentally stumbled on the revelation that the party-political 'cottage hospital' where they were operating on war casualties, was simultaneously a conduit for Saudi and Kuwaiti middle-class funding for 'illegal' fundamentalist political activity. They were investing long-term in the expectation of re-importing less autocratic Home Rule, either by osmosis or backlash.

Long before the pot had time to call the kettle black, it transpired that another establishment to be succoured by the British medical team, in league with the German Afghanistan Committee and Orthopaedics Overseas, was not only cover for arms for drugs traffic, but also the subject of tear-jerking alms raising from the German Government, the European Community and the ever-generous, if gullible, German general public. Grants and donations were then systematically plundered long before they had a chance of leaving Germany. Conversely, large quantities of medicines, donated by manufacturers, were shipped to Karachi or Islamabad, where, with creative accounting, they could either be sold on or bought in, according to prevailing market conditions.

Whilst adopting the position of innocent bystanders, the Americans applied their stock solution of throwing money at the problem, without necessarily knowing where it was going, nor having the means of checking if it ever got there, since Afghanistan was officially off limits to them. One such dream project was to fund an internal refugee re-settlement programme destined for one of the world's most desolate and dangerous places, Baghlan, with next to no chance of ground truth verification. For this purpose, the State Department elected to entrust US $1.4 million to these same German Afghan aid industry operators in recognition of their known expertise on the ground. These war swindlers were the only people in a position to check themselves out and were now poised to milk large sums to their own ends, with no call for accountability. All the Americans required of them was 'advocacy', meaning propaganda, not accountability.

The book discloses how this racket, together with another known as the 'by-pass operation', was facilitated by its very clandestine nature. Not content with being the best paid politicians in Europe, this practice was to reach the highest levels of the Bonn political *élite*.

On a more positive note, the book tells of the outstanding contribution made by some exceptional expatriate women in their war effort for a society not renowned for honouring their sex. The story is embellished with humorous anecdote, since, at the time, humour went hand-in-hand with survival.

Part 1
Foreign Bodies

1

Banking on my help

In theory I used to work to a day-sheet 'organiser', which had space to demand 'action this day' for as many as thirty-six pieces of entrepreneurial trivia. Any leftovers would be carried forward to the top of the next day's list, ad infinitum. So two items on today's menu constituted very light duties indeed.

My first obligation was to see the bank manager, yet again on a 'personal' matter. When was it not a personal matter, I wondered? The other item on the agenda was a pleasant surprise - it was an altogether unexpected invitation to breakfast with the then Editor of *The Times*, Charles Douglas-Home.

The bank was in Hammersmith. To reach the manager gave the impression of going aboard some eighteenth-century man o'war. The gun deck was reached by an internal gangway. Access to the wardroom was heavily guarded with coded door locks. I wondered if the numbers were changed daily. As the door opened, the decibel count shot up, as if hit by a ghetto-blaster on the Underground.

Far sooner than expected, the manager himself appeared. His name was Bill Stokoe. His father had been a general manager in one of the joint stock banks and Bill had ambitions in that direction too. Clearly he was earmarked for top management. He was always, and genuinely, extremely pleasant, with the most natural good manners and that essential talent of putting you immediately at your ease, however grave the matter in hand.

Everything had seemed so cut and dried, at our last meeting little more than a week ago, that I wondered what could have caused him to call me back so soon. Anyway, here he was, beaming as always, a big-boned man with his large hand outstretched in greeting.

'Thank you for looking in. I hope I haven't dragged you out of your way. Strictly speaking, I should have called this meeting on neutral ground but the last thing I wanted to do was to cause alarm by calling at your office. What I am about to ask you has nothing to do with bank business. You can see what life is like in this branch - hectic, overloaded and understaffed. We are always pushed for time. Do you mind if we perch in here?'

He led the way into some kind of secretarial cubby-hole, one better than the broom cupboard. I could not imagine what was coming next, but we had hardly sat down, both on the same side of the pokey little desk, when he came out with it.

'Over the years we have known each other, I have picked up some idea of what you do. Rushed demands for telegraphic transfers to Grindlays, Peshawar, speak volumes to someone like me. So I have been wondering if you might be willing to extend a helping hand to my wife, Anne?'

I am seldom taken completely by surprise, but this was not a question one expected to be asked by one's bank manager. However, before I could utter, he recovered himself and explained that his wife was a voluntary worker at the Royal Surrey County Hospital, near their home in Guildford. Her part-time job consisted in looking after an enterprising Pakistani gentleman with the improbable sounding title of 'Associated Orthopaedic Specialist'.

Bill Stokoe helped me to digest that mouthful by explaining that the National Health Service was now riddled with status concerns. Anyway, Anne's job was on the administrative side, principally attending to the needs of this specialist, whose name was Anwar Chaudhri. He was billed as 'part of that backbone from the sub-continent, without which the Health Service would collapse'. Anwar had come to England from Lahore some sixteen years earlier. He had married an English wife, the daughter of an Anglican priest. He had taken British citizenship. They had a daughter. Confusingly, his wife was also called Anne. In all my years I had never met an Indian doctor in England, although there were said to be some 14,000, but in my mind's eye I could only see Peter Sellers.

Apparently, Anwar Chaudhri had succeeded in motivating a group of surgeons and their support team into volunteering their holidays to go and treat the wounded Mujahedeen in the North West Frontier Province of Pakistan. It was 1987 and there was a war on there. The Russians had invaded Afghanistan over Christmas 1979. Substantial sums of money had already been banked, raised by Anwar and his colleagues from all the usual local sources - Rotary, Round Table, Lions, church groups, on the knocker, whatever. It had been agreed that any shortfall would be made up from the team's own resources, meaning their own pockets. I couldn't see the snag, nor, for the life of me, why they needed me.

Bill's wife had come home one evening in an agitated state. She had not expressed this in so many words, but began by castigating the whole British race in general and the current government in particular. With the best will in the world, Guildford had put together a superb surgical team, capable of going anywhere and operating in almost any conditions, dedicated to helping the Afghan freedom fighters at no cost to the government. All the government had done in response was to discourage them by warning that it might be unwise because it could turn out to be an unproductive waste of time. No sooner would they be organised than it would be time to come home, with nothing achieved and, no doubt, with untold and unnecessary anxieties for HMG.

I was now beginning to see what might be expected of me. Mention had been made of the 'powers that be'. So, I asked Bill if he could give me some precise idea of who was being referred to. He could not, but from the finality of the thumbs down, he assumed it could only be the Foreign & Commonwealth Office. They had told the Guildford team to forget the whole idea.

I had three immediate questions to ask. What were the existing contacts, if any, in Pakistan? Was the operation to be based in Lahore? How long was the team proposing to stay? Bill had no clear answer for any of them, but promised to ask his wife.

I then jabbed somewhat below the belt. There was always the chance that somebody had done a smear job, suggesting the whole idea was some kind of jaunt - a joyride in the cause of medical tourism. In which case they could find themselves in for a bit of a shock!

Bill assured me there could be no question of that. He knew all the parties concerned. Most of them had worked together for fifteen years or more. In addition, they had been battle-hardened by the Guildford bomb back in 1974. Then, they had had to cope with over sixty simultaneous casualties. They were simply not frivolous people; indeed, they took themselves desperately seriously.

There was a pause. Bill then asked me, point-blank, would I be prepared to take an interest and maybe shepherd them along, where others so far had failed? Now that I realised Bill was not about to demand the immediate repayment of all the money the bank had so rashly pressed on me without security, I, equally rashly, said I should be happy to meet his wife and the Guildford team and that we could take it from there.

He said he would get Anne to give me a ring. Rather than do that and add to the confusion in my office, I asked him instead to give me her number. I explained that I was also due to go away again.

Bill seemed to take notes, but he was actually listing his wife's telephone numbers. He handed me one of those meticulously annotated slips of paper one imagines bankers using to record the overnight money market rates. I placed it in my pocket diary, where it fitted a treat.

Guildford Surgical team including Shaiq, Peter Stiles, John Stoneham and Iqbal

Photo taken by RC in Taramangal Gap

2
The Times Takes an Interest

Breakfast with the Editor of *The Times*, Charles Douglas-Home, proved an altogether different occasion, but it also related to Afghanistan. I remembered feeling twinges of early morning resentment as I headed off for Belgravia. Surely, I said to myself, any influence-peddler worth his salt dines with the Editor of *The Times*, in sufficient time to catch the late editions. The early editions would be put to bed around 9 p.m. I would coincide with the paper's delivery.

The compensation was the Caledonian Club venue, as if there were some need of Charlie's to emphasise his Scottishness. In fact, he explained that people there, if they knew who he was or cared, had the good manners not to bother him. I had known and liked Charlie since he had been made Defence Correspondent of *The Times*. Also his sister was a friend of my stepmother, and our wives also knew each other professionally. However, once set in motion, our collision course had accelerated, as so often happens to a point where it seemed we should never stop meeting.

He had undoubtedly heard of my latest Afghanistan excursions, more than likely from his step-brother Christopher Wills. We had each been told to expect the other out there. There was no mistaking Christopher. At the time, there was a dearth of Englishmen anyway, but he was a figure distinguished by sporting those ragged-edged, Bermuda-length khaki drill shorts which might have begun life as trousers. He and I had collided in Rawalpindi, and then in Peshawar, where he introduced me first to some of the less obvious but highly relevant embassy people, and then to the essential key to the Pakistani Ministry of Tribal Affairs, Jamshid Burki.

Charlie Douglas-Home told me that Christopher had brought back a mass of black and white photographs of the Afghan War, some of which he was planning to use. Most of them graphically illustrated the effects of high-altitude bombing on the civilian population. What he now required, and was apparently looking to me to supply, was half a dozen articles of two or three thousand words each, on such topics as

The Russian point-of-view. What had they stood to gain over the past eighteen months?

Why should their adventure prove any more successful than former British punitive expeditions?

The Mujahedeen response.

The missing factor, or Pakistani ambivalence.
Finally, *American inertia with an election year looming.*

All this was way above my head. I reminded Charlie that I had not filed copy as a journalist in thirty years. Undaunted, he continued by telling me that 'we' seemed to be faced with a media black hole, if not a media black-out. We needed more journalists of international repute prepared to risk going to Afghanistan for longer than it took to be photographed in native costume while gazing across a Russian-dominated landscape. It was, undeniably, a photographer's war.

In order not to be entirely negative, I mentioned one or two people who might supply what he was after if he could accept French or German text. He said he would be only too happy to do so and it was agreed that I should pass the word.

He wanted to know if I had run into Sandy Gall of ITN or Nigel Ryan of Channel Four. I said as far as I knew they had both been in the Panjshir in the north east of Afghanistan, which I had not. This brought us naturally to television and comparisons with the 'living-room' war, Vietnam.

Here I did have a valid contribution to make. I thought I understood why it was no easy matter to make undetected satellite transmissions from within Afghanistan. I had not only worked peripherally on behalf of Advance Warning and Control Systems (AWACS) in Australia; I had also played a small part in getting some freelance cameramen paid a proper rate by the American media. This in turn brought me into contact with the United States Information Agency (USIA) as well as our own Central Office of Information (COI). As the Americans put it, 'all yer needed to broadcast live was to walk in a sack of cement.' For some as yet unexplained reason, nobody wanted to crank this war up that much. Obviously they were content to let it fester at the current level of hostilities.

Knowing that I was part American, Charlie next wanted to know if I could recommend an outsider to him, somebody to mark his card for his forthcoming visit to see President Reagan. I began to suspect this could be the real reason behind his asking me to breakfast.

Firstly, we roughed out between us the likely stepping stones Charlie would take, as he went through the Washington maze, on his way to meet Mr President. It was sure to be a well-established route by now, via such notables as Jean Kirkpatrick, Senator David Patrick Moynihan, Senator Charlie Wilson, 'Little John' Tower, Senator Tsongas and no doubt countless others. Then I told the Editor he should look out for Reagan's bandleader friend Wicks, who currently headed up the USIA. It was he who proffered authentic pictures of Russian tanks running down Afghan kids; plus photographs of lethal butterfly bombs that blew off their arms and legs to stop them running away.

After thinking it over some more, I told Charles I might just know somebody who could help him sort the political Hollywood hype from the State Department action pad. However, I warned him that my candidate was an old-timer, a crypto-Brit, who had made his reputation early in life, reporting on Hitler's war for Beaverbrook with the immunity of an American passport as each succeeding European city had capitulated. Not surprisingly, he had been recruited to 'Wild' Bill Donovan's staff at the Office of Strategic Services (OSS). On the basis of last out, first back, he had staged a pre-D-Day invasion all his own.

In post-war career terms he had taken much the same soft option as Colonel Maurice Buckmaster of 'F' Group and had become a press and public relations adviser to Henry Ford, Howard Geeneen, and other such tyrants. He knew the traps well. Charlie said he liked the sound of him, so I told him his name - William Sydney Morrell.

I promised that if Charlie gave me his flight details, 'Bill' Morrell would come out to the airport to meet him as a matter of course. When asked how Charlie would recognise him, I said that, by now, the air-conditioning and iced water had so got to him that he had one of those grey india-rubber American faces that were so malleable you could squidge it into almost any pasty shape you chose, so long as you stuffed the putty under a porkpie hat. I then told Charlie some more about Bill Morrell's contribution on the Afghan War front. I had introduced some independent correspondents and their work to him, in particular a German called Dittmar Hack. Not only had Bill succeeded in getting the rate per foot of film used jacked up from a derisory £100 to a meaningful $1,000, he had also managed to root out rooms full of 16mm and 35mm equipment going for the asking. All the stations were in the process of switching to video, but in the Afghan context, video was less than satisfactory. By the time a Russian Hind helicopter gunship, which was the dominant feature of the war, reached the screen via video, it had become a meaningless blurr reflecting a buzz. For proper definition there was no substitute for 16mm.

I explained to Charlie how the time delays caused by having to walk the film out of Afghanistan were often exceeded by the delays in getting the film screened. In some sorry instances the film had been rushed over on Concorde, only to wait six weeks to appear. The thought that, for once, newsprint might have the edge over television cheered Charlie no end. It also put our discussion back on the printed-matter track and so I raised the subject of Professor Sayed B. Majrooh.

I felt sure Charlie must know all about Majrooh already, but he appeared not to. The Professor ran an 'alternative' news service out of Peshawar, the capital of the North West Frontier Province. It double-distilled the facts from the Afghan hyperbole, making due adjustments for party political bias. This dedicated attention to the facts tended to ruin the Professor's relations amongst the seven-party political dwarfs who all spent their days playing leapfrog in the cause of personality cult and kudos. The American media were known to have given Professor Majrooh's press service *carte blanche* telex credit. This meant he could now afford to send them everything that he had got to offer. Charlie said he would look into it and ensure his people did likewise. It might then come to match the welter of Russian propaganda material that arrived every day over the wire from Kabul.

Next, Charlie asked me what I thought were the most important issues he should raise with the President on Afghanistan.

I replied that the unresolved matter of the alleged use of chemical weapons by the Russians would be high on my agenda, plus the fear of famine being wielded as a weapon of war. After that, the paramount need was for ground-to-air missiles to even up the Russian helicopter gunship domination.

To illustrate the indifference he might encounter, I cited the extraordinary buried case of a Mr Richard Smith, who was based in Geneva, representing The Dignity of Man Foundation of Washington DC. As Bill Morrell had reported it to me, this Richard Smith had irrefutable evidence of Soviet use of chemical weapons in Afghanistan, but his long-awaited television interview had opened ominously 'Afghanistan, yes, we haven't heard much about it since Haile Selassie died!' That was only the beginning. Smith's Soviet chemical warhead container evidence was duly passed on to the State Department, who undertook to have it analysed and let him know their findings. This was subsequently amended to 'When the State Department decides that this would be appropriate.' (*i.e.* Anything to avoid escalation.)

Some six months later, Smith found himself invited to attend a meeting of chemical warfare experts at the Defense Department in Washington. This included several four-star generals as well as a Nobel Peace Prize winner, none of whom had the least idea of

Smith's contribution. Charlie suspected that this was a clear case of politicians being mesmerised by the opinion polls with elections looming on both sides of the Atlantic. Support for the Mujahedeen would be at an all-time low. *Détente* and dialogue were all the fashion and nobody wanted to mention to Gorbachev anything so tactless as Afghanistan.

Indeed there was so much 'Walk in the Woods' style (a remarkably prescient play by Lee Blessing with Alec Guinness) pussy-footing going on, that Charlie asked me if I had heard of any tacit agreement between the Russians and the Pakistanis. The theory was that, so long as the Mujahedeen restricted their activities to attacking and killing Kabul regime militia (*i.e.* other Afghans) and refrained from attacking Russian bases and Russian personnel, there would be no hot-pursuit air attacks in reprisal over Pakistan. I said I had heard of no such thing, but added that it would help to explain the recent high incidence of cross-border incursions and bombings. It also helped to explain why most convoys were manned by Kabul regime militia.

This led on to the thorny problem of arms escalation. Charlie, all in favour of arms limitation, felt that this was one aspect of the war that the Americans had got right, whether it was for Jewish lobby reasons or not. The more the weapons were up-graded, the greater would be the repercussions once the common enemy had been defeated. Afghans had always reverted to fighting each other once there was nobody else around to divert their attention to richer pickings. With more sophisticated weapons, they would only do each other that much more damage. It was like giving six-year-olds a darts game for Christmas. And once the Afghans' immediate need diminished, there was no knowing who would be next in line for them to sell such weapons on to.

I forebore to mention an article, which Charlie must have seen in his sister newspaper, the *Sunday Times*, which identified both Christopher Wills and myself as offering 'Blowpipe' (the British ground-to-air missile) to the Mujahedeen. It was much the kind of rumour the Afghans liked to spread abroad to highlight the need and hopefully accelerate delivery. Christopher had passed the buck, saying it had to be me who made the offer as I spent my time dashing around in all directions, resembling nothing so much as an out-of-control Exocet! In fact, unknown to us, there were two other former Grenadier officers there at the same time, either of whom could equally have fitted the bill.

Presumably because we had gone so far down the track of

trading names, Charlie now determined that I should meet both Nigel Ryan and Roger Scruton. I could think of no good reason for or against. Who was I to question the wisdom of the Editor of 'The Thunderer'?

He would let me have his flight number and expected time of arrival. I would then brief Bill Morrell and we would leave the rest to fate. With that, time was up and the breakfast over.

Charlie offered me a lift in his chauffeur-driven but modest limousine. I said I would prefer a walk in the park to collect my thoughts. I would go through Green Park and St James's Park, which would bring me to the most reliable telephone boxes I knew in those days, beside the Broadway Post Office.

It was time to telephone the bank manager's wife. Just as Bill Stokoe had explained to me, if and when I got through to the hospital exchange, they would signal Anwar's bleeper, which would invariably result in Anne Stokoe coming to the telephone. And so she did.

3

Meeting The Team

Anne Stokoe and I agreed to meet within the week. The arrangement was that I was to go to one of the last of the old-style red telephone boxes at the footbridge exit to Guildford Railway Station. If I found myself in the middle of the never-ending improvement works with a sluggish taxi rank, I was on the wrong side. Once inside my little red box, I was to telephone Anne at her home number and await collection. She would be looking out for Peter Sellers; likewise I would be seeking a Margaret Thatcher lookalike, behind the wheel of a car. Just in case I was obliged to quit my sanctuary, I said I would be carrying the *Economist*, the *Financial Times* and the *London Evening Standard*. I also described the boring pin-striped clothes I was wearing. No sooner had I rung off than I realised I had given a description which could cover half the people on the 5.55 p.m. train from Waterloo - the other half being women.

In the event, I had no difficulty spotting the much more glamorous, much more cheerful Margaret Thatcher. Also, she was every bit as well groomed, as if a film-set hairdresser were in constant attendance. Likewise, Anne had no difficulty in recognising me. Much later, I was to learn that her husband had expanded considerably on the Peter Sellers' cachet, even to suggesting the role I might currently be playing - a short, dark, dapper, larky saboteur!

As we drove off towards the hospital, Anne explained that she and her boss, Anwar Chaudhri, had arranged a small beer and sandwiches acquaint session for me to meet the Guildford volunteers, and for them to take their measure of me. It was all to be informal.

Anwar was waiting, bouncing up and down like an india-rubber ball in the hospital car park, which, in common with so many modern buildings, was its salient feature and only saving grace. Anwar was the epitome of those extremely charming, persuasive Punjabis, who are a delight of the sub-continent. He was shortish, plumpish, with the most engaging smile. His hair was pommaded after the old Denis Compton fashion, with a thirties' period parting rather high up the crown. Brylcreem was back. But it was his voice that stole your heart. He not only spoke that impeccable English commandeered and preserved by Indians and Nigerians alike, he purred it, replete with a Welsh lilt.

'So glad you could make it. So good of you to come. We have heard so much about you. I am sure we shall all get along famously.

Your experience must be so very relevant to our purpose. Will you be so kind as to outline to us this evening how you think you will be best able to help our worthy cause?'

All this between getting out of the car and walking the few paces to the hospital annexe door.

'Not quite so fast, my friend,' I said. 'I've come to listen first. Then perhaps I might have an idea or two. I need to know roughly where you are all coming from. What is the real motivation behind this determination to serve the Afghan cause?'

'All will be revealed. All will be revealed, directly.'

I may have sounded unduly cautious, even cynical. Only recently, there had been a special case of Afghan wounded being flown in to be treated at the Cromwell, one of London's most expensive hospitals. The owners had over-spent the building and equipment budget by some $40 million. No-one had counted the cost and there seemed little prospect of the investors ever seeing their money back. The ownership was said to be Gulf Arab with Pakistani management - not unlike the *Banque de Commerce et Credit Industrielle* (BCCI). Such high-profile antics on behalf of the Afghans would enjoy compensatory propaganda value in the Muslim world. There was no question the Afghans had received exceptional treatment, but I was guarding against the stunt aspects of such philanthropy.

The hospital annexe building we now entered was one of those economy, school-house 1960s designs, which seem preoccupied with keeping the square-foot cost down to the minimum, whilst concentrating on fire regulations. It had once been intended as a temporary structure, but with the passage of time had now stayed up long enough to qualify as a permanent building, at least in the eyes of the regulators.

Somehow, it had escaped the usual desperate afterthought attempts at humanising, such as the introduction of silver birch-tree mountain-scenery wallpaper over sparse sections of the concrete wilderness. For the remaining acres, patients could count on soothing pastel shades of emulsion paint. No hot colours and, if all else failed, child art could be added *ad lib* on rafts of pin-boards. This building, however, was so utterly bare and uninviting, so totally devoid of any improvements, it could only have been designated for staff use.

Finally, we reached the reception room. It was intended as a common-room or canteen. It had a floor-to-ceiling vertical dividing screen made of concertina-grey plastic panels, the purpose of which was to make the room supposedly more intimate by making it appear smaller. To me it felt like the closing stages of Edgar Allan Poe's story, "The Pit and the Pendulum"! Only notice boards decorated the wipe-clean walls. Nothing relieved the utter drabness. It was as if distraction was superfluous to the nature of hospitals. The pathological approach - what was wrong with the patient instead of what was right with the world.

Set in the right-angle of the retractable concertina, there was a focal point - the bar counter. This could cater for two competing functions or, flung wide, take on all-comers. This evening it was dispensing the said beer and sandwiches, but little else, to half its capacity.

It was not the most welcoming ambience in which to meet a whole set of new people, but although the volunteers were in no way lined up - rather standing in informal groupings of threes or fours, chatting - I had the feeling of being introduced by the captain to his football team on the pitch. There was the added disadvantage that the field positions held little meaning. Until that evening, in my ignorance, I had no idea that 'theatre nurse' could, and more often did mean a male nurse, certainly in the surgical theatre context.

It was all a bit confusing. There was no apparent hierarchy. The captain was not to emerge for some time from his hermit-crab shell. As if determined to see what colour the litmus paper would turn before committing himself! Meanwhile he would play second fiddle to a giant of an anaesthetist. It may all have been a ploy to escape the hidebound over-structuring of the National Health Service, but a demonstrably democratic persona was on show as befitting a volunteer force for an humanitarian medical mission. The appropriate keynote of informality had been struck. They were all very natural and at their ease.

There was no way I was going to master all their names, let alone their relevance, first time round. But I did manage some rough groupings in my mind as between surgeons, anaesthetists and theatre staff.

Some instinct made me tackle the largest man in the room first. He was the giant anaesthetist. He looked to me the type to have been hand-picked at eighteen by Guy's or Bart's to play prop forward in their rugby team. Any medical knowledge required would be fed intravenously at some later date. His name was John Stoneham. He had that calm, cool, composed demeanour the English prize above all others, and would be the prop, anchor-man and mainstay of any team in a tight spot anywhere.

He keeps himself in a permanent state of peak physical fitness and strides up mountains with consummate ease. There is nothing of the swank about him. On the contrary, he exhibits that peculiarly English characteristic of understatement, except when it comes to eating, when he has a giant frame to fill. There are one or two other surprises too. He sports unlikely bow ties, once thought to signify an inferiority complex, but nothing could be further from the case with John Stoneham.

I wanted to know what made him want to help the Afghans. He said that he and his colleagues in Guildford all enjoyed security to the point of affluence. The Afghans, who had nothing, had shown the will to stand up to the Russians, whilst we in the West had the means, but fell sadly short on willpower. At this point Peter Stiles, with whom John Stoneham worked closely, joined the conversation, to add that world opinion mattered, even to the Russians.

I asked how they all came to be working together for so long. Didn't any of them get any better at it after fifteen years?

They explained it was the way the system worked. You qualified and then you were appointed to a hospital for life ... barring serious misdemeanours! I said that must mean that they got to know each other extremely well. Wasn't there a danger they would get sick and tired of the same old faces?

Long associations, they explained, could have their advantages as well. For instance, this little gathering didn't represent some flash-in-the-pan fit of enthusiasm. The germ of the idea probably came after some chance remark following a particularly bloody atrocity seen on television, maybe as long as a year ago. It then got kicked around, moulded and developed - just to see how viable it was.

I said I only had to look around at the cars in the street in Guildford to recognise a very high standard of living indeed. What I should like to know was what they would be like at roughing it, making do in primitive conditions. I said I was thinking as much of the lack of proper operating facilities as ordinary day-to-day living. They wanted to know how bad it could get. I said conditions were generally lousy and could only get worse. Flies, filth and no proper sanitation. I exaggerated in anticipation of a time of trial.

Peter Stiles said he thought they could put up with most things. They would, of course, attempt to impose their own standards of hygiene from the outset; although he recognised they would have to compromise. As for creature comforts, most of them had had to cope with camping at one time or another; and they would always be able to fall back on their reserves of medical student humour.

I said that that could well be the saving of them and it was the most encouraging thing I had heard all evening. It should be prescribed in large doses and they were not to bother to bring anyone without it.

I wondered whether the Hippocratic Oath might have some bearing to complicate matters. So I asked how impartial they would want to be as between the seven political parties.[1] I explained that the more apolitical we appeared to be, the better would be our chances of personal survival as well as of conducting smoother operations. They expected to leave all that to Anwar and me. So far as they were concerned, it was a purely administrative matter!

I moved on to join another group, where a highly articulate theatre assistant, Tony Bray, was holding forth. The point he was making was that, whilst the Russians were busy destabilising the world, all we could do was witter on about whether or not we should play pat-ball with them at the Moscow Olympics. What we should be doing was standing up and being counted alongside the Afghans. Someone else in the group said how uneven the struggle was with a super-power pitched against a rabble armed with Lee Enfields. There was talk of giving David a better chance against Goliath.

That particular analogy was pertinent. The combatants were all children of the Book. I speculated how odd it was that in this Godless age, the mighty atheist Russian Empire should have been thwarted by two of the most spiritual nations on earth - the Poles, champions of Christianity since the XII century, and the Afghans who, amongst many other things, claim two of the lost tribes of Israel and early conversion to Islam. More likely, they were late arrivals - but all the more devout for that. The Poles and the Afghans also had charging tanks with cavalry in common. But, what the Russians had most to fear was that, by the end of the century, their Soviet Empire would be Muslim-dominated. It would then be time for their history to begin all over again.

I added that in all the team's dealings with the Afghans, they would find it was very much a question of praising God first, five times a day, and only then was it time to pass the ammunition. Everything stopped for prayers.

In answer to my enquiry about any existing connections on the ground, Anwar told me about the Lady Reading Hospital in Peshawar, which had a fine reputation and longstanding accords with the Royal Surrey County Hospital. Over the years they had taken in any number of interns.

In my time I had visited the International Committee of the Red Cross/Red Crescent (ICRC) hospitals and knew them to be first rate. The problem, as I saw it, was going to be how to co-ordinate efforts on a short-term basis, without getting in their way! The key to success would be thorough reconnaissance and detailed planning. That, I assumed, would be Anwar's job ... and mine.

Amongst the first fifteen or so people present, there was a hard core, clearly determined to make their contribution. Then there were the waverers, who presumably had been asked along in the hope of reassurance or Pauline conversion. I began to have a feel for the sheep and the goats. At the same time, of course, they were making their assessment of me and the chances of my looking after them in a tight spot, in a strange land.

For this embryo MASH type team, the shared experience of the IRA bomb had been the bonding factor. By all accounts, they had coped magnificently in that emergency. The fact that they had handled some sixty-four simultaneous casualties convinced me of their ability to switch into battle gear.

As two more women joined the party, I asked Anwar whether he was thinking of taking any women team members. He gave me an ambivalent answer. He said that Anne Stokoe would be staying behind this year, as they would have to have somebody they could rely on at base to give the necessary back-up, calm anxious wives, man the telephone etc. And there were sure to be things forgotten that would need to be sent on. Just as I was beginning to think he was avoiding the question, he told me that their top gynaecologist was thinking of bringing his female assistant; and his wife had hinted that she would be coming as an observer. It appeared they were planning to combine the medical mission with a holiday in Swat. Anwar told me he was very high-powered, very much the big cheese around Guildford. He said I could even have heard of him in London. I had not. I was more concerned to know what chance Anwar thought there was of us finding them anything to do. He must be aware of all the prejudice against western doctors interfering with Afghan women. The mullahs never stopped shouting from the minarets 'Let not the infidel defile your women.' Anwar was confident, however, that these little local difficulties could be overcome, once we got there.

With that he implored me to take up the challenge. As further inducement, Anne had put together a mass of background information for me to take away. It was said to incorporate all the groundwork done by the American organisation, Orthopaedics Overseas. The British group, World Orthopaedic Concern, was said to be bigger, but it did not have Afghanistan amongst its current concerns.

Not to be side-tracked, I insisted to Anwar that I could not remember having seen a single hospital for women's complaints, or maternity for that matter, although I had witnessed regular weekly clinics, held for women and children in refugee camps. Anwar replied that I would see the Americans had a Dr Momand listed with an Obstretrics & Gynaecological Hospital and there was always the Lady Reading.

I remained to be convinced. I remembered meeting a powerful and vocal French or possibly Belgian lady, who appeared to be in charge of *Médecins Sans Frontières* in Peshawar in the early days. She had been on the admin side and she let me know, loud and clear, that there was nothing in the way of interface on the highly sensitive subject of female Afghan patients. Perhaps the world had moved on since then?

My instincts told me that, in the Afghan context, women meant trouble. They would restrict mobility. They would more than likely cause petty strife and jealousies amongst the male team members, even over a short period. They were best left behind. Also, once we had one wife on board, all the others would clamour to come along too. In addition the presence of women would also increase the risk of our being swept up in the pointless social life which follows in the wake of proxy wars, a merry-go-round of self-justification as funds are squandered in the cause of furthering political awareness; the seamier side to aid. But this observation probably said more about my social shortcomings than anything else.

Anne Stokoe appeared at my elbow, signalling. One of their number, Phil Jones, a recently qualified general practitioner, was volunteering to drive me back to London, whenever I was ready to leave. They were taking no chances of my overstaying my welcome.

Phil was a rare breed, a Welsh Devonian. Unable to find a practice to his liking in Britain, he had elected to spend six months with the Lady Reading, followed by six months inside Afghanistan. For the time being, he lived in digs in Tooting.

For a first meeting, it seemed to me to have gone rather well. The casual informality had worked. They all knew each other so well there could be little standing on ceremony. They certainly seemed positive and, above all, cheerful. The bleak surroundings counted for nothing, and indeed there had even been a hint of serenity in the air, a prevailing atmosphere of peace. Was this the reward for a lifetime spent in the service of others? Or was I reading too much into the situation?

I agreed with Anne that, as I was London-based and already had dealings with the Pakistani embassy people in Lowndes Square, I should handle the group visa applications. She would deal with all the other documentation, notably the meticulous flight manifest listings of drugs and equipment, which would be accompanying us. On this she would be working with John Stoneham.

It was also 'agreed' that I should follow up Anwar's initiative on group travel arrangements with contacts of mine in British Airways. It was unlikely I would be able to improve on any discounts offered, but there was also the tricky question of excess baggage, to cover all the extra medical kit that would be accompanying the team.

Willi-nilly, it looked as if I had let myself in for the job, if it existed, a lot sooner than I had anticipated. But I had one final question for Anne. Her husband Bill had made references to the 'powers-that-be'. Who, I wanted to know, had given that definitive thumbs down? She told me it had been Sir Oliver Forster at the Afghanistan Support Committee, not the Foreign & Commonwealth Office as such. That was a big relief.

Sir Oliver had been the British ambassador in Islamabad until quite recently (Pakistan had yet to be readmitted to the Commonwealth). So, on his retirement, it was to be expected that he might become the *éminence grise*, if not the Director of the Afghanistan Support Committee. Fortunately I had met him once or twice in Islamabad and more recently in London. He was delightfully unstuffy and approachable.

I asked Anne why she was sacrificing herself by staying behind. She explained that, as the only volunteer, she was the natural first choice. I said that seemed rather unfair. At which she laughed heartily and agreed that life could be horribly unfair. She then handed me the fat file of background papers which I should need to digest, long before I went anywhere near Sir Oliver Forster's office.

I promised to reciprocate with a stack of press cuttings on the war, refugee camps and anything else I thought relevant ... like modesty strictures incumbent on women's, and to a lesser extent, men's clothing. I would leave it up to her to distribute at the Guildford end. She assured me it would all get read. Their job required them to read reams of bumf and mine would be that much more interesting .

At this point, she remarked there was something else I needed to know, which Anwar might not have got around to disclosing. Every four years or so, surgeons for sure, and possibly all medical practitioners, were encouraged to widen their experience, by practising in a different environment. They could accumulate up to a month of such 'study leave of absence' on some such basis as a fortnight's paid credit for every three years. The point was that most of the team had substantial periods owing; indeed, there was a significant backlog standing to their credit. The other point to note was that travel and subsistence costs on such occasions could be set against tax liability. I promised not to mention that to British Airways.

On the other hand, Anne said, theatre staff neither had the means to pay their own way, nor would they be entitled to the allowances if they could. We therefore agreed that there would be a need for some creative Robin Hood accounting to restore such imbalance. I said I would be sure to let Anne know how I got on with Sir Oliver.

I then purposely went round shaking everybody by the hand; trying to put correct names to faces and mumbling where I could not. Any full-blooded American would have deemed it a cake-walk. John Stoneman, Peter Stiles, Frank Schweitzer (was he related to Albert?), Tony Bray, Robin Jago, Geoff McLeod, etc., etc. Phil Jones then led me, with Anne and Anwar, towards his car, a ramshackle student banger. It was too late to opt for the train.

As his Parthian shot, Anwar said he had thought we should have a policy of 'work hard, play hard'. We would need to think of some suitable rest houses to go to and get a breath of fresh air at half-time, clear the lungs, what? I agreed that Peshawar had terrible inversion problems - the polluted air simply rises and falls again, seldom blown away - then there was the open sewer system. But we had to be sure of getting the work done in order to deserve the break. We must not earn a medical tourism label.

'Definitely, definitely. Quite, quite right,' were his parting words as Phil and I juddered away.

*

During the hazardous journey on the A3 I distracted myself by ruminating on what I had let myself in for. Unlike most volunteer groups - which tend to get thrown together at the last minute, to serve the cause of the moment - here was a close-knit body of men (and maybe women), who were proposing to do precisely what they always did on a day-to-day basis as a team, but with a change of venue. The seeming lack of protocol mattered not a fig-leaf, because their extra-curricular activity would be no different to their everyday one. Their over-riding strength was their long-established procedures. The chain of command was a chain of operation - a routine drill, mastered over many years to the point of being semi-automatic. The discipline was of the best - self-discipline.

Then, given time, their contributions could be a logical extension of other initiatives and activities in which I suspected AfghanAid, if not the Support Committee, to be engaged - notably, an ambulance programme for the evacuation of casualties from the battlefields.

Next, I speculated on how the team might cope if it was faced with any real nasties, like revenge atrocities, mass disembowellings, flayings alive - and rapidly decided that they would cope a damned sight better than I would. Who but me in my biology class of 1947 had chucked up all over the dismembered frog and the dissected bull's eye? Then, not so long afterwards, I had let the side down again, whilst visiting the French in Algiers in 1952. The sight of small children, whose parents had twisted their limbs into spiralling contortions to improve their begging chances had convulsed me.

But my real misgiving was still the threat of the accompanying women. I would just have to hope that they had second thoughts.

I could see that Anwar would certainly make an excellent counter-balance to me. I visualised him sitting in the old Aga Khan's birthday scales. Instead of diamonds in the balance, was his mother tongue, Punjabi. He also had Urdu. There had been mention of a brother, who was some government official in Islamabad. That could be useful. All I had to offer was French and a different native cunning.

The long and the short of it was that I found this Guildford team of surgeons and their back-up people entirely to my liking. They were highly motivated, but in a calm unsentimental way, deserving all the help they could get. What I must remember to bang home to Sir Oliver Forster was all that dedicated reflex action; Taylor Woodrow type teamwork! Thanks to him I was not going to have to go through the normal channels of the Foreign & Commonwealth Office.

[1] Seven political parties and their leaders, forming the Afghan Interim Government based in Peshawar, North West Frontier Province, Pakistan.

4
Red Tape

It was early days in the Afghan War and I had teamed up with some ex-Special Forces friends, who held a brief that melded neatly with my own. I sought suitable company to witness some of the early ambushes. They wanted to attend so as to be able to report on Russian equipment and, where possible, to bring some of the more portable pieces back - particularly if they substantiated the use of chemicals. There was also the possibility of offering some specialist training, ideally for a US or Saudi fee.

To me at the time, 1983, it had seemed the most natural thing in the world to first get the co-operation of the Pakistani Special Forces, who deny it as they might, were definitely fully engaged in Afghanistan. They had agreed readily enough, but, not unreasonably, asked for our bona fides to be endorsed by our own government along the way - 'purely as a formality, old boy!' In my naïveté, I thought nothing could be simpler.

More by happenstance than contrivance, I had met Lord Carrington, then the Secretary of State for Foreign Affairs, on a number of occasions over as many years - all of them easy-going informal ones. But I knew his number two at the time - the Lord Privy Seal, Sir Humphrey Atkins - even better. He had sought my advice some twenty years before over an investment in an advertising agency specialising in marketing financial services in the City.

The circumstances of our meeting could not have been more auspicious - tea for two in the Lord Privy Seal's Office. Naturally, it overlooks St James's Park. What is surprising, once you have taken in all the fine paintings and high ceilings, is that it has two equally imposing entrance doors, side by side. Sir Humphrey took delight in explaining their purpose. They had been specified at the height of the Raj to cater for the peculiar precedence problems of admitting equal ranking Maharajahs. By this singular means, they were able to make their entry simultaneously, two by two, as if into Noah's Ark. Since the tea and cups were both of the highest quality, the whole atmosphere struck me as charged one hundred and ten per cent positive.

Sir Humphrey said he could not have been more in agreement with my purpose, 'unofficially, of course, you understand.' The war needed reporting properly, with 'more in-depth coverage'. The world needed to be told what the Russians were up to. In similar circumstances, the Russians never hesitated to arm and train insurgents in the communist cause.

It was high time for us to take a leaf out of their book. Why should they always have the initiative? It was time to cease being knee-jerk reactive and become 'pro-active'. That was the buzz word for the eighties. Sir Humphrey knew exactly the person to arrange everything. It was just the job for the 'quite excellent Chief Clerk'.

To begin with, I made no comment. I thought I must have misheard. It would not have been fitting or seemly - might even sound unappreciative, ungrateful. But, even at the time I feared the Pepysian title spelled doom.

Unheralded, as if operated by a Smersh button, the left-hand of the two identical pairs of doors opened and we went out to the ante-room. Here Sir Humphrey, to emphasise the informality of modern conservatism, sat on the hall table swinging his legs, as if on the brink of delivering a public school sex lecture. There was a clatter of inferior teacups as the permanent civil servants jumped to pay attention. They were all young, keen and alert. All Sir Humphrey had to say was would they kindly arrange for me to see the Chief Clerk 'on a matter of some urgency'. In the event it took a week for me to be fitted in, and my lasting impression was that I was being treated to an exclusive episode of 'Yes Minister' - being unsure where illusion ended and reality began.

The Lord Privy Seal's Office is a political appointment of the utmost gravitas confirmed by the pretensions of the premises accorded. So, perhaps I should not have been so surprised that his Chief Clerk, however excellent, should have inhabited a drab *eau de nil* hutch with an electric clock for embellishment, slung high on the wall opposite his gaze.

The actual building may have been temporary premises. Finding it was an initiative test in itself. It was in that maze of doglegs which take over where Queen Anne's Gate runs out. As if privy to some Civil War romance one is told confidentially that all these offices are linked to Downing Street, the Foreign Office and Whitehall by a veritable rabbit warren of underground passages.

Gauging the likely importance of this interview with the Chief Clerk, I elected to take with me a retired army major with over twenty years service with Special Forces. Let his pseudonym be 'Spike'. As we were ushered into his office, the Chief Clerk summoned some reserves of his own. I suspect they were due anyway, if only for window-dressing. It was on the tick of 3 p.m.

All I had to go on was that the Chief Clerk had a 'very fine half-Blue for hockey'. To give him his due he was every bit as aware as his colleagues were somnolent. To bully-off, I asked how much background had been supplied already, to which it was suggested that it might be as well to begin again at the beginning. I then explained our joint purpose as best I could and our need for some measure of endorsement, to satisfy a request from the Pakistani military authorities. A note or the right word to their military attaché, at Lowndes Square here in London, would suffice.

The reply he gave was as unforgettable as it was unequivocal 'I think you had better ask your Minister friend for that. It is definitely not a job for us.'

Whereupon, recognising the interview was at an end, the three wise men filed out. I was livid. It made such a monkey out of me, a most frightful loss of face before my special friend. Fortunately, he had been expecting as much all along. As we took our leave, I muttered to him, but ensuring that all could hear, 'It must have long since ceased to be a function of these people to have ideas - least of all any *new* ideas.' I refrained from saying that I would revert to Sir Humphrey. I would not. If this was the best he could do to pave the way for me, there was no point.

Spike told me to forget it. He was long experienced in never counting on official support - least of all from the Foreign Office! Always only too happy for their dirty work to be done by others; just so long as everything was 'deniable'. Spike said he could even ventriloquise the report one of the sleepwalkers would file on our meeting

'Foolish and utopian expectations, stemming from wild, unbridled enthusiasms etc., etc.'

Better by far to
'Do what thy manhood bids thee do,
From none but self expect applause,
He noblest lives and noblest dies
Who makes and keeps his self-made laws.' [1]

On which note, I determined to perpetrate an off-white lie to this Pakistani military attaché in question, Brigadier Ayaz Ahmad. I told him I feared my past links with the media had made my people supra-cautious, so that my application and the relevant approvals were going to take a little longer than usual. I said I was sorry, but I was going to have to ask him to bear with us. I said we didn't propose to hang around waiting for ever, but had asked them to get in touch with him, directly by name. That part at least was true. It was precisely what I had asked for and I had been at pains to leave the Brigadier's visiting card on the Chief Clerk's desk. It was dispensable.

For good measure, I added that the war would most likely be over and done with by the time these pen-pushers had found the correct formula to advise him of our relevance or otherwise. At which we all had a good laugh. In terms of deniability, it was now at least debatable who was denying whom.

The bluff had worked. Within the week, Brigadier Ayaz Ahmed had brought round the commanding officer of Pakistani Special Forces, 'incognito, of course', to meet some of his opposite numbers in the attic voids of half-derelict houses at the back of the old St George's Hospital at Hyde Park Corner. These were awaiting demolition and re-development by the Grosvenor Estate. The address was St George's Crescent, leading into Old Palace Yard. Surprisingly, perhaps, it was possible to give effective demonstrations there of a number of startlingly original and economical devices of the Bond 'Q' type - without making a whimper, let alone a bang. Infra-red night vision scopes were at the obvious end of the spectrum, but also on display were silent means of intercommunication on night patrol, and equally silent means of taking out sentries. Everything, short of how to catch and kill your cow in the field. After which, with appetites sufficiently whetted, a substantial steak lunch was to be had round the corner at the Grenadier pub.

Old Palace Yard was both handy and discreet for Lowndes Square, only a short walk away. The officer commanding Pakistani Special Forces was another brigadier. He was on an official 'inward mission' to the United Kingdom. Whether his visit to us was on his official programme, I rather doubt, but I had had enough of asking questions first. The brigadier was known universally by his two initials "TM". They stood for Tariq Mahmood. "TM" was known to be a favourite of the Pakistani President Zia-ul-Haq. After all, the President had been a fellow brigadier not too long before. For his 'incognito' meeting with us, "TM" wore a fisherman's jersey and slacks and had he succumbed to a beret and a string or two of onions and garlic, might have passed muster as a Breton on a bicycle.

There was a happy sequel to our blocked initiative. The three wise men of the Foreign Office may for once have anticipated correctly. Let us in charity give them the benefit of the doubt. For in the case of Afghanistan, they met their match, as on so many other occasions, in the Prime Minister, Mrs Thatcher. There was no pussy-footing about once she had arrived on the scene. She didn't think twice. She didn't have to. As surely as day follows night, she knew where the moral high ground lay and made sure she stood on top of it. From the appropriate eminence of the Khyber she authorised the despatch of a training detachment of the SAS forthwith to the North West Frontier – to her eternal credit and the ensuing gratitude of that senior commander, Abdul Haq, and others, who had the good manners and public relations *nous* to come and thank her afterwards in person.

[1] Sir Richard Francis Burton
British explorer & orientalist(1821 - 1890)

5
Organising Charity

"TM" was an obvious contact to help channel the Guildford Surgical Team's efforts in appropriate directions. I would call on him for advice at the next opportunity. He had given me his private line home number for just this kind of purpose.

Between them, Anwar Chaudhri and Anne Stokoe had handed me a formidable file of background material and I took my time to flog through it. Characteristically, the Americans had collated everything you needed to know on the ground - plus plenty you could do without.

Merged with the basic American peanut-butter and jelly sandwich survival kit abroad was a comprehensive index of all the Government and Non-Government Organisations (NGOs) to be found in Peshawar, plus all the Afghan organisations, together with their party political 'cottage' hospitals. Some of these hid behind box number anonymity. Then came a comprehensive mailing list of all those past and present surgeons, who had volunteered to operate in the Peshawar hospitals, or otherwise, States-side. There was yet another listing, described as the 'Roll of Honour'. This did not illuminate those who had perished in the call of duty, so much as those who had, to date, undertaken the arduous journey, entirely at their own expense, to perform many worthwhile operations. In time, with luck, the one list would come to embrace the other. Likewise, over time, teams of American surgeons would come to represent the American contribution as much as valuable individual efforts. Of course, all were more than welcome, but as evinced from the correspondence and reports, overall planning and co-ordination of effort was going to be a major element in the mix. Could this have been the underlying reason for Sir Oliver Forster's caution?

One of the most constant factors of this guerilla war in Afghanistan, was that it was obliged to be seasonal. The fighting slackened as the summer heat took its toll. Likewise it ceased during the extreme winter cold. Peak fighting conditions produced peak casualty periods in spring and autumn. Nobody knew how many of the wounded died between the battlefield and the border. It was assumed that the majority did so, but there was no means of knowing for sure. This factor had no doubt been the inspiration for the AfghanAid ambulance programme for the timely evacuation of casualties.

With any luck it would also manage to cut out some of the taxi vultures, who hovered on the border. Their purpose was to extract as high a toll as possible for ferrying the wounded to a productivity-oriented hospital, where a further fee might be demanded for the delivery of a live patient, depending upon their triage skills.

So long as they could be properly co-ordinated then, there was every need for qualified Western surgeons to give their services *in situ* at peak casualty times. From what I remembered of previous visits, before I had any expectation of medical involvement, the International Committee of the Red Cross/Red Crescent (ICRC) had been responsible for ninety per cent of all casualties handled on a round-the-clock, year-round basis. All other efforts needed to be seen in that context, *i.e.* all outsider efforts were puny by comparison. The counter argument ran that any effort made by foreigners to further the Afghan cause, was of major psychological benefit. The Afghans appreciated that they had not been forgotten and that their sacrifice and spirit of resistance held the admiration of the world.

The next organisation of note was the high profile, Franco-Belgian *Médecins Sans Frontières* (MSF), who were heavily committed with large numbers of (mostly young) doctors working a year at a time inside Afghanistan. Some of these may well have been contributing their National Service. Then came the efforts of individual countries. Prominent amongst these were the Scandinavians, particularly the Swedish Committee, the Norwegians, but there was also the occasional, highly active Finn. And there were Danes too. The Germans sent teams of plastic surgeons and made special efforts through their HELP organisation. Their world-famous pharmaceutical companies were especially generous. It was said that the German constitution forbade more active cross-border participation.

The more you studied the picture, the more aware you became that, so far as the Guildford Surgical Team was concerned, they would be subordinate to the whims and dicates of the American Orthopaedic Overseas planners. The marshalling of all this volunteer effort could only be fully grasped once you were there. No Afghan would believe you were coming until you had arrived.

One thing was for sure. There would be no shortage of patients. The next problem, therefore, was to fit in the availability of operating theatres. This was further complicated by the political requirement that the patient ready for operation needed to be in line for the correct party hospital operating theatre! By that stage I could see it beginning to resemble a three-dimensional game of solitaire.

I could also foresee *prima donna* surgeons throwing fits

because of double-booked operating tables, or patients, limbs permitting, wandering off after a change of heart or family veto.

As far as possible then, schedules would need to be pre-planned. This whole headache appeared to be the remit of one remarkable man, whose appointment, according to the papers I had, was Chairman Peshawar Program. If the signature was to be believed, his name was Dr Kermit Veggeberg MD. If his up-coming schedules were anything to go by he seemed to have the whole circus firmly in hand. A continuous flow of American surgeons was listed, intensifying to cover the two peak periods of fighting. Their addresses showed they came from all over the United States and their only apparent grouping was under the double 'O' (Orthopaedics Overseas) banner.

So, from the outset, our team would have the advantage of self-sufficiency. There would be no call to hang around waiting for a qualified anaesthetist or other absent theatre staff. On all counts, therefore, we must constitute ourselves in autonomous four- or five-man teams, consisting of surgeon, anaesthetist, plus two or three theatre staff. Then, in theory, we should be able to go anywhere.

Finally, I found two further copious listings of ethical pharmaceutical donor companies, together with details of their local Pakistani representation. And the last list of all was of those hospitals in the United States, which had hosted referred Afghan patients. These were selected by a visiting panel. By now, it had become every wounded Afghan's dream to be picked out for such special treatment, with all the inherent expectation of a one-way ticket to El Dorado.

6

Sir Oliver says 'Yes'

The offices of the Afghanistan Support Committee and its sister organisation, AfghanAid, have moved about a bit over the years, depending on the fortunes of funding and the 'grace and favour' disposition of their most active chairman, patron and landlord - Robert Cecil, Viscount Cranborne, who has since become The Most Hon. The Marquess of Salisbury, P.C.,D.L., sometimes a peer of the realm, sometimes a courtesy title commoner and Member of Parliament, often a cabinet minister; but always highly active on all matters Afghan.

However, in the early days of the Afghan War in 1982, the whole Foreign & Commonwealth Office and Overseas Development Agency (FCO/ODA) annual budget for Afghanistan amounted to only £50,000, plus any funds subscribed by a largely indifferent public, which, at a pinch, might have produced an equivalent sum, but by no means every year. As with all registered charities, the accounts were assuredly available for inspection, but they might not have told the whole story. There were certainly no hidden agendas, but that isn't to say there were no hidden subsidies. The rules governing registered charities are strict and have to be rigidly adhered to; so, the chances are that the church-mouse poor appearance was a true reflection of the balance sheet.

Having begun life in two tiny interconnecting rooms the size of *wagon-lits* - two floors up and two light wells back, which could only be approached along a succession of abbatoir passages of lavatorial tiling - the Afghanistan Support Committee had, by the time of Sir Oliver Forster's installation, grown into larger premises at the front of the same building - No. 18 Charing Cross Road. The precise location of tenants within the building was indicated in signwritten gold or black lettering on heavy mahogany boards, perpetuating Victorian school or law courts values and practices. The rent no doubt remained in the peppercorn range. Beggars can't be choosers and whatever these premises may have lacked in modern comfort and facilities, they made up for in compensating old-world charm, superb open gas-fires, West End and theatreland location.

The address and the offices themselves were therefore suitably understated, befitting a charity; although some of the neighbours had high-falutin' names like the International Institute for Defence Studies, Committee for a Free World, cheek by jowl with the Society of Distillers and Vintners Gazette. Only slightly incongruously, there was also a discounted airline ticket 'bucket shop' on the first floor - disarmingly named 'Terminal Travel'.

The elaborate filigree wrought-iron communal front door was, however, shut and heavily bolted each evening at 6 p.m. sharp, effectively putting paid to any question of late working. But it was well-established that Sir Oliver liked to catch the 4.30 p.m. train. He was, after all, officially retired.

On arrival, I was greeted, as of old, by Rosemarie Askham (I used to help with the Afghan Support Committee house magazine in the early days). Rosemarie, one of those immensely reassuring unflappable English ladies who seem incapable of a cross mood or a sharp word, was aware that I had come to see Sir Oliver and prepared to usher me in. To be shown in is hardly the right phrase. His door is always wide open, mainly to create a through draught to help waft out some of the tobacco smoke-screen. But he is welcoming.

Rosemarie's purpose was now to attract enough of his attention for him to realise he had a semi-approved, semi-expected visitor. He was standing, engrossed in speed-reading fists-full of reports, press cuttings, two or three in each hand, seemingly simultaneously, as if making some long-ago computerised cross-reference. All the while, he inhaled furiously, and then, as if to punctuate the absorption of so much information, he would spasmodically convert it into a curt *curia* smoke-signal.

'Hello, Rupert, and what brings you here?' - his habitual cheery greeting.

It must have been four years since we had first met. I had been loosely attached to a group of all-party MPs visiting mainly refugee camps in the North West Frontier Province of Pakistan. The group was under the leadership of Robert Cecil, Lord Cranborne, who made all the speeches, and the visit was undertaken in the name of the Afghanistan Support Committee. (Neville Sandelson represented the all-party element.) Sooner or later the party was bound to call on the ambassador in his new riot-proof concrete bunker of an embassy. The Americans had had theirs burnt down not long before, as an indication of what we might expect in future. As I was very much an unofficial adjunct, I kept myself well in the background. I had nevertheless been a keen observer. I was aware that first impressions could be deceptive in such circumstances. So, when, at my distance, Sir Oliver reminded me of Arthur Askey, the comedian, I kept any such observations to myself.

I told Sir Oliver that I had come to ask for his advice, as

usual and, maybe, a favour too. I went on to explain how I had been approached by the group of well-meaning orthopaedic surgeons from Guildford, who wanted to volunteer their services in Peshawar and all places north west.

Sir Oliver said it sounded interesting and asked what the problem was. I said that they had already approached him and had been given a thumbs down, and that he had been quoted as saying that, by the time they had got out there, been accepted and settled in, it would be time to come home again; having achieved nothing worthwhile. I asked him if the name Anwar Chaudhri rang any bells.

Indeed it did. He seemed to remember they were thinking of going for a fortnight and asked if I didn't agree with his forebodings. So there was the rub. I explained that it was now proposed to stagger and stretch the programme with a recce over a slightly longer period.

I then quickly outlined the one or two advantages I thought the Guildford team had going for them. The fact that they had been together for fifteen years or more, enabling them to work their magic blindfolded on a windswept moor.

Before I could get carried away any further, Sir Oliver said he thought he knew what I meant; although he could not accept my Afghan hyperbole, I should know that his wife was a nursing sister. She never stopped reminding him that post-operative care was as significant as the operation itself and what had I planned for that? It hadn't entered the equation.

He then went on to ask how I fitted into all this. I replied that I had reached a bit of a watershed, and was contemplating a sabbatical. I thought I might benefit from the sea change of shepherding these volunteers as a kind of acting unpaid assistant administrator.

Sir Oliver thought that should prove most humbling, for, normally, they only had utter contempt for the admin role. To which, stung, I said it would be a challenge for me to make them revise their ideas.

There was a long pause with some extra hard puffing and blowing of smoke. The *curia* was in plenary session.

He then said that, if I was prepared to be responsible for them, take them there, look after them, full-time, bring them safely back, then, I could have his go-ahead. But there was to be no shooting-off on any will o'the wisp flights of fancy - leaving the team in the lurch. He also counselled that, whatever else we had in mind, we should concentrate on the most thorough of reconnaissances.

If possible, we should leave ten days ahead of the main party.

Nobody would believe we were coming until we had arrived. No amount of letter writing would alter that. He then softened the lecture a bit to say that it wouldn't be at all what we were expecting, but it would certainly be interesting, possibly rewarding and anyway different. As he had told Anwar Chaudhri, it would take at least a week to establish any kind of bridgehead.

I told Sir Oliver that I was planning to let Anwar conduct the recce, adopting the support role myself. After all, Anwar had set the ball rolling. His very name was said to mean born leader. (*Nomen est omen.*) I also touched on Anwar's language facility and the civil servant brother - all of which should be useful. Furthermore, we had six unprecedented months in which to plan. We could write all those letters nobody was going to read. More to the point, we should have no excuse for any failure to work ourselves into the American master plan.

Sir Oliver reminded me that I had a favour to ask him.

I said that it had occurred to me that his people on the ground in University Town, Peshawar, could be helpful in weighing the balance between the various political parties and their 'cottage' hospitals. I assumed AfghanAid had a clear idea of preferences from the ambulance programme. Of course, if problems arose, we could always hide behind the apolitical apron strings of the Hippocratic Oath. But the favour I wanted was a two-part one.

Our other pressing need was to organise our own transport - one or two reliable vehicles plus the all-important 'captive' drivers, who needed to know the different 'cottage' hospitals and the shortest route between them. Otherwise, we would be in danger of becoming beholden to whichever party sent its transport. I said we could pay, but some long-term planning was needed, if we were not to become hostages.

Sir Oliver had been thinking along similar lines. There was an American organisation called SERVE that might fit the bill. It was probably listed in the material I had. In the meantime, he would telex his people and see what they came up with. The cost of transport was not so much the problem as the reliable driver. He could see how important independence of movement would be to us, plus the local knowledge of the hospital locations. He asked where we were planning to stay.

I expected we would put up at Dean's Hotel. Dean's was discreet, cheap, adequate and, so far as I personally was concerned, more sympathetic than the Khyber Intercontinental (since renamed Pearl Intercontinental). Failing that, I supposed we would have to

Dean's Hotel in Peshawar - nest of spies. *Photo by Peter Stiles*

settle for Green's. We could always cut along to the Khyber for a meal or a swim if things got too desperate. Part of my problem was that I really had no idea how fastidious medics were.

Sir Oliver remarked that his wife would have us believe surgeons expected somebody to be standing there full-time handing out the man-sized tissues!

I told him that, nearer the time, the latest political briefing would be much appreciated. That, he said, would come as a matter of course. But he would be asking Juliet, whom I might remember from 'this office',[1] to give some thought, and perhaps some time to us, on our arrival. Her maiden name was Crawley. She was now married to a Frenchman, Dominique Vergos, who was most knowledgeable on Afghan affairs. Juliet excepted, however, Dominique was said to be none too fond of the Brits. The old language barrier might have had something to do with it. Almost as an afterthought, he said Dominique was thought to work for the CIA, which, he added, would be enlightened of them.

I remembered Juliet, with great affection. She and Romey Fullerton had had the two little *wagons-lits* rooms at the back of the office. Her Jack Russell used to hog the gas fire all winter long. Sir Oliver said she now had a whole menagerie ... camels, horses, donkeys, as well as dogs and parrots. They may have arrived as company for her first child, Fynn.

More to our purpose, it was she who was now running the highly efficient and much praised casualty evacuation programme (CASEVAC), using mostly Toyota pick-up trucks as 'ambulances'. They went to pre-determined (party) pick-up points well inside Afghanistan. The beauty of it was, I suspected, that there was no back-haul wasted journey problem, because drivers could take in essentials - but not arms or ammunition - for the survival of those who had stayed behind. Unfortunately, this did not include seed corn, most of which was destined for the far north of the country; whereas the casualties came predominantly from the south. This meant that the cost of transporting a sack of corn could often be more than that of the contents. In these circumstances, it was to prove more effective to carry the cash to the Oxus instead of the corn, but this required, of course, reliable couriers. AfghanAid's other main activity, at that time, was to sustain the agricultural livelihood of all the stay-behind farmers. That way they might be able to stem the flood of refugees, ease Pakistan's burden but, more importantly, maintain the resistance infra-structure. Of course, the Russians knew that resistance fighters needed feeding and were busy laying waste to the land, expecially the

Juliet Crawley Peck. *Photo by Gerhard Stromberg*

intricate irrigation systems. Their objective was to control the cities, leaving the countryside deserted.

I said how much I was looking forward to meeting Juliet again and, if she welcomed suggestions, one of the Guildford team, Peter Stiles had National Service experience in Cyprus to draw on, which could have relevance. I said I would keep in close touch and in due course would let Sir Oliver have our itineraries.

Not surprisingly, Sir Oliver's successor as ambassador at Islamabad, Nicholas Barrington, took a keen interest in AfghanAid's activities. Either he or another key member of staff, visited Peshawar once or twice a month. It would be as well to let them know what we were doing. I said I should not have dreamt of doing otherwise. Sir Oliver was delighted to hear it, but not altogether convinced. He wanted to know what would have made someone like me settle for the mundane task of co-ordinating an humanitarian medical mission, which was all about fussing and nannying, when his impression of me had been one of living for kicks, preferably in the enemy's camp.

Timing could have something to do with it, I told him. My father had died recently. He often said that some of the most rewarding years of his life had been spent fund-raising for the Sheffield Voluntary Subscription Hospitals, before the Second World War. I was planning a sabbatical without daily, weekly or monthly deadlines. I wanted to take time off, to do less and be more. The Guildford effort struck me as more meaningful than my own daily round. We then agreed that there was nothing quite so dead as yesterday's news, which, at present, was all we were getting from Afghanistan.

At this stage, Sir Oliver seemed to devolve into some Sherlock Holmes state of trance. Inevitably he was suffused in tobacco smoke, but there was also a faraway wistful expression on his face as if Doctor Watson were about to arrive hot foot from Maiwand. Now, a knowing twinkle crept into the corner of his left eye, the one which said *I know what you want*, whilst the other said *I'm damned if you'll have it*. It was the look he probably kept in reserve for Civil Service Selection Board interviews - where not-for-nothing was he Chairman.

He mumbled something about it making more sense for Mohammed to go to the mountain. He then explained he was thinking that it made more sense for surgeons to go to the casualties, than for the casualties to be brought back to western hospitals. It had to be more cost-effective, especially by the time their vastly extended families, with whom they could find themselves saddled for months at a time, were included. The morale effect would be just as visible there on the ground, for all to see. And the press could surely demonstrate as much concern. I could not but agree.

Then, as a final thought, he added that, if I should ever find myself anywhere near a place called Bannu, on the way to Miram Shah, I was to be sure to call in on Ruth Coggan at the Pennell Memorial Hospital. She was a truly remarkable woman running an amazing operation.

By way of rejoinder, and speaking of remarkable women, I asked if there were any more reports on famine as a weapon of war coming along from Frances D'Souza.[2] Sir Oliver asked how I knew about that. I pointed out that I had not only been included in the original press conference to launch the initial research findings, but that the last time I had been at Jamshid Burki's house in Peshawar, I had met Ahmed Akbar, who has the Chair of Pakistani Studies at Oxford and who had told me to follow up Frances because she had something highly germane coming along. So, now he knew my impeccable source. I said I had only mentioned it because Charlie Douglas-Home wanted to know if there was anything special enough for him to raise at his imminent meeting with President Reagan. I had suggested AfghanAid might have something promising, in draft form.

I knew I could now leave it to Sir Oliver to have the appropriate word in the appropriate quarter at the appropriate time and the oiling of the wheels and the smoothing of the way would follow, for Charlie, for Bill Morrell and for me.

*

I walked slowly and contentedly across Trafalgar Square and St James's Park until I reached the telephone booth beside the main Broadway Post office. I put through a call to the Royal Surrey County Hospital and, like clockwork, got Anne Stokoe via Anwar's bleeper. I told her she could tell Anwar and the team that it was all systems go now for end-October or early November, this year.

She congratulated me and said she had always known I would pull it off and how pleased Anwar would be. I said we would need to call a meeting in a fortnight or so. Then we could get down to some detailed planning.

[1] Strictly speaking, 'this office' is correct since Juliet was there at Afghan Support Committee when Sir Oliver was in post at Islamabad.

[2] Frances D'Souza conducted research into Famine as a weapon of war in Afghanistan. She has subsequently championed Salman Rushdie.

Rupert with Dr Ruth Coggan daughter of the former Archbishop of Canterbury at Bannu, Waziristan. *Photo by Peter Stiles*

7

To Kill or Cure - a Reconnaissance in Force

I soon came to the end of the matters outstanding on my 'organiser'. I was free to take my leave from the daily grind - a new lease of life was about to begin. I was ready to return to the North West Frontier . . . and the quest beyond.

According to Michael Taussig[1]

'There is a weight of Old World traditions which support a view of Saint Michael the Archangel as containing within himself the dual powers of healer and warrior. Donald Attwater, in his *Dictionary of Saints* (1948), says that the reference, in the book of Revelation, to the war in heaven contributed to Saint Michael being honoured in the West, from the beginning of Christendom, as Captain of the heavenly host, protector of Christians in general and soldiers in particular. In the East, however, as in Constantinople, it was not his status as warrior but his power to heal the sick that was important.'

What the British and the Afghans may have most in common is a mutual admiration for lunatic bravery, plus a sneaking respect for genuine eccentricity. What other races have claimed descent from the lost tribes of Israel? At one time or another, both British and Afghan have done just that.

A fierce independent spirit was common to those attracted to the country in the first place. Amongst the Afghans themselves some found affinity with the wandering Galandar - 'The wearer of the patchwork coat of many colours, symbolising the world's ninety and nine lost illusions and hailed by us, via Sicily, as Harlequin.' Or pass for the even more mysterious Malamati, equally renowned for their eccentricity of dress and odd behaviour. 'Madmen, fools, lunatics - all are sacred to Islam ... for only children and madmen speak the truth.'[2]

By now, the British were on well-trodden, hallowed ground, which gave added purpose to every step. We had been coming for one good reason or another for many generations. This time our intentions were the purest of the pure, our shining sincerity manifest, which wasn't to claim it had always been so. As ever, it was time to restore some balance. We had long given up the white man's burden, which the Americans were ever loath to assume, unless there were money or votes in it. However, in our small way, we would continue to make our contribution to 'The savage wars of peace, Fill full the mouth of

Famine and bid the sickness cease!'[3] The acts of the good Samaritan would transcend the outmoded notion of Christian revenge.

An early part and parcel of my duties as acting unpaid assistant administrator to the Guildford team was to obtain group discount fares and as generous a baggage allowance as possible from British Airways. I was fortunate to know Gordon Dunlop, the Financial Controller, from a previous incarnation at Commercial Union, and Lord King, who had provided the containers which I had helped to fill for Lady Salisbury's[4] relief missions to Poland during Jaruzelski's reign. Gordon came up trumps with a very generous baggage allowance of 1,000 kilos, which would enable us to take all the impedimenta as well as some relevant medical donations. This was a most welcome bonus on top of the already heavily discounted group fares.

In those days the Government was the only shareholder for BA to satisfy, which not only made such decisions easier, but possible at all. It was an offer we could not refuse. It was also a relief to find there would be no case for attempting to play one airline off against another, with the chance of alienating them both. This was to be an all-British effort from the outset.

Newcomers to Pakistan are tempted to take the domestic flight on from Islamabad to Peshawar. By the time you have waited four hours for the non-existent incoming aircraft, or landed back at Islamabad a couple of times due to unexpected turbulence, you learn you are better off taking the longer haul by minibus up the Grand Trunk Road. Endless security checks are an added hazard at all times. On one occasion, we were delayed unbearably whilst trying to make the domestic flight connection. The security guard insisted on minutely examining and even rattling a Cox's orange pippin, as if it were some clockwork orange about to explode. What he did not tell us in our panicked state was that the plane was being held for us anyway. It was one of the ones that had returned to the start line twice, before we elected to travel by road.

As an early indication that he was destined to teach me my job, whereas I could never do his, 'Pathfinder' and Lead Surgeon Peter Stiles would admonish that all one needed was a sharp eye for the Nicholson Monument.[5] If it was not on the left-hand side of the road, it meant you were headed back to the airport!

If you are fortunate to have your arrival heralded in any way, the chances are that, in this land of unlimited hospitality, somebody will have been sent to greet you. So, before succumbing to a minibus tout, look first for a huge notice worthy of a political demonstration, which may spell out your name and who has come to meet you. I was once reprimanded for not looking hard enough. The driver had missed out on school and did not understand the magic of writing. He was frantically waving the banner, but all rolled up. We only found each other when there was nobody else left.

Therefore, if you have any say in the matter, go by road and preferably the first time at least, by shared 'flying' mini-bus. There is so much more to be seen and learned along the Grand Trunk Road.

Save the wonders of Taxila and its Hellenic Buddhist stone carvings and Babur's Wah Gardens for your return journey; or you may get no further.

From the moment you reach Attock, it is as if some outside supernatural force takes over. Attock is at the confluence of two mighty rivers, the Kabul and the Indus. Their very different characters are reflected in the peoples who border their respective banks. At Attock stands the vast fortress of the Mogul Emperor Akbar (built in 1586). The only competing attraction, placed discreetly, almost out of sight where the river bends, is one of those indestructible British box-girder Callendar-Hamilton bridges. But it is the Mogul fortress that demands a natural staging post, as a break of pace and journey is called for. There are many *chaikhana*s (tea houses) to choose from some with impressive views, matched with indifferent fly-blown food, drink, sloppy service and no amenities; others making up for what they lack of the famed view, which supply all those other needs of the weary traveller. Anwar had supposedly penetrated Akbar's castle, but I know of no other mortal who has done so. They are still frequently used for police internment and interrogation, which could be reason enough for deterring tourist interest. As a 'Prohibited Area' photographs are officially banned, but it is rather like trying to stop photography of Windsor Castle. The trick is to flatter the bridge sentries by taking their photographs.

It is now, on setting out again, that a sense of impending excitement begins. It is hard to analyse this exhilaration. It is a sensation said to be particularly familiar to Scotsmen and the Welsh; and so, presumably, to all mountain and hill tribesmen. Nobody has expressed it better than the former Governor of the North West Frontier, Sir Olaf Caroe, the region's most renowned scholar and administrator.

'For the stranger, who had eyes to see and ears to hear, always as he drove through the Magalla Pass, just north of Rawalpindi and went on to cross the great bridge at Attock, there was a lifting of the heart and a knowledge that, however hard the task and beset with danger, here was a people who looked him in the face and made him feel he had come home.'

For the friend and frequent traveller, old memories return to flood the carburettor of the mind. Driving along the Grand Trunk Road has few equals for excitement, anywhere in the world. Massive Bedford trucks, with their sides enhanced with boards like old garden wheelbarrows, brilliantly decorated with primary colour naive art common to Sicilian cart, canal barge or gipsy caravan, all over-loaded with sand, rocks, bricks or jumbled people, career headlong towards each other at breakneck speed and only manage to avoid collision by a mirage of Max Sennett film-splicing magic. Before much longer there will be hard rock face to smash into on one side and sheer chasm on the other.

Peshawar has its old city. As old, they would have you believe, as Rome, and with good reason, for Peshawar was the winter capital of Kanishka, the contemporary of Julius Caesar. There is a much more recent cantonment area, which was very much a British creation. If the trees alone were left to proclaim our former presence, they would be ample testament. But, despite minimum maintenance, the buildings still remain; hardly in keeping with quarters originally intended to be occupied by troops 'on a more than temporary, but less than permanent basis!' Yet more *arriviste* is University Town. The university itself can only have been the former Government House and is a gem of Islamic colonial architecture.

However, the similarities between the old town of Peshawar and Rome have more to do with traffic activity than architectural pretension. It is the intermingling of people, bicycles, motor scooters, artisans' hand-carts, trucks, cars and lorries and the ant-like way they all merge and cross over with the minimum of bumps, scrapes, collision or casualties, which confirms world crossroads status. Peshawar, however, is more animal picturesque; many more tongas (horse-drawn carriages). donkey carts, and camels come into the mix. Picture postcard drawings of the Rome Ghetto of a century ago have much the same feel. But even today, they definitely share the same frenetic sense of purpose, the same determination to win this race of life to the death. To add zest, youth dashes across the tracks, leaps the crash barrier to risk life and limb in the errand of the moment. Those that failed to make it can be seen, limbless at the roadside, scudding along on wooden trolleys, mounted on sofa bearings. There are so many wounded from the war and the mines that there is no stigma attaching to the halt or the maim, who frequently profit from their plight. Alms giving is a major tenet of Islam.

The inversion[6] pall of pollution that hangs over Peshawar can be seen for twenty miles or more. But like in Rome, San Francisco or Sydney, you soon acclimatise. There is little alternative until you can escape for a breather in the mountains, while inversion continues to play its killing-ground havoc.

Accommodation choices range from the Khyber Intercontinental (since renamed Pearl) through Dean's to Green's Hotel and below and beyond. In the early days of the Afghan War, the Khyber had been reserved for visiting groups of VIPs, anyone thought likely to have an influence on US or other aid. President Reagan's special envoys, who could vary from Caspar Weinberger to Kirk Douglas, would put up there. Mohammed Ali also appeared there to promote his brand of Muslim power and powdered milk.

The Khyber boasts one of the few, if not the only accessible, swimming pool. In the summer heat this is a major drawcard among the expatriate community. As if the army needed to boost its manning levels under President Zia-ul-Haq, armed sentries were placed at the lift and stairs of every floor of the six-storeyed building and then again within eye contact at every corner angle and, if you warranted it, outside your very door.

Like all such places in wartime, there was no shortage of journalists crowding out the Permit Room (bar), where home-brewed Murree whiskey and beer were available to the non-believer *faranghis*, but only after a great deal of form-filling and the surrender of passports. Old friends and adversaries were free to meet up here again for a convivial drink in a tobacco haze fit to exceed the pollution outside. The barman was simultaneously censorious and supercilious. On our first and last visit, Anwar was banned as a bad Muslim, despite his protestations that he was a British subject, married to the daughter of an Anglican priest. No wonder everybody who wanted a drink preferred to go to the American Club, so long as they could gain admittance.

However, for our privately-funded budget-conscious expedition this purpose would be much better served by Dean's Hotel. Dean's is an altogether remarkable establishment. A hangover from the heyday of the Raj, it must have served as some kind of hostelry or even transit camp on the periphery of the cantonment area - used for shuffling married families around between quarters; a stop gap, whilst awaiting allocation.

To this day there remains an incongruous dining-room/ballroom duplex, which suggests that Dean's might also have hosted mothers, aunts, cousins 'trawling' eligible young ladies around India in search of a husband. This conjures up visions of distant *thés dansants* as the 'fishing fleet' moored in yet another hopeful haven.

Dean's modest comforts consist of well laid out bungalow accommodation with individual access. Private entrances with porches, lead into a sitting-room area, which leads on to a bedroom, which in turn opens into a bathroom - en suite. Living, sleeping, bathing - the whole ensemble has a suitable roof void overhead to allow a through draught to alleviate the effect of the midday, all-day sun on the galvanised hot tin roof. Revolving ceiling fans, electric replacements for the punkawallah, waft you to sleep as you lie exhausted beneath them. The cries of the mullahs' dawn call to prayer rouse you from over the high garden wall in good time to greet the new day.

The thermos of twice-boiled and cooled water, standing on the living-room table is as good a guarantee as any that you might get through another day without falling victim to Delhi belly or worse. 'Fleaseed', the stand-by Indian remedy, tops the survival kit list for any stomach ailment. Like most devotions, mine can become repetitive. Once you have suffered you will understand why! Forget the Amex Card - but don't leave home without Fleaseed. It consists of the upper coating of *plantago orata*, which is highly purified by sieving and winnowing.

The prime reason for favouring Dean's, however, was certainly not the Room Service, nor the charms of the night-duty telephone operator, whose location was a closely guarded secret and whose 'deep throat' services were mandatory. Nor was it the competitive manoeuverings of the Christian room boys, who vied with each other to remove the stinking sodden *shalwar kamees* or western shirt off your sweating back, as you dashed for the shower. Muslims are forbidden to look upon nakedness, which is the explanation for this peculiarly Christian monopoly. Nor were the touching little flowerbeds lovingly tended outside each makeshift 'home' the compelling attraction.

No, the prime reason for our picking Dean's was the fact that each and every bungalow apartment afforded a separate meeting point, which was to prove the only satisfactory means of simultaneously coping with the seven different political parties and their emissaries. Once the word was out that doctors had arrived, the pressure groups would be unleashed.

However, Pathans[7] tend to keep Italian time. Two minutes equals more like twenty. A little hour can mean four hours. Disconcertingly, appointments can be kept bang on time, but two days late.

Dean's copes with all this through the total calm of its Front Desk Managers, who are a byword for discretion. Mohammed Youssuf is entirely wasted on Dean's. He should be installed at Claridge's or the Connaught tomorrow, for he is the all-powerful custodian of precedence in chalet allocation and the sole conduit for all incoming callers and telephone messages. He has impeccable handwriting and takes pride in keeping a meticulous ledger. By all accounts he is a Kashmiri. A very different character, a Punjabi with rather obviously dyed orange hair, has 'security' responsibilities for monitoring the movements of foreigners. He lurks in an obscure office tucked away behind the tourist information shop. We adopted a policy of saving him trouble by always asking him the way.

The public rooms at Dean's are, if anything, a bit too public, but fun for all that. There you can meet Australian overlanders and any number of international aid organisation personnel. Scandinavians predominate, good English speakers and good for comparing notes. As usual, the French have got themselves organised. There are generally more of them, including Belgians, and as much for culinary as cultural and conversational reasons they congregate at the 'French House' in University Town.

Green's Hotel comes a poor second to Dean's. Whilst Dean's is spacious, Green's is cramped. There is no garden, just a central light well. There is a feeling of prison-like confinement. In making for the staircase, you must take especial care not to cross the prayer mats. Privacy is minimal. The restaurant 'Lalia's Grill' is said to surpass Dean's for delicacy. Neither will poison you, but one or two meals a week at the Khyber are counselled. It is no great indulgence as, by Western standards, the cost is derisory. 'Meatless' days have to be suffered under the Muslim (Sharia) law, but as the vegetarian fare, which includes chicken, is often better, the self-denial of fly-blown sheep and goat carcasses is no great hardship. One glance at any butcher's shop should be enough to convert the most avid carnivore to pulses and potatoes for life.

[1] Shamanism Colonialism and the Wild Man - A study in terror and healing by Michael Taussig. University of Chicago Press (1987) p.206

[2] Afghanistan (1980) Editions du Chene, Paris, Roland and Sabrina Michael Michaud. English translation (1980) Thames & Hudson, London

[3] Rudyard Kipling

[4] Molly, Lady Salisbury, is Robert Cranborne's mother.

[5] The Nicholson Monument commemorates John Nicholson, soldier and administrator in the Punjab, who made a celebrated dash from Lahore to Delhi in the Indian Mutiny. He died relieving the City at the assault on the Lahore Gate in 1857. His monument was raised at the site where he had previously distinguished himself holding the Margalla Pass during the Second Sikh War in 1848.

[6] Where the layer of air next to the earth's surface is cooler than an overlying air.

[7] Pathan is the old British Raj word covering those tribes, which are now described more ethnically correctly as Pashtoons, from their language, Pashto. I suspect Pathan was a refined compromise, avoiding the less guttural spit of Pachtun. In my turn, I have failed to find a more politically correct term for tribe!

8

Dressing the Part

Having settled our accommodation and our diet, the next objective was to get ourselves properly dressed for the climate and local custom. Opposite the mosque beyond Green's, there is a fine outfitters called The Novelty Stores, which could pass for the Aquascutum of Peshawar, if not the Austin Reed. Here you can buy almond shaving soap for 25p and at the next counter a *pakool* hat for £1 or £2. Next, sandals, or *chapli*, made to measure out of old car tyres come for another £2 and, again, designed like the box-girder bridge, are indestructible. A superb *patoo* blanket will cost rather more at £10. The *shalwar kamees* - pyjama suits - one on, one in the wash and if you are flush enough, one spare, come in many shades and ranges in price. Unless you fancy yourself as the white panther (ultimately Anwar's downfall) it is wiser to eschew the whites or cream materials and settle for Diana Duff-Cooper beige. For well-camouflaged obscurity, there is nothing to beat field grey or baby-shit brown.

The *shalwar kamees* gives the freedom of relatively cool movement. The *chapli*, which must be made locally to the local pattern, are mandatory and should preferably fit so as to slip on and off without stooping. The reason for this is that Muslim custom requires the removal of shoes on entering most buildings. Europeans are sufficiently ungainly as it is, without adding to their gawkiness by bending down. Footwear is the universal giveaway. It can be make or break at border crossings. Border guards are long trained to look at feet first.

You can get away with just two sets of *shalwar kamees*. Usual underwear. No socks. A turban or neckcloth, especially for sandstorms, and the standard *patoo* blanket and that, plus the all-purpose Afghan waistcoat or flak-jacket just about completes the rig-out. Do not attempt to wear a turban unless you have done so since infancy. It will take the rest of your life to learn how to balance the blanket nonchalantly on your shoulder so that it doesn't fall ignominiously into the open drain. It is not good enough to fold it over your arm. Keep trying, and don't forget that what you now need above all else is a water bottle, preferably insulated in some way.

Our personal kit just about complete, and now knowing the ropes for the others to follow, Anwar and I headed back to Dean's, after taking careful note of all prices, although it must be said that no attempt was ever made to sell us anything, superfluous or otherwise. Next, we changed and handed over our now highly impracticable European clothes for *dobi-wala* (laundry) attention and retention until the return flight. I always made it a ritual to bring anything requiring expert sewing repairs. This warrants extra payment but the standard of invisible mending surpasses anything affordable in Europe.

Now that we had settled accommodation, diet and costume, we could perhaps get down to the serious business of organising the work programme for the main party - due to arrive in less than a week. As outlined before, we needed to be careful to give our time and services in as impartial and apolitical a manner as possible; or so we thought at the time.

Try as they might to restructure their politics into two basic groups of 'traditionalists' and 'fundamentalists', the Afghans always seemed to fall apart again, just as quickly, into the original seven recognised political parties. The Afghans blamed the Pakistanis for this and the Pakistanis the Afghans - *ad infinitum.* The cultural basis of Afghan society is vehemently anti-organisation anyway. That is, anything over and above the immediate tribal structure. They are congenitally opposed to any higher authority - other than God.

Everyman would be king and another *shibboleth* to note is 'Honour is in the mountains, only taxes in the plains!'

To help us through the minotaur's maze of all this, we had two invaluable guides. The first was our own British Afghanistan Support Committee and its sister organisation AfghanAid. The other, which was ostensibly more directly aligned to our purposes, was the extraordinary American organisation, Orthopaedics Overseas Inc. Orthopaedics Overseas is in turn linked to a British organisation with worldwide ramifications called World Orthopaedic Concern, to which the Guildford surgeons belong. For once, World Orthopaedic Concern is bigger than its American counterpart. However, for the present, in Peshawar, the American organisation was the high-profile party already well-established, well-known and respected, with a semi-permanent representative and presence; and, being American, it also afforded ready access to the American Club, which was the only ex-pat watering hole permitted to serve alcoholic drinks without requiring the rigmarole of a government-issued individual permit. Membership alone was enough to damn you in the eyes of Allah.

Whereas AfghanAid had issued us with a two-page list of useful addresses and telephone numbers, the Orthopaedics Overseas manual resembled the Yellow Pages. It had been compiled over many years largely by their Peshawar Program Director, Dr Kermit Veggeberg. Anwar used to describe him as giving a wondrous impression of the wrath of Jehovah complete with swirling smoke-screen. He is a vast, unshaven, sweet tempered (till crossed) prime optimist of a chain-smoking walrus of a man. More than likely it was he who put Anwar up to all this in the first place. He not only believes that Faith and Mohammed can move mountains, but that man has been placed on earth with the sole object of by-passing such trifling obstacles. At times this can prove a tall order in the Hindu Kush. When in Peshawar, he resides at Dean's alongside his compatriot and a knowledgeable scholar on all matters Afghan, Dr Louis Dupree. Dupree's wife, Nancy, is also an authority on the country, and has compiled the only reliable modern guidebook.

Armed with our extensive guides, therefore, we set out to reconnoitre the various hospitals on the basis that it was better to ascertain what was feasible, do-able from a surgical perspective, before getting bogged down in political niceties. The only immediate snag to this plan was that a number of the party political hospitals gave box number addresses for fear of reprisals. Assassinations are commonplace. Corsican-type vendettas are part of the order of every Afghan's day.

So, we elected to introduce ourselves first to those hospitals with published addresses, beginning at the top. As was to be expected, the International Committee of the Red Cross/Red Crescent (ICRC) was far and away the most impressive. I had been there four years before. Highly receptive as they were in the person of the current British medical co-ordinator, Dr Robin Gray, who gave us a masterly tour d'horizon, including a privileged political overview, there was simply no way that they could embrace volunteer surgeons, however skilled, for less than a six months' stint. Indeed, they did have British and Australian surgeons on the strength, working without respite for six months at a time. Sadly, there would be no place for us there.

Next, we called on the Lady Reading Hospital, under the direction of the charming and urbane Professor Jamil. They could not have been more accommodating. They bent over backwards to demonstrate their desire to welcome us. At the outset, Professor Jamil offered to house our theatre staff - Tony Bray, Robin Jago and Geoff McLeod - in enviable self-contained VIP lodgings in the hospital grounds, together with breakfast, cleaning and laundry facilities thrown in, all free of charge. We accepted with alacrity. It would make a handsome reduction to our overhead.

In return for such open-handedness, we agreed to give a

series of early morning lectures, but this turned out to be our first big mistake. As Anwar might have known, Peter Stiles was against preaching, believing that osmosis was the better lecturer. Too often lectures were on subjects and techniques that were inappropriate to the local situation. Too late, the damage was done. If we had waited a day or two longer before committing ourselves, we might have sensed the point from the racks of (replacement) hip prostheses which were to confront us on our rounds. These had been shipped out by well-meaning donors to no good purpose. Afghans are blessed with particularly mobile hips from a life-time of hunkering down. However, to maintain goodwill, lecture we would and at dawn if necessary. But Stiles was to be proved right again. Clinics and ward rounds were the best teachers in the long run.

There were soon other dilemmas to concern us.

The Pakistani authorities had attempted to change the name of the Lady Reading a number of times, in their search for something less colonial. But all the alternatives suggested had failed. One wonders what they would have made of Rufus-Isaacs, if the Reading title had not conveniently intervened!

The major problem with the Lady Reading was that, ostensibly, we had come to treat Afghans. Their patients, whilst being predominantly Pathans (Pashtuns) were not necessarily Afghans. It would take greater experience than ours to spot the difference. At the outset of the war there had been little doubt that upwards of ninety per cent of the patients were Afghan War casualties. Now, it was nearer fifty/fifty, or so they said. The nature of the injuries would show.

There and then we were automatically expected to join the hospital rounds. This turned out to be like elbowing our way through a railway terminal concourse, with all the panic of the streets running with blood. The statistics we were given were horrendous. Four hundred patients were seeking new admission status daily for a hospital with eight hundred beds. There was no after-care annexe. We found ourselves being jostled by today's supplicants, who, on recognising European doctors and pseudo-doctors alike, were no longer so concerned about the bed, but just wanted to get on with the consultation, then and there, anywhere, in the corridor, on the stairs. Privacy, if it existed as a concept, had gone out of the window long ago.

Under the Muslim *majlis* (open court) system anybody can chip in at any time, which is what can make getting on an airplane, let alone an operating table, such a hazard. X-ray negatives and diagnoses are thrust under your nose in Roman scroll form. Sometimes they are secured with an elastic band, otherwise more formally, like a QC's brief, with strands of pink or other multi-coloured ribbon. Everyone looks most profound. No doubt it is often a matter of life and death, but it is how to handle the patient, who has the same bad news from a dozen different international authorities, that requires the master's degree, and more, in tact and understanding.

Hospitals can be such laughter-shy, lugubrious places. No wonder medical students sometimes break loose and run amok whenever released from the unnatural internment of their youthful energy and high spirits.

When the team finally made it to the actual wards, we had to face up to all sorts of horrors and conditions that were seldom encountered in British medicine. 'Not in living memory in Guildford,' became the oft-repeated lament, and added justification for our presence.

Among the usual horrors of war, there were also weird cases of self-inflicted wounds. This was particularly true in the female wards. It was not so much attempted suicides as the ignorant administering of totally inappropriate drugs. Pakistan boasts the highest number of lawyers per head of population in the world - including even America. To this record should be added the highest number of quack and other chemist shops, with hardly a qualified pharmacist amongst them. Anybody can buy what they can afford and administer what they feel like. On the whole they might be better off prescribing opium, as the British used to do until this century.

Whether they were Afghan Pathans or not we did witness remarkable stoicism. Once we had completed the ward rounds and observed all the Pashtunwali tribal code of hospitality, tea drinking and quiet chats required of us, it was high time to head off by tonga taxi to the Afghanistan Surgical Hospital.

9

A Triumvirate of Treaters

The Afghanistan Surgical Hospital, where we supposedly had long been expected, is the finest by far of the party 'cottage' hospitals in Peshawar. It is sponsored by Jamiat Islami, Pakistan, which, confusingly, is the Pakistani equivalent of the Hesbe-i-Islami, Afghanistan, fundamentalist party of Engineer Gulbuddin Hekmatyar.

As you approach the hospital, a short distance along the Jamruddin side-street off the main Grand Trunk Road, you become aware of its presence by the clusters of family groups, squatting in the scanty shade opposite the entrance. In common with most Peshawar villas, the actual entrance was a Judas portal in a massive pair of sheet metal gates. Nobody could see what was going on inside or out. Admittance was gained by a hefty bang on the door, which brought forth a *chowkidar* or, since he was armed, even on hospital premises, guard. We found ourselves beckoned into a small parking area taken up mostly with two ambulances. We proceeded up a short flight of art-deco steps to our right into what had been the hall and was now the reception area, where we were greeted in the traditional Afghan manner 'Salaam Alaikum', to which we knew how to reply with much the same 'Alaikum, Salaam'. The first person we met was the hospital administrator, Firdos Khan. On his desk there was one wire basket. There was only one thing in the basket, our letter from Guildford. Nothing else. As it turned out, it was unlikely it had ever been read and, if read, certainly not understood. No hope of a reply. It had simply become an international status symbol, part of the high-tech world. At the top of an impressive flight of stairs, again of art-deco-derived 1930s design, was a suitably impressive door marked 'Doctor in Charge'.

Dr Sayed Iftikhar Hussain, the doctor in question, has been captured many times in print and more often on camera. Iftikhar is one of nature's more engaging creatures. We were not kept waiting long before he burst forth from his gilded cage and descended the sweeping curved white staircase, like some rare elusive butterfly.

'What indeed is your good name and your honourable profession?' came, at long last, the classic greeting.

Iftikhar could well have been of the tribe that claims descent from the Israelite diaspora, along with the British Israelite Welsh. The young Benjamin Disraeli may well have resembled Iftikhar, the oiled black ringlets bobbing to near shoulder-length, as if in compensation for dearth of other facial hair. His was the most winning of smiles and the most charming of manners as he flitted and weaved his way between us. Sharp, aquiline, saturnine features from which emanated a surprisingly high-pitched squeaky voice.

Neither Anwar nor I had expected anything quite like this; although Anwar and Iftikhar were both originally from Lahore.

'Welcome, welcome, welcome - thrice welcome. We have been expecting you. What has taken you so long in coming?' L-o-n-g was protracted indefinitely.

Without waiting for a reply, Iftikhar now led the way back upstairs to his office, which doubled for laboratory and dispensary as well. He told us reassuringly that everything was kept securely locked at all times.

On entering the room, he introduced us to his number two, another doctor and fellow surgeon, Faisal Rabbani. Faisal Rabbani could not have been a greater contrast, either physically or in personality. Equally charming as Iftikhar but much quieter, more subdued - a contemplative man, resembing more the heavily bearded Afghan we had come to expect. His eyes smiled all the time and, unlike the chirpy Iftikhar, his voice, when he spoke - which was seldom - flowed like milk and honey. He was always diffident and deferential as if we came bearing untold gifts.

The third man in this triumvirate, whom we had already met on arrival downstairs, now reappeared by a side door. Firdos Khan had us guessing, on our toes, for a long time and no wonder. To all outward appearances he was pleasant enough. He spoke perfect English. But then, so he should, for he'd been an accountant in Willesden for sixteen years and must have hated every minute. It soon transpired that he had a general loathing of the West and all its decadence, so much so that we came to suspect him of deliberately confusing our programme.

On arrival, we learnt to expect him to tell us we were not scheduled, as we had got the day wrong. Then, not content with telling us that, despite our both holding copies of the same programme, he would go to the games-playing lengths of sending a vehicle to collect one of our teams when they were operating at another hospital. So we were obliged to produce individual programmes for each hospital; so that he would not be able to know where we were. From the outset he seemed to want to do his utmost to discredit us. He was quite capable of telling us that Iftikhar had gone to Lahore on other business, when we could hear his infectious laughter in the next room.

Above Firdos Khan's desk there was the most wonderful and extraordinary of all maps of Afghanistan. We never saw another like it, and came to covet it, but had to content ourselves with a photograph. It may well have been more of a propaganda poster than a map.[1] Hard to tell, maps of Afghanistan are so bog-basic and bad, and inaccurate as to be utterly useless on the ground. As Freya Stark so aptly put it 'Place names seldom agree with the maps, which never agree with each other.' This was all the more exasperating when one knew that documents captured in the Panjshir revealed that a very high standard of large-scale map-making had been achieved by the Soviets. And what had become of all those much-lauded British surveys?

Anyway, what made Firdos Khan's map special was not the cartography, but a highly romantic bayonet-charging figure superimposed in blood red. It was a representation of Alexander the Great (Sikander to the Afghans) suitably metamorphosed into Mujahedeen valiant pose, replete with plumed helmet and a squirming Russian cobra impaled on the bayonet's blade. The rifle was a Lee Enfield Mark 1 and the bayonet the long WW1 model.

My first thoughts had been of Aaron's Rod, but clearly there were non-medical overtones to this whole hospital. However much the doctors protested their political impartiality when selecting patients for operations, the fact remained that the Afghan Surgical was a fundamentalist hospital and there was more than one war being waged. Quite apart from the testimony of the patients, the whole of one large area of wall, opposite the poster, was plastered with gory colour photographs of the halt, the maimed, the blind and the burnt; plus those totally disfigured - left sucking and blowing through a single facial orifice that looked more anal than oral.

The Afghanistan Surgical Hospital was sufficiently in tune with Western methods of self-promotion to issue ring-bound photopacks, featuring the worst afflicted cases they had handled so far. They were given out like free sets of holiday hotel postcards.

On this occasion we explained our reconnaissance purpose and promised to return to join the statutory ward round the next day. There were a number of differences which singled out Afghanistan Surgical.[2] One of them was the absence of families undertaking nursing duties. Here that was done by professional permanent staff.

At the call to prayer, we just had time to study the layout of the place. The inner courtyard was still given over to garden, with whispy grass and a few rose bushes. Obviously, once, the whole back area had been a large garden. Now all four sides had been built up to match the three-storeyed main building, so that the ward floors were indistinguishable. The two operating theatres were one above the other with scrub rooms adjoining.

At prayer times, all those capable of movement came out on to the balconies ringing the garden and lined up in rows to face Mecca. We were hard put to know what to do with ourselves. There was no slinking away. It was never too late to drop to our knees. All too self-consciously, we stood and gawped, as we came to do so often in the future. Thank heavens, nobody ever took the slightest notice of us, or cared. We were beyond the pale.

Goodness knows why we were constantly caught so unawares. They knew instinctively the moment before the moment, when you couldn't tell a white thread from a black one. We never twigged it. Either we thought the truck was slowing to a halt for lack of fuel, defect, refreshment or change of driver, or even to relieve nature when, more significantly, it was to refresh the soul. A need which we ourselves would come, in time, to overlook at our peril.

Prayers over, we were driven back to Dean's in one of the two ambulances we had noticed on our arrival. Anwar said he was looking forward to telephoning his wife Anne - a treat which took four hours to consummate for four minutes' chat. To his enquiry, I replied that I never did ring my wife if I could help it. It usually ended in acrimony over trivia, which led to remorse and regrets. Rather than have expensive long-distance arguments, it was better to stay silent and send a letter, which with any luck would arrive after my return and any discrepancies could be explained away. I once made the mistake of taking up a generous offer to use the lead-lined bug-proof radio satellite telephone box in the Islamabad Embassy, just to let her know I had returned safely. Unfortunately, the reception was so good she refused to believe I wasn't next door in London.

The next day we duly witnessed, at first hand (as opposed to the photographs), all the horrors of the ward round at Afghan Surgical. Unlike at the Lady Reading, there was no doubting that these were war wounds, many needing urgent secondary surgical attention. Some of the guillotine amputations had been altogether too rough and ready. Anwar took careful note. Again, we had to explain that today we had not come to operate, but to draw up lists.

It was also time to move on to the Kuwaiti Red Crescent Hospital. This proved to be such a terrible experience that, ever since, whenever we drove past we averted our eyes involuntarily. The notice board with its elaborate red and white, part Arabic, part Roman signwriting was enough to induce shudders of apprehension from me.

The establishment stands four square on the University Town road, just opposite a string of good restaurants - Usmania (Pakistani) and Shirnawaz (Afghan).

It may have been a particularly bad 'off-colour' day, or perhaps we struck unlucky with the duty staff. A bit like a Sicilian hospital, the whole place hadn't been swept in weeks and was deep littered with cigarette butts. The exclusively Egyptian doctors did not hesitate to tell us that they were only there for the pay and cared little for the patients, whom they seemed to treat on a conveyor-belt high-productivity basis. Since their pay was performance related, they resorted to bribing taxi ambulance sharks to bring their charges straight to them; like so many West End hotels competing for taxi patronage.[3] So, those unscrupulous drivers who lay in wait on the border to rob the dying and the dead, before delivering them to the doubtful mercies of an Egyptian surgeon, were being paid twice over for their pains. Which *sura* of the Koran did they take as their refuge and their hope?

The Kuwaiti Red Crescent Hospital must surely have had its finer moments, but with our limited itinerary, we never went back to discover them. For the record, the doctors happened to boast that they were earning ten times what they would be paid in Egypt, which at least explained their chain-smoking. When they learned the basis of our own voluntary contribution, they laughed us to scorn. There could be no meeting of such disparate minds.

[1] Reproduced on the cover of this book.

[2] We knew it colloquially as 'Afghan Surgical'. Strictly speaking, I suppose it has to be Afghanistan Surgical.

[3] Part of the reason for establishing the Afghan CASEVAC programme was surely to bypass these charlatans.

10

Cottage Hospitals

Having dealt with what could be loosely termed 'real' hospitals (although Afghan Surgical was really an expanded 'cottage' hospital) we next decided to call on the more homely, or cottagey, of the cottage hospitals.

Invariably, these were in rented standard villa accommodation, which could be 'converted' to their new purpose. The living/dining-room became the operating theatre, the kitchen was the scrub room, the bedrooms became the wards. Bathrooms remained vaguely bathrooms. The number of beds that could be crammed in varied between 40 and 60, depending on how much spillage occurred into the passages, landings etc. Outpatients waited patiently strewn over the garden area. Sometimes an outpatients' consulting room was improvised in the chowkidar's hut, or porter's lodge.

Over the time remaining to us, we managed to visit all these medical establishments. However, I shall only describe here those finally selected as being eligible for our purpose.

Although Afghanistan Surgical had given us repeated assurances that patients were treated irrespective of their party political allegiance, and we had no reason to doubt them, equally we had no means of confirming their impartiality. It was noticeable that there was no means of cross-referring patients between hospitals. We had little idea of who made the initial recommendation for the patient. From the chits that some carried, it looked likely that choice was determined by the commander in the field or the flag that was being followed at the time. There would need to be a leavening at some stage, but our next call was to the other main fundamentalist party cottage hospital.

This was also Hesbe-i-Islami. There was an added complication here though, since the party is sub-divided. The faction better known to Westerners is that headed by Engineer Gulbuddin Hekmatyar, mentioned at the beginning of the previous chapter in the Afghanistan Surgical Hospital context. But the other, just as worthy of recognition, is under the inspiring leadership of Younis Khalis. At the venerable age of seventy-four, he is the only Peshawar-based political leader to take to the battlefield if not the battlefront. He was also memorable for his henna-dyed beard and the fact that he had a penchant for 15-year-old brides. So, we hoped that by embracing his hospital we might bridge some degree of schism. The location was every bit as obscure as the politics, because this time, it really was one of the Post Office Box Numbers. So, for this, our first visit, we had to be guided there.

The establishment was by any reckoning a long way down the hygiene scale, but, fortunately, the assistant administrator's assessment counted for nothing. What I had noticed were only the superficial indices. The fans might be too few and too sluggish. The tattered mosquito netting might be left unrepaired. The walls were certainly besplattered with saliva and worse. No sooner was a dressing removed than a swarm of flies would settle to gorge on the bared wound. Surely, I ruminated, this must cause widespread cross-infection. But, as I learnt later on, what mattered far more was the quality of the treatment. After his first ward round, Peter Stiles was able to tell me that here - in the person of Ali Abdul Rousta, the Doctor-in-Charge - was a man who not only knew what he was doing on behalf of each and every one of his patients, but also that he genuinely cared for them. This was reflected in their morale and the morale of his staff. Ali Abdul Rousta, who was also the lead surgeon, resembled a benign fairytale sultan of outsize girth and grin. Given time his patients would recover.

Seen overall - excepting the ICRC, which perforce received the lion's share (90%) of the fresh casualties - there wasn't much to choose between the range and type of wounds to be treated amongst the patients in each of the party hospitals. This should not have come as any surprise, since they had, after all, been fighting much the same kind of battles, involving the same weaponry. There was one unexpected new category - bouncing walls. This referred to those crushed by mud walls after high-altitude Russian bombardment.

So far as we could discover, hospital selection was more a matter of accident of birth, tribal origin or political allegiance than anything else. To have reached the Pakistan border in the first place was the surest sign of a strong survival streak. There was no means of assessing the numbers who failed to make it. The evidence of the wards was that casualties with wounds of the thorax and abdomen failed to survive their injuries, whilst those with wounds to their extremities frequently did. There was no doubting the amount of work to be tackled, but there did seem to be an inordinately high proportion of secondary surgery cases - with all the criticism that implied. There were any number of above and below knee guillotine amputations without any allowance having been made for skin flaps to cover a neat and healthy stump. This would mean long debates to persuade patients to have more off to effect the more desirable result. Any diminution of the temple of the soul was anathema to Islam.

What we now needed for balance was a leavening of 'traditionalist' patients ... This brought us to the last of the 'all-male' original party cottage hospitals to be selected by us. It did wonders for our morale because, although it was one of the last to be visited, it turned out to be by far the best. Not on account of facilities, where Afghanistan Surgical had the advantage, but on account of its inspired leadership. We had come to it last because it was far and away the hardest to find. In fact, we went on having difficulty locating it for some time. One continuous smooth high mud wall can look much like another.

This hospital was the Ibn Sina Balkh (Ibn Sina was the great Persian physician known to the West as Avicenna, 980-1037 CE) cottage hospital of Pir Sayid Ahmad Gailani's National Islamic Front for Afghanistan (NIFA). There was no doubting the motivation here or the patronage. His picture was everywhere. Pir Gailani is not only descended from the Prophet's brother, and consequently a religious sect leader as of birthright, but also a distinctly pro-Western as well as pro-Royalist political leader. Politics and religion are still inseparable in Afghanistan. Pir Gailani has a fairly large following, with a wide-ranging influence over vast areas of the south-eastern parts of Afghanistan - all amongst the Pashtoo speaking tribes as far flung as Kabul and Qandahar.

Here, in the Ibn Sina hospital, there was a totally different kind of atmosphere, readily identifiable as right-wing paternalistic and somewhat closer in style, if not in spirit, to Guildford. It was only day four of our survey and if we were not careful, there was already some danger of our compromising our even-handed ideal. For once, I found I had an added value too, in that their administrator, Dr Babrakzai, was, like myself, a French linguist. But the single most impressive feature was not so much the quality of the religious leadership as the sheer charisma of the Chief Surgeon, Major Abdul Satar Paktiss - an early defector from the "Russian-supporting" Kabul regime Afghan Army.

From the moment you first set eyes on the man, you knew you were in the presence of a whole man, replete with wholesome aura, albeit a most pragmatic saint of the Calcutta slums stamp. Or if it had to be another man, an Albert Schweitzer or a Leonard Cheshire. Either way, a very big little man, with the most penetrating intense black eyes, set in the handsomest of bearded happy positive faces. He had an excellent command of English, gravelly tones which could talk the birds out of the trees; he was also a born organiser. Surgically speaking, he wasn't just highly competent, but also highly innovative.

His claim to fame stems from an amazing external fixator, which he either 'invented' or at least developed to match the war need. Its function is to restore whole a shot-up half-destroyed limb.

High velocity bullet wounds cause extensive tissue damage, as never before - far worse than the dum-dum bullet. A massive hole the size of your fist or bigger can be blown out by the tumbling, blasting bullet.

The surgeon then has the problem of cutting out and removing all dead tissue along with any dirt (foreign bodies) and, above all, dead bone. This sounds easy enough on paper, but tends to be a lot trickier in practice. He then has to make the most of what he has left, which may not be much!

Paktiss's magic, as I understood it, consists of salami-slicing what bone remains and re-positioning it over the former full-length of the limb. These bits are then held in place 'externally', by the external fixator. It resembles an inverted cradle or maternity frame from which prongs or skewers protrude into the limb, through the flesh, 'fixing' the position of each succeding salami slice of bone.

To the layman, the miracle is that the bone then grows together again between sections, which can be as much as an inch apart, to recreate a full-length limb over a six-month period. Full-length, that is, to the same all-important length of matching limb. If all this were not enough Brighton Rock to swallow, such external fixators do not come cheap in the West. Paktiss has his fabricated in the local bazaars from spare bicycle parts, at a fraction of their stainless steel cost. Bicycle spokes become the skewers. They may not be as sterile, but they make up for this deficiency in availability, economy and effectiveness.

On our statutory ward round with him, we were pleasantly surprised to be ushered into a female ward. At first glance it was empty, a sham. In fact, if the patient had had her way, we should never have noticed her. She was a whimpering bundle of once bright, but now grubby rags ... shuffling about on her haunches in a corner of the room, trying to get out, but not knowing how to go about it. Her head and face were completely covered. She was more like a hedgehog left scrabbling about in a motorway storm-water sump, unable to find the non-existent exit, than a human being.

Paktiss managed to soothe and calm her and somehow reassure her that we were not systematic rapists. He then coaxed her up on the edge of a bed with her leg extended beyond the fringe on the bundle of rags. I couldn't help noticing it was as hairy as mine. So, finally, we came to examine her external fixator. It had a fine patina, like an old ship's sextant, much used, with a wealth of two-toned brass or copper furniture and screws as if counter-sunk by Cartier. It was a thing of great beauty, a Florentine guildsman's artefact. It must have been used over and over again to good effect.

Abdul Satar Paktiss went on to introduce us to each and every one of his patients and spoke to them and of them with all the concern and tender loving care that Ali Abdul Rousta had exhibited in his hospital.

The visit culminated in a crescendo of impact, which can only have been intended to make a final lasting impression. As if staged on the way out and not there on the way in, we met a father who was sitting caring for his boy, who had lost all four limbs and was blinded. A mine injury. The boy had either been clearing the mine or laying it. There was no telling. It made no difference now. It would be a long gruelling death before the father could bury his son. As Bacon wrote, 'In peacetime sons bury their fathers. In wartime fathers bury their sons.'

We never had any hesitation in recommending Abdul Satar Paktiss and his hospital to all and sundry. If there was ever any choice in the matter, where AfghanAid's ambulances were concerned, we endorsed NIFA. It was always a pleasure to operate there. Interestingly enough, it was also always spotlessly clean.

*

There was only one other hospital left, which we had to include in our reconnaissance survey for the sake of our high-powered gynaecologist and his female assistant. We had heard that the Afghanistan Surgical Hospital, Jamiat-e-Islami, Pakistan, had a women's hospital, but there was no question of our gaining admittance. However, there was another possibility, which Anwar had researched from the Orthopaedics Overseas listings. This was the Afghan Obstetrics & Gynecology Hospital of Doctor M. Hossain Momand, MD. Dr Momand was said to have strong links with the United States. A brother-in-law was a practising gynecologist in America. He came to give his services on a devoted annual basis.

We were keen to find any opportunity for our specialist and his assistant to offer their skills. There was always the fall-back opportunity of the Lady Reading, but it might not be a true reflection of original intentions. Dr Momand's establishment, therefore, seemed, initially at least, a heaven-sent blessing.

Dr Momand himself created a lasting impression of an anxiety-

Dr Abdul Satar Paktiss with his renowned External Fixator at Pir Gailani Hospital in Peshawar. *Photo by Peter Stiles*

ridden chain-smoker. He was desperately seeking funding. He had a very neat formula for calculating the sum required. What made it memorable was that it was the same figure as the number of days in the year. Allow a thousand dollars a day and you reached the big figure. He went blank at the mention of a business plan.

In truth, of course, such a sum could have been justified many times over, when applied to the stark refugee statistics. There was a minimum of three-and-a-half million refugees in the camps, 75% of whom were known to be women and children. These were served by visiting clinics on a once-a-week basis, at best. Very soon you came full circle to face the fact that there were no qualified doctors to cope with the female patients, and you then reached the conclusion that they really didn't give a damn about their women. Nobody cared. Either they were stifled at birth, or they could be dispensed with on whim or they died in childbirth. If, worldwide, a thousand women a day die in childbirth, one can but wonder how many of them are Muslims, and how many of those are Afghans.

Which brings us back to the one-day visit to Dr Momand's hospital. Our high-powered specialist's assistant was sent to examine a patient. What she found was a suffocated female baby, nonchantly tucked away in the bedding. Afghans are known to stifle unwanted female babies at birth. Simply not wanted. Males only need apply. She could have been stillborn. It looked very much like the close of the chapter.

From our observations on ward rounds, we were able to anticipate some of the more unusual problems which would have to be faced by the teams, once they arrived. One such was the constant frustration of gearing the patient up to the operation. Invariably, permission had to be obtained from other members of the family. Blood donors had to be solicited from the same source. Often the patient had come from a far distant camp and had changed his mind, or simply failed to complete the second arduous journey back. Or, all he was after was the perennial objective of selection for America, with no intention of returning from there.

Sometimes, we noticed, there was an elaborate game of substitution. A list would be drawn up and agreed from the previous afternoon's ward round, only to find that for 'political' or possibly even pecuniary reasons, some altogether different candidate, with different symptoms presented himself.

To some extent, professional performance and Thatcherite productivity could be affected by the obligation to take in vast quantities of green tea during long breaks in order to cement social ties. Since discussion invariably revolved around surgery, these periods would have to be re-classified as lectures.

Having completed our *tour d'horizon* of the full range of hospitals and having chosen those we intended to service, we now needed to draw up the detailed programme and tackle the vital question of independent transport. I had roughed out an outline programme with Anwar, as we went along. It was now time to call on AfghanAid.

11

The Team Arrives

In contrast to their London peregrinations, AfghanAid have managed to keep the same pleasant premises in Gulmohar Road, University Town, Peshawar, for as long as they have had a base of their own. Before that, in the very early days, they shared accommodation with the Austrian Mission, over the wall. The outward appearance of the villa changed with each succeeding director. Sometimes there was a peaceful garden. At others, it was converted into a volley-ball pitch. Once the emphasis was on training schemes for the disabled; so, self-taught wounded tailors' shops predominated. These, in turn, gave way to mechanical transport maintenance bays, as the all-important ambulance programme for casualty evacuation got underway. Which was how it was at the time of our visit.

The girl who sat with her Jack Russell shivering beside the gas fire in the Charing Cross Road and the young woman now running the CAS/EVAC ambulance programme in Afghanistan were barely recognisable as one and the same. Surely, the slight figure remained unchanged; although the vicar's daughter was now a married woman with a child of her own. Juliet had never lacked self-assurance, but now she was unmistakably 'in charge'. In control. In command. She must have been all of twenty-four.

Somehow her personality and shining inner goodness had captivated the very souls of these grisly Afghan tribesmen. They appeared to be her most willing slaves. It was uncanny and so out of keeping with their perceived attitude to women. They could hardly be expected to recognise the cast in her right eye or the enigmatic smile so reminiscent of Beechey's portraits of England's frail hero, Nelson.

Her French husband, Dominique Vergos, had been billed as cussed and uncouth, hard to get along with. This was not at all our experience. All that was needed was a working knowledge of French. He was also heroic in our eyes, as he had been inside Afghanistan countless times for extended periods - not just border hopping - and he worked for the CIA, as Sir Oliver had hinted.

Fortunately, Juliet did remember me from the early days in Charing Cross Road. She had also heard about us at length from Sir Oliver. Once we had outlined our programme, she had no hesitation in allocating to us, full-time, one of her prized drivers, Sabur, with his Toyota pick-up truck. He had recently been wounded by a shell fragment to his right shoulder and needed a break from the forward areas. Even more to our purpose he knew the way to all the hospitals at first hand. He also knew the direct routes between them. We arranged for him to meet us at the Queen Victoria red letter box at Dean's at 7.45 a.m. each morning, save the Sabbath, Friday. He was invariably a quarter of an hour early.

The first job we had for him was to help us to hire suitable drivers and vehicles for two quite different excursions, where his truck and time would be inappropriate.

Sabur was a gentle soul, very quiet, obviously very brave. He had little English, but seemed to understand most things instinctively. We were going to need a minibus to take twelve people minimum, preferably up to sixteen, to bring the whole team plus kit from Islamabad to Dean's. This trip would require an overnight stay, either with Anwar's brother in Islamabad or at Flashman's Hotel (same Government ownership as Dean's) in Rawalpindi, next door. The plane was scheduled to arrive at 5 a.m. It was essential to be there in plenty of time to brief, not bribe, the Pakistani Customs officials. By letting them have copies of the flight manifests, there was a good chance our group would get waved through to a quick getaway.

In addition to the minibus, which would be contracted at the massive transport hire emporium on the outskirts of town, we also needed to visit the taxi depot. Conveniently this was behind Dean's. There we would take our pick of driver and vehicle to go in search of a suitable rest house for recreation in the mountains, somewhere within a hundred miles of Peshawar. The better rest houses came under the aegis of the Forestry Commission and could be rented very reasonably; otherwise, Green's Hotel had a second establishment at Dunga Gali. There was plenty of choice.

By comparison to European or American chauffeur-driven car or bus hire, Pakistani rates are ridiculously cheap. But you do have to check the state of the vehicle and the state of the driver. Tyres always need a thorough inspection, plus spares. They change a wheel quicker than in the pits at Brand's Hatch. Oil changes are less frequent. The state of the driver is another matter. More than likely, he is on *naswar* and most of the time is as high as a kite. This puts him in just the right frame of mind to take on those head-on collisions, but like long-distance lorry drivers, they never get enough time off to sleep. They are the hirelings of whomever owns the vehicles, so are only due a fraction of the hire; so handsome tips at outset and end are a good insurance.

Although we never saw any of the AfghanAid drivers taking anything, the use of *naswar* is widespread. It is very obvious, as it is ingested in the pouch of the cheek and discolours the teeth and burns the gums a lot worse than aspirin. It looks like *wasabe* - the green Japanese mustard or nasturtium snuff - and can be seen for sale in little clear plastic bags at many a street corner. It is said to be a tobacco derivative, but, if so, how does it acquire the alarming property of making the driver totally fearless. Also, he can switch instantly from a waking to a sleeping state, which can be as startling as the fearlessness when over-hanging a precipice.

The universal imprecation throughout the Muslim world is 'Insha-allah' - God willing. The full meaning and significance of this is brought home to every traveller. God either wills it or He does not. There is only one course of action open to you and that is to accept your lot.

*

The Peshawar bus depot is initially daunting. It is the sheer scale as much as the confusion. It is a highly competitive market place with fine rates over the distances and times quoted. Anwar was initiated in all these rituals and could drive a hard bargain, but it was as well to have Sabur along for local back-up. The essential is to have a linguist on your side.

Taxis were another matter, much easier to commission. Far more chance of an English speaker. They were used to dealing with the idiosyncrasies of foreigners. Drivers often initiated itineraries; especially long remunerative hauls to Swat or Chitral. Americans dominated the market, because they were known to pay over the odds and tip generously. There was no alternative but to compete on their terms.

For the first weekend of rest and recreation we settled rather idly for Green's second hotel at Dunga Gali, where a booking was made without any fear of competition. We then set off, with a clear conscience that all preparations had been made, for the home of Anwar's brother - Inam ul-Haq - where we were expected to dine and stay overnight, before collecting the main party at Islamabad airport the next morning.

The family connection proved invaluable. Through Inam ul-Haq's good offices we had been accorded Pakistani VVIP (very very important) status. He came with us to ensure that we got it. At the airport we were swept through to the VIP arrivals/departures lounge with an all-important parking slot, next to the security and Customs offices. We were given a special chit which afforded us freedom of the

Customs and Immigration area. From such eminence, it was a simple matter to approach the senior Customs officer, explain our purpose and bypass all the hassle of the usual time-consuming queues, delays and frustrations.

John Stoneham's presence in the passport queue stood out like a Hore-Belisha beacon. In next to no time, the team was ushered through. All sixteen hayboxes with matching manifestos were piled high on trolleys and waved through by the senior Customs officer. After more, fuller greetings had been exchanged, we trundled the trolleys through to the VIP car park and began loading the minibus with as much forethought as possible. The driver then began all over again. He indicated all sorts of nooks and crannies for the stowage of hand baggage, which we would never have spotted. Once the baggage was in place, the team had to be squeezed in around it. It was an amazingly tight fit. John Stoneham got pride of place in the death seat. There was nowhere else to put him.

There was time now to hear more about the flight out. British Airways had been better than their word. On presentation of the high-powered letter of authorisation, covering both journeys out and back, the excess baggage had been accepted without demur. Everybody had been looked after champion. The whole of the 747 upper-deck `bubble' had been allocated to the team. They had been virtually upgraded to business class. You could not ask for better than that.

We made the one scheduled stop on the way at Attock, and then sped on to Dean's where everybody was checked in and assigned to their chalets, except for Tony Bray, Geoff McLeod and Robin Jago, who were taken on to their superior villa accommodation in the grounds of the Lady Reading Hospital. The only shortcoming to these digs, we were soon to discover, was that they were 'dry'; so we had to arrange for a supply of Murree beer to be smuggled in, after dark. They took breakfast in their place, otherwise we all messed together at Dean's. Supplements had been brought along - most notably marmite, marmalade, chocolate, peppermints and glucose tablets. There were also hidden reserves of Kendal Mint Cake and large bars of Bournville plain chocolate ... designated for emergency ration use only.

Most surprisingly, Dean's ran to HP Sauce and Heinz Tomato Ketchup and some very runny honey. Seven-up and Pepsi were available for their addicts. Best of all, was the green tea with crushed cardamom seeds - a mainstay. For the connoisseur, there was the most delicious matching green pistachio ice-cream.

The day of arrival had been scheduled for a Friday, to allow a first day of rest for jetlag recovery. But, by teatime, everybody was off to see the sights by *tonga* (one horse-drawn two-wheeled buggy), tri-shaw (motor-bicycle engined two-seater taxi) or on foot. A whole routine was in course of establishment. A tour of the old souk market - the Quisikaiwana or Street of the Storytellers - then a leisurely scan of the carpet sellers, the English bookshop, return to Dean's in time for dinner. Early to bed, early to rise, always provided the dreaded night operator could be coaxed into action before midnight.

The old Peshawar Islamic-Colonial Governor's Palace had been appropriately turned into a gem of a museum. Here are to be seen the superb Hellenic influence on the Gandharran stone carvings of the fourth and fifth centuries CE. Late by Greek standards, they are all the more fascinating for the cross-culture scenes of Buddhist veneration. The very best are to be seen at Peshawar, Taxila and the Karachi museum. Otherwise, try the Guimet, Place d'Iena, Paris. All can be visited time and again and new discoveries made. On my last visit, a delightful fox-and-grapes continuous carved-stone border motif revealed itself for the first time.

More mundanely, my biggest responsibility was to ensure that the Dean's breakfast staff were ready to serve breakfast on time. It didn't always happen. Then I had to ensure that the right teams were dispatched to the right destination scheduled on the programme. That did happen. I didn't appear to be short of things to do until they returned. Sometimes, I went with them. It never failed to fascinate me.

12

The Money Laundry

In the treatment of Afghan casualties, foreign bodies were the over-riding pre-occupation of all surgeon-patient relations. Peripheral to operations, I remained ignorant for some time as to what the fuss was about. Since, in the Muslim world, it is important to present your Maker with as wholesome a temple for the soul as possible, all foreign bodies are best excised.

Problems arose mainly after the marketplace availability of X-ray machines. Hospitals expected patients to arrive with their own negatives (not machines) and consequently let their own equipment run down and the developer run out. This meant that there really was no denying the readily identifiable profiles of ricochet bullets or shrapnel shards. For many of the patients, the offending item was often best left alone. By the time they reached us, judging by their record sheets, some of these patients could have seen upwards of a dozen surgeons of international repute - all of whom had come to the same 'unacceptable' conclusion, that is, unacceptable from a Muslim spiritual point of view.

One such patient arrived with X-rays straight on and from the side, which showed irrefutably an AK47 bullet, which looked as if it had fallen out of the sky after 'happy firing' and lodged in the patient's skull slap between his eyes. Or, it was a spent richochet. The patient was desperate to have this blot removed from his aura. He could not be persuaded that it would be much more dangerous to attempt such an operation, than to leave well alone. So, he spent his days trailing round the Peshawar hospitals, holding out his scroll of X-rays in the hope of one day finding a visiting surgeon, who might relieve him of such an onerous foreign body. It crossed our minds more than once (he came back often!) to trick the man by going through the motions of an operation, substituting X-rays minus bullet and handing him a spent round. But when we thought more about it, we suspected he would go back for more X-ray reassurance, only to find he had to bite on the bullet anew.

In simpler cases, where bullets were removed, the patient's greatest desire was to hold the keepsake as living proof that it was out. In Afghan eyes, digging bullets out of bone took precedence over all other forms of surgery. If it could be captured on film for television news coverage, so much the better. Everything stopped for the media. Operations came to a standstill as camera lights were rigged up. The propaganda war came first.

Other major problems arose from the premature sewing up of wounds. It is surely only too natural to think that the sooner a gaping wound is closed, the better, when the reverse is generally the case. Severe complications follow the closing of a wound with dirt, dead bone or foreign bodies still inside. In secondary surgery, we were to experience some exceptional cases of this misfortune. 'Debridement' is the medical term used to describe the treatment of open wounds - the cleaning of a contaminated wound to remove all foreign material and dead tissue. Usually, in war surgery, it is followed by closure three to five days later. To the layman, cleaning the wound means allowing the pus and foreign matter to ooze out, sometimes with inducement, but usually of its own accord.

On one memorable occasion, the patient had been half stitched up. The matter being agonisingly excreted was thought to be gangrenous. It was a horrendous black slick. He would have to be opened up again to forestall amputation.

In fact, at the moment when the patient had been blasted under a truck, some foreign body had been imploded into his buttock wound. Unnoticed, it was slowly finding its way out; causing maximum pain and discomfort. What had been anticipated was a fragment of trouser material. To the patient's relief and the surgeon's delight, what arrived instead was a six-inch strip of radial tyre! It was to become a star trophy. That was one 'foreign body' that decidedly did need removal!

The vast majority of cases handled by the Guildford team fell into the category of secondary surgery. This term is used to cover a multitude of sins. It may be recognised, from the outset, that secondary surgery is going to be needed. Other cases arose because of mal-unions or non-unions of bone. Or, as we have seen, the wound simply failed to heal, usually because inappropriate action had been taken at an initial stage. It was depressing to find so much of the workload consisted of putting right the bodge-ups of other, less experienced, surgeons. This, in turn led to the team wanting more variety, to include at least some primary surgery.

Of course it was absolutely right that the fresh urgent cases should go directly to the ICRC, where emergency facilities were readily available, including life-support systems. The staff were permanent, and sophisticated back-up and after-care existed. But I could already sense a groundswell urge for a move up to fresher cases. The Kuwaiti Red Crescent can hardly have cornered the market, surely?

The work programme conformed to a routine formula, following

Guildford Surgical Team in convoy. *Photo by Peter Stiles*

a clearly defined pattern of certain days of operations in each given hospital, after careful patient selection during the previous afternoon or evening round. It was quite a simple matter to ring the changes between the various teams and the hospitals.

However, by the second week, we found we had played ourselves into the Afghan Surgical Hospital rather too stolidly. What we were finding was that the more we did, the less they did. Until, on one particular day, we had all but taken over the running of the hospital.

Iftikhar was, as usual, away on 'other business' in Lahore. We were beginning to imagine he ran a successful private clinic there. Rabbani was out, attending an inter-party *jirga* (political conference) and the semi-hostile administrator Firdos Khan was absent for no declared reason.

I found myself chained all day to Firdos Khan's desk, working out the team's personal expenditure accounts - mostly telephone bills. Meanwhile, I was taking an interest in all the general comings and goings and wondering what it would be like to have this as my whole life's purpose. At that moment, there were three intern student doctors between us and the total administration of the hospital. So we seriously began to wonder if we would indeed be able to leave at the end of the day, week, month or year!

It was then that the guard announced the arrival of some Kuwaiti VIPs. Three very non-medical-looking businessmen were led into reception - to their apparent consternation and my own. Each of them was carrying a similar sizeable overnight sausage holdall.

It may have been paranoia, but they did seem particularly put out to find me sitting at Firdos Khan's seat of custom. They repeated his name time and again.

Fortunately, somebody had the wit to fetch one of the interns. A general search began for keys. There was no sign of the key to Iftikhar's office. However, they seemed to be satisfied with finding a bunch of keys which opened the three metal clothes-lockers in the reception area. The three overnight airline bags were then lodged, one on top of the other, in one of these, and locked again. Imagining these were modest overnight travel bags, full of spare clothes for obese Kuwaiti businessmen, I thought no more about it. However, they had not returned by the time of our release; finding myself left alone again in the same room for much of the next day, my mind kept returning to them. Why three? Why had they been so keen to see Firdos Khan and horrified to find me? Why the request for safe deposit in Iftikhar's Aladdin's cave?

Of course, communications were so bad, there was no knowing precisely when they could be expected. They were used to just turning up. Quite obviously, they came regularly.

Not long afterwards, the mystery was part solved. We were all back at Afghan Surgical and for once Iftikhar was there too. To my surprise, and quite undaunted by my presence, he went to the same clothes-locker, unlocked it and took a sizeable wad of US dollars out of the uppermost zip bag to pay off a visitor. I couldn't think why he hadn't moved so much money to a safer place, like his office.

I naturally assumed that all this loot was generous Kuwaiti funding for the hospital (but why weren't they supporting their own Kuwaiti Red Crescent Hospital?) I developed this theme along lines that suited my book. Since these drops of large quantities of US dollars took place on such a regular basis, there must be more than enough to fund both hospitals. So, perhaps it was also to fund some first aid clinic activity inside Afghanistan. However, this theory was scotched when we learned that Iftikhar had left for Lahore with all three bags and no escort!

This convinced me he was just a brilliant con-man feathering his own nest in the name of succouring the Mujahedeen. I now envisaged the most lavish of private clinics, peopled with odalisques after Ingres. However, Iftikhar's double life, as it transpired, had little to do with medicine and nothing to do with voluptuous slave women. How disappointing. It was, in fact, all open and above board and everything to do with politics. He was standing as one of the Jamiat candidates for Lahore in the forthcoming elections. All this boodle was needed to buy votes, or respectability. The party had been illegal until only recently, as I understood it.

In any event, the money was well wasted. Jamiat only achieved 6% of the vote. But that was by no means the end of the saga. It took a long time to learn that this funding was no Saudi government or Kuwaiti government money. Not a bit of it, this money came from *soi-disant* middle-class intellectuals, funding fundamentalists in the hope of a backlash, so as to achieve some measure of democracy in their own countries. The hospital provided excellent cover for siphoning off such funding. Some of the voluntary subscriptions could be shown to have gone the route of hospital funding, no doubt other sums had gone to buy arms. It was a second-to-none laundry for a qualified accountant to re-allocate money.

How horrified indeed must the Kuwaiti couriers have been to find their faithful fellow conspirator, reliable accountant and link man replaced by a total stranger and Westerner. How could Afghan

Surgical have handed over command and control of their preferred conduit to Westerners for even half a day, without warning them? They could even have suspected a kidnap plot at journey's end ...

Of course, telephones were all tapped and the mails unreliable and no doubt read too. Any means of advertising their expected time of arrival were limited to word of mouth, cleft stick and runner. The same was true of the other direction too.

*

On a day-to-day basis, I couldn't help hearing of the difficulties our surgeons were experiencing in obtaining enough blood for operations. First call was always to the relatives of the patient. It was a sure sign of how much they cared for him. But the problem was deep-rooted. Much the same as the foreign bodies dilemma. Muslims believe their life blood is sacred to God and is part of their presence before him, hence their marked reluctance to be blood donors. The very poor can sometimes be persuaded to part with some of their indifferent quality blood for money, which is then sold at a mark-up in the bazaar. Even then it is in short supply. The haeomoglobin count amongst Afghan patients is well below the level at which operations would be contemplated in a British hospital.

Ever aware of Tony Hancock's 'Blood Donor' sketch, I decided my contribution to the war effort was wholly inadequate and a supplement was called for. Some leeway might be made up for this wet admin role by offering a pint or two to fill the veins of some valiant Mujahedeen warrior. I had suffered from a surfeit most of my life, given to frequent nose-bleeds as a lad, etc. I suffered none of the Muslim misgivings that any wholeness I possessed in the eyes of the Almighty would be damaged by the loss of the odd pint.

My offer was greeted with such acclaim that Iftikhar himself insisted on playing Count Dracula then and there before I changed my mind. Grinning like Vincent Price, he stabbed my forearm twice with a needle a horse would have shied at, before penetrating a clearly visible vein at the third attempt. I don't think he'd done the job before. I was beginning to doubt he was a doctor at all, let alone a surgeon.

Anyway, as I tried to relax and let the vacuum bag take over, I got the impression it was all going on forever. I began to feel like a Roman senator sent home by his emperor to commit suicide. I wondered if and when I would lose consciousness. I thought more about Hancock. Should I spend my last moments drafting a will? I had nothing to leave, so that was taken care of.

Then my mind wandered off to the last time I had been a donor. It was in Australia. I was in St Vincent's, Sydney. As an inspired promotion, Sir Robert Helpman had offered preview tickets to all blood donors to his forthcoming production of Dracula.

It was high time Iftikhar returned. I had been forgotten. The bag was full to bursting. It was all going to waste and I was an interesting shade of verdigris. Then I heard his twittering Bloomsbury voice: 'Clench the cotton-wool swab as tight as you can between forearm and bicep. Here is the cup of tea you expect in England, I believe.' Yet another cup of green Afghan tea with sand-like sugar that never dissolved. It wouldn't do to ask for a biscuit. What I had meant to ask him was what had taken him so damned l-o-n-g. Instead, I took it out on the cotton-wool to an exaggerated extent.

At last he stuck an elastoplast over it and I was allowed up. Dizzier than usual, we debouched on to the landing, just as another group of three VIP visitors were doing the rounds of 'their' hospital - maintained entirely by voluntary subscriptions. Yet more Kuwaitis, or were they Saudis, indistinguishable in their Yasser Arafat headscarves and outsize *jellabas*, cloaking their obesity and their money-belts? I wondered whether they had dumped any holdalls in Iftikhar's office along the way.

Following Itfikhar's lead, I was now obliged to go forward and give the traditional long-lost-brother Afghan greeting. This consists of a right-hand side, followed by a left-hand side, full body-length embrace, with corresponding arms encircling the other's back. The sort of clinch we normally reserve for the dance floor and the opposite sex. On this occasion, the first person to step forward and disengage himself from their Arab guests was Iftikhar's number two, Dr Faisal Rabbani - that large, lovable, huggable bear of a man. He had no need to greet Iftikhar, so he made straight for me.

As my right hand extended up Rabbani's back, what should happen but the cotton-wool should choose this poignant moment to detach itself, heralding a great geyser of blood, which gushed over the back of Rabbani's *shalwar kamees*; as if it were his own blood surging from the most vicious of stab wounds. Pandemonium ensued, as the VIPs adopted a horrified back-to-back huddle. The young interns rushed forward to restrain me. Only when they saw Rabbani remain unaffected and then my forearm, did they realise what had happened. And alarm turned into all-round mirth. But there had been a loss of dignity, a loss of face.

In future, I restricted myself to donations to the ICRC blood bank or insisted that John Stoneham administer proceedings.

13
The Heroin Trail

It was Eid-ul-Adha, a religious feast which marks the end of the Pilgrimage to Mecca. It sounded ominously like the Ides of March, but this was October instead.

Thanks to Christopher Wills, I had received a formal invitation to lunch with Jamshid Burki at his house in Peshawar. It may have been his home, but it was more likely some official residence. On the back of the invitation was the clearest of maps to show exactly where the house was in relation to the Khyber Intercontinental Hotel. Dean's was off the map. However, the house would be within easy walking distance after a cooling swim at the Khyber pool.

There was no covering letter. No hint of order of dress. No requirement of insider knowledge. I fondly imagined other staff members from the Ministry of Tribal Affairs, enjoying a day off, and rather hoped Ahmed Akbar might be among them as he was an authority on tribal matters, holding, as he did, The Chair for Pakistani Studies at Oxford. Jamshid himself was perfectly capable of inviting anyone. The Wali of Swat, the Mir of Dir, Imran Khan, Mohammed Ali, Danny Kaye. He, and Ahmed Zeb between them, had the responsibility of looking after most of the VIP visitors to the North West Frontier Province. Jamshid is immensely personable and attractive in the classic Afghan *émigré* Pathan way. His background and breeding crossed all frontiers. If he'd been around at the time, he might have captained India at cricket in some Boy's Own Paper story, circa 1910. Of course, he would have outsmarted 'Kangaroo Kennedy, the whizzbang bowler,' and he would have had to be every bit as good as Imran Khan. (In fact, his brother is said to have played for Gloucestershire.) Jamshid speaks far finer English than most of his English contemporaries - ever so slightly clipped, always concise and above all, clear. His father had been a general in Monty's 8th Army, which may have accounted for Jamshid's staccato Noël Coward enunciation.

His other guests for luncheon that day were not staff, but half-a-dozen tribal leaders from among the Tribal Areas under Jamshid's protection, who had come to town to celebrate the Eid festival. I was the only non-Pathan guest. I wondered if I had been invited to play court jester. Jamshid had to translate laboriously for me as we went along. Through his filter, he allowed me some clue as to the drift of their questioning, but not much.

By way of background, Jamshid explained that he had been tour guide to this jovial but sinister looking lot of cut-throats on an official 'inward mission' visit to the United Kingdom. This can only have meant it had a degree of official government backing, if not Royal assent. It all seemed highly improbable, but by Sunday afternoon, the party had gravitated to Smith's Lawn, Windsor (the polo ground), which was to be the climax of their visit.

The most voluble tribal leader began by making various flattering or possibly derogatory comments about my person, which Jamshid, ever the gentleman, reduced to a 'Mai Harris title version', by telling me that one or other of them would like to invite me back to his place that afternoon, but Jamshid had explained that it would not be possible.

We then got on to more searching questions. They took me back to the golden moments of lengthening shadows on Smith's Lawn. They had come to recognise that the game of polo might be a variation of *bushkashi*, an Afghan game occasionally played by Pathans, the ball and sticks replacing the headless goat and lead-lined whips of the Tadjiks and Uzbeks.

They had also just about come to accept the concept that we should have not one, but two women as head of state. After all they had vaguely heard of Queen Victoria, but what they wanted me to explain was, if our Queen was so very rich and powerful, why should she choose a coachman for her consort?

They could see and relish how disarmed I was by this novel interpretation of Prince Philip's favourite equine pastime, four-in-hand dressage. I felt like Mervyn Peake's Yellow Creature facing Captain Slaughterboard's crew for the very first time. I made some feeble attempt to explain outside interests and hobbies, which meant nothing to them. Floundering, I next tried to amuse them by saying that a cousin of mine had once fallen off the top of the royal coach, breaking her hip. The Queen had sent round a bunch of daffodils for comfort. Jamshid, knowing it would all fall on deaf ears, acknowledged what I was saying with an embarrassed nod, cutting me short and made no attempt to translate.

As it was undoubtedly meant to, the next question took me completely by surprise.

John Fullerton, who was the husband of Romey Fullerton, the field director of AfghanAid immediately before Juliet Vergos *(later Juliet Crawley Peck)* was a journalist of high repute. On assignment as a Delhi correspondent he had, only too recently, published an article, which had made the front page. It pinpointed the heroin production in the Tribal Areas and exposed how the Governor of the North Western Frontier Province, Fazli Haq - Jamshid's boss no less - was responsible for masterminding the transportation of the processed product to the Port of Karachi, from where it was shipped out to an eager and receptive world. According to Fullerton's article, this was achieved by army truck drivers returning empty to the port to pick up more material for the Afghan War effort or refugee relief. The drugs were said to be neatly stowed under the driver's seat. It had indeed been one of the cuttings I had issued to the Guildford team as part of their background briefing. I knew it well. What made the story all the more convincing was the knowledge that army trucks were the only ones never to be stopped or searched by the high-profile Drugs Enforcement Agency road blocks, which made everybody else's journey such a misery every few miles along the Grand Trunk Road.

The question I was being asked was: did I think the article was true?

Clearly, any doubts as to why I had been asked to lunch alone were now resolved. As nonchalantly as I could I replied that one should not always believe what one read in the newspapers. If one knew a subject well, it was surprising how inaccurate they could be. As a throwaway, I added that, anyway, barely a hundred and fifty years ago Britain was conducting the Calcutta opium auctions on a regular annual basis.

I waited for Jamshid to translate and studied their reactions, as they must have been reading mine. They seemed to be satisfied with what I had to say. I wondered what the hidden purpose might be. Either Jamshid wanted to indicate to them that it was time to curb production or, more likely, that they need have no fears of increasing it!

There was nothing innocent about their inquiry, and in my view, nothing would deter them. I thanked Jamshid for his kind invitation. I thought it better not to write. I only saw him once again, in his office, to make formal application for a pass to his Tribal Areas. He was full of useful suggestions of things to see and do. He was going on to higher things and was soon promoted to Islamabad. I have not seen him again from that day to this.

I took my time walking back to Dean's and kept the detail of the lunch to myself.

I had once been told that Fazli Haq had been allowed to buy himself a retreat in Gloucestershire.[1] I wondered where it was and whether he would live long enough to reach his funk hole.

On the footpath along the banks of the River Wye, not far from the Slaughters, is to be found my favourite notice in all of England. It reads: 'Extreme Caution - Adders.' Then, in much smaller beautifully signwritten palace script, it continues: 'Should you be bitten, send your companion for Doctor Blenkinsop, Bourton-on-the-Water.' There was then a telephone number, added at some later date, but no telephone for miles. There was no alternative proposal for those unfortunate enough to have no companion.

So, things need not be all plain sailing in Gloucestershire ...

[1] In the event, Fazli Haq 'died by the sword' before reaching retirement.

14
Preparing for a Push

By now we had instituted a programme, which worked like clockwork, on an annual visit basis for the month of October for the next three years. These tours were, of course, timed to match peak casualty periods.

On average, some 500 patients would be seen each year, of whom 100 would be selected and operations performed. Naturally, some operations took longer than others and we had no desire to compete with the Egyptians. However, during a five-day week, it would be fair to say that each surgeon would manage at least two major operations a day, plus numerous smaller procedures. The day began at 8 a.m. and finished any time around 4 p.m. Sometimes, with complications, later still.

I do not intend to make any clinical analysis here of operations. Indeed, as a non-medical administrator-cum-trouble-shooter, I have no competence to catalogue the surgical achievements of the Guildford Team. However, I was able to research the overall Orthopaedics Overseas statistic of which the Guildford Surgical Team effort formed a contributory part.

In all, from 1985 to 1992 a total of 263 visiting orthopaedic surgeons, trauma surgeons, and health care professionals travelled at their own expense to Peshawar to teach and to do surgery. A total of approximately 4,300 'teaching surgeries' were thus performed. By no means would these all have been war wounds, for these statistics would have included large numbers of polio and tuberculosis cases as well as other congenital deformities. All the surgery performed, however, would have been vital and necessary.

As we anticipated the turning of the tide in the war, what we sought next was some means of taking surgery nearer to the wounded. *Médecins Sans Frontières* were the prime exponents of this; but again on a full-time basis. It was a full-time job. The nearest link we had to anything of the sort was through AfghanAid and its ambulance programme, where some constructive advice had been given and well received. This related to bean-bags for making the casualties more comfortable in transit. Otherwise, there were tenuous links through to the Sandy Gall Afghanistan Appeal and the Medical Refresher Courses for Afghans, which was organised and run by the French under a Belgian umbrella.

Peter Stiles had not been idle and had set out his case for a detailed study of medical problems, including the primary care of the wounded, treatment of casualties inside Afghanistan in writing to Sir Oliver Forster at AfghanAid. He was promised action, which was not long in coming.

In the meantime, I decided to look up some old friends from earlier visits. First of all, I tried to telephone 'TM', Tariq Mahmood, the brigadier commanding Pakistani Special Forces, at the number he had given me in London and which had been used successfully on previous occasions. It was his private home number in Cherat. I was politely told that he was not at home, but was expected shortly. As this message was relayed from his wife, I thought it reliable enough to go on spec. The problem was, Cherat was a 'Prohibited Area' and without a military vehicle to lift you in, it was the devil to get anyone to take you, however pressing the invitation. No taxi would go beyond the first prohibited area sign. With baksheesh persuasion, I did finally manage to get a driver to break down within five miles of my objective. It was a most convincing performance. It was a hot walk, but gave me plenty of time to think through what I hoped to gain from my visit.

What I was after was the best place to locate one of Orthopaedic Overseas' more ambitious plans for setting up one of their re-cycled disaster hospitals. We had heard of this through Kermit Veggeberg's newsletters. "TM" would be more likely to give an objective view than any Afghan. The best informed opinion would come from the Red Cross, but they were, of course, proscribed from divulging any information on the course of the war.

Recognising the hearts and minds purpose behind the move, I trusted that "TM" would be positive with his advice. He had always been candid in all his dealings with us, and the most approachable of men.

Cherat was formerly the Headquarters of the British Commander, North West Frontier Forces. It is an imposing, stand-alone hill on the edge of the Indus Plain. Unfortunately, it is better known today as the trademark of a leading cement factory. Be that as it may, handsomely carved into the rock face are numerous regimental insignia of those county regiments which served there over two centuries of British Rule. The coloured carvings are meticulously maintained to this day, to the credit of their current successors.

Security was better than I had expected. There was no bluffing my way past the guard. I promptly found myself under open arrest in the guardhouse, but with the door left ajar. The photostat of my passport, plus spare colour photograph stapled on top was removed and I was asked politely to await the outcome of 'further enquiry and deliberations'. Nobody was going to accept my word that I was an honoured and expected guest, until they had the word of "TM" himself. I thought it better not to compromise his wife.

"TM" had a notoriously hard head, both for bashes and booze. I began to wonder if I had been altogether wise in coming on spec. There was no means of finding out how long he was going to take getting home this time.

Somewhat to my surprise, I was offered neither drink nor food. From what I could see through the open guard-room door, nobody else was eating or drinking either. It wasn't Ramadan. I could only imagine that they had over-indulged at Eid. There was a tethered goat and that was all. I had thought to bring my own water bottle, filled with Dean's double distillation, and some hard tack rations plus some canned pork luncheon meat - fit only for infidels.

Early the next morning, after a particularly sleepless night on the cell floor, my fortunes changed immeasurably for the better. My ersatz identification was returned, all smiles, and a jeep arrived to whisk me up to the camp proper, where keys were produced to open up the guest suite adjoining "TM"'s married quarters. I could only suppose that "TM" had telephoned ahead of his arrival, because he had not passed the gate.

I was to be left for over an hour freshening up, saying my prayers, kicking my heels. In my continuing enforced idleness, I took to photographing the whole panorama from my superior vantage point. The buildings, all from the turn of the century, were solidly built. From up here, the regimental insignia were closer and more distinguishable: the Somersets, the Gloucesters, of glorious Imjin River memory, the Devons, the Dorsets.

A smart servant came to disturb my reveries and conduct me to "TM"'s quarters along the verandah passage. To my delight, I was ushered into a living-room, which was occupied by him, his beautiful wife and small children. This was the only time I was ever received amongst the military in such a relaxed Western manner.

He asked when I had arrived and, once he realised what an uncomfortable night I must have spent, was full of apologies. We both had a good laugh. As if in compensation, he indicated a dumb waiter, covered with every conceivable brand of hard liquor. I had heard tales of Jinnah, the founding father and revered first president of Pakistan, and his medicinal whisky, and had often wondered how far down the ranks the prescription had penetrated. I assumed that, under President Zia-ul-Haq, the army was dry. I said it was a bit early for me to indulge; although in truth I was teetotal, which was supposed to

Two American Friends Kermit Veggeberg MD and Charles Berges

make Islamic countries less of a trial for me than some.

I said how impressed I was with the way all the old British army insignia had been maintained. He said an extra high standard may have been achieved recently because they had had another British visitor. Unlike me, she had a pass for the prohibited areas and was free to go almost anywhere she liked. She represented the British War Graves Commission. He asked if I had ever heard of a Miss Farrington. I said I had once known somebody of that name, long ago in Monte Carlo. She had been a swimming champion. Her father was a retired army colonel, who had introduced himself to me as the Senior British Resident! So I should know my place. It could hardly be the same, but you never knew ...

"TM" said he thought her job consisted of ensuring that the graves of British servicemen were properly maintained. He asked me what I thought. I said that my impression was that a much better job was done out here than many a place back home. I had been amazed by the polish on the brass memorials I had visited in a number of churches, and told "TM" how I had made a chance visit to a deserted Anglican church, miles away in some Murree hill station, or it may have been above Abbotabad. Anyway, the door had not been locked, so we had entered. It looked as if we were the first visitors in fifty years. Cobwebs and dust everywhere. Then we saw something you would never see any more back in Britain. The Victorian silver communion plate, chalice and patten and a pair of silver candlesticks were still standing on the altar, tarnished but untouched. When I said it was a phenomenon unlikely to be matched in Europe today, not just Britain, he took great delight in reminding me that I lived in a heathen, heretic world, whereas here they still said their prayers five times a day.

Next, he asked after all his old Hereford friends by name. Then he wanted to know what brought me to see him.

I explained how Orthopaedics Overseas, the American organisation with whom we worked, believed the war had now reached a stage when a calculated move might be made into Afghanistan. There was no shortage of equipment. Nothing would be done to upset the existing system for evacuating casualties. It would have to be complementary not competitive. I thought, for medium-term reasons, any site for a field hospital would need to be within reach of Jalalabad. Did he have any suggestions?

He said the problem was entirely political. The local commanders had no respect for the Afghan Interim Government. The only place he could think of for the moment was at Azrow. There could be a problem getting there in winter, but that was true of many another place. He thought there might even have been a hospital once at Azra.

No doubt prompted by a bulge in one of my pockets, "TM" said he would prefer it if I didn't take any photographs during my stay. My visit was unofficial and had not yet been cleared!

I said I understood but, at the same time, felt terrible, like some thief in the night, who had ended up stealing from his best friend. I wondered if I had been reported taking photographs. My camera was an Olympus, not obvious, not a spy camera. In this light any bloody fool could take good pictures. I was in luck. "TM" went on to invite me to a 'wings' passing out parade in 'Pindi that afternoon. I asked if I would be allowed to take photographs of that. He said that would present no problem.

We left almost immediately. "TM" drove and we dropped in on any number of Afghan 'friends' on the way down. Most of them seemed well off, established in large farmsteads. I knew that one of the anomalies of the Pakistani Army was that they were farmers in a big way. To a large extent, they were obliged to live off the land of their holdings. For all I knew, these farms were now being tenanted by new Afghan 'friends'. Alternatively, these were wealthy Afghans, who had arrived with ample funds to invest in new farms. Farming may well have been what they had most in common. Even Special Forces army pay was not that special and a lot of the fringe benefits of army life sprang from good husbandry. And provided you lived to retirement age, there was always the hope of a smallholding to go to.

We were allowed a break and a shower along the way. So I made a special effort to be properly turned out for the parachutists' passing-out parade. I took all the remaining film in my camera. There was no doubting "TM" was a big shot amongst his own people. He took the trouble to introduce me to several of his brother officers, but one especially. He was known as 'TR', Tariq Rafli, and he was in charge of security at Karachi Airport. This introduction was to lead in time to a major inspection audit, the recommendations of which were ignored. Some years later, the PanAm hijack took place precisely in the manner predicted in the report, *i.e.* a uniformed team masquerading as military guards. One only hoped it hadn't fallen into the wrong hands ... "TM" was asked to recover the grounded plane, which he duly did.

15
Meeting the Mujahedeen

When I got back to Dean's, Peter Stiles told me we had a pressing invitation from the number two surgeon at Afghan Surgical Hospital, Dr Faisal Rabbani, that very evening to meet his political bosses. Somehow I had managed to fall into a trap of my own making. I had assumed that Dr Faisal Rabbani was a Jamiat Afghanistan supporter. Nothing could have been further from the case. He was a Hesbe-i-Islami party member, in other words a supporter of Engineer Gulbuddin Hekmatyar, or more likely Younis Khalis.

That evening, therefore, we had no clear idea what was happening to us. Because we had no command of the language, we learned everything at second hand, through the filter of Dr Rabbani's translation.

We were to be taken in the back of a closed van, under cover of darkness, to one of those anonymous box number accommodation addresses. Why the mystery?

On entering the van, we noticed there was a carpet on the floor and a rear window. It was no help. We had no idea where we were being taken. Nobody trusted anybody any more, least of all the political parties, which were in constant internecine vendetta. As if dealing with the Soviet super-power wasn't enough! Indeed, the official reason given for all the secrecy was that the Russian-trained, Kabul regime secret police - KHAD - had started infiltrating Mujahedeen forces with the object of 'turning' them. They were becoming increasingly competent at cross-border shoot-outs, assassinations and bombings, culminating, it was assumed, in the sabotage of the Rawalpindi ammunition dump.

There was, however, no great advantage in learning an address, because everyone's standard practice was to keep on the move, always renting 'builders' finish', bare-board, accommodation and simply moving the carpets in and out. All we knew, as we went like lambs to the slaughter to what ostensibly had been billed as a social visit, was that we were no longer in any part of town known to us.

From the outset there was a distinctly hostile feel about our reception. This was all the more surprising, since medics are, on the whole, *persona grata* everywhere.

Dr Rabbani led the way into a large living-room, with a strange sunken floor area. For doctors there is usually a flatteringly large assembly. This turned out to be just the two of them to the two of us.

For the most part, Pathans are a singularly handsome race. Tall, slim, agile, with aquiline features. By contrast, Rabbani's political boss was remarkably unappealing. Instead of the taut, spare, muscular figure we had come to expect, we were now faced with a puffy, gross, podge of a man who would have made a convincing Nero in a Hollywood epic. Indeed, as we entered, he was reclining in the Roman fashion, engrossed in the all-absorbing business of inserting luscious ovaloid 'bride's little finger' grapes into his mouth. For greeting he gave us the most dismissive of imperious waves and returned to his grapes.

We were not offered even a glass of water, let alone a grape! By now, we should have got the message. We had been invited along solely to be insulted. What made it even harder to take was that it was so completely out of character for Dr Rabbani to be party to such behaviour. Since he was a mild gentle man in his everyday dealings, he must have been put up to it.

But there was to be no getting up and simply leaving the Pasha's party. We were obliged to grin and bear it, until the grapes came to an end and there ensued a gabble of guttural, saliva-throttled words. Then our interlocutor opened up.

They had noticed that we were taken to and from the hospitals by an AfghanAid driver in an AfghanAid pick-up truck. Did this mean we were part of AfghanAid? If not, what was the exact relationship?

I said, first of all, that we should like to know who our gracious host was and what interests exactly he represented. Rabbani said he would tell us all we wanted to know on the way back. However, he did add that we were now at the Hesbe-i-Islami party headquarters.

I told him he knew perfectly well that we were a team of volunteer surgeons from a British hospital with no formal links as such, although we did operate under the aegis of the American charity, Orthopaedics Overseas. AfghanAid was a registered British charity and it was only natural that the one should be prepared to help the other. We were compatriots. We left Rabbani to ramble through all that.

We were then asked if we knew the personalities and policies of AfghanAid. I said that over the years I had met most of the personalities and the policies were an open book - offering help to all Afghans; both external refugees, but more especially the internal ones, those who had stayed behind. I attempted to make this sound like a pointed barb - suggesting just about anyone, except present company. I went on to say that I knew of no hidden agendas, if that was what he was after.

I was then asked why AfghanAid had such a clear-cut policy of not helping Hesbe-i-Islami people? I replied that this could not be the case. Their charter as a registered charity would not allow them to practise such discrimination. Of course, with hindsight, all I had to do was point out the even-handed way we were operating in their hospital, if they wanted any proof of lack of prejudice on our part.

We were then asked, rather ingenuously, if we would report this meeting and this conversation to 'our' people at AfghanAid. I said I could give them every assurance that I would and that Dr Rabbani would bring back any reply or explanation offered.

We never did get to know the name of the grape devouring politico,[1] but from then on we always referred to him as Nero. It was getting late and we were thankful to escape to the sanctuary of Dean's. We decided that, rather than bother Juliet with it all now, we would sleep on it, and, if we still felt the same way about it in the morning, call on her in her office.

Calmly, dispassionately, in the air-conditioned light of day, we told her what had happened to us.

She hit the ceiling. She told us to tell that fat slob that as soon as he stopped attacking and robbing her couriers and stealing their money and smashing their cameras and generally harassing them and beating them up and intimidating them, then she would reconsider extending aid to his group and evacuating their casualties. Reprisals were the only language they respected.

She went on to explain that Hesbe-i always complained as a matter of policy that the Non-government Organisations (NGOs) favoured Ahmed Shah Massoud and Jamiat, when Hesbe-i deserved all the support. What the Hesbe-i people did was pursue their jealousies to horrendous lengths - flaying people alive, thirty at a time, and disembowelling others. In fact, Jamiat was far better organised to receive and re-distribute aid - whether food, money, seedcorn or medicines. They were more efficient in the field and far more deserving of AfghanAid's support.

Hesbe-i had enjoyed Pakistani support and consequently American backing since as long ago as 1974 - five years before the Russian invasion. They had creamed off the best arms and equipment for themselves and could not bear for anybody else to take the limelight, let alone the credit for any success. Everything had to be focused on them - especially media coverage.

We were getting such a thorough briefing that I determined to prolong it. So I asked Juliet if she could give us her overview of the essential differences between the two fundamentalist parties. She said that John Fullerton had put it best. The great strength of Jamiat Islami, Afghanistan was that it managed to bridge the divide of urban sophistication and country tradition, which was the contradiction which beset other groups.

Jamiat Islami, Pakistan, was politically nearer to Hesbe-i-Islami, Afghanistan, and this was a source of widespread confusion. At one time, Jamiat Islami, Pakistan had been a proscribed political party in Pakistan as being too rightist. Paradoxically it had played an important role in bankrolling Afghan fundamentalist leaders. (This may have been one of Firdos Khan's more impressive sleights of hand.)

So far as Engineer Gulbuddin Hekmatyar and Hesbe-i-Islami was concerned, his following transcended tribal allegiance, but occurred most frequently in Pashtoon areas amongst young intellectual groups, especially where tribal structures had broken down or where there was a mixture of groups originating from different tribes. Hekmatyar was a Ghilzai from the east. The other great Pashtoon group, the Durrani, were mainly from the west. Their allegiance tended towards the great families and royalty, whereas the Ghilzais were more *hoi polloi* with stronger tribal ties.

With all that, and her remark that reprisals were the only language Hesbe-i-Islami understood, still ringing in our ears, we promised to report back everything she had said to Rabbani. Which we duly did. He said sheepishly that he would be sure to pass the message on. But we very much doubted he would - not even a watered-down version. There were too many irreconcilables. However, it had served to give us our first political insight on the medical front and demonstrated how we could so easily become the rope in a tug-of-war.

It also served to show Juliet in her true colours. I had never seen her so angry, or half so beautiful!

Not long afterwards, Rabbani tried to recover face by inviting us all for a traditional Afghan feast at his home. As so often happens, there were too many of us and we were taken instead to a quasi-Afghan restaurant. The only thing to mar the evening was Anwar Chaudhri's refusal to attend. He would not divulge the reason. All he said was that they were a bunch of rogues and vagabonds and thieves - every one of them. One day, he added, we would find that out for ourselves.

No amount of cajolery would make Anwar budge. We reminded him that the idea had been his in the first place. There could be

'One Afghan on a donkey is worth four Russians in a tank'
- General Alexander Lebed.

Photo taken on the Baghlan Plain by Rupert Chetwynd

no backing off at this late stage, but nothing would induce him to disclose what had caused his *volte face*. The Good Samaritan had had second thoughts. This was no fit of temper. Either the Afghan had seen through the Punjabi, for they could see through a man in the most disconcerting way, to lay bare his innermost soul; or, conversely, Anwar had read them like a book and discovered some inner truth which, if bared to us, would destroy our whole *raison d'être*.

For the moment, and since I was Anwar's chalet companion, it was up to me to make his excuses. Following his request to blame the ravages of Delhi belly, I had little difficulty. I could truthfully endorse the most appalling off-stage rumblings from the direction of the thunder-box. I had even commented caustically how strange it was that a native of Lahore should succumb, whilst lesser mortals remained unaffected.

Dr Rabbani expressed such deep regret at Anwar's absence that it seemed his real purpose was to discover whether we yet knew of any underlying reason for such a *maladie diplomatique*. But although we thought we understood Anwar's motivations, we may well not have done. In the years ahead, he chose to go his own way, hand-picking his own team and concentrating their efforts on the new Afghan Trauma hospital once it opened in Nasarabad Road, where better facilities were to be found. Significantly, he kept away from Afghan Surgical, so his axe must either have been related to Dr Rabbani personally or to the Jamiat Islami, Pakistan party in general. One cannot help wondering whether they attempted to bring pressure to bear on the former citizen of Lahore, but what kind of pressure? Or he may have felt 'his idea' was running away with itself, no longer under his control.

From the point of view of the Guildford Surgical Team it represented tribal schism in our own ranks, as if the condition were somehow contagious. From now on there would be two separate teams.

At about this time the Guildford Surgical Team suffered another minor upset. It was contained in a report from a Belfast 'expert in amputation', who had been sent out on a visiting firemen tour of the North West Frontier Province. I never saw his report but it was purported to state that the Guildford Team 'did no useful work and spent their time enjoying themselves.' The author of the report had a particular aversion to me - likening me 'to a typical civil servant, who failed to impress!' - which only served to illustrate how superficial the findings were. The surgeons at the cutting edge, however, were deeply resentful of such hot-air-bags. It seemed to us that rich regional hospital boards, such as Belfast in this case, devised these reporting excursions, merely hoping to rid themselves of their own misfits, just as manufacturing companies used to give responsibility for exports to the awkward colleague. Nobody could remember the last time the so called 'expert' had amputated.

There was no link I could find to Anwar's outrage. And these two events were the only negative vibrations that were to come our way. Of the two, I took the Anwar conundrum much more seriously, because I could not understand it.

At some discreet moment I reported back to Peter what little I had learned from my visit to "TM". If Azrow turned out to be in the heart of Hesbe-i country, we'd have to wait for clearance from Juliet before making any recommendations.

For two years or more, there had been the promise of a brand new hospital in Peshawar. Once again, it was to be called the Ibn Sina, after Avicenna, but it was described as a Surgical Hospital and Trauma Centre. It was to be located in Nasarabad Road, University Town. We had even been shown a prospectus with an artist's impression of how splendid it would all be, with both male and female wards, two operating theatres, five emergency rooms, computers, X-ray department, laboratory, blood bank, physiotherapy, pharmacy, recovery room, laundry, kitchens, and conference room. There was no end to what was contemplated.

We took it all with a pinch of salt. And then, suddenly, much to our surprise, the very next year, it was all there. Sir Nicholas Barrington had spoken on behalf of the European Community at the inaugural ceremony. This was the hospital where Anwar Chaudhri was headed. The original team would operate there too, but at different times of year.

[1] Ten years later Peter Stiles was able to identify 'Nero' as the son of Younis Khalis.

16

The Great Unwashed

Over those same two years, we had become alarmed because the American charity, with whom we were working, had decided on a new policy. This consisted in removing the very best Afghan surgeons and shipping them to the States for a fourteen-month intensive training course in hospital administration. Inevitably, two of those selected were Abdul Satar Paktiss and Ali Abdul Rousta. This seemed to us lunacy at a time when their skills were desperately needed at the surgical front line. Inevitably, without their inspired leadership, both their hospitals went into sharp decline. This caused us to concentrate our efforts more on the new Nasarabagh Road hospital, with the excuse of its better facilities. Years later we had to admit that, in the overall plan to reconstitute Afghan hospitals and medicine inside Afghanistan, the Americans had not only been right, but had shown remarkable foresight.

At the time, all we could do, in our small way, was to give Abdul Satar Paktiss a crash indoctrination course in what he might expect to find in America. We concentrated on telling him a few home truths, the ones he might not hear from them! We tried to explain how different America was; that eighty per cent of the wealth of America was owned by the women; that they ruled the roost. Not content with just one Queen, or two, like England, America had hundreds of thousands of matriarchs - all daughters of the American sexual revolution.

The best way of succeeding with them, we said, was to tell them that whatever he was due to administer, once he returned, would embrace women and children. This would reflect the statistics of the refugee camps. At the same time we had to be careful not to alienate his affections. We noticed his alarm when we told him that the men, like worker bees, got killed off young by the competitive pressure of hard work. He should look out for the heart-attack special, delivered in good time to leave gracious young widows, ready for the blue rinse and the 'Wentworth-Brewster' world cruise. But Afghans are quicker than quick on the uptake and he was able to take it all in his stride. He had clearly identified his next mission and he was the ideal man to exploit it. He knew the Afghan refugee statistics at first hand. He was familiar with the hysterical mullah rantings, forever tirading against western doctors for defiling Afghan women. He was able to turn everything we had told him, and all he inherently knew, to maximum advantage. As we discovered two years later, his particular brand of charisma paid handsome dividends.

During the day classes Abdul Satar Paktiss absorbed the finer detail of American hospital administration with consummate ease, both as to theory and practice. Like most Afghans, he was equally quick to identify his leisure time activities - with amazing flair.

To the select few, he gave specialist lectures on the virtues of his external fixator, and, to wider audiences, he lectured on the war in general. As a former major in the Afghan Medical Corps, he could relate authentic battleground experiences. In post-Vietnam America, this gripped the matrons and daughters of the revolution where it mattered most. It also loosened their purse strings.

He returned after fourteen months, fully conversant with American hospital management practice and with a large fortune by American standards, which meant a vast one by Afghan ones. This naturally aroused enmity, resulting in a succession of back-stabbing tragedies ever since.

First of all, he stood accused of misappropriating the funds. Then he was removed from his original foundation. Undaunted, he started up again with a new hospital and recovery ward in premises adjacent to the Afghan Interim Government Health Ministry offices in Hyatabad, where he also assumed high office with responsibilities. Part of his problem, if not the major part in fundamentalist circles, could be quite simply attributed to the emphasis he continued to place on the care of women and children. The other factor, inevitably, was the tallest poppy syndrome. Afghans, who would all be king, do not like to see one of their number get too far ahead.

Abdul Satar Paktiss had done too damned well.

*

Unlike my rather fruitless walkabout excursion to Cherat when I visited "TM", Peter Stiles's painstaking written proposal for consideration by the AfghanAid committee was now assured of endorsement. His proposal was that a detailed study be made to assess the medical problems in a restricted area and produce a scheme for medical care in that area, in order to give such a matrix, once proven, a wider application to similar districts throughout the country. This 'microcosm to macrocosm' approach anticipated the refugees returning home in the foreseeable future, when the war would be over.

At the same time, since the programme of surgery was running smoothly on the annual October/November visit basis, it was time to see what, if anything, could be done to improve the chain of evacuation and the primary treatment of casualties. Increasingly, the war would be taken into the enemy camp as territorial gains could be assumed. So, the formula proposed would be: Battle Area to Camp Medical Centre; Medical Centre to Pick-up Point; Pick-up Point to Casualty Reception Centre; and Casualty Reception Centre to Hospital.

AfghanAid was to be our Long Range Desert Group. They would organise sorties to coincide with their regular itineraries. This would enable Peter Stiles to see the whole evacuation process in action. I was to accompany him as minder. For the first trip, we were to travel via Bannu and Miram Shah, with a view to crossing the border somewhere in Northern Waziristan. Our precise departure date and time would be determined by the vagaries and turn-round time of the next ambulance due out. We expected to visit at least three of the existing camp medical centres inside Afghanistan.

In the meantime, we were to cease all washing and shaving. Even above elbow and knee ablutions were out. Something had to be done to make our clothes look more lived in. Like sleeping in them. We even went one better and dutifully rolled around on the ground like a couple of disobedient Jack Russells.

After three days and nights we were paraded in front of Sarah Forster of AfghanAid (no relation to Sir Oliver). We were like truant schoolboys, pulled up before the housematron, except that, this time, she was tweaking the ears as she inspected them to make sure we had NOT washed behind them and that our necks and collars were suitably ingrained with dirt. Our feet were filthy and as much matching grey stubble as possible was being nurtured by the pair of us. Above all, we stank. Happily we passed muster.

Sarah said they had heard over the radio telephone that there was a fair to good chance that we would be off at dawn the next morning. She told us to get ourselves to Gulmohar Road by 4.30 a.m. at the latest. We were to take the absolute minimum of kit. Nothing was best. The guard had been told to expect us. We were then handed a letter containing basic written instructions on where we were going, with some idea of who and what to expect, together with the all-important Tribal Areas Pass, covering our outward journey, as issued that day by the Home and Tribal Areas Office. Our driver would be Satar and, as a special favour, Malang, whom we knew already, was being allocated to us as interpreter. We could only thank Sarah profusely.

Mindful of Sir Oliver's injunction, I promptly telephoned ahead to Ruth Coggan at the William Theodore Pennell Memorial Hospital at Bannu to say how it had been suggested that we should look her up and would we be welcome at eight o'clock in the morning? She insisted that we join her and her assistants for an English breakfast - including eggs and bacon!

The first part of our preparations was plain sailing. We were that keen to be off, we would have gone to Gulmohar Road with Sarah then and there. We reduced our kit and then each other's by three ruthless stages, until it was down to the basics: sleeping bag; patoo blanket; one complete change of clothes; one pair Baxter's boots with socks; waterbottle; water purification tablets; salt tablets; headache tablets; on-going malaria tablets; toothbrush/toothpaste; brown bumf. (We were like some walking chemist shop. I wondered if I would be taking this lot if I weren't quite so quasi-medical myself now); Fleaseed - indispensable miracle worker on the trots; photostat of relevant pages of passport - three sets each with colour mug shots; camera, film; penknife; grubby comb; grubby handkerchief; pen, paper; swatch; one paperback book each - neither choice read by either of us, so that we could swap; emergency rations - Bournville chocolate, Kendal Mint Cake. Peter also had a secret tin of curiously strong peppermints, but these were classified as 'medicinal'. And that, plus Peter's small but powerful binoculars, was it.

Sabbur, our normal driver, was up and ready to introduce us to Satar. Malang, already known to us, since he was part of Juliet's close-knit headquarters' staff, spoke wonderful English and had enough presence to talk us out of trouble. A minder's minder, if ever there was one.

Satar was about the most cheerful-to-manic Afghan it was our good fortune to meet. The greater part of his left hand had been blown off by an anti-personnel mine. We never learned whether he was laying it or clearing it, but his war effort now was to help his fellow Mujahedeen by serving as an ambulance driver cum courier. Afghans are the most awesome of drivers, and Satar the most daring and original of all we met.

We soon got the message as we were crossing the Kohat Pass in the half-light of dawn. We were to be taken up dried river beds to keep out of sight in dead ground and so cross and re-cross territory unobserved. Neither Peter nor I had ever witnessed anything quite like Satar's style. He delighted in dedicating the wheel to the mangled left stump, while, if possible, crossing arms to change gear, and talking and gesticulating to us over his shoulder all the time. We understood not a word, but he was in no way deterred.

Juliet Crawley Peck - with Malang and team on road to
Afghanistan in 1990

Malang, as interpreter, was at the polarised extreme. He was a quiet introverted, highly intelligent, civil engineer. He looked very striking. Although a Pashtun and not a Tadjic Persian he bore a close resemblance to Darius the King as seen on coins, and his English was delivered with the most perfect Oxford accent, although he had never been beyond Pakistan. For a man of action, his whole demeanour was surprisingly donnish, as were his comments. Today, he was riding shotgun, tomorrow, obviously an accomplished linguist, he might be translating some of the finer nuances of the Lion of the Panjshir's latest treatise into language suitably refined for the readers of the *Daily Telegraph.*

Both he and Satar were somewhat run to fat, but as Juliet pointed out, what would happen to me if I were to be let loose in Italy after a lifetime of being half-starved? That not only silenced me, but proved a prescient prediction!

Malang had a ready answer to all our questions and often managed to anticipate them. He was devout, sincere and quiet-spoken. The only resentment we ever heard him express was that his civil engineering course at Kabul University should have been interrupted by the war. He was convinced he would be returning there to complete his degree, just as soon as hostilities ceased. Such was his faith. He never, ever missed prayer times. They were sacrosanct. Instead of sometimes setting the pace, Satar appeared often to fall in line, but this could have been wrongly perceived.

Although we had no Red Cross/Red Crescent markings, being a quasi-ambulance, ours was an all-white vehicle - denoting Non-Government Organisation (NGO) status. Other than AfghanAid's name appearing discreetly on the doors, our only other identification was the Toyota logo, blind embossed on the tailboard. Needless to say, as non-combatants, we carried no weapons.

According to Sarah Forster's outline paper, we were to be accorded the privilege of a guard of honour to escort us across the border. This was to be mounted by Jalaluddin Haqqani's men, as we would be entering his tribal territory. We were to be his honoured guests. Our lives would therefore be protected better than his own. In theory, his tribe would defend us to the last bullet and the last man. There was only one drawback to enjoying this protection and that was to establish the initial rendezvous point. Which border was meant as the intended meeting place? There were two. The first was that between Pakistan and the Tribal Areas of Northern Waziristan, under Pakistan administration and 'protection'. And the second (which we assumed was the one that mattered) between those Tribal

Areas and Afghanistan.

All these 'Tribal Areas' were a hangover from a British buffer state invention, as a semi-autonomous attempt to control the unmanageable Shinwari, Masoud, Waziri and Afridi tribesmen. So in many ways we still had only ourselves to blame for any frustrations suffered. And, were we in for frustrations! Neither Peter Stiles nor I can claim to be renowned for calm or patience. But since I was the more experienced, I knew that, without a long-suffering acceptant attitude, we would only get turned back. Peter was permanently on a short fuse, steaming himself up for by-pass surgery. This reduced my job to getting him there and back; thus he became the one who had to be humoured, mollified and have his ruffled feathers smoothed.

The Tribal Areas access formula is conceived in classic 'Catch 22' style, no doubt by the British-instigated regulations as applied by the Home Office to the Tribal Areas, covering the issue of passes. According to the time-honoured dogma, you are requested and required to make application 'in person', by the 15th day of the month previous to the month of intended travel. That is fine for those who can plan their lives that far ahead. A hundred years ago you would almost certainly have had to. It also serves the purpose of letting everybody know you are coming, and gives an inkling of your intentions in advance, thus providing the authorities with an opportunity to balk you at every turn if they so wish.

Jalaluddin Haqqani's tribesmen wore the most glamorous of costumes. Predominantly black, they were the Beau Brummells of the Afghans, with magnificent outsize black-as-jet turbans, edged and threaded and flecked all over with finest gold. Like Highland regiments, they might have something less showy for battle order, a hunting tartan. I couldn't wait to see, but breakfast came first, breakfast at Bannu.

A British breakfast would set us up for whatever was in store, however long the day. As we were travelling on a Friday, anything could go wrong and probably would. Our safety valve was to equate any frustration suffered with British Rail engineering works or leaves on the line.

Entrance to Jalaluddin Haqani cave. *Photo by Peter Stiles*

17
Breakfast in Bannu

One of the great joys of travel with Peter Stiles was that he was extremely well-read on the subject of British India - especially the North West Frontier and Afghanistan. Typically, on our way, he had pointed out the monument where the last British district officer had been shot. Asked why he had shot a British officer in cold blood, once he knew they were leaving for ever, the Afghan responsible had replied: because they were leaving it was his last chance!

Peter had read the biography of Dr William Theodore Pennell, the eccentric Anglican missionary, who had founded the Bannu hospital in 1893. Indeed, the full title of the hospital today is still the William Pennell Memorial Hospital, Bannu. It was housed in a small military garrison cantonment area, just on the outskirts of the town, and easily found, welcoming all-comers to a long-standing enclave of Anglican conviction.

If Peter had the story right, William Pennell operated in the mornings and preached the gospel in the midday sun. Mostly he was stoned for his pains, but this did not deter him. He took to native costume, rode a donkey, sometimes a camel, and even a bicycle. It must have been an early model. He built a fine Anglican church in the style of a mosque, in his attempt to entice the converts in.

One of Pennell's regular operations involved skin grafting. Supposedly adulterous Afghan women had their noses cut off and Pennell managed an operation to restore them. Whether related or not, the hospital had evolved as the prime haven for Afghan women with obstetric and gynaecological problems. Difficult cases were known to converge on Bannu from all over Afghanistan. It was always the difficult cases, because the easy ones had no need to contemplate such an arduous journey.

Sadly, Pennell, whilst trying to save the life of his assistant, had become infected and so they both perished from septicaemia. This was just before the First World War. Since then there had been all sorts of developments under the aegis of the Anglican Mission, including, at one time, a flourishing boys' school.

It had been Sir Oliver Forster's Parthian shot that we should be sure to look in if we were passing that way. So here we were, bang on time for an 8 a.m. breakfast, and Ruth Coggan hadn't been kidding; we could smell the bacon - sizzling away!

Sir Oliver thought the world of Ruth Coggan, and with good

reason. As a senior nurse, Sir Oliver's wife had a very clear idea of what is involved in the running of a hospital establishment on this scale. Ruth Coggan is the daughter of the former Archbishop of Canterbury. Whereas our puny efforts were confined to two or three weeks' voluntary service each year, hers was day in, day out, month after month, year after year, for over twenty years.

Seemingly frail in her physique, but deceptively wiry and strong, her presence proclaimed an ascetic, sustained by prayer. One glance tells you that she is a saintly but also pragmatic person. She also exhibits a self-deprecating, yet sparkling sense of humour. Always Christian, ever cheerful. There was just a hint of Joyce Grenfell about her, 'wiser, gentler, more generous, ever hopeful, with that generous spirit born of optimism.' She gave us a raptuous welcome as though we had come hot-foot from Canterbury, along the Pilgrim's Way.

We had assumed that Malang and Satar would join us, but they made it clear that they would go and find their own breakfast back in the hypermarket buzz of Bannu proper. Plainly this was what Ruth had anticipated, bacon or no bacon. The outsize metal gates were re-opened to let them out with the clear injunction that they were to be back within the hour, an hour-and-a-half at the outside. That should allow us enough time for breakfast and a quick tour of the hospital; or, at least, those parts permitted. Being a Friday, there was a better chance of seeing more as there were unlikely to be any operations that day.

I took my opportunity to relay Sir Oliver and Lady Forster's best wishes. Ruth said that Sir Nicholas Barrington had come down to stay last weekend. She feared his visit had not been a great success. They had suddenly been faced with an emergency operation and he had been left to cope with a barbecue all by himself. While he was about it he had also tackled the garden, which somehow they never had time to do. The ambassador (or High Commissioner, once Pakistan returned to the Commonwealth) was known to be a keen gardener.

Ruth led the way into the living quarters, which consisted of a large dining-room with an even larger semi-circular living-room beyond. It had copious long-seated planters' chairs, a hand-wound gramophone for old-style 78 rpm records and an altogether common-room library look and feel of academia. The whole place was in the process of getting a new lick of distemper - whenever the pressure of operations allowed. The rooms were spacious and high-ceilinged, from the early Victorian period, when Georgian proportions still prevailed in the outposts of Empire. The Gothic Revival failed to reach

Bannu, if only because, instead of allowing the church to succumb as expected, its eccentric patron had insisted on early Islamic-colonial instead!

The main buildings, including the hospital itself, had distinct architectural similarities to Dean's Hotel: the same brick and timber construction, the same sense of proportion. Built to stay cool and built to last.

We were introduced to Ruth's team, who were at their appointed places at the breakfast table. 'Kips' (Caroline) Kippenberger from New Zealand, Alison Ffookes and Sarah Fane, who was preparing her elective year project at Bannu. Sarah turned out to have a father who was a renowned Guildford GP and she was destined to marry into the family of an old army boxing contemporary of mine.

Over breakfast, we asked Ruth to tell us about the hospital. When she had come out by ship, some twenty years previously, she told us, the word was out that her predecessor, another Anglican missionary lady, had been abducted by the Waziri. She had been in dread, lest her father hear of it and order her home. Secretly, she said, she would have quite liked being kidnapped ... preferably on arrival. But it was not to be. Once they knew she had arrived, her predecessor was released and soon sailed home.

Ruth asked what we knew about the Anglican Mission, and reiterated most of what Peter had already researched. However, she had more to add about the proselytising, for the mosque-like familiarity had signally failed to entice the converts in. However, the baptismal register showed that Pennell had succeeded in making four converts. The mission, though, would be remembered for other reasons.

We had said we could not help hearing an endless tirade against Western doctors. The outcry from the mullahs in the camps warned against Afghan women going anywhere near them for they would defile them, etc., etc. Of course, they were referring specifically to male doctors, but we wondered if Ruth and her team had suffered any knock-on effect? Happily, their reputation was far too long-established and widespread for such hysteria to cut any ice.

Breakfast turned out to be the very model of British middle-class suburban conventionality. As well as the eggs and bacon, we had cereal, toast and marmalade, and instant coffee. It brought back memories of the mess in the Suez Canal Zone forty years ago, where my then commanding officer, Brigadier Stewart-Richardson, had attempted to create an atmosphere of 'home' in the desert, by asking me to pass the non-existent Frank Cooper's Oxford Marmalade. It was a soundly-based, long-conceived game for British army officers to play when far from creature comforts. Long before, Lord Leighton, the only painter ever to be ennobled, and founder of the Artists' Rifles regiment, had laid down that the prime necessity to ensure a good performance on summer manoeuvres was coffee and marmalade; for the officers at least. Nothing else was stipulated. He would have appeared on the scene at much the same time as Pennell. They were both best vintage *fin de siècle*.

We longed to know how Ruth obtained her delicious illicit bacon, naturally forbidden in Muslim lands. It was simple when you knew. It turned out it was tinned and was smuggled in via the diplomatic bag! Whenever he knew of a safe courier, Sir Nicholas Barrington sent a consignment. It could have been us. In fact, he had delivered the last lot himself, which reminded Ruth to ask us, if we were to pass back her way, whether we would mind taking some old medical journals back with us, 'to teach the next generation'. We said we would be delighted.

Once it was established that there was a good chance of our taking the same route back, she asked if Peter could hold a clinic there too? Amongst the midwives, there were any number of cases of damaged backs, shoulders, arms, elbows. Peter remarked that he was not a bit surprised, with all the lifting they must have to do. He was then led off to inspect the newly completed operating and delivery theatres. They would only be used on the Sabbath in an emergency, in which case there would be plenty of time to clear Peter out of the way.

So, I found myself left with Kips, Alison and Sarah. We talked of home. We talked of the guerilla war and the types of wounds we had seen. Alison said that, in the twelve years she had been at Bannu, she had never visited Afghanistan proper. She simply longed to don the *chardor*, but was sweetly fearful her feet would unmask her. She was too tall to pass for an Afghan woman and, indeed, her feet were outsize. She told us of the countrywide network of women she now knew as a result of her work and how she could be certain that, if asked, each and every one of these women would afford her *pachtunwali* hospitality. This meant they would protect her life as more precious than their own. Quite clearly, she longed to come with us, but it could not be.

An alternative tour had been arranged for me. I would be allowed to visit the male wards and Sarah had been delegated to take me round. In common with all Muslim establishments, and indeed our own hospitals and some schools, the mission hospital was divided into a male and female side.

Rupert with Sarah Fane in the Wah Gardens of Barbour.
Photo by Peter Stiles

We began in the communal courtyard, where the women were usually to be seen busily washing clothes, whilst the men spent their time chewing *naswar*, smoking and gossiping generally, under their nodding dusty turbans. Most of them were TB, malaria or malnutrition cases.

Nursing care was minimal. Patients' families were expected to provide the basics and food. That explained why whole families were camped around the beds with their pots and pans and potent curries and, of course, their prayer mats. There was even the odd chicken pegged to a bed leg.

Sarah said it was a positive pleasure to make a ward round here. There was no standing on ceremony. None of the formality of our system at home! No starched white coats, mill-boards, or glum faces.

As we approached the first family, Sarah was greeted in the traditional Afghan way with a heartfelt hug. We then had to perch on the edge of the rickety *charpayee* (string bed) and drink a cup of chai or green tea. Sarah told me in an aside that they, all of them, always asked the same questions at the same time. I'd see. There then followed the stream of questions, just as Sarah had predicted. Was she married? Was this her husband? Not? How did she escape her husband? Where were her children? How many children? Why no children? How no children?

We moved on. Sarah explained how they held an out-patients' clinic every day to which hundreds of women and children came. Most of them were Waziris, but they also saw Masouds and occasionally Afridis. The women all wore magnificent costumes; tight bodices, decked in beads and coin collections. Huge sweeping blood-red skirts worn over baggy harem pants, pointed embroidered shoes, *dupattas* over their long plaited hair, plus myriads of nose- and ear-rings. I told Sarah one of the less obvious reasons for the women's bright dresses was so that no sniper could claim he didn't know it was a woman he had shot at!

Sarah admitted that the men appeared rather dull by comparison. However, whatever they lacked in peacock splendour, they made up for in bearing and proud good looks, which were, after all, their lasting national monument. But, just now, she was somewhat disenchanted with them all, for a particular reason. Medically speaking, by far the worst aspect of conditions at Bannu was the terrible shortage of blood. The standard practice was always to make a first call on the immediate family squatting round at the foot of the bed. It was hard to credit, but they would refuse to part with their blood even when they could see their loved ones bleeding to death before their very eyes. Even when asked to give just a little blood, those same tall, strong, proud Pathans, bristling with guns, ammunition belts and daggers, turned pale and pleaded 'off colour' weakness.

As we stood apart for a moment in the middle of the square, I told Sarah of my blood donor experience at the Afghan Surgical Hospital. Instead of attempting to amuse her, I would have done better to explain my strictly non-medical role, because I soon found myself way out of my depth as she explained that there had been over a hundred deliveries in the short time she had been there. Given that most Afghan women have more than ten children, she had seen all the complications of the Grand Multip! I had no idea what she was talking about and before I could put her right she was off again, telling me the one thing I did know, which was that, at Bannu, they only ever got the cases which were expected to be difficult, or at any rate would involve complications. So, only 37 of the 100 or so births attended had been spontaneous vaginal deliveries. There had been 2 horrific craniotomies, 20 neo-natal deaths and more *antepartum* haemorrhages than Sarah cared to count. I tried to look caring and above all impressed. It was probably just as well that, at this point, we were rejoined by Alison.

Alison explained that most of the other major problems they encountered stemmed from ignorant interference with labour in the patients' homes. In the twelve years she had been there, the biggest problem by far resulted from the indiscriminate prescription of drugs. Whatever came first to 'lay' or laymen's hands was ladled out. Bannu then got the job of clearing up the resultant mess in the midwifery room. It was not unknown for untrained locals to administer drugs, which caused the uterus to contract strongly in women in labour with catastrophic results ... stillborn babies, ruptured uterus. As often as not this caused the mother's death too. I told her we had been taken to see a ward of survivors at the Lady Reading Hospital.

Otherwise, it was a story of unsterile vaginal examination, causing sepsis, often septicaemia and sometimes death too. Sarah then described how horrifying it could be to see a week-old baby with tetanus, caused by cutting the cord with a dirty knife. During her short stay, two babies had died of that.

Whether I was a qualified 'quack' or not might have made no difference to my modified tour, but I was beginning to feel as if I had been through the women's ward medical complaints mangle, without crossing the threshold. If that had been the watered-down version, what, I wondered, had Peter endured with Ruth's synopsis of over twenty years' experience?

Here, at long last, clambering through a hole in an unfinished wall, came Ruth and Peter. Both were beaming. This was the last of the construction work, nearing completion. Peter was saying how very, very impressive he had found it all.

Unwilling to hang around fielding compliments, Ruth Coggan told us peremptorily that we just had time to visit the church before we had to be off! On the way we passed some highly productive kitchen garden beds. There were also two strange-looking sun ovens, which would have to await explanation at some other time.

Suddenly, the church was upon us with its twin Muslim minarets. In its way, it was beautiful, as well as amusing for its Osbert Lancaster pretensions, and most unusual. Inside, all was calm and cool. The peace of God is like a cool breeze at night after the scorching heat of the midday sun. There was only one memorial, a joint tribute to Pennell and his assistant - a brass plate put up in 1912. Ruth explained that they didn't always have time for regular full services. But they always tried to slip away at some stage during the day, either singly or in pairs, for a few minutes of silent prayer.

We needed no prompting and duly sank to our knees in a dark corner of this remote sanctuary where so many far more devout Christians had worshipped for upwards of a hundred years whilst bringing medical aid to Afghan women.

It was a humbling thought. It may also have been an opportunist thought, sprung from memories of Lady Forster's last visit and specialist relevance. But Ruth then speculated as to whether there might not be some possible future role for our wives to help out at Bannu, whilst their menfolk concentrated on casualty evacuation programmes over the border. It was a vivid vision.

It would soon be time to leave. We found Malang and Satar praying in a nearby apple orchard. I couldn't stop myself wondering if they had smelled the wafting, forbidden bacon, and what they had made of it. Malang had not succeeded in reaching the Haqqani escort by telephone. As it was Friday, he thought we should simply travel on. 'Trust in God, good luck and damn the consequences' was to be the order of the day. For us, there was not much choice in the matter. Nor was there any norm for comparison. We gave Ruth our promise to call in on the way back, if possible with some kind of advance warning by telephone from Miram Shah. She could then assemble those members of her permanent and casual staff, plus any of their immediate dependents, who wished to attend Peter's travelling consultancy.

I could anticipate a clutch of 'Guildford elbow' candidates among the midwives who had spent a lifetime humping a continuous conveyor belt of labouring Afghan mothers. The Guildford elbow is a replacement joint for arthritis of the elbow, designed by Peter Stiles. It was one of the first successful elbow replacements in the world. Once I knew Peter well enough I asked him why, as for Thomas's splint, he had not named it the Stiles's elbow. His characteristic reply was: 'What if it hadn't worked?'

We then took some photographs to record our visit, appropriately outside the church. I took Ruth with Peter. Peter took Ruth with me. By now, the others were far too busy to be bothered with such vanities.

As we drove off, I looked back at the vanishing figure of the seemingly ageless, calm, unlined, slight, sinewy saint with her halo of reddish gold hair and serenely-smiling freckled face and wondered what exactly kept her ever-alert, brisk and energetic. In a word, it had to be Faith. God alone knows how she hadn't suffered irreversible back damage, with all the heaving, huffing and puffing she must have endured over the past twenty years or more.

Simply to contemplate all those Afghan women she had succoured, let alone the countless babies, both male and female, that she had saved for the world, must make her the personification of the Christian's Revenge! Her saintly influence spread from Miram Shah to the Oxus and embraced the Safed Koh, the Pamirs and the Hindu Kush. There was no limit to her immense power for good. It was back to that ever hopeful, ever generous spirit of optimism. It was a view of the world worth sharing. Never was the OBE she received, no doubt at Sir Oliver's instigation, more deserved. That lady hadn't taken a holiday in 26 years. Do they still make them like that?

18

`Cross-border Crossroads`

The overriding disadvantage of the *Insha'allah*, God-willing, world, is that it lands you every so often in a no-win situation.

We reached the checkpoint to find there was nobody there to meet us. Only the Pakistani Army Border Guards. So, we decided to wait at a discreet distance in some rare shade, and see if any of Jalaluddin Haqqani's men turned up as promised.

Then, after more than an hour, we saw with a huge sigh of relief, a 'mirage' convoy approaching. It had a rag-bag of tribal militia for escort and their charges were two Egyptian doctors on secondment to our least favourite Kuwaiti Red Crescent butcher's shop. They were on their way back from the Miram Shah Red Crescent Hospital, headed out of the Tribal Areas, for Peshawar.

On impulse, I decided I would endure anything rather than sit around in the midday sun, waiting for people who might never show up. I would pocket my prejudices and persuade the shambolic escort to conduct us back to the Miram Shah Hospital. It was a time for action, movement of any kind.

Fortunately, one of the Egyptian doctors was a French-speaking Greek from Alexandria. He understood our predicament perfectly - all foreigners were obliged to have an escort in the Tribal Areas. Thank heavens the idea proved equally acceptable to the *ersatz* escort themselves.

So, at last, we were in good order to report to the border guard. Our names were duly compared with the official list of those expected that day, as forwarded the day before by the Home and Tribal Affairs Ministry. The guard commander was extra smart and super efficient. His name-tag proclaimed him to be Pir Mohammed and his appointment was given as 'Security in Charge'.

We undertook to release our escort once we reached the safety of Miram Shah Hospital. There was no reaction to this gratuitous offer. Pleased as Punch with such initiative, we were delighted to speed off. Imagine our chagrin, therefore, when only a few minutes down the road, we found ourselves being overtaken by a blue jeep, containing the self-same border guard commander, Pir Mohammed. As he drew level, he gave us a standing salute and, as if to assert his invulnerability, I noticed there was a neat round hole slap in the middle of his windscreen.

With our long-awaited arrival (delayed by the Bannu stopover), he had now finished his business for the day. Nobody else was listed or expected. All we had succeeded in doing was imperiously to subborn (through superfluous Graeco-Egypto-French channels) the very band of tribal militia who would have been our lot anyway. If we had checked in any earlier, we should still have had to await them. Now, we were simply being conducted back to the Miram Shah command post to await further orders.

We were duly taken to the office of the Assistant Commissioner for Refugees, Nasir Khan Wasir. Protest as we might, that far from being 'reffos', we were doctors on an important fact-finding mission, expecting only a safe conduct to the Afghan border, our guardian remained implacable.

None, but none, of the telephones in any of the government offices worked. After shouting at the various instruments for an hour and a half, as if they were megaphones, Nasir Khan Wasir admitted it might be simpler after all to try and call on the Assistant Political Agent in person; even if it did mean disturbing his day of rest and peace.

We were obviously in for endless prevarication and hanging about. At one moment we were even allowed to go in search of our mythical, mystical Haqqani contacts in a succession of mosque visits. Having drawn blanks, we took advantage of our freedom to call on the Red Crescent/Red Cross hospital.

Earlier that week we had dined with Robin Gray, the International Committee of the Red Cross senior medical co-ordinator in Peshawar, so the local doctor, Wana Waziri, had no hesitation in standing guarantee for our parole for a couple of interesting and instructive hours. Casualties had come through two days before, so they were in a state of readiness for more trouble to come. The two Egyptian doctors we had met were in fact on their way back to recruit others of their number to beef up the establishment.

As evening approached, we were told that the Assistant Political Agent, Badshan Gul Wazir, would graciously receive us at his home. We were conducted there under heavy escort and entered a well-manicured walled garden. He was tall, and of distinctly military bearing despite his civilian clothes.

He listened patiently to what we had to say and then broke out into some oft-rehearsed, pre-set pantomime about how we had to understand that this whole procedure was primarily an expression of concern for our personal safety. He was surprised we should have misinterpreted the meaning of our pass. There could be no misunderstanding. It clearly stated it was for the purpose of visiting the Tribal Areas only. There was no mention of a safe-conduct to the Afghan border. He could give us his unequivocal assurance that foreigners were never allowed to visit Afghanistan by this route.

Nevertheless, as an exception and just in case there had been some unusual oversight, he would have a word with the Home Secretary at the Home Office between 7 p.m. and 8 p.m. this very evening and convey the Home Secretary's ruling to us no later than 9 p.m. to 10 p.m. this evening at the Guest House or at the very latest by 8 a.m. to 9 a.m. on Saturday morning, tomorrow. He hoped we would be comfortable in the Guest House. We thanked him kindly. So that there could be no possible chance of mistaken identity, I insisted on leaving our Tribal Areas passes with him. They weren't proving of much use to us.

No doubt it was all hot air. If they couldn't make a telephone call around the Miram Shah area itself, what earthly chance was there of the megaphone reaching Peshawar, let alone Islamabad? It was still Friday, the day of rest and peace, all day, and there would be nobody to answer at the other end. To cover our frustration, and much to his surprise, we admired his garden and his shy children, licking their 'colourful cholera' ice-creams in the sanctuary they had found behind his ladder-backed chair. We had been fobbed off. We were getting nowhere ...

Far from reaching Afghanistan by nightfall on the first day, we found ourselves instead under house arrest as guests/prisoners in the floodlit Miram Shah Circuit House, complete with watchtower. Our transport, driver and interpreter had all been removed. What ignominy. We checked out our rations and discovered too that thanks to my distrust of a stallholder, I had landed us with a quantity of inedible 'cooking' bananas, despite being warned off them. Our prospects looked none too bright, although we had been left our boots and sandals. Also, in compensation, the floodlighting was bright enough to read by. But our 'guest' status was restored to some extent by the arrival of some rice, nan bread, and tea, kindly afforded by Pir Mohammed.

The night was punctuated by intermittent, desultory 'happy' firing - mostly the usual mix of small arms, some automatic tracer to light up the night sky, plus the odd mortar crunch. It reached a crescendo at 12.10 a.m., with a close-down *grand finale* at 1.30 a.m. It seemed all too well staged, as if put on to convince us of imminent danger and the need for that watchtower for protection; in truth, it picked us out as a perfect spotlit target.

The following morning, to our considerable amusement, we

discovered our entire guard asleep in the room next door. They slept very soundly. Now we knew why Malang and Satar had been refused such creature comforts. The compound gate was wide open. We went for a look-see, but we really had nowhere to go. The guard was still asleep when we got back. *Quis custodiet ...* ?

There was no sign of movement, until Pir Mohammed appeared, bearing sergeant-major's green tea and yoghurt for our breakfast and what I think is about the most touchingly miniscule bill it has ever been my lot to receive. It read, to food and one night's lodging for two - Rupees 150 (£6). He was far too grand to attempt to tip.

Not long afterwards, Malang and Satar reappeared, plus the vehicle. They had not been idle. They had spent their time tracking down Haqqani's men. Distress signals had been sent out. They were confident of positive action very soon now.

After our light breakfast, we set out on the trail to reach the highest possible authority available to us. Of course, there had been no message from the Home Office, neither by 9 p.m. last night nor 'at the very latest by 9 a.m.' this morning. We now had to start the peculiarly English game of snakes and ladders all over again.

We began once more at the offices of the Assistant Commissioner for Refugees. From there we played leap-frog all the way back to the Assistant Political Agent. There we were to learn that anybody who was anybody had gone out to the airfield for the day, for a passing out parade. This was not promising. Parades were sacrosanct. Our informant even told us we were missing a vision of 'Paradise on Parade'. We gathered he was referring to the Tochi Scouts in all their glory.

Peter and I began to speculate whether it might not be the same old RAF and British Imperial Airways staging post where Aircraftsman John Hume Ross (Lawrence of Arabia) had served his anonymous time. But we were really only trying to cover up our frustration. Crunch time was fast approaching. Sometimes, Malang and Satar would be allowed to sit with us as we climbed the ladders, but as we neared any apex, they were excluded.

Peter was becoming increasingly tetchy and impatient of the bureaucracy. I was only too aware that we had arbitrarily set midday as our 24 hours elapsed time deadline to abort. Then we heard that our application had been rejected out of hand by the Assistant Political Agent on the grounds that there was increased fighting and conditions could no longer be guaranteed for our personal safety in the Tribal Areas. We were told that even if foreigners were prepared to absolve the Pakistani government of all responsibility, they had to be protected from themselves. They had no idea of the dangers on a day-to-day basis, while the Political Agent did. It was his job. Of course, if we insisted, we could hear the decision from the PA himself . . .

I did insist. I could see the age-old gap in the three-quarter line, a chink of hope. It was time to sell a dummy and go for the line. But before reaching the pinnacle of power, we had to slide down a particularly slithery snake, to conform to the normal-channel procedures to gain admission to the Political Agent.

This involved crossing a compound crowded with other beseechers. We entered an immensely crowded, standing-room only, general office, where we had to elbow our way forward to gain the attention of an unctious functionary, who began by abusing us roundly for wearing ill-fitting, bad-taste Pakistani clothes, instead of Afghan clothes. I longed to tell him all we wanted was the chance to buy some Afghan clothes in Afghanistan, but bit my lip. He was make or break, all-powerful. His omnipotent role was to decide who got to see whom, when, where, but never why. For all that, we got our chit without any *baksheesh* passing hands. This took us directly to the Political Agent's office. Of course, he was 'fri-a-ghtfully' busy. He would not be the Political Agent if he were not.

Red warning lights were on. Back-lit glass panels reading 'Occupied' like some super-loo. 'No Entry' and eventually, green for go 'Enter'. We were shown in to a row of chairs against a side wall, whilst the more important meeting continued. It was all so British. There were more Rolls of Honour on the walls. Great mahogany panels with names and dates of appointments. Just like back at school. At a given moment in 1947, the English names abruptly ceased. That was the only apparent change.

The important meeting was drawing to a close. It had been decided that the most effective way would be to invite the recalcitrant tribal leader in question to tea and, over tea, it would be explained to him unequivocally what would happen to him if he were to step out of line again.

The Political Agent now turned precipitately upon us. There were no introductions. Tongue-in-cheek, he told us we must not blame him for any procedural inconveniences or problems with the system, as we should know, they had inherited it all from us! They had simply taken over where we had left off. This office was a bequest. The photograph frames on the desk looked just the same. The desk undoubtedly was the same.

He wanted to know what appeared to be our problem. I said

I thought there might have been some slight misunderstanding. We thought we had been given a safe conduct to the Afghan border, where the responsibility of the Pakistani government would cease. He cut me off by saying that we must understand that 'up there', the picture could change rapidly, daily if not hourly and if they were to be responsible for our safety, then he must have the right to decide whether or not it was safe to travel. He then wanted to know exactly what it was we had come to do. I told him and to make it sound more significant, said it was to see if any improvements could be made to save lives. He wanted us to know that they did allow ambulances to break the curfew and travel through the Tribal Areas after dark. I said indeed we had heard that, and re-iterated our purpose was to look at ways to improve the evacuation and primary treatment of casualties, from the pick-up points, all the way to the operating theatres in Peshawar. I did not go into the secondary objective of examining the medical problems in a restricted area of Afghanistan. It would have taken too long and given him a chance to change his mind. At this point, he announced that he saw no problem. He asked for our passes. I pushed them across the desk. I knew what was coming. He ceremoniously tore them up before our eyes, saying that we must understand that, from now on if anything was to happen to us, he and his office were completely blameless. We had never passed his way. As we would put it, he had washed his hands of us. We thanked him effusively.

Nasir Khan Wazir, whom we learned was also known as Ali Jan, was told. Security in Charge, Pir Mohammed was told. Our vehicle was allowed to refuel and have the tyres checked; and, as if they had been awaiting some hidden signal, our blessed Haqqani escort chose this moment to materialise. We set off in high spirits for the border. Delayed indeed, but mercifully by only twenty-four hours. A blink in desert eyes.

We had not got five miles out of Miram Shah, when we were stopped at a road block and ordered back - for want of Tribal Areas passes! No Catch 22 chits. So, we sent back our escort vehicle to Pir Mohammed with a written plea for help, as even the land-line telephone was down!

The escort soon returned with the handsome addition of a large figure bearing a close resemblance to Zero Mostel. He was to be our passe-partout to the Afghan border.

The border itself, at our chosen crossing-point, was swarming with super smart Tochi Scouts, with what looked like elaborately folded black and scarlet table napkins on their heads. No doubt they were part of that morning's passing-out parade, now destined for a lifetime of sentry duty. Malang indicated that we would be required to leave a suitable tip for the border guard, plus something for Zero Mostel, whom we should be shedding and would need recompensing, as he would now be without transport to get him back to Miram Shah, until some obliging vehicle coming out, could lift him home.

The actual physical border was picked out in an unending line of stones, placed at regular two-yard intervals. Each stone had another smaller one placed on top of it. These stretched to the mountainside in one direction and as far as the eye could see, to infinity, in the other.

A short distance further on, we came under the domination of a solitary unmanned fort. It still had large metal plates silhouetted on the parapet, for sentries to take cover. Once past that fort, we were out of no-man's land and into Afghanistan proper.

We had finally made it. Many another had had to face delays of weeks, not days, at a time; especially if coming via Iran. All we had endured was a bureaucratic game of 'pass the parcel'. If it hadn't been a Friday, we might even have sailed through. Peter had the grace to admit that, if we had turned back, he would have regretted it for the rest of his life.

19
Grandmother's Footsteps in Paktia

Soon afterwards we came to a kind of checkpoint, not unlike a toll gate. This turned out to be a casualty collection point. It was a cave in the rock face, leading into an inner cave. It was all most orderly, decked out like some 1950s Royal Artillery barracks with whitewashed stones and bomb and shell trophy flowerpots standing in pairs on both sides of the cave mouth. There were other, whole, unexploded bombs up-ended, standing on their tail fins. These had been defused and slowly gutted for cooking fuel! Some of the empty canisters had then been filled with earth to make more flowerbeds. Mostly marigolds. As if to maintain parity, there was a brace of cannibalized armoured personnel carriers. A row of *charpayee* beds made of stout string stretched over a wooden frame added a hint of *chaikhana* informality.

A solitary guard slowly extricated his toes from the unmeshed twine at the foot of his *charpayee*, raised himself, effortlessly slipped on his *chaplis* and led us, beckoning, into the cave. Almost semi-circular, it resembled one of those workshops to be found underneath the arches of railway viaducts in Britain. There were three more very relaxed Mujahedeen inside. Rapturous welcomes ensued. Each of us was awarded the most elite order of the golden marigold. It appeared that this should either be worn behind the ear, dangling from the corner of the mouth, or, if you had one, popped into the muzzle of your gun.

It was the first time I could remember ever receiving flowers from a man. So, perversely, I put mine in the top buttonhole of my bad-taste Pakistani waistcoat. Next, a pitcher of ice-cold water was produced, together with a number of battered communal 'Alzheimer aluminium' mugs. This was going to be a moment of truth we would increasingly have to come to terms with, as our journey continued. I contemplated pouching the purification tablets like *naswar* and spitting them into the mug. Peter saved the day, as usual, saying that it was western medicine and made me take some salt tablets at the same time, whilst we were at it. Unfortunately, they all wanted to try the medicine-man's potions too.

I wondered if the marigolds were the origin of the pyrethrum magic of the Italian bush tomato fields. (A cordon of marigolds keeps the crop bug-free.) No doubt, a marigold behind the ear also helped to keep the flies out of your mouth. Would a marigold in the mouth drive the flies into your ears? What would keep them away from your eyes? I was already reckoning on four or more.

There were no casualties reported that day, although two cases had passed through yesterday or the day before. Presumably these were the ones who had shown up in Miram Shah? Nobody seemed sure. We made an inventory of the medicines available. It was confirmed that the nearest Afghan doctor was Dr Mohammed Anwar in Miram Shah. (Dr Wana Waziri was a Tribal Areas doctor, under Pakistani protection.) Through no fault of his or anybody else, the dispensary racks were full of inappropriate remedies. Masses of haemorrhoid ointment, cough mixture and indigestion tablets. Is this what the donor countries had prescribed to fight a proxy war? Or, had all other remedies been consumed by now?

Tucked away under a rack, Peter found something I thought was a childhood toboggan. It was a Thomas' splint. He spent some time extolling its virtues to an attentive if uncomprehending audience. It was essentially a visual display, as he applied the splint to one limb after another, but whatever he said they would continue to use broken-up wooden ammunition boxes. Soon the inevitable green tea and nan bread arrived and we moved into the inner sanctuary of the cave, to exchange news and views. Since we were British, sooner or later the conversation would come round to the Dari or Pashtu broadcast of the World Service of the BBC. There was never enough Afghan news to suit them. The complaint this time was that there was too much coverage given to corrupt Chinese officials!

Here on the ground, we learned that Hekmatyar was conducting a huge sweeping re-supply operation up ahead; alternatively, as some suggested, removing his men from the scene of action, to conserve them to fight other Afghans another day. We were advised to steer well clear. In all fairness, it could have been this intelligence which had caused the Political Agent to delay us. After all, Hekmatyar had only recently threatened to kill all foreigners, especially doctors, on sight!

We needed no reminding that his group, as described by Juliet, had expressly killed a French *Médecins Sans Frontières* doctor, 'pour encourager les autres'. All this, plus an endless tirade against the West, whilst at the same time helping themselves to as much Western aid and weaponry as they could lay their hands on.

We could by now detect that there was an undercurrent swell, suggesting it was not too late to turn back and attempt a re-entry at a less sensitive point. However, after all the hassle we had been through, we were dead against this. Amongst other things, we no

Contraflow

longer had a Tribal Areas pass between us. We would prefer to carry on and take our chances. Psychologically, there could be no turning back. But, on setting out again, the 'ground truth' of the matter was somewhat beyond our discernment. Only too soon the road became a track, the track ran out, and before long, we found ourselves way off any sort of beaten track whatsoever, creeping up river-beds, with sometimes near-vertical rock strata on either side. Fine for October, but in the spring snow melt it would be impassable. At least, this way we stuck to dead ground and had the reassurance of knowing we were invulnerable to all but a direct hit! What map there was, was in Satar's head alone. We became hopelessly disoriented. At least Satar's driving served to confirm that 'a motor can be as good as a mule, if driven with enterprise!'

Suddenly, for no clear reason, Malang hissed a command. We were to hide our cameras, put them away - immediately. I automatically assumed we must be passing a group of Afghan women, for Afghans can be very sensitive about anybody photographing their womenfolk. But no. Instead, there was just a loose, lone grey pack mare, trotting along, with rockets neatly slung on either side of an X-frame wooden saddle. She was moving smartly, assuredly, and soon followed by a whole train of similarly loaded beasts of burden of every description. It looked and sounded like a hundred horses, camels, mules, even donkeys thundering along. Disobeying orders, the adrenalin running, Peter and I, between us, just had time to snap off half-a-dozen shots each, unobserved, before secreting our cameras.

We saw heavily-laden camels squatting momentarily unattended in the shade of an escarpment. Finally, the caravanserai camel-herder himself came into view, bustling along waving a stick, on foot. Goodness knows how he kept track of all his charges, or indeed, kept pace with them. How did his lead grey mare know where she was going? But, she surely did. She must be earning her owner a fortune. Those who were making most out of this war were in the transport business. Any day now they would have mobile cellular telephones.

Malang brought me back to earth by telling me, as if it was today's headline news, that Hekmatyar was a bad man. His headquarters, presumably only temporary, were pointed out as being somewhere over there - indicated with a broad sweep. With us on board they had to avoid contact at all costs. As we had been told, he was planning for a massive flanking attack in the Khost area. Malang said we were going to try and slip through the column unobserved. The alternative meant turning back to make a wide detour.

But it was too late for that. We could see by the sheer

This is the lead horse of Gulbuddin Hekmatyar's caravan which seemingly knew where it was going without any guidance.

overwhelming weight of the column, which had grown now to be a solid stream of Mujahedeen and materiel, that there could be no slipping through at this point at any rate. What we were looking at had to be the main force.

So, with a great flourish, Satar turned down another river-bed and we returned to another sector of the frontier with the Pakistani Tribal Areas. Fortunately, at this crossing-point, the Tochi Scout garrison was much lighter. With some fast talking and a small consideration to the guard commander, we were allowed to pass by on the other side unnoticed and head at a tangent up yet another river-bed, out of sight, which somehow miraculously enabled us to outflank Hekmatyar's column. With luck we should now reach our first base camp at Bôri (pronounced Bari), well before nightfall.

On the last leg of the way, we stopped off for a quick inspection of an open-air casualty area. It was impressive, built like a two-storey airport garage. A largish space with four rows of *charpayee* beds, with a beaten earth roof, supported on brick piers, with vegetation growing on top. This gave effective camouflage from the air and supposedly a measure of protection from light mortar attack. It also provided an effective overnight staging post for Mujahedeen to sleep on their way up to the Khost 'front'.

This time we were garlanded with marigold and with mint. There was also a faultless dispensary. This was explained by the extensive colour pages articles plastering the walls. This clinic was the brainchild of an Afghan-American doctor, who had returned to join the struggle after sixteen years in the U.S. It was normal to paper the walls with posters, propaganda and, above all, texts from the Holy Koran. This was the only time we were ever to see an English text. Of the Afghan doctor there was no sign. He was away, busily raising more money to buy more medicines. Everything was in good order and Peter made a special point of saying how impressed he was, particularly with the racks of clearly ranged, appropriate remedies.

This clinic belonged to Pir Gailani's National Islamic Front for Afghanistan (NIFA), the selfsame party as Dr Abdul Satar Paktiss's Ibn Sina hospital in Peshawar. However, I could not help noticing that the flag on the flagpole was Mojadidi's. It could all be so confusing, better not to enquire. Perhaps it was being flown like some courtesy burgee?[1]

We told them how much we admired their hospital in Peshawar. We noticed that all the cave mouths here had smart brickwork facings with iron-barred windows and, to our amazement, even some poured concrete floors. The only item missing was a patient.

Khost area April 1983 Mujahedeen positions bombarded by Russian Migs with phosphor bombs. *Photo by Dittmar Hack*

As we drove away, I noted along the next re-entry a smart house with a well-watered smallholding. There was also a garage made in the same manner as the open-plan hospital ward area, with brick piers and beaten earth roof; but it was exclusively to house one brand new light tan Range Rover. We could not imagine how it could have got there. Peter suggested wealthy Arab donors. I wondered if it had been reassembled piecemeal outside the factory gates. Or, it could perhaps have belonged to the absent American Afghan doctor.

I thought no more about it just then, but the spectacle of that free running lead pack mare and the parked tan Range Rover were to return to haunt me. These fleeting visions and the four-star overnight accommodation-cum-hospital open ward were typical of Afghan deceptions. When you thought you were being shown one thing, the chances were it would turn into something quite different.

*

The next stage in our progress was to visit a kind of cross-roads, set deep in rocky terrain, with overhanging cliff face. It was a storage and assembly area, described as the Commander's camp. It seemed to be shared in common by a great many different interests. We were shown the spot where Sabur, the driver seconded to us by AfghanAid, had been wounded with a shell fragment to the shoulder. It was surprising everybody hadn't been blown to kingdom come. There were crates and crates of Chinese artillery ammunition stacked in every conceivable crevice and rock fissure.

We were shown one captured Russian jeep. As usual it was riddled with bullet holes. There was no means of knowing whether they had been inflicted before or after the capture. Likewise, there was no knowing whether it had been surrendered by Kabul regime Afghans or Russians. Whichever, it didn't look too serviceable, more like another tired war trophy, left behind for kicks and jubilation.

Our arrival finally at the Bŏri base camp was unforgettable. The way was barred by a tethered, hobbled horse. The tether was stretched taut across the narrow path entrance. The alarm was raised by the whinnying and neighing of the horse. Sure enough, soon enough, an armed sentry sloped towards us, and after cursory inspection, waved us into a covered parking area.

We were expected. The barefoot 'auxiliary' doctor here was Said, a younger brother of Dr Mohammed Anwar, the nearest Afghan doctor in Miram Shah. It was to him that our safe conduct letter of introduction had been addressed by the first commander we had met

A stressed out Rupert at Bori. Note AK47 and false arm in
background. *Photo by Peter Stiles*

in the inner cave at the checkpoint on our arrival.

What was remarkable about this commander's camp was that, in reality, it was a perfectly normal collection of conventional dwellings built in a massive rock cleft around a well at the mouth of an extensive network of caves.

A huge awning was slung like some dun-coloured spinnaker right across the open space between the rock face and the houses. Later, we learnt its purpose, which was to cloak the flames of the cooking fires from aerial observation at night.

We were led off to our sleeping quarters, which were in one of the houses on the other side of the canopied chasm. On the way, there was a gaping hole carved out of the ground rock. We were told this was to be avoided, especially at night, in the dark, as it was the well. We only had time to dump our sleeping bags and holdalls on the two *charpayee* beds allocated to us in a pristine looking guest room, before rejoining Malang and Satar to continue our itinerary of casualty points.

[1] In fact, subsequently, Juliet explained there was a perfectly logical explanation. Unknown to us, NIFA were aligned to ANLF, which was Sibghatullah Mojadidi's Afghan National Liberation Front.

20
Shoot-Out

We had not gone far, when Satar, through Malang, announced that he wasn't able to find the next clinic. He'd had enough of clinics for one day. How about a good shoot-out instead?

We had no idea what he had in mind. He was so vital to our interests, there seemed little point in upsetting him. We may have looked lukewarm, but with the only map being the one in his head, we were putty in his hands.

As I think back, something tells me that every detail had been premeditated. There was something too set-piece and planned about it all. Although they could hardly have anticipated our time of arrival, we soon found ourselves back at that messy focal point, with all the Chinese ammunition lying around. From there we took a new track, which led out to a well dug-in gun emplacement with three light artillery pieces - the pride of any mountain gunner.

Again we were told with heavy emphasis that these were all captured Russian guns. Patently they were not, as they were plastered with People's Republic of China hieroglyphs, especially the unused range-finders and the copious broken wooden ammunition boxes, which lay open everywhere - littered with detonators slung around like deck quoits.

At this juncture, again as if on cue, an old codger of a bandit came forward. We had already caught a glimpse of him back at the Bōri campsite. He had lost his left arm. Red Crescent had obligingly supplied him with a shop dummy replacement, which was more cosmetic than practical. We had noticed the pairing of the arm with an AK47 slung nonchalantly on the same wall hook in his billet. In his belt, barely perceptible, he wore what he told us was his preferred personal weapon - a ladies' handbag 0.22-calibre six-chamber revolver. It was 'preferred' not for any killing power or aesthetics, but, as he told us with great pride, because it had once belonged to an 'Inglestan' officer in the 1920s. To me he looked just the right age and certainly the type to have shot that last district officer Peter had told me about.

He now advanced, *primus inter pares* amongst his comrades, and prepared to give us a display of markmanship. In true Robin Hood fashion he set up a slither of white willow wand at two hundred paces. He then squatted down on his haunches and pressed the muzzle of his automatic hard against one of the bipod legs of an artillery piece and

One of three Chinese artillery pieces, supposedly 'captured from the Russians'. *Photo by Peter Stiles*

let rip. With equally predictable precision the wand vanished from sight and all the merry men, including us, cheered. Was this what Satar had meant by a shoot-out? No, it was only the *hors d'oeuvres*. The main performance of the evening was about to begin with the 'laying of the guns'. This literally meant sighting them by eye! The Chinese range-finding hieroglyphs were mere embellishments to be ignored.

All the next star-turn did, more as a second thought than second nature, was remove the shell already loaded in the breach of one gun and look up the barrel to satisfy himself he was going to clear the escarpment opposite! Nothing more sophisticated than that. It could well have been an extra drill for our benefit.

Admittedly the battery was properly dug in, in an enfiladed position. Once satisfied with the elevation of all three guns, the master gunner gave a nod and other Mujahedeen shambled forward to load. One round was fired from each gun. Then, after a short pause, three more rounds were fired from each gun, at will. Each blast was shattering to the eardrums. We were confidently assured that the target was Khost Airport - some 14.7 kilometers to the north - as if some forward observation officer had paced it out beforehand. Being Afghans, they may well have had somebody sitting on the target to report back on how short the shells were falling. And that was that.

Dimwittedly, for the second time, I studied the deeply embedded bipod legs, with occasional sandbags stuffed around them, trying to work out just how long this gun position had been established. Six months maybe? By now, surely, it must be pinpointed by aerial photography. Any self-respecting artillery officer would have worked out a reverse bearing and range, with a proper range-finder - then the incoming rejoinder salvo arrived. At last, this was the shoot-out Satar had been pining for. Ever mindful of our basic training, however remote in time, Peter and I hit the deck simultaneously, fast enough to feel we'd been blasted there. All that fell out of the sky, however, was a shower of pebbles. Then, when we opened our eyes, what we saw was the others, pointing at us in the dust and roaring their heads off with laughter. Only one twelve-year-old boy had followed our good example.

What could we do, but stand up, brush ourselves down and join in the merriment? As if we too could think of nothing so desirable as their vision of Valhallah, following our *shaheed* (martyrdom). Anyone unfortunate enough to fail the entrance exam by merely getting wounded, could call on any British surgeon at hand, who would surely finish them off. Even their flak jackets were all show and no substance; whatever protection had existed had long since been removed as an unwarranted encumbrance.

The shoot-out we had witnessed was the classic 'war as a sport' formula as practised by the Pashtun. Honour is satisfied once sufficient scarce ammunition has been fired off at a distant enemy, without taking any unacceptable risk of casualties.

Satar announced that the evening's fun was now over and it was time to return to camp. But not before Peter had dealt with an out-patients' queue which had sporadically formed alongside Big Bertha. Other younger blades were set to try their skill at splitting the willow. Although the evening light was fast failing, there was just enough to take a formal photocall of the gun crews - our adopted guerilla band, to include Malang and Satar. The fun may have been over for Satar and his shoot-out, but for us, it had hardly begun. The first hard lesson in this company was that it was better to get your head blown off, than lose face. An attitude of mind, never more gallantly or aptly expressed than by Lord Longford's father with his parting words at Gallipoli 'Don't duck, the men don't like it and it makes no difference

*

We arrived back in camp to the welcome blaze of the cooking fire, which must have had some fuel additive as it was too fierce to be wood alone, even though there should have been no shortage of ammunition boxes. We were told it was sun-down prayer time, to be followed by the evening meal and went to our room to get freshened-up, in strictly limited fashion.

Peter and I felt there was a compelling need to make some kind of gesture. We rummaged through our kit to see what on earth we might have for a suitable offering. Fleaseed, water purification tablets, aspirin, malaria tablets would not be appreciated half so much as my chocolate-covered Kendal mint cake. It must have melted and refrozen a dozen times by now. No knowing where the coating might be. Likewise, there was no knowing when an emergency might or might not arise. We would keep the less glamorous glucose tablets for that. We also found that somehow we had one of John Stoneham's giant bars of Bournville plain chocolate and a dozen soggy Mars Bars in reserve. So, we voted to sacrifice the Kendal mint cake and the giant chocolate bar as a gesture of appreciation to our hosts.

Afghans have a very sweet tooth and the mint cake, even divided between twelve, was to prove a sensational novelty. It was certainly a rewarding sacrifice and came as a fitting climax to lamb, rice, nan, and a delicate watery apple.

I was particularly keen to record the homely, welcoming feast, but characteristically my flash attachment failed to function. Consternation, but not for long. To my amazement, the old one-armed bandit promptly produced two brand-new batteries from nowhere, as if he were the local Kodak corner shop. It turned out they were standard for short wave radio use, and indispensable for receiving the World Service of the BBC. There was some suggestion that they could be recharged at night with body heat, but I eschewed further detailed instruction. We were then subjected to the chimes of Big Ben and the World Service News, which Malang now kindly translated for us; so it was probably in Pashto this time.

Although dusk prayers had gone unremarked by us, as we must have been busying ourselves with laying out our sleeping bags on the unexpected luxury of *charpayee*s, or examining our meagre kit for giveaways, night prayers were to prove inescapable.

After supper, Peter and I had chosen to position ourselves on the flat roof of the highest building in the complex, to take stock of the night sky and the night's proceedings. Our perfect hosts recognised that we would welcome some time on our own, just as they were no doubt ready for some time off from us. What we were expecting was to lie on our backs counting shooting stars and generally star gazing. There was the added distraction of a certain amount of fixed-line firing, with night tracer lighting up the sky and even some distant shelling. A creeping barrage, like some electric storm. But yet more sinister, there was also the constant rumbling and droning of a slow propeller spotter plane, seemingly hovering directly overhead. We could see nothing specific.

Our attention then became riveted to the proceedings on the larger lower rooftop opposite, above our guest accommodation. It was a hundred feet away at most. Each of the twelve good men and true of the recent shooting party, plus the ten-men garrison with whom we had dined, appeared in file, each carrying one of those shiny tin Chinese storm-proof hurricane lamps. The paraffin wicks were duly lit and the lamps placed in a long row along the leading edge of the roof opposite and below us. The effect now was as if we had middle front row dress-circle seats at some Victorian Music Hall. The playbill tonight offered a vision of blind faith, grand opera and fantasia.

The men knelt in two long rows facing in our direction, which must have been west, towards Mecca. They then began to pray as if there was nothing in this world that would distract them. One amongst them, hard to identify as they may have taken turns, led in the singing of a kind of Gregorian plainchant.

At the same time we could hear what sounded like a sublime descant coming from a neighbouring valley to our left, further west, but not half a mile distant. It could only have been a large group of women and children. Their singing sounded like a medley of patriotic hill songs, with strains of the Marseillaise, but it was more likely to have been religious. The quality was Welsh or Vienna Boys Choir.

All the time there was that other background *muzak* of the droning twin-engined turbo-prop aeroplane. More and more I dreaded lest it was an Antonov carrying sensors, operating as an airborne command post, which at any moment might shower down flares to herald yet deadlier toys of war.

The most awesome sight of all, as ever, was the whole panoply of heaven above; putting man's occasional puny distant flashes in their proper place, and offering an alternative vision of peace on earth. Our eyes kept being drawn back to the row of lanterns, the praying Mujahedeen and the cooking fire. It was still flickering fiercely beneath the ineffectual screen of the coarse flapping jute canopy; placed there like a giant *pattoo* blanket, through which the 'Muj' fire their Dashaka heavy machine-gun in the hope of masking its giveaway flashes.

Either time stood still for us, or they continued praying a long time, or both. But by the time prayers were over, we were beginning to droop and I, for one, was keen to turn in for the night. There was no guarantee of sleep as such; just some rest would do. It had been a long full day and, for sure, we would have the earliest of starts in the morning.

We headed off to our generous quarters, giving that black hole of a well, without parapet, the widest berth. It was clearly visible in the bright starlight. In fact, for the unwary, there was every bit as treacherous a drop on the outside edge of the terrace leading to our upper floor room. A balustrade would have been superfluous, but a warning 'string handrail' would not have come amiss. Inside were our welcoming twin *charpayee* beds, discreetly placed against opposite walls. I had chosen the outside wall, indicating to Peter that his talents had more value here than mine. From our scant knowledge, picked up here and there from bouncing wall casualties, we understood there was a better chance if there were two mud walls with a cavity between you and the impact. So, we were as safe as houses, mud houses.

As we drifted between sleeping and waking, laughingly recounting some of the highlights of the day and hearing mostly dogs barking, Peter surprised me with an absurd request. He wanted to know if I had brought a tooth-mug with me. I said he knew damned well I hadn't. It was not an item that had ever been considered. It was high time he learnt to clean his teeth with his finger. He said, in all seriousness, it wasn't wanted for his teeth. He wanted to amplify the voices he could hear through the wall. I said what was the point, he wouldn't understand a word they were saying. The walls were too thick.

More asleep than awake, he droned on that these were high-pitched, squeaky women's voices. I didn't know how I was going to handle this new side of him. I remonstrated that we had probably been put next to the women's quarters, an honoured position of great trust, which must not be abused.

But he persisted. He was now hearing strident, English female voices. Sloane Rangers, born to command - Daddy said so. It must have been something he ate, but we had all eaten much the same. Only the sun could have made him hallucinate like this. That knotted handkerchief had done the damage. In future, there could be no question of removing his *pakool* hat, however prickly.

Fortunately, however strident these female voices, they could not compete for long with the cacophony of howling dogs and neighing sentry horses, which came to dominate our state of mental and physical exhaustion before blissful sleep finally enveloped us.

The next day began, as normal, with a pre-dawn call to prayer. Once out of the sleeping-bag it was surprisingly cold and the preferred obligatory ablutions freezing. It woke us up, but was nothing like as welcome as the tea and nan which we seized on with real gratitude.

As we stood around, stamping our feet and taking deeper and deeper draughts of the hot sweet green tea, I teased Peter about his tooth-mug aberrations. I asked if he'd heard any more sirens in the night. But he wasn't to be deterred. He persisted that we could all tell the rhythm of our native tongue, without necessarily catching individual words, let alone whole sentences. He meant to ask Malang if there had been any other visitors in camp overnight. But if Malang knew, he wasn't telling. He had, however, reacted a little too sharply, I thought, with some riposte about supposing proper doctors always carried stethoscopes.

Intermittent flashes lit the pre-dawn sky at ever-shortening intervals, like thunder and lightning, approaching and then, as suddenly, departing again.

It was agreed that our inspection of the large double cave clinic could wait until we all had a clearer idea of what was going on above ground. It was no time to bury ourselves counting bandages.

It was looking as if the Pakistani Political Agent might have known a thing or two we hadn't, and, perhaps, we should not have been so incensed at being detained and delayed. What this growing barrage must mean was that the warrior poets had begun their inexorable march towards the sound of the guns. For the first time massive Resistance reinforcements were moving up cross-border from the camps. What was different this time was that they were marching to the drum of leaders and local commanders other than their own.

21
Mujahedeen on the Move

At last the tide of war could be seen to be turning in favour of the Resistance. For the very first time they might hold the Russian bear at bay from a fixed-line defensive position - against all the tenets of guerilla warfare, as practised from the time of the American War of Independence and the Peninsular War, to the Boer War and Vietnam. This time, they had elected to run the risk of static annihilation, rather than engage in the more normal small-scale 'hit and run' tactics of the ever-mobile, ever-fluid, running-sore conflict of which they were past masters. By the time of the Russian invasion, the traditional *Qazaki* methods of guerilla attrition were already three hundred years old. This was the familiar small force fighting born of Afghan inter-tribal conflict more than a hundred years before the word guerilla was coined.

Amidst a fanfare of publicity and prediction, what the Russians had planned as the decisive victory, was fast turning into a telling defeat. No longer would the Soviet Army be free to move at will in Afghanistan.

The main road leading from Gardez, the capital of Paktia province, to Khost had been closed to the Russians for about eight years. More recently the other three roads to Khost had been blocked off too, while the only airport, if it hadn't fallen yet, was surrounded and besieged. Obviously, in the fog of war, we could only be vaguely aware of all these implications. These were some of the peripheral factors which might or might not have any bearing on our tiny sector, which was anyway far removed from the sharp end.

The little that could be seen, however, formed a very vivid picture and, when subsequently related to the whole, broader, fuller story, became that much more positive.

As dawn broke, long files of Mujahedeen could be seen on every mountain ridge and track, breaking all known field-craft rules! Rising from their prayers, some in groups of as many as fifty strong, the 'Muj' were setting out on a long day's trek across familiar rough terrain to take up their predetermined battle positions. All were moving north towards the line of the Gardez - Khost road. They appeared to be arriving in bevies, staggered like reinforcements, just as for a set piece battle.

What had been the rag, tag and bobtail mob of yesteryear had now become a properly co-ordinated field force. Their fabled courage and fighting spirit had never been in any doubt, but this now exhibited the additional outward vestiges of military order and discipline. Some even displayed a novel 'uniform' appearance.

If an Order of Battle could have been compiled that day, it would have read like a Roll of Honour compiled of all the leading commanders from all the seven major political parties in Peshawar. It showed, for once, that they could work together in common cause. What had begun as an ideological war of influence between the tribes, had moved on to be a populist cause and now, at last, was an issue of national survival. If only the coalition could have lasted.

What gave added spring to their step that morning, was the knowledge that at long last, heat-seeking ground-to-air Stinger and Blowpipe missiles were arriving in sufficient quantities to change the course of the war.

As often before, the air superiority, which had been expected to give the Russians early victory, had signally failed to do so. Now, at long last, roles were to be reversed and the dreaded Hind and Hip helicopters driven from their murderous gunship dominance. The whole problem of Russian re-supply, particularly of Khost, way out on a limb, was becoming increasingly difficult - even by night. Heli-borne troops, including the elite Spetznaz Vysotniki special forces, were less and less inclined to venture far behind guerilla lines. From now on, the Russians and their Kabul regime adjuncts would have to rely more on artillery than air strikes.

Those helicopters which did venture out were obliged to stick to low-level hedge-hopping missions to evade the Stinger's most effective field of fire. This, however, placed them at the mercy of heavy machine-guns, often sited in the mountains above them. All their armour-plating was now in the wrong place. There were even cases reported of helicopters falling victim to rocket propelled grenades.

Any misgivings about illiterate Mujahedeen Jihad fighters being incapable of mastering sophisticated weapons proved stillborn. Ever resourceful, the 'Muj' were known to have fired rockets, minus launchers, from 'rock' bipods, over open sights, with telling results, in much the same manner in which they brewed up on explosive scooped from 'Italian' mines.

As to sophistication, we did hear reports that Ahmed Shah Massoud was training his reconnaissance teams to take video films to improve the standard of briefings! They had technology tamed. Massoud may not have had the capability to install a secure radio link, but he knew he needed one and had no difficulty operating it, once it was supplied by us.

But when it came to strategy, however, he had always been careful not to allow himself to be drawn into any pitched battle in the Panjshir. He preferred the well-tried traditional approach and his example was usually ignored , at everybody else's peril.

Visually, the only remotely similar scene I had witnessed was the bicentennial re-enactment of the gathering of the Clans at Fort William in 1945. Although the weaponry was different and the spine-chilling drone of the pipes was missing, in bearing and spirit there were distinct similarities, not least the 'highland' mentality and tribal code of honour, the bright-eyed spirituality and courageous willingness to fight to the death. There were other superficial similarities too, the close resemblance between the plaid and the *pattoo*, the Glengarry and the *pakool*. All this headgear may appear mediaeval, but the Chitrali *pakool* could possibly date back to Alexander the Great. But, most of all, there was the same broken step devotion to the clan leaders. What these two traditions have most in common is undoubtedly bred of long-standing internecine strife and shared hardships - 'a stringent code, a tough code for tough men, who of necessity live tough lives in one of the toughest terrains on earth,' as Louis Dupree has expressed it.

Now, from our point of view, and thanks entirely to Juliet and Sarah's perspicacity, we had been judiciously placed with Jalaluddin Haqqani's Zadran tribe. There could not have been a better, wiser choice. Jalaluddin Haqqani had emerged by sheer force of arms. 'Commissioned in the field,' twice badly wounded in the thick of battle, he had proved himself to be the outstanding natural leader in Southern Paktia and Paktika.

He had the great advantage of being based on the Tribal Areas border at Zhawar. This gave him ready access to a safe neutral haven which is the sustenance of every successful guerilla operation. Guerillas are not expected to destroy armies in the field nor capture territory, which was what made the battle for Khost so very different from everything that had gone before in Afghanistan. It was as if the Chinese had slipped in a copy of the 'Thoughts of Chairman Mao on Revolution' with each of those artillery pieces as they trundled down the Karakoram highway. 'Guerilla struggle must develop into conventional war combined with popular uprising.'

The essential difference with the Afghans was that, although they had no shortage of young people prepared to take high risks, they lacked the normal quotient of women. Women are essential to any successful guerilla operation, since they supply the vital social support - including food, medicines and spies. The vast majority of

Mujahedeen wives were to be found disconsolately confined to the refugee camps in Pakistan.

So, the battle for Khost would be concentrated on the airfield we had supposedly been shelling. The struggle had been engaged for a long time. Logistically the airfield was essential to the maintenance of the Kabul regime forces garrisoned there and in the surrounding fortresses, which changed hands in regular ding-dong fashion. The ground routes from Kabul had already been effectively cut. The time-honoured strategy was never to take the cities as such, much simpler to starve them into submission. Or, better still, subvert them into wholesale desertion, along with their arms and ammunition.

It would be as well to acknowledge at this stage that the massive laying of minefields without proper record in Afghanistan (estimates vary between ten million and fifteen million mines) was intended by the Russian-backed Kabul regime forces as much to discourage desertion to the Mujahedeen as to deter attacks by them.

The heavily mined hilltop outposts, surrounding the airport life-line, became, therefore, the subject of continuous and increasingly determined attack and counter-attack. Until now, whenever the situation became too desperate in Khost, Kabul would take retaliatory action, mainly in the form of airstrikes and the occasional heliborne interdiction of Spetznaz Russian special forces. But since the arrival of Stinger, these had become increasingly hazardous. Knowing this, the Resistance were determined to infiltrate all the strong points, subjecting them to constant attack, as part and parcel of their overall objective of closing the airport - regardless of cost.

Then, as always in war, the hand of God and the weather played a decisive role. Torrential rains of unprecedented duration caused the airport to close down completely.

There was now no other alternative, no easy option. The Russians would have to send a 'punitive' relief column - a massive retaliatory ground force, said to be 20,000 strong. The land area between Kabul and the Pakistani border in this sector of Paktia, is as many square kilometers. The more you studied it, the more it resembled the British Afghan Wars. Punitive raids ending in annihilation. From all we had heard, it sounded highly unlikely that this column could ever get through. The Mujahedeen had had all the time in the world to lay many more extensive minefields, which were 'covered' by well placed *sangars* - rock built gun emplacements - built up rather than dug down, as the ground is too hard, and concealing heavy machine-guns.

This then was the major additional ingredient on the ground, which made for a first-class defensive position. However, these uncharted, indiscriminate minefields would prove a hazard and a scourge to the civilian population for twenty years or more to come.

22
Kismet, Triage, Cairns.

That was enough strategic and tactical speculation on our part. Our job, of course, was to make a report on the first-aid clinics, the very clinics which would be required in earnest at any moment. It was time to inspect the caves, and Peter asked me to help with the copious listings of drugs, bandages, splints etc. While we checked the dispensary, Peter subjected the barefoot auxiliary doctor, Said M. Anwar, to the most ingenious and subtle of questionnaires, by which he could make an accurate assessment of his true capabilities. Said M. Anwar happily passed with flying colours - a credit to his doctor brother and to his tribe.

Peter had one immensely practicable suggestion which was to prove unacceptable on religious grounds. The most reliable method of recording drugs administered, was to write the detail on the patient's forehead. There was a Muslim proverb which specifically countermanded this 'It was the writing on his forehead' meaning it was his fate, like the writing on the wall. 'First in prayer. First in fight. Sleeping poets that woke up only to die ...'

Otherwise, debate centred on the relative merits of tailor-made packing-case splints versus Peter's favourite - the Thomas. Then the approved methods of cleaning wounds were discussed at length and procedures agreed. Finally Peter touched on triage. (*Triage* is a French word covering the sorting of casualties into groups on the basis of severity and urgency: Urgent, Not so urgent, or Hopeless - leave to die.) At a pinch there was room for thirty casualties in the bomb-proof inner cave, plus another twenty in the outer cave.

Either Malang had waited until our inspection was through, or his arrival coincided with the completion of our detailed listings and discussions with Said M. Anwar. What he came to tell us was that we were effectively cut off from our next port of call, because we were now virtually surrounded by Hekmatyar's sweeping right-flanker movement. There could be no question, for now, of the planned return to Miram Shah, Bannu and Peshawar. Furthermore, unless we had casualties on board, there could be no question of our travelling through the Tribal Areas after dark either. This meant that the later we left our departure, the more chance there was of staying in the Khost area to see the action, at least until the next dawn.

Our dilemma was simple and classic. Should we await the first casualties and travel with them - adding to the authenticity of our mission? Or, hightail it back to ensure that all was in place and ready to receive the increased flow anticipated? What we had witnessed to date was the usual lulling period of stalemate - often involving a negotiated truce, allowing both sides an opportunity to recoup and regroup. What was coming now had to be on a grand scale, as never before experienced.

Although there were no casualties yet, there was every prospect, as the Russian offensive built up, that they would start coming in, even before nightfall.

Despite our earlier aim to take the surgery nearer to the freshly wounded, we now found ourselves obliged to think strategically, not tactically. As Peter put it, our purpose was to evolve a long-term casualty evacuation programme, through to aftercare, prosthesis and physiotherapy. There was also the question of the medical care scheme study. This in turn reminded me of my undertaking to Sir Oliver Forster not to sky-lark. Anyway, the fact of the matter was we would have to do whatever we were told by Malang. We learnt much later that Juliet's orders to Malang were that, whatever he did, he was to take no risks with us! This accounted for the cautious, overcaring way he protected our every move, thus undermining my minder role!

To soften the blow, Malang prepared the way by telling us that he would have to get in touch with the ambulance control to confirm if we were to stay put, or if the ambulance was needed in another sector. He said that he and Satar would be back shortly. We assumed they had gone to make some secure radio contact. It was unlikely to be a foghorn exchange on the Pakistani public telephone system. However, there was no radio set on the vehicle, so they must have had access to a set somewhere nearby. At the same time Satar would assess our chances of cutting across Hekmatyar's columns, on the reverse tack, unobserved.

Whilst we were wondering what to do with ourselves next, our attention was caught by a group of, as ever, brightly dressed Afghan women. As there was nobody much about, it looked like a good opportunity to take a surreptitious photo. I would keep watch while Peter took one or two shots. Then he would give me a turn. There was something unusual about this group of women. Firstly, they were standing around - rather like we were - at a loose end. Why weren't they busying themselves as usual, or at least hunkering down? More surprising still, there were no children clinging to their skirts. Then we saw the most anomalous detail of all. Some of them had notepads, the kind of notebooks market research ladies have on clipboards at airports, railway termini or along Oxford Street. The more we looked at them, the more convinced we became that they were European women; *burqa* or no *burqa*, *chardor* or no *chardor*. It was their size as much as anything, but also the way they held themselves and carried themselves.

They could well have learnt deportment balancing half a dozen books stacked on top of their heads at a convent school, but they had never coped with five litres of water and ten kids. Anyway, their feet were too big. It began to look as if Peter's dream-time abberations of the night before had sound foundation. We took it in turns to snap away. Just as we were proposing a more positive, more familiar, if strictly forbidden approach, Malang and Satar reappeared to tell us we had our marching orders. We had to leave then and there.

Very few Europeans can pass for Afghans on close inspection. Their feet are never horny or hard enough. The men have that peculiarly springy loose-jointed lope to their walk, which comes naturally to them and is impossible for us to imitate. Our hips are made differently. It shows up most when seated on the ground.

We asked Malang outright who those European women were we had just seen. He said he didn't know and rather pointedly told us we should ask Juliet or Sarah.

We were soon distracted, because Satar had brought us this time to a particularly high point from which we could see what we took to be the whole of Hekmatyar's force on the move. Again we were told not to take any photographs, which was particularly galling but no doubt wise. However, we were allowed to use Peter's fine pair of miniature binoculars. From our vantage point, we were now on the inside looking out, as it were, and so not subject to such obvious scrutiny or curiosity. It was like watching an ant heap. Malang again pointed out what he said was Hekmatyar's headquarters. This time, since he pointed in a specific direction, we had less reason to doubt him. We just wondered how anybody could be so sure about a man who was always so secretive as to his whereabouts. As far as we knew, it could just as well have been the camp of any one of a dozen different Hesbe-i-Islami commanders. The 'captured' Russian jeep and the 'captured' Russian artillery had made us sceptical. Were we being fed what was expedient for us to hear?

It was likely that the whole meandering snake was his main force. It was on too massive a scale to be otherwise. But would it reach the Gardez road in time to do battle? Or were we witnessing a ploy, as darkly hinted, to evacuate his main force to turn their fire-power on his rivals at some later date? There was no substance, in fact, to such allegations, just long-founded suspicions. It turned out that the engagement was to last over twenty-four days and nights, much longer than anticipated, so there was ample time for this decisive force to join all the others along the line of the Gardez-Khost road, which it duly did.

Satar thought he could see a gap in the line down below, and, being the born gambler he is, determined to make a dash for it. The purpose of our reconnaissance was now achieved. We had visited two of the three main forward area clinics in this sector. If we hadn't indulged in the shoot-out we might have managed all three but lost Satar's goodwill. It could be construed as irresponsible to take up any more valuable ambulance time, unless we were accompanying casualties, and there was no guarantee of that. The counter-argument ran that we had absolutely no right to return over such a distance empty-handed! There could be no question of leaving any wounded behind. Where were we to position ourselves to maximum advantage? As often happens, the solution worked itself out. You can't invent casualties.

The irony of our position was that here were we, for the second time, running the gauntlet of the Hekmatyar Hesbe-i column, as if they were the enemy, when they were supposed to be the staunchest of allies. It was all too absurd. Who indeed needed enemies with friends like these? I should have preferred to be going in the opposite direction and taken my chances facing the Kabul regime enemy. At least one would have a better idea of where one stood, with less chance of being shot in the back as a lookalike foreign doctor.

We were now cautiously edging our way forward towards the cross-track, which Satar had identified from the high ground, and where the snake column was wending its way.

Suddenly Satar surged forward and we shot, like a rat up a drainpipe, into an adjacent *wadi* or dried up river-bed. No shots came, no attempts to stop us. It looked as if we were through. We now travelled at breakneck speed to reach the Tribal Areas before curfew.

Next, we recognised the fortress we had seen before on our way in - at Ullam Khan - and began to appreciate for the first time the huge circuit we had completed as part of our evasive action, in both directions! We could be sure now of returning via Miram Shah and Bannu. There hadn't ever really been any alternative. Soon, as the light began to fail, we were passing through the vast Mujahedeen war cemetery at Nullah. All the tattered, multicoloured banner flags, made of torn strips of clothing flapped forlornly in the evening breeze. Each one represented the unquenchable spirit of a slain *shaheed* (Jihad martyr). Each body was buried under a cairn of gathered stones; with one or sometimes two larger stones set jutting jaggedly upright at one or both ends. With rock as hard as this the graves themselves would be shallow - not unlike a *sangar*.

> 'A time to cast away stones and
> A time to gather stones together;
> A time to embrace and a time
> to refrain from embracing.'
> *Ecclesiastes III, 5*

Had Europe's crusading knights, I wondered, gone as happily to their graves, seven hundred years before these holy warriors? Or had their cause been as good or as just?

23

Border Hoppers' Return

In next to no time we found ourselves back in Miram Shah. Pir Mohammed, our gaoler of only two days ago, had now become our greatest friend. The guard was turned out for us - all grins and solicitations. The greeting was genuine. It was openly admitted that they had never expected to see us alive again and certainly not back this soon, with our mission accomplished. A 'Security in Charge' pix photocall was *de rigueur* and we were all lined up accordingly.

Whilst our vehicle was being refuelled and serviced, an impromptu clinic was called, which invariably follows moments of euphoria, as Pathans and Waziris, with an ever open eye to the main chance, remember their less fortunate brothers (seldom their sisters) and their own minor ailments. The complaints are often trivial, but all have to be handled with gravitas, for fear of causing offence or loss of face.

Of all these parties, who have to be attended so considerately, the most common contingent are back-pain sufferers, which is scarcely to be wondered at when account is taken of the huge loads they carry over rough ground. One or two may sit at desks, but not many. Masses of exercise is taken, of course, walking, climbing steep rocky paths. Physical jerks as such, however, are unknown. For me, one of the highlights of any clinic conducted by Peter is when he decides the moment has come to give everyone a pep talk on Physical Education. I can see it coming and my joy is complete when he swings into his Jane Fonda aerobics display. Of course, the music is missing, but the commentary, unintelligible to all but me, makes up for this loss. As his head is often down, touching opposite toes, legs wide apart, he cannot see the look of consternation in every Afghan eye. They can only think of it as the most demoniacal piece of witchcraft and the mullah had better not hear of it. If I am stupid enough to get caught smirking, Peter calls on me to demonstrate my 'well-known' sciatica cure. This requires me to stand on a chair and hang by my hands, slipping gradually to the fingertips from one of the ever-present poplar roof beams. I have to kick the chair well away for dramatic effect, or he does! I then lecture the assembly on the virtues of Dr Cyriax and Dr Henry Sanford's home traction and posture methods from the hanging position. From what I have seen, Pathans prefer this performance. It is more congenial.

However, this can mean I am left hanging from the poplar

beam rather longer than is strictly necessary, until the Fellow of the Royal College of Surgeons says I can let go. We know that none of the Afghans will ever take up the exercises. In their eyes, they are superlatively undignified. But if they won't participate, they now at least know they have only themselves to blame. And, after all, some of their gyrations at prayer time are well on the way to limbering up. Just as swabbing the decks must have had beneficial side-effects for sailors.

When the only answer is a placebo, Peter has an inexhaustible supply of curiously strong peppermints, the kind that take your breath away.[1] These have never been known to fail, distributed one only at a time as something infinitely precious.

Peter told me that the one prescribed to our one-armed geriatric contemporary to relieve the pain in his missing arm had, Peter noted, been surreptitiously removed half-sucked and passed on later to the sentinel horse. Obviously, a very special relationship existed there. In any emergency, the old bandit would, unlike Shakespeare's Richard III, have been able to save his kingdom.

As soon as the Toyota arrived back, we begged to be excused, explaining that we had a job to do. But Pir Mohammed would not let us go unless we took the whole twelve-man escort in the back of our pick-up, which was hardly possible or wise. Surely, they had their own vehicle coming?

We next delivered auxiliary barefoot doctor Said M. Anwar, who had travelled with us, to his brother Dr Mohammed Anwar. Peter went out of his way to congratulate him on the expert tuition he had given his brother. At the same time, Peter warned that they should both hold themselves in a state of permanent readiness.

We left Miram Shah in high spirits, only just remembering to shed our faithful Tribal levy escort at Barakhail checkpoint, as we exited the Tribal Areas at the precise point we had entered and engaged their services only two days previously. We had begun by resenting their attachment and wound up enjoying their musical comedy company, which can be the relationship which grows over time, we are told, between hijackers, hostage takers and their charges. It is known, after one particularly notorious incident of shift in allegiance, as the Stockholm Syndrome.

Interestingly, Malang points out that all the graffiti on the rockface along our way are texts from the Holy Koran and not the Iranian/Iraqi political scrawls we had grown accustomed to, such as disfigure the London Underground and underpasses. Although we may be none the wiser, Muslims can tell at a glance. Obviously, from what is said, but also because the beauty of the calligraphy can be as much an expression of faith as the text itself.

Between us we had managed to remember to ring ahead to Ruth Coggan, who had assembled her patients for Peter to see. None of them had far to come, as they were nearly all staff members or their families. So, no time was lost, and, unlike so many other impromptu line-ups, none of their complaints was trivial. As expected, most were strained, over-worked elbows, shoulders or backs, caused by lifting patients. Following Sir Nicholas Barrington's good example, I tackled the garden. I also slipped into the amazing Anglican church to give thanks for our safe deliverance.

Top priority for Malang was to reach Juliet on the telephone, or radio link, if there was another set in Bannu, and get her latest instructions as to what was expected of us.

We told Ruth she was much too busy to be bothered with feeding us and anyway the sun ovens had not been primed. I still had no idea what one did with a sun oven, but priming it sounded right!

Peter and I had a hard-tack picnic under the trees, whilst we waited to hear our fate. It may not have been the wisest move because horseflies picnicked off him. Happily they found me distasteful. The upshot was that there were two casualties waiting at the Zhawar checkpoint. Malang and Satar would go and collect them and pick us up on the way back. As it was already prohibitively dark, we could not afford to run any risk of causing further delays by inclusion in the party. Any casualty not up to the journey back to Peshawar could be left with Dr Waziri at Miram Shah.

Peter could now afford to extend Ruth's clinic list, which couldn't be more deserving. And we might just manage to return to Peshawar, not quite so empty-handed from such a significant battle area.

Ruth said that, if necessary, Peter and I could be accommodated overnight in the recently redecorated pristine guest quarters - a riot of white calcimine paint, no doubt done over for Sir Nicholas's recent visit. Where on earth did they find the time? Ask a busy woman. However, any hopes of our relishing such creature comforts were soon dashed by the precipitate return of Malang and Satar with the ambulance full to capacity. The severe nature of the wounds had caused the Pakistani authorities to have no hesitation in waiving the curfew. Miram Shah hospital had reached saturation. All these cases were for Peshawar. Mine injuries, way beyond the local capability.

Some murmurings and the occasional moan were emitted. No cries. Such stoicism is beyond belief. Their pain threshold still unassessed, Peter immediately wanted to know what drugs had been administered. There was no record and Malang knew of none. He sent me to ask Ruth for whatever morphine she could spare. He then set about gently separating the bodies, inserting the bean bags his wisdom and foresight had led him to commission in England the previous year. When these ran out, we were obliged to resort to Ruth's bundles of *Nursing Times* - neatly tied with string and incongruously labelled 'smooth bottoms on top'. In all there were six casualties - four Mujahedeen and two kids - teenage children, warriors in their way. There had been two more 'own goal' cases, too serious to travel, which had been off-loaded at Miram Shah. Every one of them had at least one limb blown off by the blast on impact. The next limb had so much dirt blown into it that it would have to be amputated. In all cases it looked as if the crutch had been blown clear away, and whichever arm was leading at the time, had also been hit. Injury invariably followed the striding action. Dirt had been blasted into all the wounds. Dirt would do more damage than quantities of old-style fragmented metal.

We had been told what to expect, but I had never believed it would be as bad as this. Robin Gray's homily at Red Cross/Red Crescent had given us an uncompromising picture of what we would be up against. Now we were face to face with the reality.

[1] These peppermints were called Altoids and had a slogan to say they were curiously strong and had been made since the reign of 'Mad' King George III. They came in a neat white crush-proof tin box, with an illustration of the peppermint plant - all of which added considerably to their 'medicinal' mystique. On other occasions, Dr Hack's or Fisherman's Friend have served a similar purpose.

Part 2
The Enemy Within

<h1 style="text-align:center">24</h1>

'And there's mines to be laid and works to be done, look you ...'

Captain Fluellyn - Henry V

Since the beginning of the Russo-Afghan war in 1979, there had been at least ten million mines scattered indiscriminately, on all sides by all sides - that is to say by the Russians, the Russian-backed Kabul militia, and the various Afghan guerilla factions.

Even allowing for Afghan hyperbole, mines are going to be the biggest single problem for the foreseeable future. The solution is not just medical or surgical. It must begin with mine awareness programmes - aimed at the returning civilian population. Then there is the overriding need for efficient mine clearance. The latest estimates we had, based on actual rates of clearance, indicated a time-scale of 4,300 years merely to sweep the known one-fifth affected surface area of Afghanistan. That is virtually to say - for ever.

This in turn means that there will be mine casualties in all sections of the community for the foreseeable future, but particularly for civilian peasant farming families in the countryside. Modern mines are increasingly manufactured to be virtually impossible to detect.

A recent Red Cross manifesto has described land-mines as 'fighters that never miss, strike blindly, do not carry weapons openly and go on killing and more likely maiming long after hostilities have ceased'. In short, blind callous terrorism. Not only do they fail to discriminate between combatants and civilians, but in truth concentrate on the civilian population and returning refugees. Yet, in addition to killing, maiming and terrorising civilian populations, mines have the latent power to deny refugees their fundamental right to return to their native homeland. The few ground rules that exist apply only to conflicts between international armies. Most of today's wars are internal civil ones. Civil war was ever the worst kind of war.

None of the available statistics from either the Red Cross, Red Crescent or the UN account for those people injured, who subsequently died or failed to make the journey to hospital. If and when 'social animators' are in place we may ultimately get a fuller picture. However, the pattern of injuries indicates that, with many victims suffering the loss of as many as three limbs, without loss of life, there can only be a clear intention to cause maximum disability and consternation in the community - just short of death.

Originally conceived to protect military installations, mines have now become offensive weapons. There is no more perverse or pervasive use of modern technology.

Consider the Falklands conflict. It is more than twenty years old now. Mine clearance began the moment the two-months fighting ceased, but clearing them was found to be so difficult, it had to be abandoned. Those mines are still there ... live.

If this is what happens where the armies are conventional ones and the areas are clearly identified and defined, what will become of those where the fighting has continued for decades and where the mines have been sown indiscriminately and on a massive scale?

*

At the time, back in 1989, we felt the case had been overstated. Now, looking at our charges, we knew it had not. So, with Robin Gray's admonition ringing in our ears, we bade a fond farewell to Ruth and her outpost and were soon on the road again, night-driving like the proverbial Jehu. We took it in turns to squat in the back with the patients and yell out if we thought the bumps were unbearable, or might dislodge us. In truth we were alarmist, Satar knew what he was doing. In four hours we were over the Kohat Pass, with only one stop for prayers and a pitcher of water. We were soon back in Peshawar and delivering directly to the Red Cross/Red Crescent Hospital.

As soon as Peter Stiles was satisfied that all that could be done for the casualties was being done, we went on to Dean's. We were both more than ripe and ready for a bath and bed. The meal could wait.

The next morning Sarah Forster called round to debrief us. She appeared pleased with our findings, which Peter subsequently put into a written report. Quite unknown to us, our perseverance with the Pakistani authorities for the Tribal Areas contained valuable lessons for the conduct of future operations. We had been willing but unwitting guinea-pigs.

The Assistant Deputy Commissioner for Afghan Refugees, whose 'name' I had listed as Nasir Khan Wasir, was also known as Ali Jan. He, and indeed Pir Mohammed, were both due to feature often in future.

Our experience had proved valuable for a variety of reasons. principally because it constituted an official approach and entry by ex-pat visitors. It was, of course, much simpler to hop on a flying bus or Bedford van and run the gauntlet of detection; but the bus would not always be going our way. When it was, we'd be on it. That way took a lot of perseverance and, above all, patience. Very early on, people had come to the conclusion that if Harriet Sandys could take the bus to Kabul, so could they. But it still took bottle.

We remembered to hand-over Ruth Coggan's giant pile of back numbers, still labelled but now patchily blood-soaked. Peter explained that these were destined for the Khyber Teaching Hospital 'to help train the next generation'. Sarah kindly undertook to ensure delivery. She then told us that Juliet would appreciate a visit to her office sometime that afternoon. We said we would call round at 4 p.m., after Peter had looked in on his patients. Although he would be unable to operate, he still took a professional interest in following their progress.

Juliet Crawley Vergos (Peck) had a number of reasons for wanting to see us. Her driver's brother, which in Afghan terms did not necessarily mean a full brother, but could do so, had suffered a serious car accident and was lying in a paralysed state. Were we prepared to go and see if anything could be done for him? He had already undergone one major operation, which had strung him together internally with stainless steel wires like some puppet. But somewhere vital between neck and collar-bone it had snapped and now nothing worked. Peter muttered that such devices never did, but he agreed to see the patient, as it was obviously important to Juliet. Although to me he looked a complete write-off, he was subsequently flown to Germany and, after appropriate surgery, was up and walking within six months!

Next on her agenda, word had evidently got back to Juliet that we had observed something on our travels better left unnoticed. Malang's report had included our suspicions. Juliet had obviously decided that, having dealt with her driver's brother, she could now tackle the other matter head-on - that we believed we had seen some English women in the guest quarters at Bōri. I said that it was a question of hearing them rather than seeing them; but we had both been surprised the following morning to see a group of 'Afghan' women looking distinctly European. I had always understood, I said, that the famine research had been conducted amongst arriving refugees as they crossed the border. Were the findings subsequently verified inside Afghanistan? Juliet confirmed that they were. However, she went on, the girls we thought we had seen inside Afghanistan could not possibly have anything to do with AfghanAid, because they had a strict policy of only using men inside Afghanistan - never women.

It was the subsequent confirmation of facts on the ground

that determined the amount of cash and comfort that was going to be allocated to any given area. Afghans were prone to exaggeration, part of their poetic nature. With the intention of persuading them to stay put, where they belonged, AfghanAid had to start with the most accurate possible picture of the truth on the ground.

I was embarrassed. I felt we had wandered by mistake into forbidden territory. But, much as I wanted to change the subject, I found myself only getting deeper into it. Something compelled me to ask how starvation was assessed, anyway. Back came the answer that a series of upper-arm measurements were taken with a tape measure and that these were checked two or three months later. I made a snide mental note to look for yellow tape measures round the necks of our gaudily dressed Bōri ladies when the colour prints came back.

Peter and I then touched on Ruth Coggan's *alma mater* network, all of whom would make first-rate referrals for women, with automatic overnight accommodation thrown in. Very few of the 'hostesses' would be either numerate or literate, but at least their loyalties would be assured.

Despite Malang's *muerta*, he must have had a very clear idea about all these 'research' trips inside. He would have been responsible for ferrying them in and bringing them safely back out again. His was the Long Range Desert Group that fitted them in according to the priority of casualties. They constituted his back-haul problem. With luck, on the outward journey, our 'researchers' might find themselves sitting astride a sack of seed corn for delivery to the very stricken area they were being sent to monitor. I visualised young female students of Social Anthropology from the School of Oriental and African Studies.

Furthermore, I suspected that Malang's dilemma yesterday morning had been ours. He had orders to take us in preference to 'them', because that had been the priority laid down by Juliet. If there had been no mine casualties, we might all have returned to Peshawar in the same truck. That would have set the cat amongst the pigeons.

Notwithstanding Juliet's denial, Peter's face was a picture of I-told-you-so smugness. There would be no more ribald references to 'Operation Toothmug'. Careless talk could cost lives.

However, once the Russian war was over, the denials turned into articles in AfghanAid's magazine featuring English women working throughout Afghanistan!

25
We meet Santa Klaus

Juliet had told us in so many words that our last operation had been little more than border-hopping. We were to come to think of it as a game of Grandmother's Footsteps in British India.

She was now keen to tell us of another sector, which might benefit from our attention, and which could even bring about our objective of taking surgery nearer to the casualties. The organisation she was referring to was the German Afghanistan Committee with whom AfghanAid enjoyed a mild flirtation and one or two joint operations.

Although Juliet had yet to meet him, the whole operation was in the capable hands of the German Field Director, a charismatic figure called Dr Reinhard Erös. It was suspected he might be on secondment from German Special Forces (GSG9)[1] At present he was in Germany but due out any day. Juliet had made a tentative appointment for us to meet him at 3 p.m. in two days' time.

Strangely enough, Dr Kermit Veggeberg, the ever optimistic chairman and director of the Peshawar program for Orthopaedics Overseas, had also given us glowing reports of this unit and its operations, and had even mooted a link-up sooner or later. It was known to have at least two very smart set-ups. One was up the Kurrum Agency, towards Parachinar - meaning Parrot's Beak - strategically placed near the Afghan border at a place called Sadda. The second was inside Afghanistan at Chak-e-Wardak. It all promised well and was, in fact, based on some historic German achievements in that very area.

Earlier in the 20th century, whilst the French had trained the Afghan Gendarmerie, the Germans had made substantial investments in hydro-electric generating schemes and hospital equipment projects - both master-minded by Siemens. Their initial thinking, arising from the strategic requirements of the First World War, had been the natural extension of the German/Turkish Axis towards British India.

Indeed, an epic German expedition from that time, undertaken by Otto von Hentig and Oskar von Niedermayer, out-performed any previous British expedition by reaching Kabul across the Persian desert. Their very first project on reaching Kabul in October 1915 was to establish a 'hearts and minds' hospital. They had managed to recruit a dozen skilled craftsmen from amongst a hundred prisoners of war, mostly Austrian, who had escaped across the Oxus from

Russian camps in Turkestan. In von Hentig's words, the hospital was to 'embody the latest German principles of light, air and cleanliness - concepts then entirely new in Afghanistan'.

The German Afghanistan Committee had now built on these earlier German presences by siting their new operating theatre at Chak-e-Wardak, between two of the three generators which Siemens had installed in 1938. They were thought to be functioning still - albeit spasmodically. The theory was that the Russians were less likely to rocket the utility that supplied twenty per cent of the light and power for the city of Kabul.

However, even if that was only half true, it looked as if we might be about to walk into precisely what we were looking for - ideally located operating facilities inside Afghanistan on the doorstep of Kabul, where there was sure to be fighting and a steady demand for primary surgery.

If the reality lived up to its advance billing, it would be a fitting reflection of all those other German efforts made on behalf of the Afghan cause. Compared with Britain, large sums had been raised in Germany by public subscription. No doubt there was added incentive for them with the Russian bear grinning over their garden fence. The German banks, unchanged since the Weimar Republic, had suffered none of the inhibitions of British institutions and had proudly displayed emotive posters in their windows - particularly at Christmas time - to highlight the anniversary of the Russian invasion of Afghanistan. These called the public's attention to the plight of the Afghans and invited over-the-counter contributions. Likewise, documentary television programmes made no bones about how and where donations should be sent through a special direct debit system. None of the pussy-footing that we Brits went in for to satisfy the Charity Commissioners! One sample slogan translated from the German read 'Everybody talks about war. Here in Afghanistan, we have it!'

The other notable contribution was the number of young German war reporters and cameramen. Many of these were freelancers, like an old friend of mine, the film photographer Dittmar Hack and his friend Christoph Hörstel. No doubt they had good reason to loathe the Russians. Dittmar was totally fearless and near fanatical at times, but the film footage he brought back never failed to inspire us. Germany was participating responsibly on the world stage in a significant, if strictly non-combatant role.

Appropriately enough, the headquarters of the German Afghanistan Committee was based in Bonn, at that time still the capital of the Federal Republic of Germany, which we called West Germany. Before the fall of the Berlin Wall and German Reunification, there also existed the Kremlin-supporting half of Germany, the German Democratic Republic or East Germany. With the collapse of communism, this state has gone the same way as the USSR, into the dustbin of history. Germany is now one country and the capital has relocated to Berlin.

After this brief digression on recent German history, we return to the German Afghanistan Committee's public face nearer the front line. Their Peshawar, Pakistan, establishment was housed at 23c Park Avenue, University Town, and there were other dependencies as well. The Field Director, Dr Reinhard Erös, and his wife Annette and their large family lived comfortably in a grand villa, 'over the shop'. At the end of a short verandah, facing the lush watered garden, stood the office complex. This consisted of the Director's Office and Command Post, which was kept locked at all times. There were two subordinate offices.

Part of the garden had been given over to a vast lock-up container warehouse. This was in the charge of a dedicated German student youth worker. We assumed he was a volunteer. We sat with him in adjoining chairs, awaiting the arrival of 'Colonel' Erös. We had deliberately arrived a quarter of an hour early. Just as well, for, with only the short distance to come from his lunch table, he was the regulation five minutes early.

Reinhard Erös was of medium height, and very dark and swarthy for a German. He was so heavily bearded he could pass for an Afghan. We were subsequently told that his name suggested, rather too obviously, Greek or more likely Hungarian origins. *Nomen est Omen*. He certainly gave the lie to the Aryan *Hitlerjugend* type. He even had a penchant for proper, Winston Churchill size cigars.

He greeted us most affably in English and led the way to his Command Post. After he had battled with all those keys, the first thing that struck us was that the walls were papered from floor to ceiling with NASA satellite photographs of the whole of Afghanistan - all in glorious technicolor.

There we were, muddling through with hopeless maps, whilst he had the very latest in SAT/INT pictures. If we looked hard enough we could probably identify the cooking fire and well at Bōri.

We sat down and, at his invitation, outlined what we had done during the last three annual visits and what we should like to do next by taking our 'MASH' team services nearer to the casualties front line. By way of illustration we cited the secondary surgery which had

Dr Reinhard Erös, Field Director of GAC -
German Afghanistan Committee. *Photo by Peter Stiles*

been our original engagement, followed by injuries that were some fourteen days 'fresh'; then there was the case of the Mujahedeen who had ridden for twelve hours with a bullet in his leg; and the six and finally four hours-old injuries at Bannu, on which we had been 'unqualified' to operate under International Red Cross/Red Crescent regulations.

Erös said he fully understood and proceeded to give us a rundown on his operations, which struck us as widespread. Two of his lead surgeons, Michael Müller, a Swiss national, and Ortwin Joch would operate as 'Mobile Units', mounted on horseback but based on Chak-e-Wardak for two or three months at a time. It was hard physically to sustain a longer period. The heavy workload, but more especially the climate and the deficiencies in diet, took their toll.

To service Chak there was a permanent staging-post 'cottage hospital'-*cum*-clinic at Sadda, just on the Pakistani side of the border.

At this point Peter Stiles proffered the services of two British or British/American volunteers - Bryony Williams and Kate Straub. This was to inject a short-to-medium and ultimately long-term view of any contribution we might be able to make over and above our annual visits. Erös agreed that such personnel could suit the German Afghanistan Committee admirably.

What, he said, he would like to propose for the present was that we should divide our team into two or three units. One should remain in Peshawar and continue with its work under the existing programme of surgery. The second unit could proceed to Sadda to spend a week or ten days there, making itself generally useful conducting outpatients' surgeries etc. Then, if all went to our joint satisfactions, the sub-units could swap round. Or, better still, provided it was safe to travel, the first unit could move on to Chak, leaving its replacement to acclimatise at Sadda.

In many ways, the purpose of Sadda was acclimatisation. The German Afghanistan Committee had assembled teams of barefoot doctors (also known as paramedics or dispensers) there from all over Afghanistan. This week there were eight, but there could be as many as twelve at a time. Along with the permanent staff, these would help simulate living conditions inside Afghanistan, whilst foregoing the dangers.

Once a week, every week, on Fridays, the German Afghanistan Committee 'flying bus' service operated to Sadda. So transport was the least of their problems. The Germans were known and respected throughout the Kurrum Agency. The back-haul return journey was made to Peshawar, either on Friday afternoon or on a Saturday. Without hesitation Peter and I volunteered for the first leg.

With that settled, Reinhard, as we were now calling him, treated us to a tour of his warehouse and 'treat' was the operative word. It proved an Aladdin's Cave stuffed with medical goodies. Peter went green with envy when he saw the quality of the surgical instruments destined to be transported, packed in sorbo rubber, to Chak. He said they would be the envy of any surgeon in Europe. No doubt they had been donated by their manufacturers. We expressed unqualified admiration and went on to discuss pack-animal transportation over the mountain passes, which in turn triggered visions of Chindit operations and recent, and more apposite analogies known to Peter in Cyprus.

It soon became clear that Reinhard had taken a shine to us, or had worked out a way in which we could be slotted into his overall scheme of things. Mention of the attachment of no fewer than one female doctor and two female registered nurses and midwives may have made an undue impression on him.

To give us a better idea of the range of their activities Reinhard handed us a 75-page Manual on the 'Deutsches Afghanistan Komitee'. Happily the text was in English. There was also a 3-page summary of 'The achievements of the German Afghanistan Committee'. At the time, we had no time to give it more than superficial attention. However, given time, we would come to refer to it again and again.

The climax of our tour came when we found ourselves gazing in wonderment at rack upon ordered rack of German manufactured medicines - from Bayer and Hoechst. Although he said they bought most of their stocks locally in Pakistan, it looked as if they weren't short of generous sponsors too. This container warehouse was said to be the conduit for fifty tons of medicines and material a year - a through-put of nearly a ton a week.

It was agreed that we should parade fully kitted up by first light the following Friday morning. We had spoken for John Stoneham too. We knew he wouldn't want to be left out and he and Peter would constitute our first basic surgical unit.

In fact, the Sadda option worked out admirably. Not least because some team members had given undertakings to their wives not to go into Afghanistan. Sadda was everything short of breaking trust. In fact, when the random Scud rockets started to arrive, in the Taramangal Gap, it turned out to be every bit as dangerous!

On boarding for Friday's dawn departure we found that Reinhard had allocated a fourth passenger exclusively for our care.

To my less than silent rage, he was to be the minder's minder and interpreter to us all. He was introduced as an ex-Kabul University professor. As time went by we began to suspect that Kabul University had more professors than undergraduates. The root cause of the problem was that he would treat us with the same pupil patronage as his former charges, when we were his senior by at least ten years.

Fondly imagining that we were a lot brighter than we were, he elected to give us simultaneous private tuition in Dari and Pashtu. We muddled everything and failed lamentably. Realising that we were, after all, idiots, he next attempted to teach us a string of the simplest everyday words, concentrating on correct pronunciation. We began, for some unexplained reason, with 'b' for *burqa*, which one might imagine was hard to hash. No translation possible or necessary. Not a bit of it. He made us repeat it again and again and again - at least forty times. We were all near despair rattling along in the back of the canvas-topped utility van. Perhaps it was his way of tackling boredom? John Stoneham dropped out and adopted a steadfastly silent brown study. It appeared that the desired intonation required that the *qa* of *bur-qa* should be emitted as if on the point of vomiting. Neither Peter nor I achieved this to the learned professors' entire satisfaction.

Whenever mealtimes beckoned, our minder would pop up with his hands spread over his distended stomach, to ask, 'What is the state of your stomach?'

Reflecting John's other prowess, we would chant back 'Pregnant with flatulence!' He never got the point but couldn't bring himself to ask for an explanation. Instead he pretended to understand. He looked incredibly out of place, a wet fish out of water. Still dressed for city life, he was effete with beautifully manicured hands. His face was hairless, which might have accounted for the antipathetic impression on our part. Being more used to Pashtuns, we expected our Afghans to be hirsute.

Along the Kurrum river highway, we were waved through every single roadblock set up by the Pakistani army. This was obviously one of the advantages of being a regular-run 'flying bus' service, recognised as a Friday-morning out and Saturday-evening back feature. Like G.K. Chesterton's postman it had become part of the landscape. Everybody was aware of the high moral ground of the German Afghanistan Committee, and the schedule ran like clockwork. Always the same vehicle, always one of two drivers. The border guards were past caring in this, the Kurrum Agency, which was all the more surprising since it was so often the focus of Sunni/Shi-ite strife. Stops were minimal. One was memorable for the local apples we were invited to pick off the tree at the roadside. They were exceptionally juicy and thirst-quenching, and the flavour slightly perfumed like rose water.

Just when we were beginning to think it was high time to run out of the Kurrum Agency, beautiful as it was, we had crossed the river and were in danger of taking a wrong turn, or so we thought, when suddenly we had arrived at Sadda. It is just short of Parachinar, which, as noted before, is said to mean Parrot's Beak. This refers to the proboscis sticking into the soft underbelly of Afghanistan at this point; as if it were possible to contemplate Afghanistan ever having had such a thing.

Sadda is sited between Via Dera and Kohard, about an hour from the Taramangal pass, one of some 350 passes into Afghanistan. The German Afghanistan Committee had chosen an ideal site for their cottage hospital staging-post. It is a large establishment surrounded by a fourteen-foot high mud wall. This is sparsely floodlit at night by half a dozen naked light bulbs; just enough to keep a sentry peering. In common with most such compounds it has massive metal gates at the front, with a small Judas door to allow individual access. Both gates have to be opened to admit vehicles.

Apparently secure from without, once inside, it is a vision of idyllic charm and innocence. The pathways are flanked with pretty pastel-coloured flowerbeds. Inevitably variegated poppies feature prominently, both Siberian and Himalayan. These pathways lead to all the principal buildings, with their mature eucalyptus trees. However, by far and away the most striking feature is the 'Mechanical Cow', which looms on the right-hand side as you enter. It is a large cylindrical, stainless steel tank. Early each morning, Fridays excepted, a long queue of children forms up at the metal gate. Each child comes bearing a container for a litre or slightly more. The mechanical cow is then set on stream to disgorge x times the number of children/litres of ready-mixed dried milk plus added protein. It is a bit like counting the host at mass. Somebody must make a guesstimate of scampering late arrivals. These brightly coloured little boys and girls, all in highly decorative national costume - each girl and boy splendidly Biblical in their coats of many colours - squat in the dust beside the magic flowerbeds awaiting the equally magic moment when their mechanical cow will spout their sustenance. Sometimes they get given a high-protein food bar as well. All diminutives are charming to our eyes, but these kids, as well as being colourful, are world-beaters for sheer high-spiritedness.

As if to add authenticity to the 'cow', further along on the right-

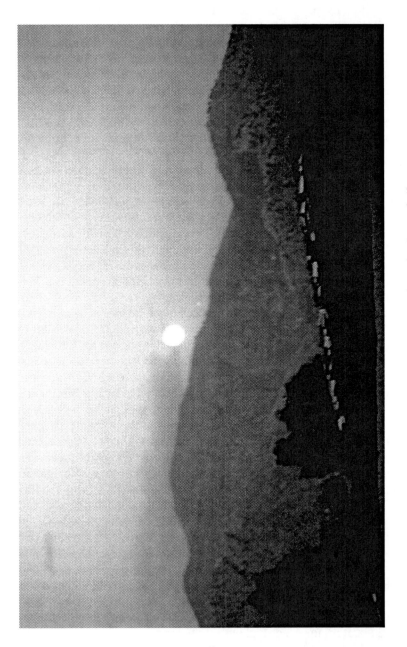

Moon rising over Sadda Clinic. *Photo by Peter Stiles*

hand side of the compound is a row of a dozen stalls. Each contains a tethered stamping steed - the wildest wide-eyed *soi-disant* domestic animals known to man. Proud descendants of the ponies of Genghis Khan, crossed with much later Arab introductions, each one stands longing to be saddled and girthed with one of those ball-breaking X-frame wooden saddles hanging from a wall hook in front of its muzzle. They rarely get exercised as such, but once let off the hook, they could be away for maybe a month or two at a time, as the mainstay of one 'Mobile Unit' or another.

Just beyond the horses was the mechanical transport park. A sorrier and less Germanic sight it would be hard to imagine. One care-worn tractor, a clapped-out Jeep, a broken-down minibus plus the predecessor of today's 'flying bus' utility van, whose sole purpose now is to supply spare parts. Finally, there was an immobilised ambulance, all like some museum to mechanised transport.

The entrance wall and all the retaining walls are blank, except, that is, for the impressive metal entrance gates, set in the smooth yellow mud.

The cottage hospital/clinic buildings are ranged along the left-hand wall, opposite. First comes the guard house, then the clinic, surgery and operating theatre. The queue waiting for the clinic is entertained in true busker style, with a grandstand view of the current operation. On the other hand, those suffering from toothache are attended on the spot by 'Doctor' Iqbal. He is an English speaker, but with the odd word of German too.

There is also the ubiquitous factotum, a stunted sergeant-major, much in evidence here. His name is Shaikh. He has a navel-length black beard, topped with large humorous twinkling black olive eyes. He bears a close resemblance to the headmaster in Jean Vigo's *Zero de Conduite*. Unusually short for an Afghan, he brandishes a large switch of eucalyptus as his badge of office, taken daily fresh from the convenient compound tree. He uses this to usher out the legion of flies through a handily broken dart-shaped gap in one of the surgery window-panes. Like some Austrian St Nicholas he employs the same switch to round up laggardly children for their early morning milk. Although gnomish, he is always good-humoured and has the most bewitching smile. Shaikh is the true friend of everyman.

Beyond the hospital building comes the cookhouse, bath-house, dining-room and dormitory building. And next after that comes the school-house cum lecture hall for the barefoot doctors. In an emergency these spaces could become wards as well as being used for student accommodation.

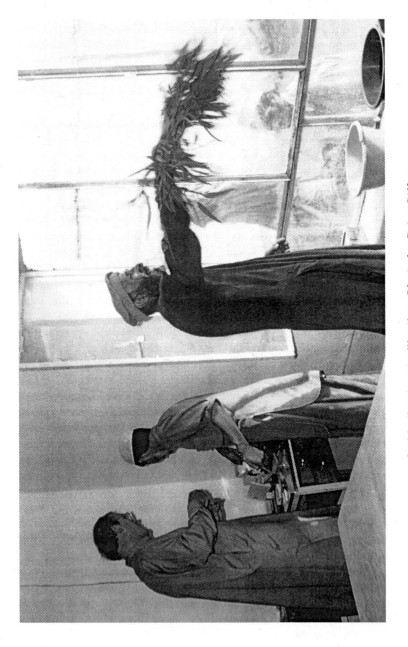

Sadda theatre sterilization. *Photo by Peter Stiles*

The barefoot doctor programme is one of the best of its kind. Fit young candidates are brought in from all over Afghanistan. They are given a two months free induction course in basic medicine and first aid. Surprisingly, they also come to learn English, as most of the text books they will be using are written in English. Then, most important of all, they return to practise what they have learned in their home villages. The problem with many another similar programme is that the nearer the school is to a town like Peshawar, the greater the temptation is to stay and go into 'quack' business on 'graduation'. By contrast, Sadda had a clear-cut policy of re-implantation.

Whilst there, I was given a real job, teaching English to the students. Fortunately they were already sufficiently advanced for me not to have to find the non-existent, English equivalent to the *bur-qa* word. The words that gave them most trouble were *the* and *teeth*. So, we were able to while away hours struggling with sentences containing these two words. Otherwise, conversation would soon degenerate into impertinent interrogation of my love life.

Every morning, therefore, save Friday the Sabbath, as soon as the ritual milk dispensary was over, the outpatients queue would be admitted from the gate. Any refugees requiring medical attention along the border were welcome. Goodness knows how they counted them, but there were said to be 35,000 souls in the immediate 'catchment' area. None of them was registered with the Pakistani authorities, so they did not qualify for the official refugee aid programme. It was all a sickly 'Catch 22' situation, involving iniquitous bribes to petty functionaries who, having taken payment, neither could nor would then do anything.

One day I was admitted to attend a minor operation in the 'theatre' and so saw the scene from the other point of view. There was Iqbal drawing more painful teeth. There was a long benchload of out-patients awaiting their turn, whilst being entertained watching us and the sufferings of others through the broken fly-blown window. A sea of curious expectant faces. Being Afghan, nobody ever showed any sign of pain. As I had half expected, I was only called in to hold a man's leg down, as it was being sawn off! Paradoxically, it was frequently obvious during outpatients' consultations that symptoms were being fabricated, with appropriate noises off, to extract a prescription. This might happily result in a quick turn on re-sale in the bazaar! There was a keen sense for secondary markets.

Whatever else they may have had in mind, it was clear that the German Afghanistan Committee had little intention of letting us get any nearer to Chak than Sadda. There had been a general alarm

Shaiq (Administrator for GAC/Sadda)
Photo by Peter Stiles

when a passing commander had offered to take us on a day trip to Azrow, which was way beyond Chak.

Then one evening a number of sages and commanders congregated around the same communal table as ourselves, (there was only one) for the evening meal at 7.30 p.m. First came ablutions, effected in a basin and ewer carried round from person to person. Then, curiously at 7.45 p.m. for some longitudinal reason, there followed the World Service News of the BBC in Dari. We couldn't help noticing that there was an excessive amount of photography going on during this 'joint session'. We were repeatedly told that this was the 'full German Afghanistan Committee' in plenary session. There plainly wasn't a German amongst them, barely any one who could even speak German. So far, the only hint of a German flavour we had were, apart from Reinhard Erös himself, the volunteer student warehouseman, mention of one German surgeon and another Swiss at Chak , where there was also said to be a resident German nursing sister. Then we had briefly shaken the hand of a Dr Tilman Hilber, who was leaving in a great hurry just as we arrived - he was one of Reinhard Erös's 'recruits'; they had been medical students together in Munich.

When we got back and reported these things to Juliet, she showed not a glimmer of surprise. Ever camera shy, it crossed my suspicious mind that we might have been set up as Kodak fodder to beef up the German participation for somebody's records, but whose?

[1] GSG9 was officially anti-terrorist only.

26

Uncle Sam's Disaster Hospitals

Not long after this we learned that Dr Kermit Veggeberg wanted us to help solve a particular problem for his newly constituted charitable institution, Afghan Hospital Relief Inc. To our surprise and delight it involved the German Afghanistan Committee, their Chak-e-Wardak facility and their relationship with the Afghanistan Interim Government.

While Sadda was undeniably most attractive, even cosy, as a base camp, it was clearly kids' stuff, not geared for war casualties and would be ill-equipped to cope with any that happened to pass that way. Its role as a key *serai* was undeniable. The barefoot doctoring paramedics course was highly commendable, but that alone was hardly justification for such a high-powered infrastructure. It was always possible that it was an elaborate ploy to please the Pakistanis, whilst actually being a subtle front for something else. But what? It left a lingering but definite suspicion of some grand deception, the hint of a hidden agenda. Highly articulate travellers in the early 1970s, such as Peter Levi and Bruce Chatwin, had even reported sightings of fully uniformed SS, armed with Luger pistols being thrown into the swimming pool at a New Year's Ball at the Kabul International Club!

There was also the acknowledged infiltration by Germans as head foresters in Paktia on the Pakistani border. It was claimed that nobody else could keep proper tabs on the timber smugglers. Three hundred had been killed in one pitched battle - 'shot like ivory poachers'.

However, there was another, simpler explanation, based on the premise that the German constitution forbade active participation inside any hostile territory. In this case, Sadda was as near as the Germans could officially get. The corollary of this was that everything that happened at Chak had to be 'unofficial'. Could that be the explanation for the remarkable dearth of real live Germans on the German Afghanistan Committee in plenary session?

Despite all sorts of come-ons and promises, we were to get no nearer to Chak under the German Afghanistan Committee (GAC) auspices, than the Taramangal Gap border crossing. At every attempt we were turned back with irrelevant tales of Sunni/Shiite strife. But there simply were no mobs and no riots. A well-aimed and equally unpredictable Scud missile did land in the Gap whilst we were at Sadda, but, otherwise, there should have been nothing to delay us. On the second week changeover, Dr Sarah Fane did make it across the border, but not to Chak.

What happened next was one of those peculiarly American 'wild cards', which played right into our hands. Orthopaedics Overseas, in the person of their local program director, Dr Veggeberg, whom we by now knew well, was never exactly short of original, ever optimistic, often over-ambitious ideas. Each successive year, his ebullient mental attitude would 'guarantee' us unlimited operating opportunities from the Oxus to the Jumna, but somehow we always wound up back at the Peshawar cottage hospitals, still buoyed up with 'jam tomorrow' expectations.

In fairness, the advent of the Afghan Trauma Hospital,with its male and female wards, had undoubtedly constituted a major facilities breakthrough. But that was surely as much a European Community initiative as anything to do with Orthopaedics Overseas or the Americans; although Kermit could certainly take credit for much of the kitting out - including the piles of entertaining video cassettes. This time, however, we were to be privy to some of Kermit's yet-more-ambitious aspirations.

He had long harboured ambitions of transplanting an unspecified number of obsolete US-packaged Disaster Hospitals. For them to be available in the first place, and affordable in the second, could only mean that the technology had long been superseded or the disasters now anticipated were becoming ever more cataclysmic! As ever with Kermit Veggeberg, the original concept was thoroughly laudable, so long as a suitable site had been found and talked through.

But no sooner would his scouts locate a discarded 'package', than it would be earmarked for a specific province. You might have thought that the Afghans would have jumped at the idea of such a facility in their midst. Not on your life. Azrow, as recommended by Brigadier "TM", was one such option, but Kunar Province had been approached first. True to form, they wanted to be paid before accepting anything. This wasn't to be a payment to cover first-year start-up costs, but a hip-pocket consideration for the lads!

Not surprisingly, the World Health Organisation took a dim view. AID Afghanistan and Operation Salaam[1] withdrew their support and Kunar Province found itself ruled out.

Meanwhile, the packages were left to rot in the warehouse of the Reconstruction Authority of the Alliance of the Afghan Mujahedeen in Darra - much more famous for its armaments manufactures and widespread destruction.

Next, the doctors Najibullah Mojadidi, Rabbani and Iftikhar of the Afghan Surgical Hospital were sighted looking into the possibility of establishing this aptly named disaster hospital on the site of the old provincial hospital building at Azrow, Logar Province - precisely the spot originally proposed by Brigadier "TM". It was also said to have been the scene of some of the most vicious reprisals by the Russians in their war against the Mujahedeen.

Although we received the usual pressing invitation to come and operate there next year, it was not where our services were immediately required. What Kermit had us in mind for, was more of an initiative test for hand-picked 'volunteers'. If Azrow was Project 1, then this was Project 2. And Project 2 was clearly something quite else.

We were given to understand that a well-intentioned group of Cuban-American doctors had formed themselves corporately into the Miami Medical Team Inc of Miami, Florida. Their purpose was to bring down the 'Evil Empire'. To this end, substantial donations had already been made to the Contra cause in Nicaragua as well as to the anti-Castro forces in Angola. The logic was that anything which brought down the Russians, would in turn bring down Fidel. With Castro gone, the Cuban doctors of Miami might once again practise as Cuban doctors in Havana.

Wise in the ways of the world and in the misappropriation of funds in other hands, they had amassed, for the Afghan cause, surplus hospital equipment to a supposed nominal value of $2 million. Once dedicated, the McCullum Humanitarian Airlift had packed up all this miscellaneous kit and airlifted it - lock, stock and barrel - to Islamabad airport. The involvement of MHA indicated CIA involvement.

Some, as yet unknown, guardian angel elected to marry this Cuban doctors' gift to the 'expertise, personnel and resources on the ground' of the German Afghanistan Committee. This could have been Kermit's brainchild, or that of his assistant 'cohort in crime' (his words), Dr Mohammed Nabi Housaini - a veterinarian from Pennsylvania, who subsequently became the Administrator at Chak and later still the resident Administrator of the German Afghanistan Foundation in Peshawar. At an appropriate stage in these proceedings, he also became an American citizen.

Whatever the facts of the matter, Housaini certainly enjoyed Veggeberg's endorsement, because he also did a stint as the Orthopaedics Overseas 'liaison person' at Peshawar. This involved greeting visiting surgeons and looking after them, as well as more mundane tasks like doling out cash.

At this juncture some fairly standard complications arose. The seventeen-ton consignment had been kicked into demurrage[2] limbo because the bill of lading and the consignee were at loggerheads. This was an untoward, but by no means uncommon occurrence. To some extent the complication was compounded by the fact that the German Afghanistan Committee had a second name, which was the same as the first, but in German - Deutsches Afghanistan Komitee.

The crates themselves had been clearly designated to GAC, but the bill of lading/flight manifesto chose to specify the Afghanistan Interim Government (AIG). This suggested that there had been either a last minute change of heart, or the original choice had been to donate to the AIG and let them determine the ultimate beneficiary.[3]

It was decided to call in the Agency for International Development to arbitrate. They ruled that AIG and GAC 'between them' should 'mutually decide' who should get what, something they were quite incapable of doing. The only satisfactory development of this unresolved arbitration was that the whole consignment, other than what had already been stolen, was moved to the US Government warehouse in Peshawar, where it now languished.

Karachi docks were a bottle-neck stranglehold on most bulk consignments. Any keen-eyed observer there would have had little difficulty identifying the Pakistani Army trucks and their drivers who were the conduits for the heroin harvested in the Tribal Areas under Fasli Haq's aegis. Once they had passed on their neat parcel, usually stored under the driver's seat, they were ready to load up again with anything from war *materiel* to dried milk for the refugee camps. Tinned goods, charitably donated and clearly marked 'Not for Resale' simply had a price label stuck over the disclaimer. Normal outlets in Karachi were full of such goods, which had fallen off the backs of army lorries in the port area. The general public was none the wiser and largely indifferent. Karachi had its own internecine wars and, if not openly hostile to Afghans, was certainly defensive, since they saw them making inroads on their livelihood, expecially in the field of transportation.

On this occasion we were past that problem. Fortunately, Kermit Veggeberg was right, we did hold the means of cutting the Gordian Knot, at least so far as the Afghanistan Interim Government was concerned.

Mainly by strict adherence to a policy of apolitical even-handedness, the Guildford Surgical Team had established such credibility with the Medical 'Ministry' of the Afghanistan Interim Government-in-exile that we had no difficulty in persuading them that we would play honest broker in the distribution of the Miami doctors' donation. Their key people were friends of long standing - particularly Dr Abdul Satar Paktiss and Dr Najibullah Mojadidi.

The President of the Afghanistan Interim Government - another Mujaddidi, a name as common in Afghanistan as Smith in England - was also known to Peter Stiles. Peter had been asked to give a second opinion on the President's damaged knee. Professor Sibghatullah Mujaddidi had made a long three or four week tour of Afghanistan on horseback in September 1988. He even went out of his way to meet Ahmed Shah Massoud. His purpose had been to demonstrate that his Interim Government held sway in Afghanistan as well as in Peshawar. It was not to be dismissed as just some Pakistani puppet regime. Unfortunately the President's horse had managed to damage the President's right kneecap by going too close to the overhanging cliff-face. It was obviously a painful hairline crack, for which nothing could be done surgically. Painkillers and rest were prescribed. The exposure did no harm to the Guildford team's reputation.

Likewise, our solution to the Miami donation problem was to take full responsibility for everything listed on the Bill of Lading; whether it was there or not. We would sign for whatever might or might not be behind the shed! We would then think about how to make an equitable distribution.

*

Not long before this, we had recruited a new team member in order to beef up the administration. His name was Peter, or '"Scrubber"', Stewart-Richardson and his re-appearance in my life after an absence of over forty years was nothing short of a miracle. The intermediary was a distant cousin of his, another doctor, Henry Sanford. Henry's family and my mother's had been friends in Somerset for at least three generations. Henry, who was a past master at manipulating parachutists' backs, had also taken a vicarious interest in the team's activities - including introducing some female physiotherapists - which I put down to his having a home near Guildford and some White Russian ancestry. Henry had passed the word that Peter Stewart-Richardson was keen for me to 'acquaint him with Afghanistan, as it was one of the few remaining countries left in the world that interested him and he had yet to visit.'

"Scrubber" Stewart-Richardson was the perpetuation of Evelyn

Waugh's Brigadier Ritchie-Hook from the Sword of Honour trilogy. A Coldstreamer, he always held himself ramrod erect, but he was far from being rigid. He possessed a singular sense of humour and a demoniacal laugh. He was branded early on as a 'bit of a military stickler', so I had been eager to join his column from the outset, as it seemed the most likely route to survival. After a legendary lifetime of 'biffing and bashing', renowned for derring-do from the Palestine Mandate to French Indochina via St Cyr, and all the forgotten wars since, it now looked as if, in the interests of 'good form' and having 'fun', his energies in retirement were to be devoted to good works for the Army Benevolent Fund.

On re-meeting him, "Scrubber" didn't seem to have changed at all. He looked every bit as fit and tough, wiry and wily as a fox, electric with energy, exactly as I remembered him from our very first encounter. That had been in the Suez Canel Zone, when I was a raw subaltern of nineteen and he the Acting Commanding Officer of No 1 (Guards) Independent Parachute Company.

At the first opportunity, I took "Scrubber" down to Guildford to meet the team and, from the outset, he gained their confidence. It was just as well, because I had 'done a wobbly' the year before, which made them realise that our 'admin' lacked strength in depth.

What had nearly done for me was not in the least bit heroic or glamorous. In the Afghan context, it could have been cholera. It looked like Aids and was said to be caused by anxiety or bad conscience. It had a fancy name - thyrotoxicosis. It loooked like I was losing my nerve. My body was giving up on me. Thirty years earlier it would have been a death warrant.

We used to joke about our Afghan excursions being the best slimming cure this side of Tring's famous diet farm. The daily drawing tighter and tighter of the *shalwar kamees* pyjama cord went unremarked. I had long given up shaving and Muslim countries are notoriously short on mirrors. We were all far too busy to be ill ourselves. However, I had managed to lose two stone in less than six weeks. Then I had a bad night, shaking like a leaf and drumming my heels. It was Dr Sarah Fane, the most recently qualified and freshest from general medical school, who diagnosed my condition. All that vaunted energy had turned inwards. I was eating my heart out and all else besides ... consuming myself.

My surgeon mates were clamouring to operate, but the Karachi General Hospital determined otherwise, and prescribed some tiny pink pills at ninety pence the bottle. I remember complaining that the bottle had been opened and that ninety pence did not inspire

Rupert with Peter Stewart-Richardson in Anobar Panjshir

confidence. Confidence was restored when Boots, Piccadilly charged £28 for the same bottle sealed. I was told by a Harley Street specialist that there was a forty percent chance of success over eighteen months.

When "Scrubber" joined us, I was halfway through the course of pills; so there was every reason to encourage him. In many ways he was more relevant than I was. A large chunk of his latter-day soldiering had been with the Sultan's Armed Forces in Muscat and Oman. He spoke some Arabic and many of the soldiers under his command would have been Baluch tribesmen. Also, his whole appearance, bearing and devout presence would be highly favourable in Afghan eyes, for, while the Afghans have many heroes, the greatest by far is Alexander the Great. A highly idealised Alexander at that. To them, he is Sikander, and, of course, an adopted Afghan. Alexander certainly left his mark and their image of their hero has a lean and hungry Afghan look. He also has red hair and watery pale blue eyes like, surprisingly, so many of them; but, more particularly, just like Peter Stewart-Richardson, who could look them in the eye, unflinchingly. They would appreciate that. He had another attribute which the Afghans would like in a *faranghi*. Over and above his twinkling sense of humour, he had an infinite capacity for attentive listening, and often resorted to claiming abject ignorance of subjects he knew better than most. He was also masterly at cloaking his opinions. All these patterns of behaviour were in stark contrast to my own. But his greatest quality, which they would admire most, was his total fearlessness.

His 'Greek meets Greek' charm would be a match for the wily Pathan. His patience would work wonders in the committee of the *shura*. The only risk we ran was one worth taking. We were now a team in danger of having one too many born leaders! At least we could afford to go in more than one direction at a time, if needs be.

[1] A Saudi charity

[2] A shipping term relating to charges made on goods that fail to clear a port area in a specific time - i.e. equivalent to storage charges.

[3] It was possible that the Pakistanis had changed the consignee's name on the documentation as part of their determination to control donations by channelling them through AIG which was their creation.

27
Dawn Raid

Our immediate task bore a close resemblance to an army G 1098 kit inspection. Our inventory was based on the bill of lading, but, in the US Government warehouse, none of us could remember when we had last been confronted with such a shambles. The nearest equivalent was the rag and bone merchants on the periphery of the old Peshawar market.

In the name of checking crates for contents, the 'Grazing and Shrinkage' searches had reduced 17 tons to 15 tons. We vainly attempted to marry contents with crate numbers and crate numbers with the bill of lading. For some reason, the storekeeper only spoke French, so we then had to think fast of the French word for any missing specific. Part of the mess suggested an outside job.

The only readily identifiable item was a 10-ton generator. It appeared intact. Next in size was a mobile field kitchen and a mobile field laundry; neither of which could be guaranteed further active service. The X-ray machine would survive for as long as the developer lasted. There was a serviceable operating table with lamps, which might, with luck, run off the generator.

The rest was a hotch-potch of second-hand junk. Some unserviceable stretcher beds with torn green canvas - the beds, metal, folding flat, had long vanished over the wall. There were miles of unravelled crepe bandage. Less familiar and useless were vast quantities of disposable rubber gloves which were rotting and sticking together in the intense heat. Equally disposable were untold quantities of syringes, enamel kidney dishes, and incongruous emery nail-files, strewn inconsequentially as far as the eye could see.

What the eye could not avoid was the most glaringly vulgar item of all - particularly in a Muslim context. It was a female foam rubber window-display model - pink, nude and highly malleable, a life size Barbie doll. The only explanation was that the patient was expected to indicate the affected part on the model. Any justification was only exceeded by the challenge of assessing how a $2 million price tag could have ever been put on this load of pharmaceutical and medical trash. My only solace in the whole proceeding was a close study of Peter Stewart-Richardson's total calm. No doubt he had witnessed far worse chaos in better-class homes.

We told the storekeeper, in my fluent French, that we would be back with a loading gang and transport first thing in the morning, and nothing else had better go missing between now and then. We then went to follow up the 'freight forwarding agents' enquiries we had instituted at AfghanAid.

Engineer Raz Mohammed, their transport manager, told us that he had thought through our request and that there was really only one operator who could undertake such a hazardous assignment. It had to be the brothers Rashid - Ebrahim and Khalid.[1]

Imagine our surprise and relief when, half-an-hour later, Michael Müller arrived at AfghanAid's offices with *Haji*[2] Ebrahim in tow. Nothing could have convinced us more of the wisdom of our choice, than that the German Afghanistan Committee should have independently found the same solution. It had to be the best of auguries.

Terms, which it seemed were no longer our concern, were agreed. We arranged to rendezvous back at the US warehouse at dawn the next day. Momentum would be maintained. Everything must be done to avoid any further Pakistani bureaucratic SNAFU (Situation Normal - All Fucked Up). All the paperwork was in order. The real administrators of the Royal Surrey County Hospital, Guildford must simply never know that for a whole twenty-four hours, they had had $2 million nominal worth of Cuban-American doctors' donation reject equipment on their books.

Although we expected to be the first on site in the morning, we were not. A twelve-man gang with two Bedford lorries was already hard at work.

They had with them block and tackle and a large wooden tripod, which was made of three stout telegraph poles lashed together at the apex. With this contraption, unchanged surely since the time of the Pyramids, and a lot of heaving and sweating and shouting and doubtless swearing, they managed to raise the ten-ton generator and lower it with some hesitation on to the back of the first lorry. They then piled everything that came to hand, higgledy-piggledy all round it, to obscure it from covetous eyes. They then stuck the female window-display cheekily astride the top.

By now, the temperature was climbing to the reputed 105 degrees - measured - in the shade. We busily pretended to marry off items on the lorries with items on the listings. We ticked and initialled the same officiously and pointlessly - stabbing the recycled bronco paper with our indelible pencil stubs. Any underlying hint of excitement on our part was that, here at last, was good reason for one of us at least to visit Chak, to establish that good delivery had been made and audit the same to the satisfaction of the donors. The Rashid brothers said they would arrange for a more comfortable conveyance for this purpose once the material was set up in situ. There could be no question, they asserted, of anybody travelling with the already overloaded Bedford van. Anyway, Michael Müller was already on board.

Peter Stewart-Richardson was the ideal choice for our follow-up. The sheer force of his personality prevailed. He had never missed any opportunity of meeting commanders back from their respective fronts - usually whilst visiting their wounded in hospital. He had the single-minded objective of making an extended trip inside and had set aside six extra weeks for this purpose. Undisclosed, he also had a hair-brained scheme all his own to persuade Afghans to bury the hatchet and take up full-time agriculture instead. The golden key to this pastoral idyll was some 'grass roots' irrigation scheme, to increase the overall fertile lands area. He already had a captive British organisation (British Executive Services Overseas) to sponsor travel and provide specialists and expertise - all free. His task was to find the appropriate microcosm. Whether the Afghans would then pile arms to assuage his complexes was another matter.

As the trucks drove out of the compound on their way to Chak, via Sadda and Taramangal, we could not help noticing that we had been joined by the quietest of all native Americans.

He had been squatting watching the proceedings from an obscure patch of shade by a pillar. He looked as if he had been innocently sketching the scene. He was readily identifiable as one of those Peace Corps American students, complete with pony-tail, sandals and jeans. He was as identifiable in his way as the German student at the German Afghanistan Committee warehouse had been in his.

The American had a visiting card which proclaimed him to be Michael A. Knowles of the Refugee Policy Group of Washington, whatever that was meant to mean - probably precisely what it said. Only appearances were deceptive.

We busied ourselves paying off the loading gang. The bill for all their labours, all morning, came to 400 rupees or £10. We added another 100 Rs for good measure, and because it cost so little, to make everybody happy.

We assumed that Mr Knowles had come along to see fair play, or to ensure that the US warehouse was left in the state in which one would like to find it. Perhaps he was expected to get it ready for whatever consignment was due next? What was more natural than to find an American in the US warehouse, for heaven's sake?

Half in jest, we invited him to come along to Chak for the ride. At this, his demeanour took on an altogether different, more serious cast. Gravely, he told us that he could accompany the consignment no further, and that Chak was most definitely off limits. So, we waved him a cheery goodbye and went on our way.

Why, I conjectured, should that be? Either the whole of Afghanistan was 'off limits' or not, but why the specific mention of Chak by name? Chak was in the Hekmatyar sphere of influence. The Americans had backed Hekmatyar unreservedly since 1974. It simply did not figure.

Then my imagination was suddenly racing. Was it possible that, for some reason, the Americans had issued a diktat that precluded them from any association with this 'German' effort? If so, why?

Had the CIA had too close a hand in the setting up of the German Afghanistan Committee? That would certainly make them windy of too close an identification with this cross-border German effort. Was such an establishment really in breach of the American-drafted post-WW2 German constitution? Was there any need to be quite so sensitive about what, after all, was only a strictly humanitarian activity? Or were the CIA funding GAC through their International Rescue Committee. Or, for that matter, Mr Knowles's Refugee Policy Group in Washington?

I then began to speculate madly on what, exactly was the 'German' involvement. Two memory chords struck simultaneously.

The first concerned a wandering Galandar Afghan student from the very early days of the war. He had been based, mostly for his studies, but also for the sake of his girlfriend, in Vienna. All alone, Nassim Jawad had managed to set up the Austrian Afghanistan Friendship and Co-operation Committee. AfghanAid had shared accommodation with him before moving into their own premises. Austrian funds had been cross-pollinated to pay for London surgery for wounded Mujahedeen. What was simpler than for the same formulae to have wider application? The question was, at whose instigation? Afghan, American or genuinely German?

The other chord of memory was the nagging recollection of a strange incident at a charity ball held at the Café Royal in London, organised by the Afghanistan Support Committee in 1983. The German Ambassador had attended and at some euphoric moment had seen fit to offer a grandiose sum - like $250,000 - towards the fund-raising. In the event, the money never materialised, which in turn suggested that some exclusively German operation of recent formation had enjoyed the re-allocation. But which?

Weeks later (long after "Scrubber" Stewart-Richardson's return to England) we learned that our lorry loads had reached their destination without incident. An independent, thoroughly reliable source confirmed there had, amazingly, been no ransom demands and no pay-offs. The combination of this remarkable intelligence, together with the veto preventing "Scrubber" travelling with the consignment, was unnerving. Frankly, it stank. It could only mean one thing. The Rashid brothers were habitually shipping in arms. And the back haul was more than likely to be heroin.

It was the only way the Rashids could guarantee safe passage for their vehicles. They had to be masterminding something much bigger, more significant than second-hand medical supplies. There was no other way they could sail past so many different commanders' checkpoints without loss or pay-off. Not long after this, the German Afghanistan Committee began to get a reputation for losing an inordinately high proportion of its vehicles inside Afghanistan.

Hand on heart we were able to advise Dr Veggeberg that good delivery of the Miami consignment, or what was left of it, had been made to Chak. There was no come-back on our high-handed behaviour from the Afghanistan Interim Government. If there had been, our response was to have been that other party interests had been served on a self-help basis, whilst the goods had been warehoused, and that precise records at the time had not been kept.

Kermit's response was to tell us that two more complete disaster hospitals had been packaged and a third acquired by Afghan Hospital Relief Inc., his side-show recently established with charity status. These had been located in the State of Mississippi. However AID/Afghanistan had sensibly ruled that no more packaged disaster hospitals were to be shipped to Peshawar until the first two were up and running. It was this same communication which confirmed the detail of Dr Mohammed Nabi Housaini's status 'He is a veterinarian, who is become (26 July 1989) an American citizen. He was to act as dispersal agent for the money on behalf of Afghan Hospital Relief. He would also act as the welcoming person and co-ordinator between hospitals and Orthopaedic Overseas volunteer surgeons.'

We advised Kermit that "Scrubber" would be visiting Chak in due course to follow through, and at the same time, to introduce our Anglo-American nursing candidate, Kate Straub, who was going to help out Karla Schefter, the resident theatre sister, for a few months.

At the first available opportunity, I made it my business to seek out Sir Oliver Forster at AfghanAid and tell him of my newly aroused but nevertheless grave misgivings about the German Afghanistan

Committee. In return, he gave me a particularly blank, poker-faced stare. He simply did not want to know. It was not his bailiwick. Masterly inactivity was to be the order of the day.

As if to emphasise his lack of concern, he asked if Peter or I knew of anybody going to Herat. This was the standard formula to see if we were thinking of going ourselves - like headhunters handing out a job description which exactly fits you!

Sir Oliver said he had first approached Nick Danziger, author of Danziger's Travels, who had been willing to act as a gold belt courier, but only on his terms, which were to travel via Iran. This was thought far too risky. By happenstance, Peter Stiles had recently treated a patient in Peshawar with a severely stiffened knee. Peter had counselled rest and the avoidance of too many stairs, almost as if the patient were a Guildford housewife. The patient had replied that Peter's advice was out of the question, as he was leaving the following morning to walk to Herat!

At the time of this meeting with Sir Oliver, AfghanAid's offices had been moved from the salubrious theatre, gallery and clubland circumstances of Charing Cross to the seedy nether reaches of the Pentonville Road, where they were to be located 'above a leather-goods and rubber-wear shop of kinky artefacts'. Somehow, it should have signalled a change of emphasis, a revised level of political interest. No doubt, the bells of St Martin-in-the-Fields would soon ring out for another, fresher, worthier cause.

[1] Ebrahim is the German spelling of Ibrahim for Abraham. He appears mostly in a DAK/GAC context so, Ebrahim.

[2] Denoting that he had made a pilgrimage to Mecca.

28

Russian Exodus - Victory Parade

There must have been many more concurrent factors at work, but four of them at least stood out. Whilst Mujaddidi may indeed be a common name to Afghan ears, two of that name had reached the highest office in the land: while Peter Stiles was busy massaging the knee of the Professor-cum-President of the Interim Government, now no longer in exile, Peter Stewart-Richardson was equally busy massaging the ego of his brother in London, where he had been appointed Afghanistan's Ambassador to the Court of St James's.

The third force at work was our old friend Dr Abdul Satar Paktiss. The fourth, far and away the most important, was the voluntary departure of the Russians and their cohorts (February 1989 - the last Russian tank re-crossed the Termes Bridge out of Afghanistan).

We had now reached that period of post-war reconstruction when Dr Paktiss would be able to put into practice all those useful lessons in administration that he had learned during his fourteen months course in the United States of America - whilst the war was raging.

In terms of the enigmatic ways of an Almighty Providence, what should be more surprising, however, than that on reaching Kabul, en route for Chak in October 1992, "Scrubber" Stewart-Richardson should run straight into not only a brace of Mujaddidis, but also Dr Paktiss, now very much to the fore in both the Ministries of Defence and Health - all together in time and space.

There was in fact a very good reason for these parties to be congregated at the Afghan National Liberation Front Headquarters in festive mood. They were simply getting ready to receive the President with a victory parade.

"Scrubber" found himself lionised by a very senior commander, already known to him, Azad Ullah Fallah. The triumphal entry was scheduled for the next day. In the meantime, "Scrubber" was covered in confusion and embarrassment. In typical Afghan fashion, he and his team, as 'visiting dignitaries', had been given the customary comfort of the best guest room. To the uninitiated this means warm water for washing, a constant supply of green tea and Russian sweets. "Scrubber" dreaded that all this luxury was really intended, if not for the Professor President himself, then surely for his brother the ambassador or, at least, some other aide. The only person he could trust to give a half-honest answer was Dr Abdul Satar Paktiss (now more simply known as Satar). Satar made it plain to "Scrubber" that, far from overstaying his welcome, he was being ordered to stay put. This was because there was renewed fighting reported from Maydan on the main route from Kabul to Chak. He would be told by Dr Najibullah Mujaddidi, the President's nephew, when it was safe to travel again and Commander Azad Ullah would provide a suitable escort.

The funny side to all this was that "Scrubber" had spent a lifetime putting up with privations and eschewing creature comforts. Now he was actually being ordered to indulge himself. The next day, 28 October 1992, he was taken off to witness the triumphal entry of Professor Mujaddidi into Kabul.

It was the nearest they would ever get to a victory parade. "Scrubber" found himself in the company of senior commanders and members of the provisional government: Suliman Yasir, Minister of Food; Fasil Karen, Mayor of Kabul. More disconcertingly, he found himself being driven along beside the President himself - like some Household Cavalry shield. The celebration was genuine enough, the welcome was ecstatic. The whole route from Pol-e-Charkhi to the presidential palace was lined with bystanders, chanting and firing off their AKs, machine-guns and even rockets, in support of the Professor.

"Scrubber" counted over five hundred vehicles, full of supporters, making up the motorcade. These thousands of people, including women, who had turned out to greet him, and the volume of firing from their weapons, was ample testimony to the popularity of this, the candidate of compromise. Such a quiet, self-effacing, unassuming university professor was now expected to keep the peace between the many diverse warring factions. The common enemy had been seen off, but with such massive arsenals left behind, the war was by no means over. There never was so uneasy a peace.

Indeed, by 7.30 a.m. the very next morning, whilst travelling on their approved route along the Qandahar Road via Maydan, Sheykhabad to Chak-e-Wardak, the euphoria of the big hello victory parade had turned into a tragic false dawn.

"Scrubber" and his team were halted at the first Hesbe-i-Islami road-block just short of Maydan and asked for identification. On presentation of their *laissez-passer*, they were taken off to the local commander's camp, where they wisely stopped their truck outside the gate. There was some heated conversation, which they did not catch between their guide (Engineer Langor) and the Hesbe-i-Mujahedeen.

Their pass was then ostentatiously torn up in front of them. Langor just had time to warn them that the Muj were contemplating 'dealing with them' so as to steal their vehicle. As "Scrubber" put it in his report, things became a little tense. At the Hesbe-i-Muj moment of hesitation, "Scrubber" told his team to 'mount' and they all returned safely to Kabul.

Grave concern was expressed all round by the doctors Mojaddidi and by Abdul Satar Paktiss. Both they and Commander Azah Ullah Fallah suffered considerable loss of face, and were forced to follow a new route plan to Sheykhabad via Pol-e-Elam. This time the Commander produced an escort of four hand-picked veterans.

By now, the situation in Kabul itself was also becoming 'a little tense'. The Prime Minister, Professor Rabbani, was arbitrarily planning to extend his period of office to two years. The only party leader not to be included in the Government, Engineer Gulbuddin Hekmatyar, was protesting his exclusion by blockading the city, to deny it both food and fuel. This was what "Scrubber" had encountered on the contra-flow at Maydan. Market prices were escalating and big trouble was forecast.

Fortunately, this time, Professor Mujaddidi was able to persuade Hekmatyar that such behaviour was not in his best long-term interests. On the other hand, he was less successful with Professor Rabbani, who succeeded in laying claim to two more illicit years, but all this achieved was a major re-alignment amongst the parties and yet more serious fighting. It didn't stop "Scrubber" and his team reaching Chak at the second attempt; but it was only now that they realised they had not seen a single other European during their Kabul stopover. When "Scrubber" asked fondly after the British Embassy, he was told that it was to be closed as an economy measure in favour of opening a more commercially viable alternative at Kiev. His highly characteristic comment was: 'Since when have members of Her Majesty's Foreign Service put personal safety before duty and the national interest?'

No wonder that famous verse:

So be it, Lord, thy throne shall never
Like Earth's proud empires pass away [1]

had so stuck in Curzon's craw that he always insisted on its omission whenever the hymn was sung in his presence.

*

Whatever the facts relating to Chak as a prohibited area for American Government employees, like Michael A. Knowles, or her citizens in general, it was plainly no inhibition to one half-American, half-English woman named Kate Straub. A highly trained and experienced nurse and midwife, she was an early Fellow of the Royal Geographical Society as well as being a Farsi speaker. She had originally written to Peter Stiles offering her services either to the German Afghanistan Committee (presumably in response to his suggestion) or to Ruth Coggan at Bannu. Her *curriculum vitae* mentioned that she had done sterling work for the HALO Trust at Kabul and Pul-i-Khumri (subsequently confirmed by Colonel Colin Mitchell). HALO is a registered British charity engaged in the business of mine and ordinance clearance and of mine awareness programmes.

Peter Stiles had no hesitation in recommending Kate Straub to Reinhard Erös and the German Afghanistan Committee. Peter Stewart-Richardson somehow arranged payment for Kate's airfare out. It was then only a simple matter for "Scrubber" to co-ordinate his visit to cover the three fields in which he now found himself engaged in Chak - namely, confirmation of the Miami doctor's donation in situ, the safe delivery of a highly qualified nurse and the search for a suitable microcosm to introduce 'his' British irrigation technology transfer.

Most European travellers in Afghanistan will attest that the climate, the food and the general health hazards can reduce a healthy man to a walking skeleton in two or three months. The two visiting German surgeons fell into this category, as had I. Curiously, perhaps, the women appeared more resilient and had greater survival reserves. They were also less emotional, and primarily concerned with life-giving forces - midwifery duties, i.e. aiding and giving life, as opposed to patching up and pathology, that is everything that is wrong with the patient. The women not only undertook longer stints, they managed without wasting away.

On arrival at Chak, Peter Stewart-Richardson would introduce Kate Straub to Karla Schefter, already firmly established as the resident theatre sister turned field co-ordinator *en poste*. At last we were able to identify a second full-time German representative at Chak.

Whatever else Reinhard was up to, however, it didn't take place at Chak. Karla averred he couldn't take the 'battle fatigue'. To me that didn't sound like a GSG9 man. Furthermore, the surgeons seemed to be at permanent loggerheads with their Field Director. It was even rumoured that he had been replaced. This was the norm I had been told to expect - a running battle between surgeons and their administrators. What we could not discover was the root cause. If rumour was to be believed, Reinhard Erös had been replaced by a certain Peter Schwittek. He had been a mathematics lecturer at Kabul University and I was sure I had seen him listed in a Berlin context. I couldn't be certain, but unlike Erös, whose background was medical, Schwittek's had been more to do with fund-raising.

There was nothing specific to put our fingers on. Perhaps if we had taken a closer look at the 'Deutsches Afghanistan Komiteee' handbook, which Reinhard Erös had given us, our suspicions would have been aroused sooner. DAK/GAC was so different to all the other non-government organisations we had come across. Maybe it was due to the quadripartite nature of the beast. Whilst the animal always seemed to be jogging along well, there appeared to be a total lack of co-ordination. What was missing in natural aggression, was made up for with sex over-drive. Nevertheless, it remained ungainly, since the left foreleg was never allowed to know what the right hindleg was up to.

We had learned never to expect a reply to any of our communications to Afghans, but it came as even more of a shock when our copious letters, reports and even Christmas cards remained unacknowledged by the German Afghanistan Committee's offices in Bonn. Then, a £64 box of Winston Churchill cigars sent by registered mail as a Christmas present for 'Lt. Col. Reinhard Erös, care of Herr Dietrich Kantel' failed to elicit a thank-you note, whilst a larger, if less extravagant, tin of Mackintosh's 'Quality Street', sent to Dentist/Doctor/Professor Iqbal at Peshawar, elicted the most prompt and charming of replies.

It seemed more and more probable that the Field Director in Peshawar was wholly innocent of whatever was happening, or not happening, in Bonn.

The organisation structure from the DAK/GAC handbook that had been pressed on to us showed that the Bonn office was manned by Dietrich Kantel and Denny Hundeshagen who, we learned, did not necessarily always share the same 'objectives' - although everything, including a much vaunted, increased secretariat, was subordinated to them.

The Bonn office in turn sired a Peshawar office, which we knew well. The confusion began with the wholly autonomous Rashid brothers' parallel office nearby at Circular Road, also in University

Town. This was operated independently in the name of being the only Non-Government Organisation allowed to be managed entirely by Afghans. The Germans had a long tradition of non-interference in Muslim countries, which the Kaiser had instituted - see *Greenmantle*[2] - and the German Afghanistan Committee were obviously keen to continue. The Rashid brothers then had their cross-border links with their own sister organisation in Jalalabad, inside Afghanistan proper.

Nobody doubted the professional integrity of the medical personnel engaged in the cause of supplying humanitarian aid to the Afghans. The rub seemed to lie between the Sadda and the Chak operations which owed allegiance to more than one master. Hence the surgeon-administrator strife.

However close individual relations became, they were invariably overshadowed by a feeling that there were 'background factors', secrets even, a suggestion of 'unknown' activities. There was no free exchange of personal confidences. The other party always had greater freedom of information to offer.

Of course everybody was extremely busy and, as often as not, the differences were then dismissed as some inherent character defect. But at other times, it went beyond that and appeared as if the German Afghanistan Committee personnel themselves had no clear idea of what was going on. It was as if a cellular structure had been purpose-made, so that the left-hand should never discover what the right hand was up to - a perfect formula in which to operate a hidden agenda.

Then we noticed that the casualty rate amongst Field Directors was on the increase. Sooner or later, one way or another, each and every one of them, through their differing methods and priorities fell foul of Bonn. Naturally, all this left the doctors and their wretched staff subject to additional stress and conflicts of loyalty.

Outsiders, mostly, limited themselves to sympathetic listening, recommending compassion and mercy at all times for small sinners; but the only problem with compassion is that you can get so bogged down that you miss the main point - especially if you find yourself, however unwittingly, on the threshold of a drugs-for-arms bazaar.

[1] J. Ellerton 1826-93

[2] John Buchan, author of *Greenmantle*, also wrote Nelson's weekly history of World War I and was well enough informed on German aspirations and policy to be employed officially by the Foreign Office. According to Buchan, the Kaiser at one stage contemplated embracing Islam to further the German war effort.

29

German Propaganda and Disinformation - A Prospectus for Potemkin Hospitals.

The next thing we heard was that the German Red Cross had, uncompromisingly and unequivocally, labelled the German Afghanistan Committee as arms dealers.

Then somebody remembered an article that had appeared in *Der Spiegel* Nr 44 for September 1988, the full text of which is reprinted here as an Appendix, which blew the whistle with an opening gambit which highlighted the strange 'it's all done with smoke and mirrors' constitution of the German Afghanistan Committee itself. The subject was so complex, involving tightly held family foundations in Liechtenstein, that it passed over most people's heads; and the excitement died away just as quickly as it had flared up. *Der Spiegel* was relying on Kantel and Hundeshagen to bring an action against them. This they had no need to do so long as the gravy train lasted.

Somewhat oblivious to all this, from "Scrubber"'s point of view, the prime objective of his visit, with so many experts in tow, was to assess the viability of a dam. As well as a visiting hydrologist, there was competent assistance on the ground in the person of Engineer Langor, a trained surveyor, and Engineer Mujtata, an irrigation engineer.

On arrival at Chak, "Scrubber" first sought out Karla Schefter at the 'hospital' and introduced Kate to her. He also handed over some standard gifts from us all - mostly Nescafé and Tetley's teabags. Once he had satisfied himself that the generator was in working order and that the operating theatre equipment had been adequately installed, he felt free to pursue his other interests. He assured the ladies that he would return before nightfall. "Scrubber" then went up the mountain alone to pinpoint the site and earmark the hundred hectares he suspected would best benefit from the dam.

A dawn start was scheduled for the next day. Assistants, tools and equipment would be ready. After a wash, prayers and a light breakfast, the whole team set off up the mountain, picking up more helpers along the way.

Commander Saddiq told them of two prohibited 'off limits' areas. The first was the leat catchment area for the hydro-electric scheme. Presumably the water and valuable silt would be removed from this area for agricultural purposes, although the reason they were given was that there was a security risk in that they might be mistaken for Russians! The other spot was the old British fort, where the garrison had been massacred to a man, as at Maiwand.[1] In this case, "Scrubber" suspected that it could well be the Mujahedeen arsenal.

After making his preliminary geological survey, the hydrologist had sent a party to dig a pit to check the water table. Sometime before, it had been noticed that water was flowing below the site, but not above ground on the site of the proposed dam.

Later they all walked back to Chak together and planned what they were going to say at the *shora* of village elders - meeting later that evening. They really needed more facts about the method of farming, crops, and also population statistics, before going firm on any decisions.

One of the three big Siemens hydro-electric generators, dating from 1938, was still working. The maintenance engineer had been paid by the Kabul regime throughout the war with the connivance of the *shora*. The point was also made that, although anybody could take a three-hour bus ride to a hospital in Kabul, most of the locals preferred to come to their own cottage hospital at Chak. They would also travel all the way to Peshawar if it was a serious matter, in preference to going to a Kabul hospital.

That evening, when "Scrubber" outlined his objectives to the *shora*, he felt it necessary to make an initial statement, which was translated as he went along by Engineer Langor:

"Scrubber" and his team supported no particular political party, but simply wished to help in the post-war reconstruction of Afghanistan, in whatever way they could.

The hydrologist would survey the proposed dam site in detail and an alternative weir site in case the dam site should prove geologically unsuitable. Whichever solution was adopted would irrigate the same 100 hectares to assist the three villages of Rashidan, Samakhat and Maddoo.

The decision as to which solution would proceed, would rest solely with Afghan Engineers, whose advice would be accepted and whose decision would be final.

Provided the £25,000 could be raised, work would begin immediately after the rains in 1993.

After seeing how behind-hand the hospital works were, further assistance would also be forthcoming there. General approval was then expressed.

As nothing could be achieved on this trip, it was decided to head back to Kabul, this time via the Khawak Dam. "Scrubber" had a letter of introduction to a Dr Mohammed Jaffar, who kindly supplied hot water, a most welcome hot meal and equally warm blankets, as it was very cold up in the mountains.

After visiting the dam the next morning, they drove to the Afghanistan National Liberation Front Headquarters in Logar. Here they were able to check out the security situation in Kabul on the radio telephone. A request to continue their journey was approved.

They reached Kabul late the same afternoon and reported back directly to Dr Najibullah Mujaddidi, who again arranged through Commander Azad Ullah Fallah to organise their Pakistani entrance visas and safe conduct to the border.

*

What we had learned from this trip was that, whereas there was no denying that the German Afghanistan Committee's 'business plan' looked fine and dandy on paper, where it related to Chak as opposed to Sadda, the reality on the ground bore little resemblance to the fiction of the Handbook. No wonder they were keen to discourage visitors. After three-and-a-half years the place wasn't half-built. They hadn't even got the excuse that it had been bombed.

It was time to take another, closer look at the 'Deutsches Afghanistan Komitee' Manual. Our initial reaction had been to wonder why they had indulged in such elaborate coffee-table puffery in the first place. The next surprise was that everything after the title page was published in English. So, it was not an ego massage, nor can it have been intended exclusively for us. On the other hand, it could have been meant for general distribution to the legions of other Non-Governmental Organisations and, of course, the media. A lot of painstaking trouble had been taken to get the public relations right. The lasting impression was one of self-aggrandisement stemming from somewhat extravagant claims.

DAK/GAC was stated to be a non-profit-making organisation constituted on 28 February 1984, to comply with current tax laws (which meant donations were tax deductible).

As to funding, it was said that 'in the beginning DAK/GAC was largely dependent on small donors subscribing as little as DM10 to DM100. Many of these people were pensioners, who, because of memories of their own impoverishment, following the Second World War, felt sympathy for the Afghan people in their plight.'

However, we soon move on to the big picture. What now follows in the remainder of this pivotal chapter is a series of quotations from the DAK/GAC Handbook with my annotations, pointing out, mixed in with plausible-sounding half-truths, the more flagrant inconsistencies, propaganda and misinformation which they were peddling:

'In 1986 and 1987 the Committee received grants from the ministries of development aid of the Federal Republic of Germany and of the United States of America. The far greater part came from the American development authorities. Without this generous support, humanitarian aid in the present dimensions would not be possible. The binding commitment of funds from public authorities is important, because structures can then be set up which allow for continuity in relief work. While private contributions fluctuate greatly, pledged public funds allow fundamental planning to be worked out and continuity to be guaranteed at a minimum level. Government grants are as a rule, however, earmarked for particular projects. The European Parliament has begun to support humanitarian assistance inside Afghanistan.

'The work of the Deutsches Afghanistan Komitee has led in recent years to a great number of new contacts with other relief organisations in the German Federal Republic and Europe. Today the Committee receives support from numerous private organisations in Germany and Europe. Apart from relief organisations which confine their work to Afghanistan, those with other objectives have also undertaken in recent years to make funds and material means available for the work of the Committee. At present the Deutsches Afghanistan Komitee works together nationally and internationally with about 50 other relief organisations. Most important in this aspect are groups from Switzerland, Holland and Denmark.

'The work of the German Afghanistan Committee can be divided into four areas:

I. Medical Projects

The medical projects form the heart of the work of the German Afghanistan Committee in Afghanistan. They take up the major share both financially and organizationally. This project area includes the operation of most of the outlying stations and medical projects within Afghanistan.'

Six pages earlier these are summarised as follows:

'A logistically independent network of 13 medical stations with several secondary stations established inside Afghanistan. 16 Afghan physicians and 63 paramedics worked in these stations throughout 1986. 10 European physicians and 2 nurses supported them with a total of 7 engagements of the Mobile Units. At the same time, the training of Afghans as paramedics was begun.
    'II. Resettlement/Reconstruction
    This area is sub-divided into "Resettlement of Afghan Refugees" and "Reconstruction and Refugee Assistance". While the resettlement program was already initiated in 1986, reconstruction and refugee assistance are just beginning. The areas: I. "Medical Projects" and II. "Resettlement/ Reconstruction" are under the supervision of Mr Ebrahim Rashid and Mr Khalid Rashid.'

Again six pages earlier a summary states:

'In the Baghlan Province in Northern Afghanistan a 20-days trip from the Pakistani border, a pilot project for the resettlement of Afghani refugees was begun (again in 1986).
    'In 1987 a total of 9 European physicians and 2 nurses were sent to Afghanistan. They visited even the northernmost of the Committee's medical stations, in Talabafak.[2] The medical training project in Sadda and the resettlement project in Northern Afghanistan were expanded and improved.
    'In Northern Afghanistan 5,000 people were supplied with necessities. By the end of 1987, 20 Afghan physicians and over 60 paramedics were employed.
    'In 1988 the resettlement project in Northern Afghanistan will be expanded and similar projects will be prepared according to this prototype in selected areas of Afghanistan.'

The only problem with this open-ended contract was that the areas selected for humanitarian aid and the resettlement of internal refugees, which were variously estimated at the time to be around two million, was that they appeared to be in precisely those areas that were hardest to check out on the ground. Whereas this proposition might be easy enough to swallow in Washington, those with less superficial knowledge might prove less gullible.

    'III. Engagement of Europeans
    The areas: "The Engagement of Europeans" and IV. "Individual Projects" are under the control of the German management in Pakistan, which is at the present led by Dr Erös.
    'IV Individual Projects

This area encompasses temporally *(sic)* and financially isolated individual projects. These projects are under the direction of individual representatives. The general direction and supervision is as a rule under the control of the German office in Pakistan. The planning team which is a part of this area is an exception here. It is directly subject to the Board of Directors in Bonn and will assist the office in Bonn in the development of future concepts.'

There then follows the exception to prove the rule.

'Since the German Humanitarian Service in Quetta is geographically as well as organizationally independent, it is subject with respect to project planning to the Board of Directors of the foundation "Hilfe in Not" (Help in Need). This planning is co-ordinated with GAC/DAK. The financial control is under the jurisdiction of the Deutsches Afghanistan Komitee.

'I. Medical Projects

'Execution and control are the responsibility of a German staff member who has spent several years in Afghanistan. The headquarters are located in the Pakistani city of Quetta.

'II. Resettlement/Reconstuction

'In practice the work of the German Humanitarian Service is not separated into distinct areas. A resettlement project does not yet exist, but is in the planning phase. The medical stations operated by the German Humanitarian Service are also centres for food and clothing assistance to the regions in question.

'The Organisation of the German Afghanistan Committee:

The essential difference between the German Afghanistan Committee and other relief organisations is the co-responsibility of the Afghan staff members and advisors. A large part of the engagement planning organisation is implemented through Afghan staff members and with Afghan responsibility. Since the Afghan population reacts sensitively to promises which are not kept, the Afghan director (Ebrahim Rashid) has placed great emphasis on the importance of building stations only in areas for which the Committee can guarantee continuous and solid medical care. In addition, no clan, province, or party dominates among the Afghan staff. This geographic, ethnic, and political diversity is offered by no other relief organisation.

'Many times during the past years, the German Afghanistan Committee has had to be reorganised in order to keep pace with the unexpectedly rapid expansion of its supply network. In less than three years the Committee has become the most active among the western relief organisations in Afghanistan. At the same time as the medical care network was expanding, there successively came into being further relief projects of greater range and dimension, for example the paramedic training centre in Sadda and the resettlement project in Baghlan.

'While in 1986 most of the stations in Afghanistan were still supplied directly from Peshawar, in the course of the past year (1987) the supply system has been decentralised. The German Afghanistan Committee has four branch offices along the Afghan/Pakistan border in "tribal areas": Wana, Bajaur, Miram Shah, and Sadda. Most of the deliveries of medical and support materials into Afghanistan, as well as the engagement of European and Afghan staff, take place through the appropriate Pakistani branch office. For instance, the medical training school at Sadda "serves as the base for medicine transports into the Nangahar Province, and it is also from here that the 'Mobile Units' set out."

'While Wana lies within the borders of Pakistan in the "tribal areas", Chak and Buzdara are located far into Afghanistan. They likewise have central importance in the supply to the stations. It is possible to drive from Wana to Chak with a motor vehicle. From Chak the northern clinics can be supplied either by motor vehicle or by pack animal. From Buzdara on, the supply to clinics located further north is only possible by pack animal.

'Medical Projects - Administration

Measured by its expenditures, the German Afghanistan Committee is by western standards an organisation of medium size. With more than 300 employees in Pakistan and Afghanistan, however, the Committee is a major employer. The great number of projects and the many staff members require a considerable amount of administration, in order to maintain the seriousness of the Committee and control over the organisation. Thus the area of "Medical Projects" alone requires three accountants, time-keeping, and accounting of expenditures and income. The rendering of accounts by the Afghan management has achieved a high standard.

'Technical Directions

The motor vehicles require constant repairs, due to the high demands made on the vehicles. The Committee has therefore operated for about one year its own small motor vehicle workshop.

'In 1985 the German Afghanistan Committee put together its own construction team. In the course of the past three years it has been able to construct caves and tunnels which serve as storage spaces and shelters. The team has erected new buildings and has built bridges and streets. In 1987, for example, a cave was excavated in Talabafak with an inner space of 2x3x12 meters. In the same year the team erected in this region a new building for a medical station. In the Baghlan province a 3-kilometer long street was blasted free so that the path which could formerly be negotiated only with horses could now be driven by a motor vehicle. In 1988 the construction teams will be occupied primarily with the further expansion or new building of the medical stations Roy Doab, Chilamjoy, Chak, and Buzdara.'

There then follows a detailed analysis of some seventeen or more main and many more secondary medical stations. Chak and Sadda are singled out as qualifying for model or near model clinic status. From comments made on various pages, it can be deduced that this Handbook was published in either March or April 1988. At the end of the Table of Contents mention is made that the missing chapters on 'Reconstruction/Resettlement' and 'German Humanitarian Service' will appear in the new edition in May 1988.

One of the more surprising aspects of the publication is the frequent mention of retaliatory Russian or Kabul Regime action, once the DAK/GAC presence was known. It, therefore, seems strange to give away so many fixed clinic locations in a public document. The Mobile Units made eminent sense. There were other interesting insights:

'Activities within Afghanistan were seen from the West German point of view as intervention in that nation's internal affairs. In the media the Committee was often stamped with the stigma of a para-military organization.' This was despite the disclaimer on page one that the DAK/GAC operated inside Afghanistan, 'in accordance with the resolution adopted by the German Bundestag [Parliament].'

As long ago as a European Aid Groups Co-ordination meeting held in Geneva on 24-26 February 1984, there was a minuted reference to a restrictive clause in the German constitution. The matter had been raised by a certain Mr Kakojan Niazi in open forum, and what he had to say about the passive nature of the German constitution appeared to be well-informed, as well as expressing his personal disappointment.We shall hear more of him later.

'Germany was officially restricted to extending aid to Afghan refugees only'. The implication of the minute was that any move across the border 'could be deemed a belligerent act against the USSR, as well as being in contravention of the said passive constitution'.

Mr Niazi went on to say that 'the German Government was bound to officially deny and disown anything done inside Afghanistan, and that anything he said was, of course, said in confidence.' All of which only served to confirm his involvement in some German activity inside Afghanistan. His passion for mystery and intrigue, plus his remarkable name, suggested he was an Afghan.

Of course, it could always have been argued that Afghanistan had over two million internal refugees - the very ones that the DAK/

GAC were proposing to re-settle in Barfak, Talabafak and Baghlan!

It was at this same conference in Geneva that a British observer (described as being ex-Foreign and Commonwealth Office) made another telling point: 'The main profiteers from this war are those who own camels. Indeed, the high cost of transport would mitigate the purchase of vehicles - especially since the bombing of villages has lengthened the links in the support chain, with serais now anything up to 25 miles or more apart.'

The Handbook continued:

'The Pakistani authorities were also apprehensive of the Committee's cross-border efforts and requested the Committee to restrict its work to the assistance of refugees. After early discussions with the seven major Afghan political parties, it transpired that they were equally distrustful of the Committee's intentions.'

As was usual, the Pakistanis pressurised the parties to exercise control, so that they in turn could continue to manipulate the puppet show, whilst turning a blind eye to the predations of the politicians. 'When repeatedly urged to make financial means at its disposal available to the parties and leave relief within the country to them,' DAK/GAC not surprisingly in the circumstances of losing control, referred to the local commanders active inside Afghanistan, who happily 'held the contrary view and were dismissive of the relevance of the political parties in exile. Indeed they often declared themselves to be in favour of one or other of the parties in exile, merely out of formal and materialistic motives! The parties should only be accorded limited importance in future, and that they themselves would afford all possible support to the Committee's work.'

DAK/GAC were quick to realise that there was little hope of working inside Afghanistan without the co-operation of local commanders, so they opted for that route early on to 'avoid the road to ruin whereby support of the exile parties would have plunged the Committee into major economic and political dependencies.'

They may well have been amongst the first to recognise where the true power base now lay.

Elsewhere there is a balancing rider which states that inside Afghanistan 'one finds a collaboration between parties which would be unthinkable in Pakistan.' Inter-party rivalry is replaced by commanders vying to adopt model clinics to enhance their local standing. Relief in these conditions soon ceases to reflect actual need. But this situation is thought to be preferable to that of 'most other relief organisations who find themselves bound up with the political parties, playing a role in their conflicts.' However, it is admitted that: 'During the years, concessions have had to be made time and again in order to reach at least a tolerance of the Committee's work.'

'The Engagement of Europeans

'Since Europeans within Afghanistan are subjected to a great deal of strain and stress, which often taxes them to the limits of their mental and physical capabilities, only well-educated, experienced physicians with stable personalities can be engaged. In Afghanistan, they are seen as representatives of the German Afghanistan Committee and therefore contribute substantially to the reputation of the organisation. It is in part thanks to their efforts that the civilian population of Afghanistan is convinced of the exclusively humanitarian objectives of the Deutsches Afghanistan Komitee and thus supports its work. The European physicians assigned in Afghanistan have, with their testimony, contributed considerably to changing the European opinion of events in Afghanistan.

'The German Project Director is in charge of all European personnel. He introduces them to their duties and prepares the engagements of the "Mobile Units" in co-operation with the Afghan administration.

'Although all medical personnel are selected and prepared for their engagements in Germany, the German Project Director is responsible for making the final decision about the capabilities of the European staff members. Before their actual engagement in Afghanistan, the new staff members first work in the projects of the German Afghanistan Committee in Pakistan, in the "tribal areas". There they can acclimatize themselves and become familiar with the culture of the foreign country, and contemplate their decision one last time.'

This is probably the best of all their ideas, since it works both ways, for the Afghan paramedics whilst training and for the European doctors before going cross-border.

'Mobile Units

'A Mobile Unit consists of 1 or 2 European physicians and German nurses. The team is accompanied by Afghan personnel: a knowledgeable guide, an interpreter, and transportation personnel. The main task of the Mobile Units is the treatment of patients in the villages which lie between the various stations of the DAK/GAC, and therefore have no permanent medical care. Since the supply network of the Committee has become so extended that there is a maximum of a 2-days' trip between the individual stations, the team members of the Mobile Units now often remain for several weeks in a single supply area.

Thanks to the substantially improved transport possibilities, the Mobile Units can now bring with them enough support materials and medicines for longer engagements. Distant journeys within Afghanistan are still covered as before by night, to reduce the dangers to Europeans to a minimum. The European staff work in parallel with the Afghan physicians and paramedics and help to acquaint them with modern treatment methods.'

The Handbook mentions the following European doctors by name: Dr K.V. Freigang, Dr Reinhard Erös, Dr L. Bernd, Dr F. Paulin, Dr Schatzmann, Dr Schuster, Dr Müller, Dr Werner, Dr Dennhardt, Dr Röckly, Dr O. Joch. Mention is also made of a Frau Maria Müller, a surgical nurse with considerable experience in Vietnam, Peru, and Bangladesh. Only three Afghan doctors are named: Dr Nawaz, Dr Anwarzai and Dr Zalmei. A female dentist, Dr Czierny, was also co-opted via Medical Refresher Courses for Afghans to train up people in dentistry.

Resettlement Project - Talabafak

'The resettlement project of the German Afghanistan Committee (we are told) is located in this region. The Main Clinic in Barfak is responsible for the medical care of the people who were resettled here. Water is abundantly available in this valley even during the dry season. The security is very high. Transport routes are difficult. In 1986 the clinic was installed in a permanent building. Unfortunately, this proved too attractive to the local commander who requisitioned it for his own personal use. A new hospital was then built, which was so unfavourably sited on a hillside that it fell victim to a rock avalanche in the following winter. A new project is planned for next year. In the meantime, our clinic is housed in the old (1984) Barfak village premises.'

If all this was not unfortunate enough, there then follows news of fairly continuous attack and counter-attack between several small secondary commanders, with intervention of Kabul-backed forces 'who succeed in temporarily conquering half the valley of Talabafak. It is to be feared that the military activities of the rival clans will continue into 1988.' No doubt increasing the already high patient frequency in the Main Station in Barfak which from the description that follows sounds inadequate:

'At the moment no in-patients are accepted here. The hospital consists of two rooms. The Europeans are accommodated in tents or mud huts.'

This is not an encouraging picture. It seems irresponsible for a supposedly primarily medical charity to have made such scant medical provision for a major resettlement programme said to embrace 3,000 souls. It certainly fails to match the promise made elsewhere in the document about 'guaranteed continuous and solid medical care'.

However, buried in the text there is a throwaway line that might provide enlightenment at some future date: 'A Cash for Food project of the French organization "Afrane" is located here.'

One other report caught my eye for its authentic nature. It related to a Main Station in Kunar Province at Shah-i-Lam. The supply position of this clinic is described as

'the most strained of all areas in Kunar. Nevertheless, it often has in-patients, who come from far-flung parts of the region. However, there are major problems with the Mujahedeen here, who up to 1986 had undertaken no military activities and often distracted themselves in their boredom by hampering the German doctor at his work. An expansion is therefore not necessary!'

Individual Projects - Media Work

As with the American medical units, with which we came into contact, there appears, these days, to be as much emphasis placed on making a video film of what is being done as on what is being done in the first place: whether it be extracting a bullet from a patient's leg, or erecting a US Packaged Disaster Hospital in Mississippi to show them how to do it in Logar. The German Mobile Units were nearly all issued with 8mm video camera equipment, and the German Afghanistan Committee is nothing if not highly sophisticated where the matter of media manipulation is concerned, *ab initio*. Key medical personnel were trained in camera use to ensure proper media coverage of their efforts.

As the Manual puts it:

'The withdrawal of the Soviets from Afghanistan (in February 1989) can be attributed to many motivations. An important role has been played by the criticism on the part of the western public of the invasion of the USSR. Yearly UNO *(sic)* resolutions have condemned with unusual unanimity the offences against human rights and international law committed by the USSR in Afghanistan. Economic sanctions and political isolation of the USSR can in large part be traced to this public pressure. While in 1979 and 1980 the subject of Afghanistan played an important role in the media, the flow of news diminished considerably in the following years. Only after European physicians and journalists had repeatedly reported as eye-witnesses on the events in Afghanistan, was more public attention given to the subject of Afghanistan. From 1984 on, more and more independent reporters ventured into Afghanistan and could present films and photographs to the public. In the same year there came into being through the initiative of many different organisations media projects with the objective of training Mujahedeen as photographers and journalists. The Deutsches Afghanistan Komitee has equipped its German physicians with photography and film equipment. Thus was produced in 1985 one of the first films, shot with a Super 8mm camera. The transmission of this film by "Erstes Deutsches Fernsehen" (a television station) in Germany led to a massive protest by the Soviet Union. The Soviets denounced the German nurse who had made the film as a CIA agent and characterized the reports as lies. By the end of 1985 almost every Mobile Unit was equipped with a video camera.'

As a final note, it must be acknowledged that whatever the underlying facts of the matter, there is no doubting that the German Afghanistan Committee not only had the full endorsement of the Foreign Ministry of the German Federal Republic, but (as set out in The Handbook), also managed to obtain the permission of the Pakistani Government to establish no fewer than four operations within the tribal areas, a state of affairs seldom, if ever, achieved by a private relief organisation.

By August 1989, either because there were no prestige Handbooks published, or because Dr Reinhard Erös had none to spare, a three-page handout was issued instead. It was entitled:

'The achievements of the German Afghanistan Committee.'

Most of the claims remained much the same, but expressed more briefly. There were however a number of interesting improvements and variations.

The number of employees had gone up to 350. There were now said to be 14 clinics in 9 provinces of Afghanistan. (Potemkin Hospitals indeed!)

'In May 1989 the GAC established a 20-bed hospital in Chak, Wardak Province, including X-ray and laboratory. 4 German and Swiss medical specialists and nurses are providing special health care to a population of about 60,000 people. These specialists are assisted by 8 Afghan physicians, nurses and dispensers.

'The clinics receive approximately 55 metric tonnes of medicine per year, delivered by their own transport fleet of three trucks and pick-ups, 35 horses and mules.

'Besides the permanent staff of Afghan physicians and nurses, the GAC medical facilities are monitored at least twice a year by 10-15 (ten-fifteen) German and Swiss MDs and nurses.

'In the Medical Training Centre at Sadda, GAC physicians are training about 40 young Afghans as health workers per year. After graduation these young health workers will be hired by GAC to complement its cross-border medical staff.

'German and Swiss physicians and nurses, working for GAC cross-border, have enlightened the public in Europe and overseas on the misery and needs of the Afghan nation through more than 1,000 lectures, interviews and talkshows.

'Once a year the general assembly of the German Afghanistan Committee determines the line items for the current year. The assembly chooses its president and board of directors. Annually an independent trust-company verifies the accounts of the GAC.

'The board of directors, as the management in charge, resides in Bonn (full address, fax, telephone and telex) and is responsible for all projects in Pakistan and Afghanistan. In Bonn the objectives of the GAC are determined and the contacts with donors are established and preserved.'

Among the five items planned for 1990, the first concerns the 'opening of a new clinic in Achin/Nangarhar *(sic)*. A joint project with AfghanAid, UK', and the fifth, 'the establishment of a Medical Training Centre for nurses in the district-hospital of Chak-Wardak *(sic)*.' *Signed* Dr. Med. Reinhard Erös, Medical Director

As to the statement that 'a new clinic in Achin, Nangahar is to be opened in collaboration with AfghanAid, UK,' there had been an earlier observation that this project 'may provide a suitable opportunity to pioneer co-operation in setting up health clinics and hospitals throughout Afghanistan.' Shamefully, we had never registered the significance of this item, possibly not even read thus far, when originally handed these papers. Could this joint venture have occasioned Sir Oliver Forster's glazed, indifferent appearance at the mention of DAK/GAC's name at the time of the disclosure of my earlier, intuitive misgivings?

But far more significant than all that, for some reason Dr Erös's latest handbill made no further mention whatsoever of the Refugee Resettlement Programmes, which had been such a feature of the earlier Handbook not eighteen months previously. So much for 'the continuity in relief work guaranteed by the binding commitment of public funds!'

Chak had always been lauded as the staging post, with 'central importance' for all the other clinics 'further north', both extant and to come. But now, in the light of our recent discoveries, and more attentive reading of the Handbook and its addenda, there were serious and growing grounds for apprehension on anybody's part. The German Afghanistan Committee was apparently claiming the existence of a whole network of front line medical facilities, and generating charitable funds on this basis, when, in truth, such hospitals existed only on paper.

[1] Battle of Maiwand 1880 (2nd Afghan War). The British force was completely destroyed in the biggest defeat ever suffered in Asia - until the Fall of Singapore. There were nearly 1,000 casualties under General Burrows. Maiwand is to the west of Qandahar. Dr Watson was reported to have witnessed the battle shortly before meeting Holmes!

[2] in Baghlan.

30

The Odyssey of Brigadier General Peter Stewart-Richardson and the Diatribe of Engineer Gulbuddin Hekmatyar.

Up to this point we had begun with a rose-coloured spectacles vision of the German enterprise. We were full of admiration for their incomparable wealth and powers of organisation, dog-like devotion and determination to get through and deliver. We had never thought to stop and count the cost.

Now, thanks to our first visit to Chak and the insights revealed by their Handbook, or Induction Manual, we had some idea of the nature of their self-esteem - whoever 'they' were. Now it was time to try and discover who these people really were and what they were up to.

Thank God for fearless men like "Scrubber" Stewart-Richardson. Although it turned out he was not much better than I was at the paperwork, he had other sterling qualities. As part of my original briefing, I had shown him photocopies of every report we had ever written. Not that there were that many. However, there must have been one or two too many, because on his very next key trip to Chak, when he came face to face with Pir Mohammed - the Security-in-Charge at Barakhail checkpoint - he failed to recognise him from the written word. Incredibly, Pir Mohammed was still there in 1992, three-and-a-half years after our encounter. It had made little difference, because the driver was familiar with all the problems of tribal areas' passes. He simply detoured up the Kurrum Agency route, with "Scrubber" either 'sick or asleep' under a blanket, and so they had reached the sanctuary of Sadda.

Sadda is roughly 150 kms west-south-west of Peshawar. Chak-e-Wardak is high in the Hazarajat, some 80 kms west of Kabul (or as little as 30 kms, as the crow flies!). The best approach depends on daily reports of rival Mujahedeen activity along any particular route. In theory, Chak should be reached from Peshawar, via Ghazni in two or, at most, three days. As ever, there was a shorter, quicker route via Sheykhabad, but the short cut was more dangerous.

But this time, for other reasons, "Scrubber" was proposing to go an even longer way round, as there was some chance of seeing Khost - from the other end of the gun barrel, as it were. Also, if possible, he wanted to learn if anything remained of the former German hospital at Khost. The investment of an extra day's journeying was more with an eye to general overview, than with any preoccupation with personal safety. As ever, there was a missing essential ingredient - suitable mechanical transport from Sadda onwards. There still was not a single vehicle in the Sadda Mechanical Transport compound that could be classified as roadworthy. It was as if the only permitted umbilical cord was still the weekly 'flying bus' to Peshawar.

This was familiar ground. There was no doubting that fortunes were being made by Afghans as they moved in on the transport business in Pakistan. What the Rashid Brothers were making out of their intra-Afghanistan transport system could only be a matter for conjecture. Settlement would be in hard 'hash'.

Just as "Scrubber" and Co were contemplating giving up on the Khost excursion and settling for the half-starved Afghan ponies, which only responded to Afghan treatment - severe whacks with a lead-lined whip on snout or tail - what should arrive but a Toyota Hi-lux 4x4 double-cab pick-up replete with driver Karmal and guide Abdul Haq, under the grinning wing of *Haji* Ebrahim Rashid himself. Mr Fix-it was not going to take any chances with such a golden egg-layer. Any unwarranted delay waiting for the vehicle, guide and driver should be put down to allowing for acclimatisation at Sadda, thus perpetuating the renowned Sadda role!

Shaiq conducted the most cursory of inspections. One team member got sent back to change. He was sporting the same flak jacket that Sandy Gall usually wore, but was unlikely to be able to live up to it. It was too 'smart'. It was in a faded tan colour with conspicuous stainless steel 'D' rings for grenades and things, until you noticed that where American servicemen disclose their name and rank, Sandy's had a designer label for 'Hardy's of St James's' - a good enough pseudonym for Sandy, but Shaiq had decided that for anyone else it was altogether too showy. These waistcoats could contain and conceal everything a boy scout could possibly need and some more. They made ideal gardening, as well as fishing, wear. A string of wooden or red-as-rubies plastic worry beads would give a touch of added refinement or provide distraction at checkpoints.

It was strange to realise how, as the limited Sadda ablutions were denied, everyone would come to savour that Hieronymus Bosch boghole vision of hell, which all of us had variously squatted over daily.

After servicing body and mind, the next responsibility was to give the vehicle as thorough a going-over as might be expedient in

Haji Ebrahim Rashid's presence. It seemed to have just the right battered look, just beaten-up enough to avoid attracting unwelcome covetous eyes. The main dilemma was always the degree of tyre baldness to offer to these gods of chance. Any vehicle going inside had improved odds if presenting a generally clapped-out exterior. Much the same could be said for European personnel.

For once, the vehicle looked up to what was known of the terrain to be tackled. The driver came highly recommended, even if he was unlikely to be up to AfghanAid ambulance driver standards. The vehicle's capacity was for up to five passengers plus driver, riding three abreast inside. There was room for 'untold numbers' outside, as for the Tribal Levy imposed on us by Pir Mohammed, Security-in-Charge. Otherwise large quantities of grain, gear or cement could be stowed under a canopy, which would be lashed down for added security.

After crossing the border at Taramangal the road rapidly disintegrated. After Pakistani roads, Afghan roads defy description. Most of them had collapsed and become rutted from the sheer weight of 50-ton Russian tanks and their transporters. Small kids, armed with besom brooms, scurried around the larger craters, refilling them with maximum self-importance, in expectation of tiny charitable offerings.

Usually the going was better along the newly formed dirt track on either side, even though that option was said to increase the risk of mines.

The first objective was the much disputed airfield at Khost, which was found to be littered with the wrecks of Andropov transport planes and not a few helicopters. Likewise, on entering Khost proper, any number of wrecked armoured vehicles were to be seen. Some were being used as makeshift checkpoints at crossroads and a surprising number still had machine-guns fitted on their turrets. Yet others had that symbol of a pair of ever-open eyes[1] displayed on each mudguard; once the proud prerequisite of the Guards Armoured Division in World War II.

In the failing evening light, files of heavily armed Hesbe-i-Islami irregulars were moving through the streets to take up their guard positions for the night. The approaching darkness had helpfully cloaked "Scrubber"'s party's arrival. But not quite, as a local commander had been sent over to learn the *faranghi*'s purpose. This was when the presence of linguists once again saved the day. Satisfied, the commander left the team in peace to familiarise themselves with the facilities of the supposed 'safe house' overnight accommodation.

However, on enquiry, the commander had strongly advised against any attempt to visit the old German Hospital premises. They had long been out of commission. So, that was that.

Their superior billet turned out to be the upper storey of a modest *chaikhana* (teahouse). Like most buildings in the town, it had been badly damaged - no doors, no windows, of course no furniture and no 'facilities'. But at least the blown-out window afforded a welcome evening breeze, plus some less welcome mosquitoes. To ward off these, they struggled to light the Chinese hurricane lamps in the draught between what had been the door and the various windows. The accommodation was free.

The nearness of the kitchens, at the bottom of what was left of the stairwell, was no guarantee of access to the menu. As usual, two men were brewing up over an open wood fire made up on the floor next to the stove - just as, given the chance, they would do in the aisle of a Haj-bound airliner.

Any thoughts of sleep were soon dispelled by intermittent small arms fire. AK47 happy firing predominated, although some of it was accompanied by mortars. Packs of pye dogs howled the small hours away, as if tied to the bells of St Martin-in-the-Fields. Some of this bedlam may have been in anticipation of the imminent Muslim festival of Eid, and it offered hours of disquiet to reflect on the rapidly disintegrating war - fast becoming full scale civil war.

Khost had been the first major town to fall to the Mujahedeen. It had been a particularly long and bloody battle. Towards the end, the Russians had been obliged to throw in even their prized Spetznaz airborne *élite*, to no avail. Along with the Kabul regime Afghan troops, they had been decimated. Instead of sticking to the standard guerrilla tactics of starving a garrison into submission, Engineer Gulbuddin Hekmatyar's men had elected to fight a near set-piece confrontational battle. This could have had disastrous consequences but Hekmatyar's gamble and timing had paid off and he was out to reap all the kudos for himself and his party, notwithstanding whoever else could call that day his own. Nor was he inclined to give any of the credit to weather conditions although he had been helped by several days of unprecedented torrential rain, which had effectively closed the airfield.

That was how the official Hesbe-i handbill put it:

'The fact should not be lost sight of that the brave Afghans are not just fighting their own war. They are also fighting for the defence of Pakistan, for the benefit of Iran and the Gulf States. They are fighting for the whole Islamic world. Indeed, they are resisting the supremacy of the superpowers on behalf of the small countries of the non-aligned Third World. And in the last analysis, it can be asserted without exaggeration that they are fighting for the preservation of the entire Free World.'

Winston Churchill might have said it with more histrionics and graver cadence, but who are we to judge who have not heard or understood the original. However, unlike Churchill, Hekmatyar went on to deny the hands that fed him. In the name of the fiction that he had never received either overt or covert outside help, he bad-mouthed Pakistanis, Americans, Iranians and Arabs, each in turn, whilst helping himself and his party from all sources. His ambition was naked - his purpose long-exposed. Nothing short of total takeover, total supremacy. The only reason he supported the Pakistani view against a buffer Pashtun state, is that, quite simply, he wanted the whole of Afghanistan to himself, as manifest in his party's handbills.

'The Afghan Jihad is no mere liberation struggle. With a single leap forward, Afghan society has passed through various stages of evolution. Jihad has given the call for a revolution which has transported society to the high plane of humanity ... far above racial, linguistic and national levels. Jihad has pulled Afghanistan out of the narrow grooves of tribalism and reorganised the entire population on the basis of mature political thought, because the country's leadership never was in the hands of traditional elders and other influential personalities, but in those of the political parties which initiated Jihad.

'The materialistic world, which cannot rise above the tangible, is unable to comprehend these great changes. Russia is the adversary and simply wants to obliterate - not understand. The West is incredulous that backward and uneducated Afghans should be putting up such a tough resistance in a completely warlike manner. This sensibility can be appreciated by those alone whose hearts abound with faith.'

*

After the first five miles or so, the road deteriorated further, if that were possible, and "Scrubber"'s party were soon back on the verges. As their journey continued, they entered one majestic gorge after another. At regular ambush points along the Gardez Road, there was ample evidence that the Mujahedeen David had turned the formidable war-machine of the Soviet Goliath into so much wayside super-junk. Heaps of Russian equipment had been left to rust and rot like dinosaurs in the barren landscape. Every dwelling *en route* had been razed, including one whole village where the road crossed a *wadi*.

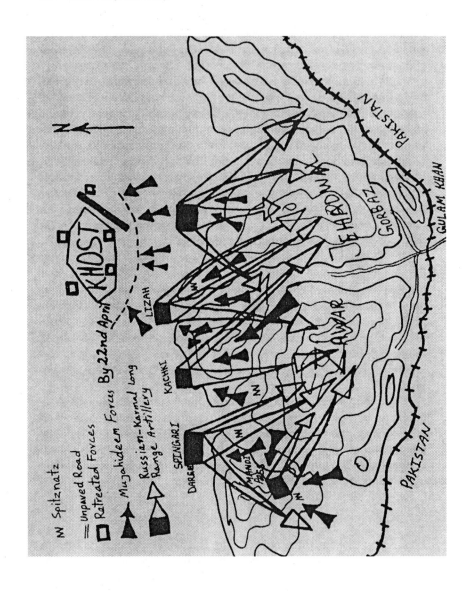

Map of the Paktia offensive - How Engineer
Gulbudin Hhekmatyar 'saw' the Battle of
Khost.

Slowly the vehicle began to climb through the ruggedly beautiful mountain passes - with occasional glimpses of the snow-capped Karakorums as backdrop - until, finally, the Hazarajat, the central highlands of Afhganistan, were reached.

Despite many more strafed, destroyed and deserted villages, the overall impression of the landscape was still of great beauty, with many another well-camouflaged community set in studded jewels of green oases or matching dun-coloured mud obscurity. Where there was irrigation, there was vegetation. Life. This was mostly poplars, citrus and vines, plus rice, barley and corn cultivation along the minuscule terraces. Lower slopes were carpeted with wild flowers, plus roses and the inevitable poppies. There were asphodels, sweet william, hollyhocks, snap-dragons - all to gladden an Englishman's heart. And at times the expedition was in danger of turning into a birdwatcher's picnic as golden orioles, rollers, hoopoes, bee-eaters, chickoos and even drongos were spotted.

With the earlier-than-planned start, they must have made better time than either their driver or guide had expected. So a tea-break was taken at Gardez. In the opinion of Karmal, the driver, a man of few words but powerful personality, Chak would be reached, Insha-allah, by nightfall.

The team was divided into two parties and toured the town. Between them, they were able to speak to many people, some in Arabic, others in Farsi. The situation was of a normal market town. The townspeople all said how pleased they were to hear the medical purpose of the visit, for there were no doctors or clinic facilities in the town, or for miles around. They said it was generally quiet in their area. The nearest fighting they had heard of was at Maidan. Most of the men were carrying a mix of infantry and hand-held anti-tank weapons. There was no firing, happy or otherwise. There were no police - law and order was maintained solely by the Mujahedeen.

Time was soon up and they left Gardez to set out for Chak, crossing the main Qandahar - Kabul highway. Unfortunately, this was a major blunder by Abdul Haq, the guide. For fear of loss of face, he would never admit his mistake, so they were forced to make a wide detour. In compensation, they soon found themselves driving through the lush cultivated area bordering the Chak river. The wheat was being harvested and the fields prepared for the second crop of rice. There were other, varied crops, including potatoes, and the trees all seemed in prime condition, with the irrigation channels brimming with water. The track itself was under repair and a further detour was necessary as a bridge was also being rebuilt - surely all good signs. Everyone they met seemed to be in the best of spirits.

On arrival at Sheykhabad, the vehicle was refuelled and they made the final approach to Chak.

[1] The Knights of St John of Jerusalem may have been the first to adopt this symbol by sculpting the eyes on the watchtowers of Valetta Harbour, Malta, to ward off the evil eye, as part of their defence system.

31

Chak - Hospital, First Class, but only half-finished

At Chak, Taj Mohammed, the hospital dispenser, was waiting for "Scrubber" and his party. There was no knowing how long he had lain in wait, or how much longer he would have done so. He was to act as host. Accommodation was provided in a small building next to the medical storeroom. It was a kind of annexe, which, with the additional luxury of mattresses laid over the floor, converted it instantly into 'guest accommodation'. To everyone's amazement, they found a separate inner room with a drain hole and a ready filled water tank and bucket for ablutions that mirrored their accustomed routine at Sadda.

After a short break to rest, wash and shake off the dust, they were taken to meet the *shora* over the evening meal. The Chak *shora*, at the time, was unusual, in that it was made up of both Hesbe-i-Islami and Jamiat commanders, who gave every appearance of getting on well together.

The meal itself was the habitual concoction of clogged rice, made easier to knead single-handed into mouth-sized balls, plus a few of those mutton chunks, which Alfred, Lord Tennyson, was said to have relished so much, but which began to pall after a fortnight or so. Happily, some days are decreed 'meatless', then the odd black bean or potato can be buried in lumps of tepid rice - all good for slimmers ... and more than acceptable to the truly hungry.

The Chak *shora* is a council of battle-scarred veterans. All of them had been wounded at least once, as if it were a pre-requisite. According to their official spokesman, all had lost a close relative in the Russian war - either a brother, a father or son. Even allowing for the extended use of the term 'brother' in Afghan family circles, this was an impressive boast. It was a matter of fact that the Russians had been driven out of Chak almost as soon as they had arrived, or otherwise some collaborative truce had been agreed.

The usual form at these informal open *majlis* assemblies was for no fixed agenda as such. Just general, somewhat aimless discussion on needs, desires, objectives - but invariably culminating in a panegyric of heroic deeds in the latest fighting - similar to the myths of ancient Greece and Rome.

However, in the case of Chak, the members of the *shora* gathered from many miles around for specific meetings, which were firmly chaired. The chairman changed every few months, so that no one party remained over-long in control. Nobody could say whether or not the German Afghanistan Committee had influenced such democratic innovation, but discussion was encouraged and decisions were then taken by the chairman of the day.

In normal circumstances, "Scrubber" would have waited respectfully until the last of the epic poems had finished and only then, when invited to do so, would he have outlined the aims and objectives of his visit. On this occasion, however, after a generous welcome, he found himself unexpectedly invited to speak first.

He began his address by damning the combined enemy - the Russians and their Kabul regime henchmen, who had caused famine by the destruction of the irrigation systems and the indiscriminate laying of uncharted minefields. He then went on to blame them for the total lack of any proper medical support or Islamic schooling, and cited the general deterioration of roads and tracks. There was a great deal to be done. Increasingly, concurrent nodding followed the translation of his successive points until it was clear the sympathies of all had been won.

"Scrubber" then switched into top gear.

He was here to conduct an inspection audit to:

raise the standard of living;

give work to returning refugees;

provide a living wage for labourers;

provide more food, and make at least three villages
self-sufficient;

provide proper medical support;

use the experiment as a matrix for other communities;

encourage all Afghans to lay down their arms.

No doubt, back home, such aspirations would have been dismissed as 'foolish and utopian' by men 'who wouldn't know Artemus Jones from Sydney Smith' and who would castigate any enthusiasm as un-English. The Foreign & Commonwealth Office had long been wary of anything that smacked of 'a showy and dangerous example of formal diplomacy, carrying us into the risk of over-extended future entanglements'. For all that, this had been a British initiative under the aegis of British Executive Services Overseas. "Scrubber"'s presentation met general and swift assent. Then, everyone seemed keen to retire as early as possible, so as to be fresh for the early morning start.

There was only the one oft-repeated but nonetheless strange limitation placed on their movements by the *shora*. As on their previous visit, there was to be no unaccompanied viewing of the three silted up Siemens generators. The explanation given was that it was a particularly sensitive Pashtun area. It was again suggested that 'unaccompanied movement' might lead to the team being mistaken for Russians and shot.

More arcane yet was the 'off limits' status of the Old English Fort, where the garrison had been annihilated. It could have been for any number of reasons, from English ghosts to ammunition storage or arms-trading arsenal, or something to do with drugs, perhaps? Any of these options has yet to be confirmed. However, waiting in the wings were more jolts and thunderbolts.

There could have been perfectly mundane reasons for the prohibition placed on visiting the generators. Two of the three generators were anyway out of commission. This could have been because of silting up or the lack of the special oil the generators required, which often vanished *en route* after painstaking efforts had been made to obtain it via Europe. But it was more likely that the water flow had simply been syphoned off for agricultural use. Anyone in the area would automatically be suspected of tampering with the water course.

German influence can be felt strongly at Chak. The more substantial buildings date from the same period as the installation of the generators - *circa* 1938. What could be described as the Schinkel look applies to all these buildings. It is as if they had come from the same German catalogue of factory-manager's houses and hotels. They were both fine and supremely functional. To an outsider it looked like the natural continuum of the well-ordered Berlin-to-Baghdad railway axis.

Conditions were rather different from the last time "Scrubber" visited, when he came to confirm the safe arrival of the Cuban American Doctors of Miami's donation. Then they had been in constant dread of a bombing raid. In the event the only bomber had been sighted over Sheykhabad, which had been bombed two days previously. But this time the pilot, anticipating a Stinger[1] ground-to-air missile response, had thrown out chaff to everyone's relief and amusement. Soon afterwards, two low-flying MIGs had caused a headlong dash for cover under the trees. Now, any night firing could be written off to exuberance, and was no longer on fixed lines. A good night's sleep was had by one and all and the next morning everyone was in good shape to get their bearings with a proper sense of perspective and orientation.

The first thing to happen was that Taj Mohammed handed the

team over to the hospital administrator, Mohammed Nabi Housaini
(Dr Veggeberg's appointee and acolyte) who gave them a detailed tour
of inspection of the medical facilities such as they were. Although a
veterinary surgeon himself, he was obviously an authorised guide
because the first port of call was the 'off-limits' site between the
generators, where Dr Michael Müller and Dr Otwin Joch had
established their wartime surgery.

Next they were taken to meet Karla Schefter, the German Field
Co-ordinator, who was to prove the mainstay, if not the mainspring of
the whole operation. Karla is an immutable, Rock of Gibraltar figure
of rent-a-tent proportions. She is of Silesian Prussian extraction. In a
way she and her mother were most fortunate to have been deported
west at the end of World War II. Like only her breed know, she had
worked extra hard to qualify as an operating theatre nurse. In her
early twenties she had been appointed as Senior Nursing Sister to
a Dortmund surgeon. As a consequence, she had been Dortmund-
based herself ever since. She retained her post for some twenty-five
years, only relinquishing it on the untimely death of her surgeon boss.
At this stage she sought a 'sea change' and applied to the German
Afghanistan Committee, who appointed her to Chak.

They could not have made a more fortunate choice, if not from
their own point of view, then certainly for the inhabitants of Chak-e-
Wardak. Over the years, she had come to be totally accepted by the
Afghans. This is no mean achievement. She is patently admired and
accepted for the selfless, painstaking work she has undertaken so
dedicatedly on their behalf.

One look is enough to tell you that Karla is a no-nonsense
operator. A good motto for her *modus operandi* would be German
efficiency within the realms of the Afghan possible!

She herself would be the first to admit, and then fiercely
defend, her move to 'go native'. Not surprisingly, since it is she who
lives amongst them for stretches of up to eight months at any one
time, she more readily understands their idiosyncratic ways. She also
shares their point of view - particularly where the whims and dictates
of visiting ex-pat firemen are concerned, who sometimes stay for all
of twenty-four hours! Given a few more years, she could well become
the Daisy Bates of the Afghan scene. Daisy, a lady of uncertain origin,
went to live amongst the Australian aboriginals, which caused quite a
stir in the nineteenth century.

Each morning Karla conducts a sick parade, which is attended
on average by 80 or so out-patients. This is of great benefit to the local
community, which numbers some 50,000 or more people.

As "Scrubber"'s team stood around in the open, it was explained that the operating theatre building was still awaiting funding after being promised for over three-and-a-half years. Something must have gone seriously wrong. It all sounded thoroughly un-German and clearly needed looking into by some competent authority. "Scrubber", who was aware of the situation, said that, although it was strictly-speaking none of his business, he was prepared to pass the word.

His immediate concern was to see that all the Cuban-American munificence from faraway Miami was being fully appreciated by its ultimate beneficiaries. The bandages had certainly proved most welcome with the recent influx of casualties from the fighting at Maidan.

When a fond, facetious enquiry was made after the foam-rubber window-display model, Karla, true to her mettle, pointed out that, when an Afghan woman wants you to know the affected part, she indicates it on *your* body *(i.e.* they indicated the affected part on Karla's body!).

Once medical matters and the hospital shortcomings had been discussed, Commander Saddiq was sent for. He was to lead "Scrubber" and the team of irrigation specialists on the long climb uphill, a good hour and a half's heavy going on foot, before the real heat of the day hit them. They would make for a village called Maddoo.

They soon found themselves climbing a valley with a beautiful clear stream rushing down it. To begin with, they found they were being taken back to the original dam site proposed by Saddiq himself. This had been discarded and everybody told, once it was discovered that the sub-strata rock was porous. (Of course, it was hard to overcome all the latent disappointment of not getting a £25,000 dam. This disillusion was expressed time and again by the team being led back to the original site!) Instead, the new scheme was to build an ingenious water course, to be used solely for agricultural purposes. However, the site chosen did not suit, as the irrigation conduit channel was out of use. These conduits are hard to describe. They are not dissimilar to the incisions made to tap rubber trees, except that they are incised for sometimes miles at a time high up on the rock face in gradual descent a millimeter at a time. When they reach their bottoming point, they can also achieve the impossible by making the water then run up-hill for short distances ... a phenomenon which has to be seen to be believed.

After a long argument amongst the party, which had now swollen to fifteen, speaking several tongues, it was agreed to move on to an alternative site. This fortunately proved to be much better.

Local knowledge prevailed and Commander Saddiq felt vindicated. However, there had been further setbacks. Electric storms had caused such atmospheric pressure that it had proved impossible to reach Peshawar on the radio-telephone. This placed the essential wire gabions beyond reach. These are galvanised wire cages that, filled with rocks and stones, are placed by civil engineers like giant Leggo to stem landslides, or in this case to channel flood waters. One of the resident doctors, Dr Maher, thought the Swedish Committee at Sheykhabad might have some.

The plan was to use local labour and local materials to construct a judiciously placed weir, using the said gabions. The specialists predicted that this diversion would irrigate an additional 100 hectares to the benefit of some 120 families in the three villages of Madoo itself, Rashidan, and Samakhat. These villages would then become self-sufficient in food production (as opposed to 70% now) and on successful completion, the project might become a matrix for other hill communities throughout Afghanistan.

This was all along the lines postulated at the *shora* meeting. However, there were to be one or two surprises in store. While the experts waited to see what might or might not materialise from behind the Swedish Committee shed in Sheykhabad, they were taken upstream to inspect some similar structures which, it was assessed, had been there for over two hundred years! The only innovation being the introduction of the missing gabion wire.

Maddoo itself is a tiny mud, stone and wood village perched high on a small plateau. Like so many others in Afghanistan, the mud-walled (adobe) houses are so weather-beaten and timeless that they blend into the flanks of the mountains behind. The camouflage can be so effective that, at first glance, any sign of habitation seems missing. There is no knowing how long a village may have been there. Mud walls defy carbon dating. Collective memory is often faulty.

On closer acquaintance, the terraces become lush with apple and mulberry, cereals and potato, to be brightened here and there with colourful splashes of rose bushes and the ubiquitous poppy.

From this village vantage point, yet more serious cultivation could be espied further down the valley. Rice paddies predominated, but there were also mature orchards of walnut trees as well as mulberry - the staple dried fruit for winter consumption - called tut. Happily, this time the invader had not laid waste the labours of former generations. All the standard farming rotations could be seen in progress. In the Chak river valley the corn crop had been harvested, and the second crop of rice sewn.

After completing the reconnaissance and the water table survey, Commander Saddiq, guide of the morning, and his brother Mohammed Nadir, invited the party into their home. The third brother, Mohammed Mansur, was away at the time. The house was wonderfully cool, especially welcome at noon. The roof was constructed with ancient wooden beams. They were most likely of poplar and left rounded. These would constitute the most valuable component of any house, and would be carted off to be used time and time again as landslide, earthquake, flood, famine, fire or war dictated. The inner walls were brightly hung with intricately woven carpets and elaborately scripted texts from the Koran, which were often framed. Like icons of the Orthodox and Catholic churches, these holy texts may be kissed as much in reverence for their calligraphic perfection as their underlying expressions of faith. No human or animal representations are permitted. These few simple possessions are their familiars, their *Lares et Penates*. They have no need of other household gods. The kaftan, the slippers and the carpet convert a hovel into a palace. The view from the front door completes the illusion, plus the desire to live nearer to God.

The fact that this visit had taken place at the time of the Feast of Eid may have accounted for the heightened atmosphere of already lavish hospitality. But it could as well have been the normal level extended to all outsiders. There was no knowing, nor was there any warning of the forthcoming festival. Everybody was expected to know. With two dates in the calendar year, determined by the phases of the moon, it is not always that apparent.

On this occasion, the guests were served first with sugar sweetened rice (not unlike Ambrosia creamed rice), then *chapattis* spread with honey and fruit. To drink, there was a choice of *lhassi*, soured yoghurt, flavoured with mint, or the more usual green tea with cardamom seeds pounded up in it.

The twelve sons of the three brothers far outnumbered the guests. As usual, the women were nowhere to be seen on this occasion, nor heard, although young girls, if there were any surviving daughters, could have been present with their devastating kohl-rimmed doe eyes.

At an unobserved signal, one of the sons, whose voice was yet to break, sang a *sura* from the Koran. His voice was beautiful and true. Somehow, this put the seal upon the great honour that had been bestowed on one and all.

The next day, to everybody's great relief, Dr Maher announced in triumph that he had found some gabion wire behind his office in

Chak. Five cages, plus the wire necessary to close them once full of rock, were coming up forthwith by donkey express. With this breakthrough and no further need to be dependent on either Kabul or Peshawar, it began to look as if the project might be completed on schedule.

However, to go with the good news, the team were warned 'anonymously' to look out for a mine on the rough track leading up to the site. It was a strangely mixed warning. It could have been either well-intentioned or malign. The fact of the matter was that they were not using either a vehicle or the track in question. "Scrubber" preferred to walk up a slightly different way each morning for variety and exercise, leaving at 5.30 a.m., to ensure being on site at 7 a.m. sharp!

But the mine story, true or false, suggested, by the timing of its release if nothing else, that somebody, or some party, did not want the job either started or finished. It could have been a faction who were still looking to be paid for a larger project over a longer time. Fortunately, thanks largely to "Scrubber"'s *sangfroid*, none of the men paid any attention to the threat and the job was completed and the men paid off ahead of schedule; and without incident. Nonetheless, somebody, or bodies, was keen to see the back of "Scrubber" and his philanthropic outfit.

However, these noises off must have influenced "Scrubber" Stewart-Richardson in his determination, born of long experience, to insist that Saddiq, as Chak's senior commander, should hold himself personally responsible to the Brigadier for the safety of Kate Straub - a British subject. She would be remaining in Chak in her medical capacity long after "Scrubber" and his team had departed the scene.

Next, the team turned their attention to the urgent needs of the Chak clinic hospital and its water supply. There was a fifteen meter well at the back of the building. Often there was no power to pump the water into the storage tank. Then, the only alternative was to use the dirty canal water. At such times the clinic was without electricity as well as water. The reason given was usually the scarcity and cost of fuel. Even when the big remaining Siemens generator was going, there was usually only one hour's supply of juice per day. The solution to the problem was to build a simple system of gravity-fed filtration tanks. There was a convenient slope, but a lot of hard work was required to get through massive tree roots. This was soon achieved, however, with extra volunteer labour from Maddoo.

The following day, the bus which had been sent to Kabul to collect cement, pipes and other plumbing parts, miraculously returned. It was a welcome sight with the piping on the roof, cement bags inside, and with all the other kit including a large motor engine. This time there was a lady passenger too, as opposed to a pink foam-rubber substitute. The return journey had been badly delayed by heavy rocket and mortar fire in Kabul, which did not augur well for the team's journey back.

They stayed on long enough to see the base and footings of the hospital filtration plant put in. The concrete pour was organised by washing the sand near the canal, where the cement was then mixed and carried up in basins by three men at a time. One basin arrived every ninety seconds. Then the rock walls were laid. Fortunately, Engineer Mahmood, who was the general factotum and doubled up as assistant administrator to Dr Mohammed Nabi Housaini, had trained in Bulgaria. He was so taken with the simplicity of the scheme, he was determined to introduce it to other communities - starting with his own.

During the course of the day a man turned up with a British chain-saw, which he was unable to start. After the most careful instruction, it was noticed that he soon lost interest in the safety precautions. It was to be hoped that he lived near the clinic.

Everything that could be done had now been done and it was time to say goodbye and move on, but not before taking the chance to entertain new and old friends. So, a goat was killed and all invited to share the feast. This was accompanied by gruesome tales of the fighting in Maidan, shortly before the Eid festival began. There were also reports of some particularly barbaric revenge killings in Kabul. These had involved Iranians mostly, but also large numbers of Hazaris. It had all been sparked off by Iranian Shias.

But, as usual with these reports, the incidents die down just as quickly as they flare up. Everything had to be accepted on a day-to-day basis; otherwise movement would soon cease altogether.

As a fitting climax to the entertainment, the World News Service of the BBC was broadcast. This caused some bitter complaint over past anti-Mujahedeen, pro-Kabul regime bias in the reporting of levels of atrocities. There was no pleasing all parties in a melée like that. The reporting had probably been accurate, but to keep the party happy, a promise was extracted to pass on their comments to Bush House. On the whole, complaints were rare.

It was in the after-glow of this farewell party that one of the team was made privy to the most surprising of sudden gratuitous confidences, that is, since the targeted mine tip-off.

Provided it was not malicious, the story was that Commander

Saddiq, no less, who was thought to be partly German, had been paid a regular retainer by the German Afghanistan Committee, for more than two years past, to ensure that any effort to complete the hospital at Chak was scotched by whatever means deemed necessary, within or without the *shora*.

The implication was clear. Once completed, the Chak hospital was counter-productive. As long as it was left in limbo, it remained the German Afghanistan Committee's star fund-raiser - their cash cow. There was no other explanation. The retainer would be hard to corroborate, but the suspicion rang true to the miasma between illusion and reality in matters Afghan. The mine warning may simply have been a more tangible expression of this same negative intention.

[1] Stinger = American-made ground-to-air missile.

32

From Kabul to the Khyber

The next morning "Scrubber" and his team left for Kabul, returning via Ghazni. On their way, they were fortunate enough to pass through a number of Koochi encampments. These are Pashtun nomads from the Ahmadzi,Mohmand and Safi tribes. In summer they move up the valleys to graze the peaks, returning later in the year to winter along the 'five rivers' of the Punjab, making a nonsense of the drawn 'border' known as the Durand Line. They dwell in black goat-hair tents and move with many shaggy camels as well as with all their sheep and goats, feeding on the hoof. The sheep are the famous fat-tailed breed, which is how they store their emergency reserve. Not unlike gypsies, the women wear the most colourful robes and the men all have gorgeously embroidered waistcoats. If they carry arms, they do not flaunt them.

Even by Afghan standards the road to Kabul is battered to bits, studded with masses of mine and demolition holes. If an average speed of fifteen miles per hour was achieved the driver was doing well.

The nearer the team got to Kabul, the more tense the atmosphere became. This was reflected in the increasing number of checkpoints. These checkpoints were strangely uniform, consisting of a clapped out tank or armoured personnel carrier with a green flag or two, fluttering or limp, usually with the gun barrel directed at the road. A chain or light hawser would then stretch across the road to a heavy oil drum - filled with rocks. Groups of four or five heavily armed, desultory Mujahedeen could be seen squatting in whatever shade was to be found nearby.

Failure to stop was an open invitation to have the tyres shot out, for starters. It was better to stop. On the other hand, it was worth taking a different view with unofficial wildly gesticulating wayside figures. Once ignored these would promptly demonstrate their displeasure by loosing off an overhead volley. It was the standard gesture of annoyance and it was essential to ignore it. When the vehicle was unarmed, there was always the additional risk of being hijacked. It was only safe to give lifts to obvious family groups.

On one occasion, speed had been so reduced that a hitch-hiker was able to nip nimbly on to the back of the truck. In no time he had helped others on board. All were headed for Kabul. Those unable to get a leg over the side, stood on the rear bumper and the Toyota shuddered anxiously along on its, by now bald, tyres, and clanking springs. In a weird way the uninvited proved a kind of insurance. They enhanced street credibility - especially at checkpoints.

Maidan showed all the signs of the reported battle. Fatigue had set in and this time, when stopped for identification, the team's purpose was approved and they were waved on with friendly smiles.

The light was fading as they crawled into the outskirts of Kabul. Happily, their uninvited passenger load began to lighten ... until there was none. Although the curfew was officially 9 p.m., it was dangerous to be out and about in the city after 7.30 p.m. The whole place was swarming with Mujahedeen, with armoured vehicles seemingly at every street corner. This was alarming, if only because the team had nowhere specific in mind to lodge or, more prosaically, get off the streets. It was here that the guide, Abdul Haq (not the Commander of the same name who befriended Mrs Thatcher), proved himself invaluable. Any previous shortcomings as a pathfinder were instantly absolved as he remembered a friend, Malik Fati Mohammad, and headed directly for his house. All six were admitted to his small courtyard and the wooden door slammed and bolted behind them in double-quick time.

Khan, the son of the house, then took them to an upper room, lit by a Tilley lamp, where a meal was soon set before them. As always in an Afghan home, they were made thoroughly welcome, even though in this case, they were totally unexpected and possibly even positively unwelcome guests! Such is the standard of hospitality demanded by the code of Islam.

That night they were subjected to the sound of a greater variety of weapons being fired than they had ever heard before. The hill areas surrounding the city were alive to the sound of shooting. However, it failed to keep anybody awake.

As "Scrubber"'s business was notionally with the Ministry of Power and Irrigation, it was decided to seek alternative accommodation nearer their city centre offices for the next two nights. Like other ministries, this one was not scheduled to open before 9 a.m., so "Scrubber" decided to pay a courtesy call on HALO (Hazardous Areas Logistical Organisation) at their residence in Lucky Five street. Here he met some very pleasant and helpful Afghans, who were so well-informed that they were able to advise him whom to see and whom to avoid in the said ministry.

HALO is a godsend in such circumstances, always up-to-speed as to the very latest developments. It has to be. It is pre-eminent in the field of mine clearance and mine awareness programmes.

It is a registered British charity. Strictly speaking, it plays a very straight bat at all times. Once accused of being an English spy by the Russians, its maverick founder, Colonel Colin Mitchell, late of the Argyll & Sutherland Highlanders, is reputed to have replied 'I don't mind you calling me a spy, but I'm buggered if I'll be an English spy!' The Russians had had the grace to laugh.

HALO was able to confirm that Kabul was indeed tense for the moment, with road-blocks everywhere and armoured vehicles stationed outside all government and public buildings. Both the Intercontinental and Kabul hotels had been requisitioned and had begun their inexorable decline towards annihilation. The city was divided between the various warring factions and incidents were commonplace.

At 9 a.m. sharp, a Mujahedeen sentry ushered the team into the ministry. The building had been stripped bare. It was completely empty, with not even a rug on the floor, nor one stick of furniture. In these stark surroundings the Executive Chief Planning Officer quietly assimilated the reasons for the visit and duly sent for various Heads of Departments.

In their turn the Heads explained that their tenure was increasingly insecure. Initially, 80% of the staff had fled. They were beginning slowly to return, but they were quite unable to do any work, since they had no facilities and no transport.

"Scrubber" then went over the Chak irrigation prototype in some detail. It sparked considerable interest, and was taken as a cue for the Afghan officials to outline their own future plans together with a hefty list of the equipment needed. This all related to the former Kabul regime's area of control. During the course of conversation the subject of the Sultan Dam came up and the ministry men were astonished to hear that "Scrubber" and his team had been there only the day before on their way back from Chak. Not one of them had been outside Kabul in thirteen years ...

It was agreed to reconvene on the following day, to allow time to assemble basic information. As a courtesy, the team were taken to meet the new minister. As with the technicians, the common language was English, the atmosphere congenial and the willingness to help self-evident. It was openly admitted that their position was chaotic. They had no money and were in desperate need of the right technical advice to rehabilitate their country. The minister insisted on sending the team back to their vehicle by pre-paid taxi.

They took the afternoon off to wander around the famous old bazaar and the Chicken Street market, renowned for its jewellery and antique shops. Many of these were boarded up, their owners fled. But one of the best was still trading, *Haji* Gada's 'Kabul House', an Aladdin's cave of furs, musical instruments, leatherwork, pottery and, best of all, some of those Koochi embroidered waistcoats, together with silver-gilt jewellery embellished with agate.

Next, they went in search of some Canadian friends of Kate Straub - she who had previously worked for HALO - and were promptly offered their UN house as sanctuary. This suited admirably because Kate was due to return to Chak with Taj Mohammed as escort, while "Scrubber" and the rest of his team would be headed back to Peshawar via Jalalabad. The Canadians happened to have an Hazari daily maid, who confirmed the horrors of the previous week's massacre - stemming from the standard Sunni/Shi'ite strife! Whilst the country mouse was getting back to normal, the town mouse was rapidly reverting to a rat.

That night was just as noisy in the hill areas all around, but gave no great cause for concern in Kabul itself. The next morning the team reconvened at the Ministry of Power and Irrigation. They met with the same friendliness and co-operation. All the information requested was in place and an undertaking was given to see what could be done to secure funding in UK and/or EC.

That night was exceptionally noisy. This was due to the kidnapping of Gulbuddin Hekmatyar's son-in-law and second-in-command earlier that afternoon.

The following morning there were more checkpoints to get out of Kabul than there had been to get in. The team's road took them first to Sarobi, the natural staging post for Jalalabad. It follows the rushing Kabul river as it cuts and curls its way through steep and narrow gorges, one of which had been the scene of innumerable ambushes during the Russian occupation. The numbers of wrecked armoured vehicles and tank transporters was dramatic. Mile after mile of tanks and trucks lay where they had been hit. Green and white flags waved over the graves of the faithful, who had been buried where they fell. Many Russians were killed here, but they had no known grave. Terrified young conscripts had climbed back into their burning vehicles rather than face being taken alive by the tribesmen pouring over the hills. Significantly perhaps, it was the self-same spot where the British had suffered their greatest military defeat in Afghanistan.[1]

Some of the burnt-out tanks now sported effigies of Soviet and Najibullah regime figures (Gorbachev/Najibullah) swinging by their necks from the gun barrels. These were a source of constant delight to the stream of lorries coming towards Kabul, crammed to bursting with returning refugees, sitting astride their worldly belongings. Whatever road surface there had been, was long gone. Every vehicle churned up a dense dust cloud, to add to the discomfort and danger.

After the standard break at the Sarobi *chaikhana*, or tea house, the team reached Jalalabad without further incident. Jalalabad is much lower and hotter than Kabul. It is also much more humid, with a larger mosquito population.

"Scrubber"'s objective was to find *Haji* Ebrahim Rashid's house, where accommodation was offered in the name of the German Afghanistan Committee. They found the house with some difficulty; *Haji* Ebrahim Rashid himself was away, in Peshawar. Nevertheless, they were made to feel at home. "Scrubber" could not help noticing the odd bit of kit, which had originated, presumably, as surplus to requirement, from the Cuban-American Doctors of Miami's donation. Not a few beds and blankets - but thought no more of it. This was the same house where there was an upper room where Dr Tilman Hilber and one of his children had unwittingly stumbled on a pile of valuable Afghan carpets - stacked from floor to ceiling. Carpets are the tally of Afghan wealth.

"Scrubber" next visited all the hospitals in Jalalabad, only one of which was of any reasonable standard. It was the only Mujahedeen one. The hand of Dr Abdul Satar Paktiss was discernible.

By now, the Toyota Hi-lux was beginning to show signs of fatigue, with ever-increasing ailments. It was doubtful if it would make the journey back to Peshawar. Finally, shortly before leaving Jalalabad, a front-wheel bearing seized up and dramatically caught fire. Kamal and Abdul Haq, the driver and guide, were left to follow on, once the vehicle had been repaired. In the meantime, "Scrubber" and two remaining members of his team would chance their arm at hitching a lift. On that stretch of road it was easier said than done. None of the gaily painted, barge-art Bedford truck-cum-buses would stop for anyone. Eventually, a Suzuki van did pull over. The two Pakistani occupants offered to take all three at 400 rupees a head (£8.80). This was extortionate but there was no option.

They careered off, but ever-increasing stops were necessary to top up the leaking radiator from wayside streams. "Scrubber" sat in front with the driver. The other Pakistani sat in the back wedged by the team. At one stage, *naswar* (a local narcotic) was offered all round and refused. The driver was undoubtedly under the influence of something, as twice he screeched to a halt on the wrong side of the road, whilst on-coming trucks hurtled past, missing him by a whisker.

Cartoon featuring Gorbachev and Najibullah, 1989

All this was happening whilst they wound up and down the hairpin bends of the Khyber Pass. The passengers could only pay scant attention to the historic scenery. Finally, the sanctuary of Green's Hotel was reached and, not that much later, Kamal and Abdul Haq appeared with the original vehicle repaired.

One of the team was clearly suffering the effects of dehydration, which can be very serious. "Scrubber" promptly opted to look after him until he recovered.

It was at this moment of stress that *Haji* Ebrahim Rashid reappeared on the scene to present an exorbitant bill for the hire of the Toyota Hi-lux, which it had been assumed was being provided free, as part of the German Afghanistan Committee's contribution to the overall Chak improvements effort. This, apparently, was not the case. Somewhere along the way, "Scrubber" must have seen the vehicle registration of the ARROS fleet, operated by the Rashid brothers, in the name of the German Afghanistan Committee. This transparent duplicity was enough to cause him to let fly. He told *Haji* Ebrahim Rashid to his face that he was dishonest and a thief, which was not the half of it. It must have been quite a confrontation. If it had taken place in Jalalabad and not Green's Hotel, Peshawar, "Scrubber" most probably would not have lived to tell the tale.

[1] The disastrous retreat of the Army and families from Kabul in 1841 in the First Afghan War. This was as much due to political misjudgement as military incompetence.

33

What Kate Straub Discovered at Chak

Back at Chak, the action was hotting up. After three-and-a-half years the promised hospital wasn't a day nearer completion. Worse still, for those on the bread line, everybody's pay was anything from two to six months in arrears. The whole community had come to hate the GAC.

Kate Straub was not the kind of girl to hang around, losing the initiative. However, her womanly intuition told her to bide her time until the ideal opportunity should present itself; but in less than a month she had struck. Over the last six months, she had witnessed how matters had developed. What Karla Schefter had to add only served to stiffen her resolve.

Then what should happen but the unheralded 'visiting circus' arrival, direct from the HQ of the German Afghanistan Committeee in Bonn, of Denny Hundeshagen himself, accompanied by the sanctimonious Khalid Rashid. For the occasion, Hundeshagen sported an outsize Nostradamus turban, the green folds of which kept tumbling about his ears.

Here was the top German promoter, throwing his weight around behind the protection of eight of Khalid's armed Jalalabad Mujahedeen, whilst Khalid himself gave cash handouts to his cronies and toadies. Meanwhile, the main body of the hospital workers remained unpaid. Their feelings of resentment were further exacerbated by the recent influx of wounded from Maidan and Kabul. Since the major 'hospital' facilities, like wards, were still not in place they had found themselves almost incapable of caring for casualties. Most of them had perforce been sent on to the tender mercies of the Arab Hospital. It had all been most unprofessional.

In addition to the stick and carrot show of force and the placatory handouts, a general invitation was issued to a big sheep roast. It was hard to refuse when hungry.

Kate Straub knew she would never get a better chance than this to say her piece. She took the opportune moment to tell Hundeshagen exactly what she thought of his own shortcomings and those of his organisation. They were not the words of a mealy-mouthed middle-American matron. Startled, he spluttered back in English 'Who do you think you are? How dare you speak to me like this?'

Khalid had undoubtedly warned him to expect trouble, but Kate, unlike Karla, had not been vetted in Bonn before her appointment. Since careful vetting had been stipulated in the GAC Manual, this was a serious lapse. Instead, Kate had been recruited on Erös's initiative at Peter Stiles's suggestion and delivered to Chak by "Scrubber". It was a backstairs arrangement, with disastrous consequences in store. From Hundeshagen's perspective it should never have happened, and must never happen again.

Something very surprising indeed happened next. Kate overheard the cook in Khalid's party muttering outside the kitchen 'Too bad she doesn't know what is happening to her in the morning!' He had no idea Kate spoke Farsi.

Shortly thereafter, two of the Mujahedeen guards to the Denny Hundeshagen/Khalid Rashid duo tipped her off that she was going to be removed by force the following morning. Kate had a good idea what her fate would be – at best, a pay-off to the self-same Mujahedeen, probably followed by false imprisonment and deportation from Pakistan, with more underhand *baksheesh* fuelling her exit. She did not dare to contemplate what the worst might be, but it served to concentrate her mind on the action she was to take next.

Kate is an exceptionally resourceful as well as an outstandingly brave girl, and the immediate action she took was to remove the diaphragm from the radio handset and fling it to kingdom come. This meant that the 'hospital' could go on receiving incoming calls, but there was no way Khalid could tip off his border sharks as to her passage.

Next, she penned a brief synopsis of her battle plan on the palm of her left hand, not altogther unlike Peter Stiles marking drugs administered on the patient's forehead. If push came to shove, somebody might at least be able to read what she had in mind from her *aide memoire*.

As Kate now suspected they intended to take her by vehicle to Jalalabad, she contemplated her chances of skipping to join a Koochi encampment and crossing the border disguised as one of them!

Then she wondered about the two or three commanders she felt she could trust. One of them (also confusingly called *Haji* Ebrahim) had spent some time in Manchester, so there was an element of bonding. But the more she thought about it the more she realised how slim the chances were. All three were bidden to the *shoora* which had been called to discuss the 'future' of Chak Hospital. With no hiding place to go to, she made up her mind to attend, too! That way at least there was more chance of word of her fate leaking out, given time.

It may well turn out to be the bravest action of her life, for it is hard to contemplate what it means to gate-crash an all-male Muslim *shoora*.

Kate initiated her intrusion by first requesting permission to speak! This was met with a shocked silence, which must have lasted an eternity for her. Then, one by one, each shaggy beard nodded consent.

Next, further to win their sympathies, she told the assembled *Majlis* that Hundeshagen and Khalid (whom, as if they needed any identification, she accusingly pointed out) were planning to remove her forcibly, very much against her will, in the morning.

By this time, Hundeshagen was demanding to know from Khalid, again in English 'What's she saying? What's she saying? What's she saying?' On and on he went, repeating his demands.

Kate told the *shoora* how Hundeshagen must be held responsible for all the delays and late payments and non-payments and that she personally would make it her business to bring him to book, even if it meant smashing the GAC in the process. She then called upon the assembled *shoora* to save her from these terrible men, who were hell-bent on killing her.

Hundeshagen's face actually changed to an ashen grey. Although his and Khalid's game was clearly up, and their days at Chak numbered, they had already set their satellites to criticising Kate and her work amongst the recently paid-off Khalid adherents. They concentrated extra effort on Yasser, who was known to be an Arab-backed, foreigner-hating Muslim fundamentalist.

Soon afterwards, another highly selective *shoora* was called, which purposely excluded any of Kate's friends or supportive commanders. As a result, she was ordered to leave, because she was unmarried. The real reason was that she had by now been sufficiently bad-mouthed by placemen, who spelled out the old party line that she had been issuing contraceptives to unmarried women, which was totally untrue and - that other old black propaganda chestnut - that she gave one-to-one English lessons with single men in her room.

Once Kate was able to set him straight on her side of the stories, one of the commanders on the *shoora*, which had passed judgement on her, was furious and had gone off to call another *shoora* to reverse the decision. But, by now, she was so sick of all the back-biting, plotting and lies, that she decided to call it a day and go quickly and quietly back to Peshawar. It was probably just as well she did.

It was also just as well that "Scrubber", with tremendous foresight, had neutralised Commander Saddiq by asking and extracting a Guarantee of Safe Conduct for Kate. Hundeshagen's more and more exaggerated demands fell on deaf ears, because Saddiq had been rendered harmless, checkmate under the terms of the Pashtunwali code of hospitality. However harmless, he did say that he could only afford her such protection until the end of the week. So, surrounded by her enemies, Kate used her time to be extra careful in the last stage of planning her exit.

This concerned her choice of travelling companions. You cannot be too careful in Afghanistan, as a wrong choice can mean you end up going to the highest bidder. So, she settled for the faithful Taj Mohammed and the Mancunian 'Muj' commander, *Haji* Ebrahim. It was also suggested that 'Doctor' Iqbal had a hand in smuggling her safely across the Pakistani border, perhaps from the other side, diverting Khalid's heavily-bribed Pakistani policemen. But only heaven knows how anyone was able to contact him, without the radio telephone.

Behind her, Kate left Karla Schefter, Dr Zaffar and *Haji* Daoud, all of whom now made pretence of rejoining the ranks of the German Afghanistan Committee team. Secretly, however, they began plotting its downfall.

On reaching Peshawar, Kate offered her services to the Norwegian Afghanistan Committee and was accepted with alacrity. Shortly afterwards, she began a new job at Chadywall, south of Ghazni, where she sought anonymity. She rather needed to, since, whilst stopping-over in Peshawar, she had persuaded Andy Price at the United Nations Development Programme that he should cancel all contracts with GAC forthwith. Somewhat unfortunately, one of Ebrahim Rashid's many relations, who worked for the UN, saw them taking tea together in the office and so was able to inform Ebrahim as to whom had been responsible for their loss.

What Kate had not blurted out was her discovery that GAC and their whole Chak set-up was primarily a front for arms and drug smuggling in support of Gulbuddin Hekmatyar. To mix with such people was highly dangerous, for they were utterly ruthless.

When the time came, she had a lot of stories to tell, to the right people. For now, for Karla's sake, she would keep silent. It was better to go underground and as far as possible, simply disappear. Which she did. She had played her part. It would now be up to others to crush the GAC in the only practicable way, which would be by undermining its bedrock support in Germany; where she had no desire or need to go.

So, there was more than one reason why Hundeshagen would want to keep Chak in a state of suspended animation. It began to look as if that particular cash cow might go dry on him. And then where would he be if word got out amongst his faithful subscribers, with their regular banker's standing orders, that he had strung them along, prolonging the agony of 'construction', stretching the time-limit to the maximum, simply to squeeze the last pfennig out of their sympathies? The one sure way to bring the house of cards crashing down would be by exposure in the German press. It had been tried before. This time there would be more to go on. Guy Willoughby at HALO had inclined Kate to have no contact with journalists. I was the one with press connections. It was a job for me.

The only other information which came to light in all this confrontation was that it wasn't a first time for Hundeshagen. There had supposedly been some other lady who had had the temerity to stand up to his intimidation. As the story went, she now lived in fear of her life.

*

The first thing I had to do was identify her, then find her before anything untoward happened to her.

All we had to go on was that she was said to be a disaffected secretary of outsize girth, who spoke English and was not to be confused with Karla Schefter! For good measure, I was advised that apparently you can get sent to jail in Germany for having an affair with your secretary. This could either be taken as a clue or a red herring. All we knew was that, if she was still around, the good lady was probably to be found in Bonn.

We are unlikely ever to know the precise cause of the altercation. However, as thieves often fall out, so did Denny Hundeshagen and Khalid Rashid. Or, more likely, it was the other way round, because it was Khalid who attempted to exact revenge in his most peculiar way!

Maybe the Kate confrontation was the beam of revelation that told Khalid that Hundeshagen had been garaging 'surplus' funds in Germany and that it had been far from being fair shares for all, and hadn't been for as long as anybody could remember! Whether or not it was a matter of money, or, more likely, a tribal loss of face, Khalid took a flight to Bonn either on impulse or to escape the Pakistani authorities and, choosing a moment when he knew the occupants would be away, he raided the Bonn offices of the German Afghanistan Committee. More precisely, the office of Denny Hundeshagen himself. Khalid went lightly armed, with a kitbag! He then solemnly proceeded to loot all Denny Hundeshagen's executive toys. They were readily recognisable because they were colour co-ordinated - yellow.

Staplers, pens, blotters, card-indexes, files. Khalid went on and on, until the kitbag was full.

So that there should be no chance of recovering these sacred status symbols they were taken all the way back to Jalalabad as a kind of war trophy. If Khalid thought that, shorn of his office trappings, Hundshagen would be rendered impotent like Sir Walter Scott without his missing waistcoat button, he was to be sadly mistaken.

However, the Rashid brothers' next act of destruction was to be utter and final. Like little Hitlers, they commanded that all that could be salvaged from Sadda was to be removed to Jalalabad and what remained should be razed. There could now be little doubt that the Rashid brothers had caught the Germans cheating at cards, paying more into their Swiss bank accounts than the combined Peshawar Swiss Franc amount for the brothers.

'He who dies with the most toys ...'

34

A Wide Tour of Enquiry and Inspection

Whilst "Scrubber" had busied himself checking out matters mostly relating to Chak, Peter Stiles and I had been given the enviable challenge of looking for suitable relocation alternatives to war-torn Kabul for the Sandy Gall Afghanistan Appeal. There was also an urgent need to assess the post-war Afghan surgery capabilities, nationwide, with particular reference to mine injuries. We planned to combine both objectives, as they were not incompatible.

The *realpolitik* of the situation *vis à vis* Non-Government Organisations (NGOs) as much as Official Government Organisations, was that the Pakistani Government was beginning to harden in its attitude towards Afghanistan in general and everything that went with the refugee problem in particular. More and more key jobs were being handed over to Pakistanis, which had formerly been the preserve of Afghans or ex-pats, in an effort to buy them off with Danegeld. The whole subject of Afghanistan had begun to suffer as much from aid fatigue as battle fatigue.

Kabul was the natural place to organise the regeneration of medical or hospital services and training. But, if the civil war continued to be centered on the capital then other alternatives would need to be considered. It was the perceived wisdom of the United Nations that the next best bet, after Kabul, would be Mazar-e-Sharif, in the far north. The only person we knew to share this view was a former Afghan colleague at the Afghan Trauma Centre Hospital in Peshawar. His name was Dadrass, and he was one of the very few Afghan orthopaedic surgeons to have gone back to his roots, which was a matter for the highest commendation in itself.

However, if NGOs were to be asked to quit Peshawar and Pakistan, en masse, the more obvious choice would be Jalalabad, primarily because it was the nearest main Afghan town to Peshawar. Essential supplies, whether medical or basic consumer goods, would still have to come from Peshawar. Other basic human requirements, like rest and recreation, were virtually unobtainable other than in the North West Frontier Province. None the less somebody needed to go and take a closer look at the alternatives.

Peter Stiles reckoned that, in the whole of Afghanistan, there were no more than a dozen trained orthopaedic surgeons and Dr Dadrass was one of them. He would be as good a starting point as any and so that was partly how we now came to be bound for Mazar-e-Sharif. Since we were going so far north, and were largely sponsored by the Sandy Gall Afghanistan Appeal, we decided at the same time to take a look at Taloqan, where there was known to be an orthotics (artificial limbs) workshop under the aegis of Mary Macmakin, yet another of those renowned intrepid ladies. She trained physiotherapists. Physiotherapy clinics were as good a guide as any to surgical needs.

Orthopaedic services in Afghanistan have never been developed outside the two main centres of Kabul and Jalalabad. The prolonged conflict has placed an intolerable burden of complex injuries on these very limited services. The fighting continues, the millions of mines continue to maim and all the time there remains an indeterminate backlog of old injuries desperately needing reconstruction. Add to these the classic orthopaedic problems caused by polio, congenital deformities, tuberculosis and other bone infections and you have an insoluble problem. These were the stark background statistics which prompted our journey.

Unfortunately, events were beginning to take an increasingly sour turn. As witnessed by "Scrubber" Steward-Richardson, Engineer Gulbuddin Hekmatyar's out-of-control commanders were tightening their stranglehold cordon on the southern approaches to Kabul. If this were not tiresome enough, there were said to be very few drivers prepared to brave the mayhem north of Charikar. Pul-e-Kumrhi began to feel very remote and the Kunduz out of the question. Robert Byron's admonition, quoting some ancient proverb, kept recurring in my mind 'He who overstays one night in Kunduz province must be contemplating suicide!' Added to this was all the comfort of a recent British briefing document, which disclosed that the UN had withdrawn all staff from the Kunduz 'after one of their convoys had come under fire from a group of unknown gunmen'. This document went on to reassure by stating 'However, it should be emphasised that Kunduz has been unstable for some years!'

At times like these, one recognises the inherent advantages of the Thesigers and Newbys, travellers who would have nothing to do with mechanised transport and thus stood a better chance of slipping through the native net. All you need is plenty of time and the constitution of an ox - including the horny feet.

It made more sense to contemplate the land journey one way only. I therefore proposed that we should take an aeroplane to the furthest point north and trek back. That way, we should at least gain the illusion of having got somewhere, from the outset. There would be no doubting our commitment. There could be no turning back either.

There appeared to be only two alternatives. Either we could hitch a ride with the United Nations or risk booking the once-a-week commercial flight with the national carrier, Ariana. This came in to Peshawar from Delhi and Lahore on Fridays only, before proceeding, *Insha-allah*, to Kabul and Mazar-e-Sharif and maybe Herat. Each alternative had its handicaps. Te UN limitation was that it could only ever fly at half capacity, as the other half had to be kept for return flight fuel. The other unknown was that mere NGO personnel could always get bumped off the flight at the last minute, to make room for more deserving UN officials. And then, as often as not, the aircraft turned out to be cargo-only in configuration.

The policy of the commercial airline was to take allcomers and take off once saturation was reached. Sound commercial sense, but uncomfortable. The pilots were more at home with the combat aircraft on which they had trained. Our 'hand-baggage-only' tended to be derisory, compared to our fellow passengers, who brought the kitchen sink.

Buying a ticket was not the problem. Everybody had one of those. The ordeal that sorted the sheep from the goats was the seven-hour wait at the 'airport' for the incoming aircraft, with a chunk of seedcake and a Fanta orange for sustenance. Then there was to be more time 'in transit' during our Kabul stopover. This would be spent squatting in the shade of what was left of the terminal building. Every now and again, a ragged line of bandit irregulars would sweep the apron, and loose off their weapons at some wreck or other. These were Hesbe-i-Islami[1] men and the chances were that the airport was only being kept open and 'secure' to protect their frequent Iranian visitors.

Finally, the news seeped out that our flight, or a flight, was expected and we found ourselves herded into a sheep pen. To my astonishment, I could see that it was a 727. The pilot was bringing it in like a 'Foxbat'. We were relieved to see large numbers of passengers were disembarking. With any luck, some of them would have had enough.

It was then that I caught sight of Mary Macmakin for the second time. Our paths had crossed originally obtaining visas at the Afghan Consulate in Peshawar. There was no way you could miss her. She was tall. Her hairstyle may have heightened the effect. She looked like one of those Norman Rockwell American pioneer ladies, who used to grace the cover of the Saturday Evening Post. Except that, instead of being crabby, she was benign. She was beautiful.

She had more shapeless pieces of hand-baggage than the rest of the plane-load put together. And the rest of the plane-load had been co-opted to carry it. She herself was like one of those dedicated eccentric derelicts who at capital city termini, trail around supermarket trolleys piled sky-high with red white and blue calico bags, full of goodness knows what daily gleanings.

In this case there was a difference, without a harsh word ever being said or a subtle request made, a crocodile of docile Afghan males of all ages was humbly helping her. Those strong, silent, stalwart 'blood donors', who believed so fervently that a woman's place was in the home, were, like unbidden lambs, lending a hand to help their helper. Perhaps, like Mother Teresa, it was impossible for this woman to travel incognito. Indeed, Mary Macmakin's *persona* shone like her good works. As there was no way she would be continuing the flight we signalled frantically to gain her attention. Once she had come up to our barrier, we told her how very much we hoped to catch up with her, sometime towards the end of the following week; so long as the road to Taloqan was still open. She implored us to do so. The American mission the previous year from Orthopaedics Overseas had been unable to proceed beyond Mazar-e-Sharif.

Happily there were far fewer passengers prepared to risk the onward journey, so we were able to board without much difficulty. As we took off, we saw one of the Iranian planes coming in to land, confirming our suspicions as to why the airport was kept open. Nobody was going to turn away geese that laid golden eggs.

The onward flight from Kabul to Mazar was short, fifty minutes at most. A glass of water was handed out to a privileged few at the front of the cabin. Our seats were too far back to qualify. We concentrated on the terrain we were so gratefully skipping. Afghanistan is always interesting to study from the air, and doubly so if a dangerous journey is being halved. At the best of times it looks barely habitable.

Less than an hour later, we had traded one desolate spot for a worse one. The big difference was the smartly unformed Uzbek militia, bristling with weaponry and sporting old style British Rail 'Africa Corps' caps. Everybody was being herded into vaguely ethnic groups.

Wisely, we had heeded some motherly advice from Carlotta Gall, Sandy's daughter. We had looked after her on her first journey out from England and now she was repaying the kindness tenfold. Her 'listen with mother' advice had been to befriend all other ex-pats at every contact, whatever their calling, circumstances or presence, or lack of it!

Just so, we had our passports grouped under an American banner, which hastened our passage through passport control. We found ourselves grouped with American missionaries, who offered us a lift in the back of their pick-up van. It was a good seven kilometers from Mazar airport to Mazar city. There was many another passenger left disconsolate behind, squatting in the shade of a newly-acquired Russian fridge.

There is no public or, indeed, much other transport at any of these airports. So, if you are not being met, you have little alternative but to walk. If you are at the destination end, it is common practice to go out to the airport half a dozen times to greet the unannounced incoming flight. It was just the way to spend the day of rest at Mazar.

We were pressed to stay by our new found missionary friends. They reminded me of Shakers or Amish. I couldn't help wondering whether they would have any more success with their proselytising than Dr William Theodore Pennell. I had long since learned never to deride, let alone abuse, such people until I had first witnessed their medical work. I usually found myself suitably humbled by their devotion. This time, we would never know, since we had to decline their kind invitation on the grounds of our need to be right at the centre of things. In truth we had to be independent.

They then offered to drive us on into town, once they had settled in a bit; meaning off-loaded the truck. They were model Christians, hard to fault.

As we waited, trying to keep out of the way of the human chain contending with their few but bulky goods and chattles (our offer to help had been declined), we couldn't help overhearing a disgruntled child's arrival comment 'Gees, mom, it's kinda dirty.'

I wondered how he would survive with no room and no garden. Like us, he would soon learn that, compared with what was to come, he was savouring the Ritz of Mazar luxury.

We weren't kept waiting long and were graciously swept on to be delivered at the side door of Barat's Hotel, bang in the centre of Mazar-e-Sharif.

[1] Gulbadin Hekmatyar's followers this time.

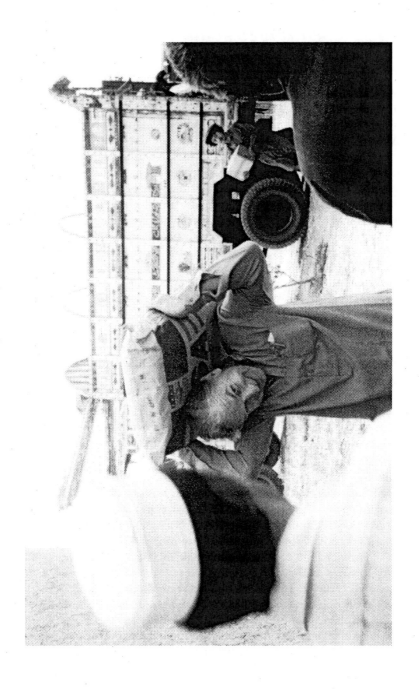

Peter Stiles unloading medical stores. *Photo by Peter Stiles*

35

Appalling Hospital Squalor at
Mazar-e-Sharif

Barat's Hotel has little to commend it - except the memorability of its name and the fact that it has the only high-rise view overlooking the only building of any interest left, which is the remoulded mosque (or 'mask' to our Amish American cousins).

The rooms are cheap and cheerful, although they are not entirely suitable for ex-pat women, unless they come in mutually protective hordes. Doors are best left open at night in the hope of catching a through draught. The rooms on the mosque side get the breeze as well as the view. Sanitation is bog-basic and consists of one, all-in-one, latrine, basin and shower per floor.

It is important to take a look at the mosque and the general layout of the place as, in our experience, most of the time it is lost in sandstorm. The mosque has some small patches of grass near it for tiny tots to play. Otherwise the public park area is given over to carpet-sellers, beggars and the ubiquitous Uzbek[1] militia. Trance-like *Muzak* engulfs all.

Besides the obvious religious focal point, there is nothing to distinguish the endless acres of municipal architecture, slab concrete radiating to eternity under bypass lighting. Like cattle sheds, their only function is to contain. However unintentional, this very drabness serves to heighten the alternative radial path to Islam.

All the major road intersections were dominated by huge cinematic hoardings featuring Abdul Rashid Dostrum. They looked mass produced by the same airbrush studio which gave us the Saddam Hussain displays. It was, as if to economise, the same 'Rambo' stencils and skyline cut-outs had been used. There was the interchangeable moustache, beret and battle fatigues. The cap badge was certainly the same extravaganza of crossed field marshal batons. It reminded me of those fairground montages with a hole for your head, but made here for interchangeable Muslim strong men.

To offset all this, there are avenues of very attractive jacaranda trees. Unlike those in the Christian cemetery in Kabul, they have yet to fall to the winter woodman's axe. However, the greatest menace in the whole place, was the packs of stray, rabid pye dogs. They would appear like ghosts out of the swirling sandstorm. The anti-rabies vaccine was deemed useless. They only respected stones or well-aimed kicks, which came reluctantly from dog-lovers. But they would have to be braved in the quest for coffee or anything resembling the coffee bean, otherwise we should be reduced, as on other occasions, to the consolations of the cardomom seed, taken pounded up with green tea from China.

But our first priority still had to be purified water. For this far-flung trip, Peter had invested in a new custom-made toy. It was an economy model stirrup pump water purifier, which had the endorsement of the School of Tropical Medicine, so there would be no more pouching or popping pills in our hosts' water supplies. Peter had convinced himself he held the panacea to all our drinking-water problems. Its inauguration was to be in the privacy of our hotel room.

Of course, being only the economy model, it was limited to the arbitrary amount of 99 litres, before a change of crystals was called for. One was left wondering, why not 100 litres? Anyway, 99 sounded enough to be getting on with. However, as it was barely the minimum for a fortnight for one person, I wondered if I should volunteer to go back on the old-fashioned pill. Peter would have none of it and began the energetic pumping action required to force the hotel tap water to pass ever so slowly from a jug to a water-bottle. After taking turns at this for some time, we allowed ourselves to savour a luxurious (and, by now, much needed) draught. In reminiscent mood we lay back, exhausted, to consider the day's proceedings.

The water tasted absolutely ghastly, but I did not dare to say anything, for fear of causing offence. At best it had an after-taste of iodine, which I consoled myself was good for thyroid patients.

Nor was Peter the picture of contentment. He nonchalantly stretched forward to retrieve the instruction leaflet, discarded at our feet. We were lying, Roman fashion, as, needless to say, there were no chairs or furniture. A look of stark comic-book horror slowly crept over his face. It transpired that 'purified' water was meant to be left to stand for at least three minutes before consumption. Any purification was busy performing in our stomachs.

Feeling more facetious than ever, I asked if, in this enlightened dual purpose age, there was any chance of such an ultra modern device doubling up as a stomach pump.

Stiles preferred to ignore me. He never gives up. Instead, painstakingly, he started all over again. This time, after the appropriate delay with a lesser quantity, he swilled and sniffed before attempting to swallow. Finally, he pronounced it infinitely preferable to the Guildford variety.

I told him that all it had done for me was bring back the horrors of childhood remedies. Taste and smell for memories. We discussed all those patent remedies, which had somehow gone by the board. Dr Collis Brown, Scott's Emulsion, Radio Malt, Dr Page Barker's Dandruff Lotion, Cod Liver Oil pills, Woodward's Gripe Water, Eucalyptus oil. We wondered how many of the old favourites had been found by the Americans in their survey of over eighty chemists the previous year. Refreshed by the drink and the slightest increase in oxygen intake, we decided it was time to do our first walkabout, but for some of our quests we would need guidance. In the event, the sandstorm was so thick our walkabout never got further than the first hundred yards from the hotel.

In the whole Mazar mix, there was only one gleam of sanity. And that, for me, was in the eye of the general factotum of Barat's Hotel. His name was Korban. He claimed to have spent eighteen years in kitchen and dining-room service in the Kabul Intercontinental. It was hard to believe it had been there that long. Whatever the case, Korban knew what was what and, when grafting, who was who. Most importantly from our point of view, he spoke good dining-room English. He was also able to write out vital addresses and our essential needs on little slips of paper, for literates in the street or taxi-drivers to interpret. Once we had made our mark with him, a Chinese 'Crown' electric fan miraculously appeared on a chair in our room. Korban's ability to distinguish quality when he saw it was only exceeded by his puzzlement at finding us in such a dump in the first place.

When Korban was not the General Manager of Barat's, he doubled up as the barman/waiter at the United Nations Hostel. Not surprisingly, therefore, during our stay at Barat's we found that most of the unexpected treats Korban afforded us could subsequently be traced to the UN Hostel refrigerator. But of course, we were not to discover that for some time. Our booking for the UN Hostel was four days away, at best. We would never have appreciated it half so much if we had not had the Barat's experience first.

We felt we owed it to Korban's past life at the Kabul Intercontinental to subject ourselves to dinner in the Barat's dining-room for the first evening at least. Indeed, there was no alternative. The dining-room was all plasterboard and chrome, with the odd homely Swiss mountain scene. There was no electricity, so we ate by romantic candlelight and the flickering firelight. The flickering firelight was in the kitchen, which we could see. As usual the fire was made up on the floor next to the stove. The food was hard to identify and harder still to eat.

However, what happened next, at least, took our minds off what we were eating. Korban's kitchen assistant, who doubled up as the waiter, removed our tablecloth mid-meal to use it for a prayer mat. We didn't know whether to laugh or remonstrate. Prayers were no sooner over than he replaced it. Was it a fundamentalist insult, or an attempt to flatter the West?

Our first need the next morning was for cash. We used the appropriate Korban slip to get ourselves taken to the bank, the only bank. It adjoined a depository for wheelbarrows. Were the wheelbarrows going to be needed to cart away the Weimar Republic Afghan currency?

We entered a large public area with heavily barred tiny windows at the far end. The manager's office was slightly more welcoming on the right-hand side as you entered. It was lined with battered Russian rexine sofas. In contrast, the manager himself affected a smart Winston Churchill siren suit. (Winston Churchill often wore a siren suit quite like a boiler suit.) In jest, I asked him point blank if he were the manager or the window-cleaner. Happily, he enjoyed the joke.

'How do you find Mazar?' he asked.

'By mistake,' I replied. He loved that.

Once we had explained what we were after, he told us we were in the wrong place. This was a bank for deposits - hopeless for exchange ... bad rates! He suggested we went to the money market, and promptly set about obliging one of his customers to take us there. It turned out to be diametrically opposite, on the other side of the blue Hazrat Ali mosque, in a large open space, teeming with open-handed traders. They were all on the 'floor' of the exchange, simultaneously shouting the odds and scrambling for the only takers in sight ... us. It was Bedlam. Bundles of notes were waved under our noses. The choice seemed to lie between fresh, minted-in-Moscow 'Afghanis', or we could settle for US dollars, which could have been forged in Iran or be post-Irangate American forgeries.

Just as we were contemplating a wheelbarrow full of each, our dreams were shattered. Our British currency was unheard of. Only mild curiosity was shown in The Lady featured on the notes. Luckily for me, as it was my responsibility to manage such detail, Pakistani rupees were, by contrast, much in demand. We were able to leave unmolested with conspicuous fistfuls of confetti to spend in the adjoining market.

This was like a Victorian Oxford Street, still made up of threepenny and sixpenny stalls. Peter and I always kid ourselves our needs are simple, but we were soon weighed down with all the survival-kit clobber we have grown used to. The old faithfuls - a

Chinese electric immersion heater, consisting of a bare element to plunge into the enamel ware teapot or tea mug. Depending on provenance, the enamel ware is decorated with bears or hedgehogs. Then we needed a kilo of karva green tea and a minimum of forty carefully counted out cardomom seeds. These came in a cone of brittle browned perished newsprint.

A Khamsin (yellow dust storm) threatened. Visibility was suddenly reduced to ten feet. The grit penetrated to the missing fillings in your teeth and turned your throat and nostrils to sandpaper.

I think Mazar is about the most destitute dump I have ever visited, although the fierce spirit of the Uzbek is still evident in every face. But the flesh is undernourished, war-ravaged, and deserving of compassion. There is food of sorts. Live sheep and goats stand tethered disconsolate amidst the hanging carcasses. Occasionally, they would shift uneasily from one hip to the other, like shopgirls.

If their Lord God, the God of Abraham and of Isaac and of Jacob, still savoured the sweet smell of the piety of their sacrifice with an exhibition of swarming flies - then, His recognition has never been more evident than here. Worse than the Australian outback, they have taken over the marketplace. They covered those exposed halal carcasses. They covered the wooden chopping blocks, running with fresh blood. They covered the axe-head and shaft and, momentarily, gave it the illusion of being borne across the already blackened diced wood surface by their slave-gang hordes. They covered all the indifferent local fruit on display. Finally, they covered even the bulked up brown leaf tea. Nothing escaped their highly mobile fleeting attention. Least of all you, your eyes, your nostrils, your mouth, or your ears. And there, at your feet, ran the ever-open sewer.

The excess of chemist shops over *chaikhanas* (tea houses) stood out. But the demand must be there, to support so many quack pharmacies - all selling much the same thing, large quantities of chemical drugs. These were doled out, as in the West, on an overkill basis for self-administration. Seemingly, the only thing to differentiate man from the beasts of the field is his propensity to pour poison down his throat. Coffee, like sterling, had gone out of style.

In the sandstorm we only just managed to make it as far as Dr Dadrass's clinic. He was out, so we left a note to say we would be back in the morning. Unlike the shock he gave us when he visited England, we wanted to give him a pleasant surprise. We never could understand how Afghans managed to give Immigration Control the slip. They needed visas, which they never had. The entry route was always the same, Heathrow or Gatwick, in transit for America. It hardly seems possible, we could only suppose they were mistaken for cleaning staff and simply shuffled through. Whatever the explanation, Dr Dadrass was definitely on the loose in England for three or four months, before returning to Afghanistan via Pakistan. He never did get to America. Maybe his impressions of Britain were enough to put him off.

The one thing to his undying credit was that he had returned to Afghanistan at all. Very few Afghan doctors returned to their roots. Most preferred what they found in the West. Dadrass couldn't have gone much deeper into Afghanistan if he'd tried, but then his origin was in Mazar. It would be an education to see him in his own back yard. We had kept the scrap of paper with Korban's written instructions and, after a cup of Korban coffee, handed it over to the taxi-driver, full of hope.

Our first call was to what Peter referred to as Dadrass's Harley Street premises. These were on the first floor of a building directly opposite the hospital where Dadrass appeared, all smiles and gentle as a kitten, in the most immaculate starched white coat. He was obviously delighted to see us. He had few visitors in his self-imposed place of exile, or was it homecoming?

Dadrass began by giving us his overview of the medical picture in Mazar, the most significant feature of which was that the Russians, in fourteen years, had done nothing to either improve conditions or institute teaching. So, what we were about to see had stood still for all that time. The only positive aspect of all this inertia was that Balkh was said to be Aids free. Any woman suspected of consorting with visitors, meaning Russians, was automatically shot, together with her whole family! The blood transfusion laboratory was unserviceable anyway.

Peter's official report read 'This is the major orthopaedic centre for civil patients in Mazar. It is under the supervision of Dr Dadrass, a trained orthopaedic surgeon. It has the advantage of a small portable X-ray machine in working order'. A rarity indeed.

'It is, however, in an unsuitable building, formerly an hotel, and lacks most basic facilities. The conditions in the wards and theatres are unhygienic and unsuitable for general basic surgery, although this is performed. I see no future for this hospital, either as a centre for ex-pat surgeons (to instruct) or for financial investment with a view to improvements.'

Almost all cases were infectious.

The previous evening we had experienced a sneak preview. As stated, Dadrass was out. He was over at the Public Health Hospital (confusingly called Barat's too), where he had other responsibilities. We were unannounced and unexpected. It would not have made the slightest difference. But it gave us an inkling of things to come. We were given a whirlwind tour, ostensibly looking for Dadrass. It was not to prove the centre of learning and modern medicine we had anticipated. There was a pipe stand with dripping tap, creating a green slime open drain, leading from the central courtyard out through the main entrance to the street. That was the water supply.

Still discernible on the flaking yellow walls, was a hand-painted notice in English, proclaiming that this had indeed once been an hotel on the 1960s Hippy Trail. It might once have seen better days, but cleanliness, let along hygiene, were long forgotten concepts. All the mosquito netting was torn. Dejected patients sat around looking resentful, sedated with indescribable smells.

On our tour, we were subjected to the charade of exchanging our sandals for felt slippers, before entering the operating theatre. Once within, we came upon a couple of students who, still in their shoes, had chosen this quiet spot for a chat and a smoke. The operating theatre resembled nothing so much as a peasant's farmyard, littered with obsolete equipment left to rust.

The scrub-room basin was blocked with sand and the taps had been rusted shut for years. Now it was relegated to the accumulation of stale swabs.

I cannot think what possessed Dadrass, but on our next visit, he took us down to the bowels of the building to inspect the latrines. The whole basement area was ankle deep in raw sewage. We were invited to walk through on duck boards, as if in some World War I trench-warfare diorama. His explanation was that the lavatories themselves were blocked long ago with small pebbles, used as their bumf substitute. It reminded me of one American tourist's tribute to Pompeii, 'The toilets were terrible!'

From there we were taken into the consulting room. It was an office with rows of planters' chairs along each of the side walls, with a low table between, displaying distillers' ashtrays. Smoking was actively encouraged. If a patient needed to be examined, a desk at the far end of the room was used. Primarily because of the Muslim aversion to seeing the naked, or even part-naked form, these examinations were rare. However, for the next three hours we were subjected to a succession of assorted patients. Dr Dadrass presided over two other doctors, his assistants. The first, Akbar, was a very big man who obviously enjoyed his food and was very cheerful and friendly. His colleague, altogether keener and more athletic looking, was called Mohammed Shafique. He was a chainsmoker.

All three hung on Peter Stiles' every word.

Apart from any ability the doctors might have, the hospital's only assets were that efficient little Japanese X-ray machine and a bank of operating theatre lights, which looked as if they might work, given power.

The lasting impression, however, was that there was nobody in charge. Certainly not Dadrass, who was wholly ineffectual. For my part, I wouldn't care to turn up there with a cut finger.

But, for balance, let us close with Peter's understated official report 'Dadrass is well-trained and competent within the limits of his environment, but has no power of command and accepts the will of God.'

---

[1] The Uzbeks crossed the Oxus into Afghanistan as the Russian Empire expanded. Racially they are the same people as found in Uzbekistan. Muslim races favour strong leadership. Abdul Rashid Dostrum was their natural champion at the time, and with short 'absences' has remained so ever since.

36

UN Creature Comforts

It was time for us to make a clean break and the only way we could do this was by moving into the UN Community Association Hostel.

What a different world greeted us there! Iced drinks and air-conditioning in front of BBC News by satellite from Hong Kong. Every chance of meeting other interesting ex-pats. Dull ones too.

Korban had the air of being touchingly relieved to find us settling into more fitting surroundings. In choosing the Barat way, we must, subconsciously, have had Dean's in mind, a wholly unjustifiable comparison.

At lunch, we fell in with a twenty-five-year-old Field Manager for the International Organisation for Migration. His name was Peter Herbert. His 'plate' was full with refugees returning from Iran. Each of them was given $25 worth of Iranian rials, a 50 kilo sack of wheat and a piece of heavy duty plastic sheeting per family.

Peter Herbert's problems began as those refugees proceeded beyond Herat. Unscrupulous Uzbek commanders were holding them to ransom for their cash handouts. Herbert's job was to persuade Abdul Rashid Dostrum to intercede. A tough assignment.

After lunch, some kindly young doctors, who had been at an East German medical school in Kabul for seven years, took us in their Russian jeep to where they said the Balkh Medical College was to be found, at the back of the premises of the Public Health, or Barat's Hospital. Although East German educated, none of them, significantly, when asked, had ever heard of any other 'German' activity, aid or otherwise.

This time we were in for a cultural shock of a different kind. As we meandered between the general ward rabbit-hutch buildings ranging over a stark and crumbling campus, we became aware that we were following what appeared to be a couple of prize hookers. Regular as clockwork, one or other of these sirens would give a furtive backward glance with heavily kohled eyes, to reassure themselves that we really were following them. They were teetering along, waggling their bottoms atop stiletto heels they could not quite manage. We needed no reminding we were on serious business and walked steadfastly past them without acknowledgement, only to find on arrival at the Medical College that the whole establishment had been overrun by hundreds of these jezebels.

Seventy per cent of the medical students here were girls. The men were away, playing soldiers, fighting each other, leaving behind them four hundred and twenty predatory females covered in warpaint. Having discarded the *burqa*, the chowdah and seemingly the headscarf too, they were no doubt getting ready to burn their bras, if they had any in the first place.

These students, many of whom had moved from Kabul, were highly motivated, but their problems were daunting. They had no books, no journals, no pens, no paper and, of course, no X-ray. They concentrated on being active in the wards of the Mazar Civic Hospital.

Although this hospital was purpose-built and structurally sound, it was run down and in need of repair. Anywhere outside the Superintendent's immediate field of view showed no sign of basic hygiene. Time and again we were to witness this phenomenon. There were never any plans to correct major deficiencies, just a strange long-suffering 'acceptance world' prepared to put up with the absence of even the most basic equipment.

Any hope that good leadership might have beneficial effects further down the line would be another delusion. There was plenty of good leadership here, but Afghans don't respond favourably to moral pressure. It is not part of their make-up.

Flypapers would have made a start. But it was going to take more than flypapers. Incinerators too. Simple scrubbing with caustic soda for the next fifteen years might get rid of the gunge of the last fifteen years. It was like looking at a Russian hangover. There was caked dried blood on all the operating surfaces. That was as nothing to the torture chamber aspect of the lithotomy position cast-iron 'thrones' in the delivery room. These were caked at base, like bottle candlesticks, with entrails and afterbirth.

Next in the chamber of horrors was the only 'working model' available to the students. It was a formaldahyde corpse in a bath with a lid. It was one of the few things that did work. And there was no end in sight of replacement corpses.

As the climax to our tour we were taken to see the pride of the establishment. It was an X-ray machine installed by Siemens about the time of the fall of Tobruk in 1942. Now it had become a museum piece. Too heavy to move, it had been given over to a pair of nesting swallows. This exhibit was all they had to teach fourth-year radiology students.

If there were streams of western visitors, it would begin to look as if this was a set piece tour, staged to win sympathy and extract donations, but everything was shown in such a matter-of-fact unemotive way, that there was no question of soliciting. Nor were there any other visitors to be seen or expected.

The last exhibits were as exceptional as the others; they just took a bit more explaining.

Over the years, the hospital had a succession of autoclaves, first Chinese and then Russian. These are sterilisation chambers into which surgical instruments are placed between operations. As I understand it, the key factors are temperature control and the monitoring of time periods. So, the gauges and thermometers matter. Here, once the original source of heat, be it gas or electricity, failed for whatever reason, the autoclave had to be moved to an outer shed, where it was encouraged to continue to function, after a fashion, by having wood fires lit under it! We were proudly shown half-a-dozen of these, being operated along the same lines as their preferred cooking methods, as if it was altogether more reassuring to be able to see the purification of fire at work.

The only other identifiable Russian legacy were masses of highly coloured, moulded plastic teaching-aids of fishes, frogs, rabbits and de-sexed humans. There were so many of these that they appeared on all four walls of each classroom.

But the most glaring shortage was exercise books and pencils. There cannot be much worse than desperately wanting to learn and being denied the means. All this on top of the accumulated despair of years of partisan struggle against a callous super-power.

*

Just as we were about to despair and ask ourselves why we were risking life and limb at our age, in the back of beyond, for no apparent good reason, we walked into one of the three most inspiring experiences we were to have on our whole trip. Two of these were under the auspices of the International Committee of the Red Cross (ICRC) and the third was the HALO operation.

We had first been introduced to Markus Thonius (Mark Antony) by Fiona and Carlotta Gall, beside the swimming pool at the Pearl Continental, the ex-pat mecca in Peshawar. Markus was on long weekend leave. Carlotta had explained that, like the Sandy Gall Afghanistan Appeal organisation, Markus was in the business of making and fitting artificial limbs to mostly mine casualties. He was a striking young man. Well over six feet tall, Teutonic to his fingertips, with blue eyes and fair hair, he was, as his name suggested, of Roman descent. Over the past two and a half years he had mastered English and Dari. He had been pressing in his invitation for us to visit him, and took obvious pride in telling us of his aims and achievements to date. If he had had any disappointments, they were well concealed.

His ICRC Rehabilitation centre was on the road out of Mazar towards the airport, just beyond the roundabout with the sky blue triumphal arch. This, made of plywood, was, for once, devoid of Dostrum's portrait.

The whole centre is a model of how the job should be done. Built to a Swiss chalet design, European visitors found themselves at once in sympathetic, harmonious surroundings. Cleanliness and efficiency were to be expected, but the preoccupation with well-regimented order and method spilled over into the manicured garden. The nurses looked like air hostesses dressed by a Paris fashion house.

Born in Switzerland, Markus had been highly trained at the Federal School for Orthopaedic Technology at Dortmund. After telling us that, he laboured his next point, which was that he was totally apolitical. He explained how ICRC had to be hyper-sensitive on this score, since the other aspect of their work was the care of prisoners of war; for which purpose they had set apart full-time dedicated 'political' officers.

Markus commanded the respect of the Afghans. Unlike other organisations, where a certain level of pilfering was accepted, he said that each of his craftsmen was trusted to draw what they needed from the unsupervised stores and there was no shrinkage whatsoever. Even when the workshop had to be closed down for four months whilst hostilities were too hot, and left in the care of five guards, there was still no looting.

We were shown every nook and cranny, including the cookhouse, laundry and latrines. All was in apple-pie order. The patients were cheerful and amazingly respectful by Afghan standards.

Patients were accommodated and fed free for as long as it took to fit them out and get them back on their 'feet' again. To 'pass out', they had to master an assault course. This was a cross between municipal golf and a children's adventure playground. There were already over two thousand registered patients, who could expect to return every two years, on average, for repairs and refits. Children had to return rather more frequently - every six months or so.

Markus told us they were currently turning out a hundred prostheses, or surgical replacements for damaged limbs, a month, or one thousand a year allowing for holidays. With the Kabul influx, the waiting list had grown to eight hundred, but with a lot of extra work this had been reduced to five hundred. They always tried to keep a three-months reserve of components in store.

Surprisingly, there were six hundred different components, of which about four hundred were available locally, either in Afghanistan or Pakistan. The rest had to come from Europe. These were mostly machinery parts for making the prostheses.

It was all most impressive. But the most inspiring part was the turn-round time for Afghan patients. Suffering few of the psychological problems of Europeans, some had been known to be up and walking - no sticks, no crutches - within four days of being fitted out!

Afghans are now so used to seeing other Afghans with false limbs that they take their calamity in their stoic stride.

Just as I assumed the tour was over, I found Peter Stiles deep in debate on the relative merits of the Jaipur, Sach and Seattle 'foot'. He was holding one of them as if it were the Portland Vase. To him, it was an object of great beauty. Seeing my bemused expression, he explained that here, in this remote spot, we had stumbled on the miracle of the Seattle foot. What it offered over alternatives, was an 'energy storing capability'. This meant that the materials used - fibres, plastics, rubber, wood - when laminated, would have extra 'latent' spring. So that, when a young energetic stride pressed down into its phantom presence from the stump above, it responded like its former living member and set its user, with sprightly step, jubilantly on his way. This was accompanied by a graphic demonstration of foot springing on the work bench.

As much to sound out whether Markus had a sense of humour to go with all the master-race efficiency, Peter told the story of the little old lady who had come to see him the previous week at the Sandy Gall prosthesis unit at Hyatabad. She wanted a new leg fitted. It was by no means her first fitting or her first leg. Amputees tend to have collections of at least two or three, for alternate days of the week. The state of the stump gives away the existence of other models.

The standard procedure on such occasions is to carry on with the fitting, but on sending the patient away, he or she is told to return the next day, bringing their alternative limbs with them for refitting or repair.

At this, the old harridan said that would be quite impossible. When Peter asked her why, she had replied that firewood had become that scarce, she had used it to cook dinner the night before! She had gone on to say that in her line of business, she was probably better off without it. When Peter then asked what her work was, she cheerfully replied that she was a beggar, which in Islam is an honourable estate.

Markus had a good laugh, but had no story of his own to match it. Unfortunately, he was also too recently established to have heard tell of any of the much vaunted German Afghanistan Committee operations in those parts.

We gave Markus all the praise that was his due and told him that, without exaggeration, ICRC were the benchmark for excellence in all our surveys and searches. Nobody ever came anywhere near them.

37

Balkh: the Mother of Cities

We ducked out of lunch that day, because Dadrass, whatever his shortcomings, was a godly man and had anticipated our need to feed the soul, for once, in preference to the body. Akbar had been detailed to eat our lunch and his number two, Mohammed Shafique, had 'volunteered' to be our guide. He had managed to requisition a recently donated Mercedes military ambulance for our only 'medical tourism' excursion.

Not to be outshone, Akbar claimed to have organised a number of commanders, who were ready to fly us by helicopter to either Herat or Taloqan, on our return. But the UN Hostel network had already warned us that there had been three total write-offs over the last three weeks - without survivors. Lack of maintenance had been cited as the cause.

As we left for Balkh - the Mother of Cities - we waited eagerly to hear what our guide had to tell us on the subject. But he knew absolutely nothing. It wasn't even certain he knew where it was. After ten or fifteen miles, we came upon a kind of garden suburb, built by King Amanullah to what resembled a German design of the 1930s. At the core there was a large and pleasant circle of giant chinar trees (also known as Persian plane trees), offering most welcome shade. Here we stopped to ask the way and take on board some proper informed guidance.

The famed shrine to the memory of Khoja Abu Nasr Parsa stood off at a tangent, shedding tiles like floods of tears. None of this was anything to do with the ancient city of Balkh, which was still two or three kilometers further on, but it was sure to be our last hope of a local guide. As it turned out, the man finally selected to fill the breach knew less about the place than I did and a lot less than Peter Stiles.

Our widely-read and well-informed lead surgeon had not only taken the trouble to re-read Arnold Toynbee's *From the Oxus to the Jumna*, he had brought photostat copies of the relevant pages with him. Half expecting some such ploy, I had brought along Robert Byron's *The Road to Oxiana*, in which he gives an hilarious account of the ambitious Nazi German plan to rebuild Balkh. In Hitler's eyes, it was not only the Mother of Cities but, more importantly, the first Aryan capital. It has never been satisfactorily explained how the Afghans managed to reconcile the adoption of not one, but two lost tribes of Israel within their host, with their pure Aryan descent;

Afghans have always been adept at acrobatic *volte face*.

The fact that Genghis Khan had razed the place seven hundred years before was only added incentive for the restoration. Nor were they deterred by a site that had been bypassed by the shifting sands of the desert and a now vanished water source. Instead they had preferred to put their faith in their Führer's mystical view of history as much as the 'myth of succeeding generations'.

Once you catch sight of them, there is no mistaking the remains of the walls of the City of Balkh. Only massive slave labour could have achieved the sheer scale, comparable to Silbury Hill, of a small section (8 kms) of the Great Wall or the Karakoram Highway. The walls are mostly down, but the foundations are still discernible after seven hundred years, running round the eight kilometers of city circumference and rising in places to seventy or eighty feet. This is particularly so on the southern approach and stretching westward. There are sections here which include the hill escarpment that could even reach to one hundred feet above the mulberry groves and fields of waving barley. The area enclosed is totally deserted and given over to scrub and weeds.

We decided to take a stroll amidst all this desolation. Peter nattered away about Alexander the Great and his wife Roxana, who came from Balkh. We wondered if the bright blue and equally bright green shards we were kicking at our feet really did date from Ghenghis Khan's sacking of the city in 1222. Surely it was more likely that it had been used as a tip much later, but, if so, by whom?

Previous visitors, both in the last century and earlier in this, had spoken of the foundations of major buildings. Of these we saw no sign. When asked about this specifically, our guide could only tell us that the Russians had done a lot of damage. One must respect the local knowledge, especially if it is not book lore. And, sure enough, it turned out there had been some earlier mad Russian incursion in the 1920s, which could well have done the final damage.

As usual, I only had to see a muddle to get into it. I had spotted a well-sited gun emplacement on the ramparts and was gently heading our party along a goat track in that general direction when, up ahead, there was frantic waving and shouting.

Wholly absorbed in our love of pleasing decay and ancient ruins, totally oblivious to the realities of civil war, we were on the point of wandering into the well-sited gun emplacement's equally well-sited protective minefield.

I felt very stupid and contrite. It would have been no earthly good saying there were no warning notices. We retraced our steps to the very foot print.

Once back outside the walls we stopped to record their remaining grandeur. The spot we chose was in the shade of some white mulberry trees, beside the wreck of a Russian tank. Two small shepherd boys came up to us bearing a newborn Karakul lamb ready for slaughter and meant for the Jewish Astrakhan merchants in the bazaar. The shepherd boys afforded us our lunch that day, which consisted of half a handful of sun-dried white mulberries each, charged with youthful energy.

That was the sum total of our cultural fun. It had been a very special experience, although we had in fact failed to view any of the Islamic remains we should have seen. They would have to await that elusive proper guide and a lot more time. We would have to come back. Now we had to plan how we were going to get to Pul-e-Kumrhi, some 180 kilometers away, by any means other than helicopter. It would have to be Herat next year, once we knew we stood some chance of getting past Dostrum's greedy commanders.

Thanks to the contacts made in the UN Hostel, we had the lucky break born of planned opportunism. It was a bit like travelling 'club'. In casual conversation a certain Jacques de Bayle of the UN Mission suggested it was always worth giving Peter Forster a call. I wondered if the world was run by Forsters. Unlike Sir Oliver or Sarah, this one was a Swiss German in charge of the UN World Food Programme.

By a remarkable stroke of luck when I rang him at 8 a.m. the following morning, he told me that there would be a UNICEF convoy leaving at 8.45 a.m. I said we were ready and would very much appreciate a lift to Pul-e-Kumrhi. They were not going any further. He told me to contact a Mr Shrestha, at a given number. At 8.30 a.m. Mr Shrestha was at the door. He took us to our next rendezvous, which was a vast UN caravanserai. It was in the shadow of a giant Russian-built bakery and grain silo. At 9 a.m. sharp, Peter Stiles and I were each allotted next-driver cab seats in two of the three Russian 20cwt trucks and our convoy set out accompanied by two Russian jeeps - one in front, one in rear, flying the right UN flags. Our cargo consisted of canned vegetable oil and seed corn.

To the untrained eye, as we sped along the straight drive over steppe and scree at the foot of the Hazarajat mountains, the agriculture looked largely unaffected by the war. Could it have been because it was next to the Russian border? It was interesting to see that it was the men who were harvesting the corn all along the plain, by hand with sickles. Vast flocks of fat-tailed sheep, goats and some cattle were grazing the stubble.

Next, we came upon what Peter Herbert had been so keen to see - a massive camp of Uzbek refugeees, escaping from a pro-communist reign of terror in Tajikistan. It was estimated there were a hundred thousand of them. Dostrum had accepted them, but only disarmed, and had promptly moved them well away from the border to discourage them from mounting destabilising incursions into their old country, which was precisely the role proposed for them by the next-door province of Kunduz, whose leaders saw in them ideal material to help establish an Islamic government in Tajikistan.

At the time, there were also concerted efforts being made to eliminate the few remaining Russian outposts along the (Oxus) border - like it was going to be their last chance to kill a Russian. It began to look as if we should have these Muslim Volunteers to add to the standard banditry hazards on our journey to Pul-e-Kumrhi and beyond. We managed to photograph the large tented camps as we passed them from the cabs of our respective vehicles.

Shortly afterwards, we entered the precipitous defile of the famous gorge of Tashkurghan. It was soon resplendent with large stretches of oasis greenery where the waters gushed forth to nurture apples, plums and figs. But only too soon this lush landscape gave way to yet another graveyard for Russian military equipment, left to rust like modern sculpture browsing amongst the giant rocks and rolling sand dunes.

In theory, we were only going to take a half-hour break on our journey at a place called Samargan. Although the map showed a more direct route to Taloqan, it was as deceptive as ever, because the road had been impassable for over a year.

The half-hour became extended to one hour, then two and finally three hours. Part of the consignment was being off-loaded, but there was no way that could take so long. We were left to our own devices. Fortunately, there was shade. We were frequently pestered by bands of robber youths demanding baksheesh. We gave none for fear of opening the flood-gates. The *chaikhana* beckoned, proffering its garrulous hospitality, with rare tables and chairs, set out on a terrace. But it looked even more fly-blown than usual and we preferred to keep our own company and go without. Still, we were to remain the focus of local entertainment, resulting in an impromptu clinic.

One old boy, noticing our grey hairs and abstinence, took pity on us and sidled over to give us each a lump of what looked like pumice - something between limestone and soda. After much gesturing and grinning, we duly sucked it and discovered it was rock hard camel cheese, korut. Once moistened, it stank and took ages to disintegrate, but it certainly sustained us. We drank very little water. There was no chance of a pee once the convoy was on the move. Because of the intense heat and dehydration rate, there was no call for one either. Dehydration was the killer.

We were much relieved when Shrestha returned. No explanation whatever was given for the delay. But we were that content to be on the move again, we forebore to comment. Anyway, we were in no position to complain! Peter had made some silent computation that we were venturing a journey of some 1,000 kilometers with no definite support!

Anyway, at Pul-e-Kumrhi we had the luxury of alternatives. There was said to be accommodation for the asking at the Cement Factory. It was known that the Textile Factory Hotel was full to bursting with 'high class' refugees paying a premium to escape the fighting in Kabul. The alternative was to look up HALO Trust, who were known to have one of their operational bases there.

As it happened, HALO came first on our road, on the outskirts of the town. We were given such a wholehearted welcome on our arrival that it was, for me, the high point of our trip. Although Colin Mitchell may have passed the word to repel boarders because of his grave misgivings that, before long, the bed & breakfast function would come to supersede mine-clearance, it looked as if we were to be exceptionally allowed. After all, mine-clearers needed medics in attendance. The purveyor of the rapturous welcome was a beetroot-red giant of a man, who was to prove to be more of a saviour to us than just a friend in need. He was another Phil Jones, a highly literate as well as computer-literate ex-Royal Fusilier.

The HALO premises are set well back off the main road, behind a large vehicle compound, in which, amongst other things, were parked two enormous white whales, which turned out to be flail-wielding tanks for mine clearance.

Whilst we were getting to know our new hosts, the UN convoy had pulled off the road and were waiting in a state of expectant trance. What we had failed to grasp, was that on 1 February that year (1993) four UN staff members had been murdered near Jalalabad. As a result, the UN had reduced its ex-patriate presence in Afghanistan to near zero. Along with The Red Cross, they risked becoming the target of choice. To some extent they had lost the respect of the Afghans. HALO, on the other hand, continued to be held in universal high esteem, and their premises were consequently amongst the most secure anywhere in the country. Mr Shrestha wanted to park the UN convoy in the HALO compound overnight, and Phil Jones kindly agreed.

The centre of the building was all staircase and window. That was where we first caught sight of Phil Jones who took us up to the living room. There was a pin-board with photographs of homely scenes in England. An array of old Gordon's gin and Johnny Walker whisky bottles was produced from the landing fridge. They were filled with chilled water. We exchanged news.

Later, we were taken along the corridor to a large bedroom with three beds and its own bathroom, and told to make ourselves at home.

HALO wisely relies heavily on resident local experts. In the case of Kabul and Pul-e-Kumrhi they are brothers. Here Doctor Nazir, an eye surgeon, lives with his family on the ground floor, in a self-contained flat, next to the kitchens and staff. He works at the Government Hospital and is well-placed to effect those facilitating bigwig introductions to Sayd Jaffir, Sayyid Mansoor, etc., as well as interpreting the local and national news. His brother, Dr Farid, is a cardiologist, who runs the HALO operation in Lucky Five street in Kabul. It makes for a tight-knit family feel.

HALO obviously attaches importance to feeding their people well. Both establishments are renowned for serving good, stimulating and varied meals. I sensed Colin Mitchell's attention to detail here and the morale boosting effect of good food.[1]

It was agreed that once we had completed our hospital visits, which had been set up very rapidly by Doctor Nazir, we could join Phil to witness some de-mining. He was keen to show us what was involved.

Pul-e-Kumrhi, which translates poetically into 'Bridge of Doves', is the natural focal point between Mazar, Taloqan and Kabul. It is a pleasant town, laid out with plenty of trees and a proper appreciation for the fast flowing Kurdiz river. Sayid Jaffir has a tight grip on the place. Nevertheless, you feel at ease walking the streets, which cannot be said of other places. The military were doubtless there, but they were less apparent.

Phil told us he had had any number of helicopter rides over the hill, to where the main force was to be found. He confirmed what I had always been told, that the Ismailis were well-equipped and in impressive shape. Sayd Jaffir himself lived in considerable style in the park-like setting we had noticed on the side of the road, on our arrival. He also enjoyed BBC Asia News by satellite and had established his own relay station.

Over the evening meal, Phil introduced us to Ali, who was to be our interpreter and guide. He began by taking us on a good sight-seeing tour of the town. To reach the German showpiece Textile

Factory Hotel, we had to cross the raging Kurdiz river, by taking a rickety, bouncing, swaying wooden footbridge with the odd plank missing. One slip and we'd be white water flotsam. There had been German factory managers with attractive homes ranged along the river bank, within easy walking distance of the factory gates. Most of the buildings showed a post-Schinkel architectural influence, but especially the smart funk hotel.

There was a Textile Workers' Hospital, which was set in well-wooded parkland. For the time being, this was given over to the military. We were asked to concentrate our attention on the Government civilian hospital.

We made our visit the following morning. This hospital was in stark contrast to everything we had seen so far. It was soundly run along military lines, with a proper appreciation of hygiene. There was a uniformed military medical officer in charge, who was referred to as the President. His name card stated, quite plainly, that he was Dr Narmgui. He had a very tight grip on affairs, no doubt reflecting his political boss.

What was missing was basic medical knowledge and basic medical equipment. This was surprising, after all we had been led to expect of Ismaili funds. Again there was no X-ray machine. Patients had to be referred to the Textile Hospital. There was only one small cramped operating theatre. It was badly equipped and had no orthopaedic instruments whatsover.

In compensation, Dr Narmgui took us to see his pride and joy. This was a new clinic block he had just completed. We were told that part of this complex could be made available for a physiotherapy clinic. A lot of money still needed to be spent on it. It was to 'builder's finish' again. It still needed sanitation as well as doors, windows, etc.

We were assured categorically that sanitation was always dug in afterwards. It was to be hoped it did not end up resembling Dadrass's best efforts.

We had also to consider that Pul-e-Kumrhi was directly in the atavistic gaze of Dostrom's feared militia. Dostrum's alliances were notorious for their brevity. He claimed he had been in parley with Ahmad Shah Massoud for all of the past five years. When asked for confirmation of this, Massoud replied that it was more like five minutes!

It was now time to go in search of the de-mining teams. Ali thought he had a clear idea of where they were to be found. But the instructions he had were muddled and we became fearful of missing out.

As we reluctantly turned back we saw the white vehicles parked in the shade of a large curtain mud wall, which was all that was left of what had once been a range of substantial farm buildings. On our way out the wall had hidden the vehicles from view. Now they were glaringly white and obvious against the mud backdrop. The track from the road to the site was clearly marked with a hundred yards or so of red and white tape.

The procedures as outlined were a lot more painstaking and laborious than we had ever imagined. It took ages to clear a very small area indeed.

The identification of an area as hazardous began, as often as not, as the result of some unfortunate casualty. The painstaking procedure would then begin with the establishment of a narrow strip corridor of cleared safe ground. This would then be expanded piecemeal, until the selected area was cleared. The patch designated that morning had included the former farm buildings and farmyard. After the Russians, the Kabul regime Afghans and the Mujahedeen had finished with it, it was hard to identify what was what. The area was suspected of containing unexploded bombs. One had been detonated the day before, and we could see the hole it had left. There were also shells lying around, and anti-personnel mines.

There were no short cuts. The equipment was rudimentary, nothing high-tech at all. Just metal detectors and remote probes. Modern mines are deficient in metal and the remote probes are no way remote enough.

Phil had a team of ten trained de-miners working on this site. They worked in pairs. They took it in turns to probe and delineate. Each parcel of cleared ground was contained within a clearly defined taped perimeter. It resembled nothing so much as an archaelogical dig. Both require unlimited patience.

Each square-inch of ground had to be scanned and probed. There was no quick way, no short cuts. No wonder it took forever and cost the earth. Not to mention the cost in lost lives and limbs. Someday soon, somebody would have to invent a laser means of detonating unexploded mines. Or devise some built-in self-destruct timing device. Otherwise, the future will indeed be grim not only for the rural communities of Afghanistan, but also for Cambodia, Mozambique and, no doubt, countless other areas of civil conflict throughout the world, both past and to come.

[1] Colin Mitchell, himself a gourmet, was reputed to complain about the standard of meals in HALO extablishments, but I suspect it was simply a means of keeping the catering staff on their toes.

38

'Sick Doctor' and Fleaseed Husk

That evening, after Ali had taken us for our evening stroll down by the river, we outlined our ambitious plan to reach Taloqan. We tried to explain how important it was to be able to see, at first hand, the workings of a prosthesis unit - so far 'out on a limb' of its own. We knew that besides the workshop run by trainees of the Sandy Gall Afghanistan Appeal, there was also the physiotherapy clinic run by Mary Macmakin. That alone would be a sure indicator of current and future surgery needs.

To get there meant going through the highly unstable military area of Baghlan, about thirty kilometers away to the north. The journey to Taloqan was altogether some 175 kilometers, but it was not a journey to be measured in miles or kilometers. On the other hand, if Mary could make it on a regular twice-a-year basis, then so should we.

Ali knew the country a lot better than most. He was an agronomist who had worked in the Kunduz as well as Taloqan itself. That had been for the communist Kabul regime, but we hoped that, as an agronomist, this would not be held against him. To have a knowledgeable guide and linguist all-in-one was more than we had dared to hope. Ali must have had a word with Phil Jones because the next thing we knew his services had been 'volunteered' for the trip! We would have got nowhere without him.

Our next task was to find a driver prepared to go that way. The first two we tried simply priced themselves out of consideration, although what Ali found extortionist by local standards would have been dirt cheap in Surrey. Only one driver, Amin by name, was prepared to undertake the three day excursion through the Baghlan, Kunduz and Takhar districts. Even then, Ali warned us, we could still get a last minute refusal - crying off for the sake of a sick child. Fathers are often landed with the sick children - the just price of greater mobility.

To test Amin's enthusiasm, we called for a briefing rendezvous at the HALO compound later that evening. We wanted to have a closer look at the Russian Volga taxi, its tyres, undercarriage, etc. As it turned out, Amin was testing our resolve. He made a first call for a hundred thousand Afghanis ($100) to buy petrol. The hire fee negotiated by Ali was two hundred thousand Afghanis ($200) plus five thousand Afghanis tip, on safe delivery back where we had started!

The earliest quotes had started at five hundred thousand Afghanis. The bus would have cost a fraction of this price, but it had no regular schedule there and the return journey was even less certain.

We pre-set Ali's fee at thirty thousand Afghanis plus a tip of five thousand to match Amin's ($35).

We tried to make only one stipulation. We felt we needed and deserved total freedom of movement. The ability to decide at any time to cut and run. We had had such bad reports of the district that we were dead against giving lifts to anyone. We wanted the option to chicken out if the going got too rough. With the driver we would already be four people, but by Afghan standards there was room for at least four more. In the event we relented over the no lifts rule - wisely, as things turned out, but there was no telling in advance.

Ali had many resourceful talents. He was highly inventive. Sickness, real and assumed, was to prove our salvation on most occasions. If the doctors were sick it must be serious. Better send them on their way, without further inquiry.

Interestingly enough, the classic British historic guises had included doctors as well as horse dealers and holy men. Each had its pros and cons but, over the years, doctors were to prove most effective. It was stressed, however, that it was important not to be too liberal with the potions, for fear of being considered worth robbing! Holy men were not only required to be fluent linguists but also conversant with the finer nuances of the Holy Koran and capable of philosophic argument. Neither that nor the search for horses was likely to fit our mission precisely. But it might have served better than the oldest, thinnest cover of all - 'just taking a spot of shooting leave!'

So we were reduced to taking turns at playing 'sick doctor'. You would have thought that by now the ever alert Afghan would have had his fill of sick *faranghi*, whether doctors or otherwise, but apparently not.

On the outward journey, I was able to give a particularly convincing performance of gastro-enteritis. In my obsession for vitamin 'C' I had foolishly indulged in flyblown apricots. My only distraction was to meet some much sicker people on our way. Wisely, they were waiting at a checkpoint, and the 'Muj' guard interceded for them. It was a poser, but we relented. In fact, the combination of a sick doctor with his sick patients became the high-speed *laissez-passer* of all time. It took epidemic proportions in the minds of some of the roadblock guards, and over the next three days it was to work wonders.

Thus we managed to ferry some half-dozen sets of genuine

emergency patients. There was a loving father with his small daughter, another with a sick child in his arms, a sickly looking woman with her ancient father, where it was hard to decide who was leading whom. Then there was a 'poisoned' youth with two male attendants. He may have been stung by a scorpion, but it wasn't clear.

We soon discovered that our idea of a veto would never have worked. We had reached an area where it was standard practice to fire over the vehicle, as opposed to at it, simply to indicate that a lift was required. Like hailing a taxi! This happened four or five times and each time we were obliged to take on board one, often two, fully armed bandits, who could have ordered us out of the vehicle on whim. Attempts to apply safety catches or gently redirect muzzles out of the window, were not always successful.

On occasion, these hoodlums proved a greater blessing than the sick. Interestingly, they never got in with the sick. Their strength lay in establishing our credibility at the next roadblock or two; sometimes, with luck, into the next township. What we could never allow ourselves to forget, was that there was every chance we should meet them all again, on the way back! There was no other road, in or out. The one on the map had been obliterated, or we would have been on it.

There was another obstacle, which in our ignorance we had failed to appreciate fully. Earlier that morning, shortly after the road had divided, the left fork going back to Mazar and the right heading for Taloqan, we had unwittingly passed through the confrontational 'front line' of the combined forces of Dostrum and Said Jaffir, as they faced Gulbuddin Hekmatyar. The two 'front lines' were barely a hundred yards apart, and those men seen loitering about did not give the appearance of intending each other any harm. But things might have taken a vicious turn by the time we came back. The landscape was blasted, with badly damaged buildings and the telling evidence of many tree stumps.

For well over a third of the distance, say sixty kilometers, the Baghlan to Kunduz road is more shell scrape than surface. For all of that distance, it is better to drive off the road than on it. Every other traveller has reached the same conclusion. So, on either side of what was the road, there is now a well-worn dust track, in places one or two lanes wide. Besides meandering all over the shop, churning up clouds of dust, there is an additional roller-coaster element. Add to this sensation the demands of cyclical collywobbles, and it may be appreciated how I was happy to be left to die in any ditch, at any time. The sooner the better. However, there is one abiding compensation for minding medics and that is they carry spongebags full of 'sample' patent remedies. Peter had brought Flagyland, the faithful standby - a nosebag of 'Fleaseed'. After a large dose, I began to take an interest in life again.

Fleaseed Husk is described on its packet as SAT ISABGOL, a natural vegetable product which is derived from isabgol seeds by a natural milking process. It is the upper coating of *plantago ovata* (Ispagul) *(sic)* which is highly purified by sieving and winnowing. Five to ten grammes of Sat Isabgol can be freely taken according to need with a glass of water, syrup, milk, fruit juice or salted curd or *lhassi*. It looks and acts like Polyfilla.

During my enforced sortie, Peter indulged his passion for birdwatching. He reported many larks, swifts, swallows, rollers, pippins, hoopoes, green parrots and a pied kingfisher. In medieval times, small boys were engaged to scare birds off crops by throwing stones at them. Here on the sides of the roads we could see small boys heaving sizeable stones into the air, without much sign of any birds. Ali explained, in his matter-of-fact way, that they were engaged in their own primitive form of mine clearance. They had no choice because, come the winter, unless the fields were cleared and sown, they would starve. More than any other image, that sight brought the whole mine-clearing problem home to me. If the kids were lucky, an animal might trigger a mine ahead of them.

The other chief hazard hereabouts is that the banditry increases with boredom, as the day wears on. The landscape was of rolling downland, wheat in the main but mixed crops giving the hillsides a delightful patchwork of tweed colours, lovat, heather browns to a deep orange. At one fertile point the road was dedicated to winnowing. The only habitations as such were straw yurts with perimeter mud brick walls, excavated from the well and irrigation ditch diggings. Otherwise we saw only nomads with long yurt poles across their saddles and families in tow. Just the place to choose for a refugee resettlement programme but if, as they claimed, the German Afghanistan Committee were the biggest and best NGO operation inside Afghanistan, how come there was so little evidence to show for it? There was no sign they had ever passed the way of any of our perambulations, yet this was supposed to be the epicentre of their impact, the staging post for all those other much-vaunted operations further north. In truth, all the Brothers Rashid had bequeathed was a dusty mirage of medical hayboxes being off-loaded from their ARROS liveried trucks to mule-train. They might just as well have never been.

The local wisdom was that all journeys should be completed preferably before 2 p.m., especially on the Baghlan to Kunduz section of the road. In the event, neither Baghlan nor Kunduz were anything like as forbidding as we had been led to expect. We could have been extra lucky, or I may have been on a euphoric high of re-hydration, but there was no question of our stopping overnight anywhere on the way. Also we would have seen the world very differently without the reassuring presence of Ali, and to a lesser extent, of our driver Amin. We were mightily relieved when we finally cruised into Taloqan with its island traffic policeman standing like a toy on a rostrum.

In contrast to what we had been through, it seemed to have the character of a resort or market town - the Buxton of the north of Afghanistan. This feeling may have stemmed from Ahmad Shah Massoud's Supervisory Council of the North. It was the same feeling of being at our ease that we had enjoyed at Pul-e-Kumrhi. In contrast to everywhere else on the way, there was no feeling of personal threat, absolutely no tension in the streets. Set at the foot of the most impressive landscape of mountains, on the banks of a large river in a fertile plain, one could understand why Massoud had given it such preferential status in keeping with Marco Polo's findings.

For the first time ever, we were to find we could walk the spacious tree-lined streets or go down to the river bank without fear of being molested. Peace and quiet prevailed. If you stopped a moment, you could even hear the river's soothing splatter.

Whatever hardware there was lying around looked very much as if it would never see active service again. There was a football pitch cluttered with Hind helicopters. There were some of the usual conversions of Armoured Personnel Carriers to guard houses, placed next to government buildings. Their tyres were invariably flat and some had even been incorporated into new mud curtain walls!

We were conducted in by Dr Hyder, the director of the Swedish Committee Clinic, but unfortunately we saw little more of him because our arrival concided with his wife falling ill. This was where the prosthesis unit and physiotherapy clinic were to be found. It was also where Mary Macmakin worked. Alarmingly, of her there was no sign, although we were assured she was on her way.

We were to be accommodated in a classroom next to her quarters and sharing her ablution facilities. Not so surprisingly, we found we were worn out by the nervous tension of our journey and lay down to recuperate. We spent the greater part of our self-imposed idleness swatting flies. There were hundreds of them. It was not uncommon to kill six at a stroke. Oh! for the Tailor of Gloucester ...

39
St Mary in Tuscany

Dr Hyder turned out to be yet another of those highly competent Afghans who had been whisked off to the United States of America to undergo admin. indoctrination. He was clearly a shining example of the outcome. His medicine was as much of the preventative variety as he could make it. A sizeable chunk of his compound was given over to the 'small is beautiful' water pumps of local manufacture - to get them drinking clean water first.

The food and facilities offered us, on the other hand, were basic Afghan. Both Peter Stiles and I now had distinct cravings for vitamin 'C'. The market stalls we visited were sadly covered in diminutive, low-grade, blotchy produce. After my apricot experience it became obvious that Afghanistan, which had enjoyed a worldwide reputation for quality fruits, now had a lot of post-war catching up to do. (Most of the world's grapevine rootstock is Afghan.)

The next day we learned that Mary Macmakin was now expected, *Insha'allah,* by bus before nightfall. We were at a loss to understand how, since our Kabul airport parting, we could have been to Mazar and back and still have arrived before her; but we had no difficulty busying ourselves, checking out the prosthesis workshop and stores and interviewing the personnel. We also met the physiotherapists, who appeared lacklustre and demoralised without their leader.

I had been particularly taken with a pair of locally manufactured crutches, which were a work of art. They had been beautifully fashioned in walnut. The underarm sections resembled reversed shotgun stocks, a pair of which would have done credit to a Purdey's window-display.

Next on our itinerary was a visit to the Takhar Province Public Hospital. In fact, we had already called there on our arrival to deliver the last of our 'ambulance service' out-patients. This time we were greeted in great style, as if Peter were on a state visit. Their senior surgeon, Dr Saidi, was very much on parade, togged up in extravagant national costume - a *chapan* or *khalat*. This consisted of a deep green *grosgrain* silk neck-to-calf surcoat with gold braid edging. All he lacked was a ceremonial scalpel. He was so dashingly handsome in his party clothes that I could have sworn it was Sandy Arbuthnot. We could only appear drab and drained by comparison. No matching Greenmantle for us!

We had no idea what Dr Saidi had been told about us, but it was obvious a big effort had been made over the past twelve hours. The floors had all been washed and the red carpet was out. This was a forty-bed hospital, capable of being expanded to sixty. There were three general surgeons and most of the beds were taken up with their patients. The conditions in the theatre and the wards were basic, but, for once, clean. Dr Saidi was Kabul trained and had spent four years in a military hospital.

However, Peter said that the facilities available were still not suitable for any visiting surgeons to perform any procedures other than the simplest soft-tissue surgery. However, that would cover the high incidence of post polio and congenital deformities. At present these had to be referred either to Mazar or to Kabul and therefore, for the most part, remained untreated. A visiting orthopaedic surgeon could see patients pre-selected by the general surgeons and Mary Macmakin. Minor cases could then be treated locally, with the local general surgeons thereby learning these procedures. All major cases would have to be transferred, but where to? It began to look more and more like Jalalabad, making it sound like a General Retreat!

That afternoon, Ali arranged an outing for us. He was friendly with Pavena M. Kohtwara, a fellow agronomist, who was a local adviser to the Swedish Committee, who arrived on his bicycle to collect us bearing a gift of cherries. He was taking us to his home for tea. So we set off, with him pushing his bike and all of us walking alongside. We couldn't help noticing the large quantities of Russian motorbikes that kept arriving by the lorry load, in see-through wooden crates. He told us to take no notice of them. They cost so little, they were almost giving them away. After a pause, he went on to say they cost twice as much as his Chinese bicycle. But there was a snag. They only lasted six months, whereas the bike was good for twelve years. (US $250 versus $125.) He lamented he could no longer buy his old favourites, Raleigh and Humber.

His home could have been transplanted from Tuscany. The villa and garden were surrounded by a high wall. All the walls were painted a sun-faded, ox-blood red. Long wooden poles were slung out from the villa to tall stuccoed brick pillars. The most luscious vines grew along the poles. There were sunken irrigated geometric beds with roses and carnations, marigold and geraniums. It was a paradiso of a garden. We were invited to sit on the terrace, surveying it all. There were many well-spaced fruit trees, but it was not yet the season for the grapes, nor for the famous melons which from ancient times were sent, packed in ice, all the way to the Khalif of Baghdad.

Nowadays they go coated in plastic.

Strategically placed, overlooking this earthly paradise, were half-a-dozen split-bamboo palatially-domed cages. These contained highly prized fighting partridges, favoured birds (three times the size of a Frenchman) who would be expected to die if necessary, for a demesne such as this. Or, indeed, find even a lesser patch of dirt worth fighting for. A very Afghan attitude. The more favoured the bird, the more commanding the view.

As we sat waiting for tea the agronomist explained how he had been obliged to give nine-tenths of his home as a billet for the local helicopter pilots, of which there was no sign. Were they the pilots for the junk heap cluttering up the football pitch? Were they all killed, or so sanitised now they were flying for Massoud? There were too many imponderables, which we hoped Ali would solve later.

The agricultural research co-ordinator's abiding interest in us revolved around British horticultural tools. He was mustard-keen to get his hands on some he had seen illustrated in a catalogue. At times he seemed just as happy to drool over the colour plates of the catalogue as entertain the prospect of ever handling one. I suspected, with the Afghan's remarkable powers of improvisation, he was about to commission equivalents in the local smithy's shop. After enjoying the *chai*, we took some photographs and walked slowly back to the Swedish Committee compound. We were told the trees on the distant hills were pistachio and that many of them had been cut for fuel. On the parting of our ways I promised to pass on Pavena's export enquiry, which I duly did.

On the way back, Ali took us on a slight detour to see the thriving grain market. We could not help noticing a large pile of sacks decorated with the European Community symbol and the words 'Donated by ...' clearly visible. At what moment do such 'gifts' become merely a part of the general trading economy? And who gains?

Mary Macmakin finally arrived at 10 p.m. Her bus had broken down, but that was not the cause of her long delay. From Kabul Airport she had gone on to stay with friends of thirty-five years standing, and found they had been virtually wiped out by indiscriminate rocket fire from Hekmatyar's lines. The father, the son and the only cow had been killed. The family was therefore destitute. In her attempts to help what remained of them, Mary found she was thwarted at every turn. The Kabul branch of her bank would not accept her written instructions. They had to have a proper instrument, meaning a cheque. Of course the cheque book was back in Peshawar. So, she had been obliged to return to Peshawar, draw a large sum in cash and start all over again - beginning with a new Afghan visa. (Multiple entry visas are discouraged.) She had been able to look after her friends handsomely, while they had guarded all her many cotton bales and the wheelchair, all of which had made it on to the bus.

No wonder we had overtaken her. Although Mary had been travelling for over twenty-four hours, excluding the previous days of reversals, she insisted on staying up half the night talking shop, without any sign of fatigue. She was clearly delighted that we had made the effort to reach Taloqan. She had an inexhaustible supply of diminutive green limes, which she offered round from the depths of her copious handbag.

Of all the people we met, she was the most desperate for surgical help. She had compiled long lists of club-foot and polio patients needing operations. She had selected 'social animators and actors', whom she dragooned into searching out the highways and byways throughout the surrounding mountainous regions. All these people were standing by, waiting for the call that never came. If the direct road to Mazar had been open last year, the American team would have made the journey. It had been terribly frustrating for her.

We had no time to get to know Mary any better. She had just returned from one of her twice-yearly trips to the United States. Along with Ruth Coggan and some hardy Irish Catholic nuns in Peshawar, she must just about hold the long service record. We had no idea, however, whether her stint was uninterrupted or not. Occasionally she alluded, somewhat vaguely, to American Embassy life in Kabul more than thirty years ago. There was more than a hint that they had been good times. One suspected there had been a Pauline conversion somewhere along the way. As the good times palled, the good Samaritan took charge.

Her grandchildren cannot be totally surprised by the antics of their Afghan grannie, because her children were partly brought up in Afghanistan. She must have been a stunningly beautiful young woman, because she is so strikingly beautiful now. She has a perpetual beatific smile and one of those soft russet apple complexions, with all the right happy wrinkles one associates with American wholesomeness, out of the mid-West. Her face shines with that goodness she spends her life distributing in large measure in the cause of serving others. Like many another before her, she leads the most frugal of lives with rudimentary accommodation – jug, basin, cistern of cold water. Saint Clare of Assisi could have moved in.

Mary was up to see us off on our dawn departure. She even had a last handout of quartered limes for our send-off. She begged us to return as soon as possible with a team of surgeons. Even the shortest notice would ensure any number of patients ready and waiting. It was a most compelling plea.

The rising sun touched the snow peaks with a soft pink. We passed a large crowd of men waiting in the hope of a day's hired labour. It was pleasantly cool with the clearest of skies and great activity in the fields - livestock driven to pasture; nomads already on the move before the heat of the day; brightly clad ladies and children with mules and pannier churns collecting biblical water from the wells and river; great piles of winnowing corn almost blocking our way time and again. We stopped at the first roadside spring to freshen-up and fill our water bottles. It was the same spot Amin found on the way up.

Rupert with twin dolls at the clandestine Swedish
Mother Child Health Clinic in Kabul.
Photo by Melissa Gibbs

40
Involuntary Drug Runners

The journey back is never as long as the journey out, until you hit trouble. On the return leg we were only once obliged to give a lift. It was just as well because, as if synchronized with the noonday gun, our undercarriage became engaged with something very hard indeed. It was not a mine, but we were brought suddenly to a highly-charged halt.

One of the sets of our vulgar Volga carriage springs had become splayed like a Chinese rotary fan, the petrol tank slightly perforated and any notion of shock absorbers a nostalgic whim. Nor was it any consolation to recognise that we were on the most dangerous section of the notorious Baghlan road. The few vehicles passing at that hour stopped for no one. There had been too many previously distressed decoys.

Ali and Amin sent us off on all four points of the compass in search of 'hand tools'. These were no artificer's fancy, fit only for a catalogue, but more akin to hard-won artefacts, which needed to fit neatly into the hand; leaving the greater part exposed to wield as a stone age hammer. Once we had regrouped around the vehicle, Amin made his selection - our specimens were all tossed derisively aside - he then set about his carefully aimed bashing of the springs. I was prepared to write the whole exercise off as a complete waste of time and effort. I considered it much more important to take a 'black box' photographic record of our last mobile moments!

Once the leaf springs were back in near alignment, Amin slipped an open staple bracket over them and proceeded to lash everything together with endless lengths of rope. And so we limped into Ailabad, as the sun reached the dreaded hour of 2 p.m.

Miraculously, Amin found a welder in the High Street and they set to work together to effect the now simple repairs. Our troubles were not over, however. This town must have been a base camp for bandits. It was given over to High Noon gun law. A commander swept in and dumped two search parties - but for whom or what? His heavily armed boy soldiers set about swaggering up and down either side of the street full of menace. Whilst the welding was proceeding two of these hoodlums syphoned off our precious petrol as their toll. Ali told us not to protest. Neither he nor Amin took the least notice. They just bided their time. First things first. One thing at a time. All in God's time.

Peter and I were invited to take tea with a very sympathetic shopkeeper, who insisted on entertaining us free 'in gratitude for the World Service of the BBC!' He plied us with endless cups of tea and Russian sweets. He had the most effective fly killer I have ever seen. It was a saucer with a tissue soaked in some substance, which they massed on and promptly keeled over. Either he could not or would not tell us what it was. Peter had no idea either. It did not smell, like chloroform. Could it have been opium? Whatever it was, it was wondrously effective.

It was he who told us that he thought the brigands were just plain bored. Like football hooligans, they had nothing better to do. Armed to the teeth, they were now reduced to either 'happy firing' or brigandry, or a mixture of both. There was also a chance that all those, who for reasons of either age or absence, had failed to play their patriotic part in the common struggle against the Soviet enemy, were itching to do so now.

As soon as Ali and Amin and the welder had finished putting the carriage springs to rights, Ali went over to the local commander, whose men had stolen our petrol, and explained to him who we were and what we were doing. He promptly produced the money for our tank to be refilled, and shortly afterwards two conscience-stricken youths returned. One of them told us he joined up aged fifteen, since he was now twenty-one he felt it was all a big mistake as he had no job and no prospects. We were then sent cheerily on our way. I couldn't help wondering whether we should have met with such gallant treatment in the wide open unobserved spaces.

We made it back to HALO's base at Pul-e-Kumrhi without further incident. Phil Jones was out on another de-mining site up towards the Salang Tunnel. This time we were the less welcome guests of Sam McLeod. Phil had somehow anticipated we might be in financial straits. We had indeed failed to appreciate that the Ismailis had no currency exchange facilities whatsoever. Phil had left us a US $200 float of his own money, which he said we could pay back to Farid, the accountant, once we reached Kabul. It was hard to know what Farid did not do - cardiologist, radio operator, factotum, accountant. The list was unending.

We had every expectation of catching up with Phil again, just short of the famous Salang Tunnel. There would be no missing him this time, because the camp was on the side of the road. With good timing, we should be able to take a breakfast break with him there, the next morning.

The usual pre-dawn start would be mandatory. So, we went

back to the Pul-e-Kumrhi taxi pool to prospect for anybody mad enough to take us to Kabul. By normal reckoning, we grudgingly had to accept that there could be up to four more passengers, making seven in all, including the driver. This time we attempted to check springs as well as tyres and were happy to settle for driver Immomali, registration number 7718. I was taking careful note of such minutiae, since Ali would not be there in the morning, to mind the minder. After three years with HALO, and with their full blessing, he was keen to return to agronomy and we only too happily promised to pass on his personal details to AfghanAid with our endorsement.

*

Having made our farewells the night before, we set our Chinese alarm clock, which was designed to waken the dead. We were outside in the road all expectation for Immomali's scheduled dawn arrival.

Peter was in poor shape. It was his turn to play sick doctor. It looked as if minimum acting skills would be required - we should have refused the colourful-cholera licks-on-sticks that Ali had pressed on us, as a parting gesture, in town the night before.

Bang on cue, at 4.10 a.m., the only dimly-shining headlamps to approach from the town direction were indeed those of '7718' - God bless Arabic numerals. Slowly Immomali turned the car around, catching each of us in his weak beam. We had positioned ourselves on both sides of the road, in case he happened to come from the other direction. Soon we were speeding back to his depot, to collect the other passengers. We had a twenty minutes wait in vain. There was no sign of any other customer. We could not afford to wait indefinitely, so we would have to pay for all seven notional passengers at 13,000 Afghanis each, but it was worth every penny to have the luxury of space and autonomy over some of the more scenic passes. It was also better from the point of view of Peter's delicate state. We would be able to stop whenever the urge overtook him. He lay there with his pale blue British Airways flannel, suitably dampened from his water bottle, stretched over his face. The bits of face that showed at the edges were a sickly grey-green. There were occasional sighs and groans. This morning, he not only qualified for a chit from matron, it was certain he would have failed the Merivale bedpan test.[1]

Then, the moment we reached Phil Jones' roadside camp, Peter's professional code of conduct took charge. He sprang into galvanised action, as if there was nothing the matter with him - a lifetime's reflex conditioning. He asked all the right bright questions of the locum British doctor. He even toyed with some nan bread over breakfast and drank a mug of tea, whilst I enjoyed double rations of cream cheese and raisins. Then, with fond farewells and our sincerest of thanks to Phil, who had generously bailed us out, we went on our way again, within the hour. Other passengers would never have put up with waiting on the side of the road whilst we had breakfast. As quickly as Peter had sprung to life, he relapsed.

I left him in peace until we reached the devastated Russian barracks, built to house the Salang Tunnel guard. Of the tunnel itself, we had read so much about it and its significance to the Russian war effort, I had come to expect something resembling the St Gothard. Instead, it was a shoddy piece of work which did not look fit to last much longer, offering at its core five claustrophobic miles of near total darkness. The road surface had long since eroded. The lasting impression was sheer amazement at anybody contemplating such a madcap project. Miles from anywhere, closed for much of the winter, what could they have thought they were doing? Then I recalled the British had been every bit as isolated coming up from the other end. A hundred years ago it had taken a month to travel from Peshawar to Kabul. At the same period, the Russians had estimated a month's march from Balkh to Kabul. One could only gape in wonder at such intrepidity. On the other hand, I didn't think the mountains here compared to the Alps. Like the tunnel.

Once through the Salang, driver Immomali suffered a distinct change of personality. Having originally struck us as a rather reserved, self-effacing, wet-looking chap, he suddenly took on go-getting, pushy characteristics.

It began to look as if he were under the territorial sway of some 'big cheese' operator, or drugs trafficker, whom he was very keen that we should meet. We would be taken to his 'hotel office', whatever that meant. In case it was bad news, I insisted on leaving the shortest of messages at the other HALO de-mining establishment at Jebel-e-Seraj. They were all out busy de-mining. But at least somebody would now register our passage.

Immomali's 'hotel' turned out to be a *chaikhana*, much the same as any other. His 'baron' pressed the most lavish hospitality upon us, but with Peter's state of health, our natural caution, and our impatience to get on with our journey, we declined.

It was then that Mr Big gave me an inkling where we might be slotted into his grand scheme of things. I was offered a large clear plastic bag of what looked like brighter, whiter Polyfilla, but certainly not Fleaseed. I was then asked in the plainest English if I should like

some hashish. Peter by now was past caring, so I ventriloquised for
him to the effect that British doctors took a dim view of drug pushers.
He chose to ignore this pontification. Either he didn't understand it,
or he didn't want to.

He was a very large greasy extrovert. Again he asked if we
were quite sure we didn't want anything to eat or drink. When I
declined for the second time, he simply picked up the Polyfilla, or
whatever it was, thrust it under the driver's seat, took massive and
firm control of the wheel - he had shoved Immomali out of the way,
as if consigning him to the glove compartment - motioned me to hop
in the back quick (Peter had never left his seat) and we set off, with
a jolt, like Fangio at the races. By now Immomali had reverted to the
shy, wet creature we had first encountered in the dim evening light of
the Pul-e-Kumrhi taxi pool. Somehow we suited Mr Big's purpose. He
was so well-known, greeted with disturbingly spirited salutes at all
the most formidable checkpoints, we can hardly have been his cover
story. Anyway, why would he have needed one? Perhaps it was a pay-
off of some kind and we were convenient dummies.

We were the label of respectability if stopped by the opposition.
We gave the journey legitimacy. We had been picked up at a HALO
location. We had stopped at two more HALO locations en route and
finally, we were to be set down at HALO House, Lucky Five Street,
Kabul. Was there some other significance we had failed to grasp?
Massoud was openly anti-drugs, perhaps we were being used as cover
to ship out. But why so little in that case? No, there had to be some
other, better reason.

We picked up and dropped escorts as regularly as clockwork
and swept through Charikar - where Hekmatyar was said to be. But
then, Ahmed Shah Massoud was said to have been at Jebel-e-Seraj.
There was never any knowing for sure. Our journey was so high
speed, it came to resemble some Moscow 'Zil' motorcade, if only
because it gave the sensation of being the fastest, most illicit journey
ever undertaken by me. There was no knowing if Mr Big was as high
as a kite on God's good air or something else. As we sped along we
were subjected to a constant wail of Arab pop music. Occasionally,
he would join in the repetitious refrains. Whilst one hand steered,
the other wielded a tin of Coke in the slipstream of his open window.
Once sucked dry, it was hurled with spite into the passing crowd. Just
the man to escort us through Hesbe-infested territory. As we crossed
the blazing plain in the heat of the day, Peter relapsed under his BA
flannel, clamped on by his spectacles. I slowly dripped water over all,
some of which he sips through the cloth to rehydrate. He makes a
convincing invalid.[2]

There was absolutely no problem with security getting in. On the outskirts of Kabul we were surprised to find the bazaar filled with first class produce and all appeared to be back to normal. It may have been a natural pause in the fighting after the rainstorms, which were said to have drowned hundreds hiding in their cellars. Then there had been landslides with avalanches of mud, which had buried hundreds more alive. Another lull before another storm. As yet oblivious to all these tragedies, all we were aware of was the stunning panorama of the hills surrounding Kabul in the setting sun.

Obviously, such a big operator could never admit to not knowing the way to Lucky Five Street, Sharhi Nau, Kabul. Time was lost as each of us in turn offered our pathfinding skills. Phil Jones had given us very clear directions. We made it in the end. To make sure we were seeing the back of Mr Big and the Jekyll & Hyde Immomali, I handed over the taxi fare in Pakistani rupees, with a substantial margin to be made on the currency exchange for sweetener.

HALO House was set back behind a high wall. Most of the garden lawn area was taken up with a massive new super-sophisticated aerial. It was assembled, but had yet to be raised on its mast, possibly for fear of attracting undue attention, so lessening its survival chances. Alternatively, these days, it might have worked just as well horizontally.

In Kabul, HALO offered a particularly sophisticated choice of guest accommodation. There is either a penthouse suite, with exposed grandstand plate-glass views of the nocturnal pyrotechnic proceedings with a backdrop of the Kolola Pushta fort, or a bed in the ground-floor explosives magazine, with airless taped and sandbagged windows. If they were not always so adamant about never taking chances, one might wonder if it were not some test of personal cool - between a bang and a whimper! I was reminded of Guy Willoughby's long ago description of Kabul 'just like Reading, but with rockets'!

In the absence of Guy, who was the second-in-command to Colin and Kabul director of HALO, the establishment was run by Dr Farid. He was not only the factotum, wireless operator and accountant, but also a cardiologist, who helped his wife Nasrene run a clinic over the road. With his ear very much to the ground, he had a keen knowledge of the state of affairs in the capital at any time. No doubt part of their daily Kabul news briefing was supplied by their patients, who came from far and wide.

We heard from him, as part of his invaluable summaries to Peter and myself, the horrendous story of the fundamentalists who had taken exception to a female theatre sister for some trivial infringement of the *shari'ah*[3] as between an operating mask and a *chardor*. They had severed her left hand at the wrist. This seems to have been the same story that "Scrubber" and Kate had been told by the maid at the newly arrived Canadian's house, about Iranian Shi'ite extremists.

Farid and Nasrene were unable to take retribution. They had accepted fundamentalists into their clinic. They stood out because they carried Iranian identity cards openly, plus anything up to two hundred dollars in forged notes, the same notes that had been around since Irangate. The Iranian identity card was said to be the most convenient for fundamentalist activists.

Over dinner, which included a special aubergine and cream cheese dish, Farid gave us his summary of the current situation.

He described Hekmatyar as a thoroughly selfish dictator, who wanted everything for himself. The problem, as always, was outside interference. Pakistan had always backed Hesbe-i-Islami, and the Iranians, for their reasons, backed Hisb-e-Wahdat.

There could be no doubt that Hekmatyar was out to establish himself as a world Muslim leader. Besides Pakistan, he could also count on support from Libya and Iraq, and we could draw our own conclusions from that.

Hekmatyar, however, had lost all credibility in his own land. First, he had rocketed innocent civilians indiscriminately, because he did not accept the coalition government. Then, a year later, he accepted the coalition government along with the premiership. It was the same story with Abdul Rashid Dostrum's militia. First he rocketed them, because they were in Kabul. Now he was on their side. Then he chose to rocket the Shia, because of their unwanted presence, now he had sided with them. Hekmatyar could never face an electorate. How would he explain killing so many innocent Kabulis and the wholesale destruction of their city?

Hekmatyar was not fit to rule. He couldn't even keep control of his own commanders on the road from Sarobi to Jalalabad. They had turned to looting the convoys and stealing from their own fellow tribesmen. What was the use of a Prime Minister who lacked even the courage to come to Kabul? How could he expect to govern from the suburbs of Charasyab?

Hekmatyar had given the appointment of Ahmad Shah Massoud as Defence Minister as good enough reason for continuing to rocket Kabul. He still went on rocketing Kabul after Massoud had resigned. From time to time, he managed to rocket his own people, including his spokesman, Qutbuddin Helal, in his own residence. The only hope was to give the man enough rope that he might hang himself. It promised to be a long waiting game.

Both Hekmatyar and Massoud had called for elections, but nobody could say what either meant by a true Islamic state. In any case, its remit would not extend far beyond Kabul and its outlying districts. The rest of the country would continue in much the same way it had always done, oblivious to the capital. However, in Farid's estimation the battles in and around Kabul were set to carry on for the foreseeable future. The problem was the weaponry had become so much more destructive and it was the civilian population who were catching most of the fall-out. More depressing still from the point of view of our visit, there wasn't a hospital worth taking a look at!

I asked Farid to tell us the story of Harriet Sandys.

She had been admitted to his hospital, he said, in a very bad way with meningitis. Farid had been able to look after her and she had recovered. He had thought nothing more about it, until she and Joss Graham[4] had sent a donation to the hospital in gratitude.

The whole KHAD secret service apparatus had been alerted by this simple act. All of a sudden, Farid found his every movement was being monitored. They had convinced themselves he was a British spy. To make matters worse he had recently attended a cardiologists' course at Leeds General Hospital, which had been arranged by Eleanor Gall. At other times he had attended Kingston and Beverley. They never stopped rummaging through his files. He was tailed morning, noon and night. He was subjected to spontaneous and incessant interrogations. Fortunately, to the chagrin of KHAD, he had no difficulty accounting for every last Afghani of the donation. It had all gone on hospital equipment, which was there for all to see.

Then, he had two lucky breaks. A new patient turned out to be one of Najibullah, the Prime Minister's, personal bodyguards. The other coincidence, so easily overlooked, was that Najibullah - in power during the pro-Soviet Kabul regime which lasted until 1992, was, of course, a doctor himself. The bodyguard arranged an interview at which Farid was able to explain, doctor to doctor, what had befallen him. Najibullah could see Farid spoke only the truth and had the KHAD tails called off.

The subject of donations reminded me of our messing obligations, signals costs and, not least, our debt to Phil Jones. Farid said they had a trusted money changer, who would never cheat us. He would have me taken to see him.

The next morning, I was driven across town to the famed money markets. Although the ordinary food markets were no way back to normal, the money market was thriving. My guard, the driver, and I had to elbow our way through a throng of small denomination dealers. We crossed a courtyard and climbed some stairs to a small back room, with tables and chairs ranged around the walls into which were set rows of safes. The HALO money changer made calculations, which he then handed to an assistant to double-check before opening the safe. I reckoned they had got it wrong. It seemed impossible, but because of the HALO 'Trust' connection, I felt constrained to point out where I thought the discrepancy lay. The problem was an old one. I wanted to change Pakistani rupees into Afghanis, but at the same time I needed to buy US $200 in notes, to repay Phil Jones in kind. In every country in the world, you are made to go through the domestic currency, giving the changer two 'turns'. When 'our' money changer got the point, he thanked me kindly and turned to lecture his assistant, rather roughly I thought. There wasn't ha'pence in it. The dollars, once they emerged from the safe, looked real enough to me. The Afghanis I would take on trust. I sorted out a suitable bundle for HALO, put Phil's dollars in an envelope and tucked the rest away for a rainy day.

We then visited the bus station and checked our chances for a bus to Jalalabad in the morning. We were assured there would be no problem, but a 5 a.m. start was strongly advised.

There would be no tourist shopping spree for us. There were no shops, full stop. Instead, we opted for a visit to the local British cemetery, which was not high on the list of tourist attractions. The museum had been looted. The Bala Hissar, the third-century CE fortress which dominates Kabul, was the object of a counter-attack. The Embassy was deserted. Where else was there to go?

One of the HALO gate guards very kindly offered to walk us there. It was just as well, because the key was kept by a blacksmith next door to the gates, and we should never have got in otherwise.

Prompted no doubt by the contrast of our own low profile appearance in the capital, Peter was reminded how, on one occasion, Lord Curzon had decided that he needed something rather more special in the way of uniform, to make absolutely the right impression on entering Kabul. He was never content with the uniform which went with the job. Perfectly respectable no doubt but too understated for him. On this occasion, he had gone to unprecedented lengths. He had sent to Nathan's, the theatrical costumiers, who obliged with something quite out of the ordinary with much gold braid, stars and other decorations. One was left wondering whether his American heiress wife had had a hand in the costume design and what indeed it had looked like. It was the Ruritanian fulfilment of my favourite Afghanistan scenario - 'All Grand Opera and Fantasia'.

We found little to interest us in the British cemetery. We somehow failed to find Sir Aurelius Stein's memorial or were in the wrong place![5] The marble had been looted, the trees vandalised for firewood. Even the franchise had been extended, since the latest arrival appeared to be a luckless diplomat from the People's Republic of China. As so many Afghans considered 'Inglestan' was somewhere next door to Nepal or Tibet, we could only accept his inclusion.

Thoughts of Curzon naturally led on to the embassy building and its future. It looked like a sorry end for the edifice that 'boasts the largest pediment and pillars between Delhi and the neo-classical opera house at Ulan Bator' [6] and 'gives the impression of having been supplied by Harrods about 1910.' [7] Built to impress the Russians, it had no doubt served its purpose. It was a pity that Guy Willoughby was not with us - he had been delayed for a week in Delhi for want of a plane - because the following was very much his story.

Apparently, Willoughy had taken an even dimmer view than "Scrubber" Stewart-Richardson of the British Embassy staff deserting their post. But all the more so, since they had left their dog behind. Guy had written a stinking letter to *The Times*. Since Foreign Office dignitaries have no right of reply, they were unable to explain. Time went by, until one day David Reddaway was sent up from Delhi to inspect the premises. Who should be asked to clear the approaches of any anti-personnel mines but Guy Willoughby. The implication was that admission was only possible across flowerbeds and through a window. Anyway, it was said that this service restored otherwise frosty relations. Certainly the dog was not mentioned. Once inside there was only one item of inventory that had gone missing - a large circular Axminister carpet! What else was there to interest an Afghan? What was more surprising still was how on earth it had been smuggled past the Gurka guard.

The Gurka guard's life had not been without incident either. Left in grand isolation for months on end, he had been attacked one night by two Afghans who each slung in a grenade. However, Captain Randhoz Rai had had the foresight to net his windows. The grenades had bounced back to kill his assailants.

*

We reached the bus station in good time before 5 a.m. and found ourselves confronted with a plethora of choice. There were minibuses and more normal sized buses, plus their barkers shouting the odds. I decided we, the only obvious Europeans, should take the biggest possible bus. We would sit apart, but right up front. The bad boys always congregate at the back of the class.

Sure enough, at each of no fewer than seven roadblocks getting out of Kabul, each requiring the driver to leave the bus to pay a toll and submit travel permits for inspection by often illiterate officials, the searching guards would then mount the bus and look straight over our heads to the very back. Once or twice they looked under the seats as well. We only attracted one piece of unwelcome attention. A youth, who had barely reached the age of puberty, or so it seemed to us, admonished Peter that it was time he started to become a good Muslim and grow a beard. Near the outskirts, our path took us past the Ministry of Health. Peter wryly noted that it had received a direct rocket hit the night before. He was glad we had not wasted any time there.

The bus broke down only three times, twice for punctures, and the third time, rather more seriously, for shortage of wing nuts. There was no excuse for this as there were no hubcaps either. Wildly gesticulating passengers on an overtaking minibus sounded the alarm.

There was an average of three wing nuts per wheel. The thread was supplemented with oil-soaked tow. They were going to need constant readjustment. There could be no question of speeding either. The road was terrible, but happily nowhere and in no way comparable to the Baghlan-Kunduz stretch. The tarmac was gone in most places and every now and again the shoulders had fallen away into the gorges. Each new twist and turn presented newer and better ambush opportunities. Nobody was the least surprised that we should both shoot off rolls of film from our vantage points at the front of the bus. They may have assumed that was why we had chosen to sit there.

By now, we had the instinctive, ingrained sense to put our cameras away as we sidled past no fewer than twenty-three of Hekmatyar's tanks, positioned on and astride the road, facing towards Kabul. It was no longer early, but I was amused to see tank crews still curled up asleep under their chassis. That was something we were always taught never to do, for fear of the tank sinking. Admittedly, the ground here was rock hard.

We could not help speculating what our chances would have been of getting by in a taxi or pick-up truck. At best we should have been turned back. Nothing like a clapped out native bus for anonymity. However, there was another aid to our concealment. We noticed that most of our fellow passengers were all much the same age as us. Grey and middle-aged, there wasn't an obvious warrior or hooligan amongst us. Just a peaceful outing of Dad's Army veterans. Or so we thought. There was only one scheduled stop, in the heart of Hekmatyar's hemisphere at Sarobi. The same Sarobi, where they had blown the hydro-electric power supply to kingdom come back in August 1984.

In contrast, our exposure proved to be a miserable experience. There was no way of staying on the bus, to await the next take-off. At close quarters we were glaringly obvious foreigners. Half-a-dozen optimistic boot-black urchins instantly latched on to us - one and a half desperate to clean each sandal. All they did was emphasise our *faranghi* status. There was no sign that anybody ever polished their shoes in this dustbowl. Most Mujahedeen were wearing shoes like ours made out of old car tyres with plastic or leather-cloth straps. And yet, these boys must have made a living somehow. All we could do was effect a steadfast indifference and drift towads the adjacent *chaikhana*. It was stuffed to overflowing with out-of-work Mujahedeen, bristling with rocket-propelled grenades and anything up to two Kalashnikovs apiece. They looked distinctly uncomfortable, sitting on all that hardware. But it served as a poignant reminder that these RPG 7 anti-tank grenade launchers had been the big bonus brought over by deserters from the Kabul regime .

It was equally fascinating to study how Afghans perpetuated their tribal traditions, whilst embracing technological innovation. Whereas in the old days, they would have lashed together any amount of brass furniture, copper wire, cap badges and metal fly buttons around their *jezail*, in the belief that barrel and stock were being made spiritually and physically secure for yet more telling accuracy, for some reason today's equivalent consisted of an endless *puttee* binding of multicoloured insulating tape - mostly black, white and green. No doubt this was done for instant recognition, but it also suggested a welcome intervening period of passively mending split cricket bats!

Once the initial curiosity had worn off and we had stood our ground refusing shoeshines, we were to be left thankfully alone. As we were in the midst of gunslingers even Hekmatyar could no longer control, we were particularly relieved when the time came for our bus to continue its uncertain journey. The landscape was to vary from barren reds and browns to lunar whites and greys, always beautiful, with here a deep blue lake and there a return to the torrent of the rushing Kabul river.

There were two further unscheduled stops, both for water. The first was riverside where the horizontal rock strata and vertical erosion of the opposite cliff-face produced a strong architectural effect, suggesting a vast Rajastani hillfort. The second was at a well where a liquid resembling lemon barley water was dispensed in a greasy Castrol can. Individual mugs were also identifiable old tins. We declined.

Just as I had reflected on the Russian purpose at the Salang Tunnel, here I contemplated the British and what had motivated such tenacity. How had they coped with all that sweaty scarlet serge and caked blanco harness? No doubt, they could fill their water bottles from the river. They might even have had salt tablets, but no sophisticated rehydration packs, certainly no glucose tablets either. It can only have been sheer guts and iron discipline, of the kind that took Lord Roberts' force the three hundred miles from Kabul to Qandahar in twenty days.

[1] Captain Merivale RAMC was renowned in 'our' day for parading sick-bed patients with their metal bedpans held at arms length. He would then pass down the line, tapping the underside of each pan sharply with his swagger stick. If the stool jumped, the soldier was fit to fight and returned to duty!

[2] Much later I learned from Juliet (née Crawley then Vergos and Peck), who had by then moved on to the UN Drugs Enforcement Agency, that what Mr Big had offered me in jestful partnership was most probably top grade heroin, known as 'China White', with a San Francisco street value of half a million dollars (based on an 'unadulterated' price of US $450-550 a gramme). If I'd known that at the time, for two pins I'd have asked him if he was in league with the Rashid brothers. Fortunately, my courage was never put to the test.

[3] Shari'ah is the strict letter of Islamic law, part of which can require women to go veiled when in public. The theatre sister's offence had been to wear her operating theatre mask instead of the *chardor*.

[4] Joss Graham is an Elizabeth Street, Belgravia trader in Afghan and other ethnic artefacts for whom Harriet Sandys and indeed Peter Stiles' daughter Francesca worked at various times.

[5] Labelled as a thief by the Chinese People's Republic, Sir Aurelius Stein is considered to have been the outstanding British archaelogist on the Silk Route. Many of his finds are to be seen in the British Museum. He was Hungarian, born in Budapest.

[6] Robert Byron in *The Road to Oxiana,* considered by Bruce Chatwin to be the best travel book of the inter-war years, 1918 and 1939.

[7] Peter Levi, *The Light Garden of the Angel King.*)

41

A Model Hospital

Of what is left of the major Afghan cities, Jalalabad, from afar, appears as one of the more inviting. Built in an oasis on the banks of the river and seen after so many miles of arid wasteland, it looks like the promised land - alive with waving palm trees and widespread lush greenery. It shimmers like a glimpse of paradise.

At the first sign of an International Committee of the Red Cross (ICRC) noticeboard, we signalled to be set down. It was precisely 12.30 p.m. The driver's mate looked as if he were about to ask for some kind of supplementary payment for stopping, but he must have had second thoughts. It may have been the mental link with ICRC, or the inconvenient memory of our last breakdown, when we had witnessed the re-jigging of those few remaining threadbare wing nuts. Since we had arrived unnoticed and unharmed, we had no cause to complain - certainly not on account of cost. The 120 kilometers journey may have taken seven hours, but at Afghanis 2,500 each it was a bargain (US $2.50).

In fact, we had got off too soon, which may have been the reason for the driver's hesitation. This was the hostel and not the hospital. But we were soon whisked on, to arrive just in time for cool drinks, a warm welcome and an excellent lunch, cooked by a former French Embassy chef, who was properly appreciated since we had eaten next to nothing for twenty-four hours.

Here we met one of those amazing, truly international characters who personify and confirm the worthy international character of the International Committee of the Red Cross. He defied accurate analysis. There was no neat pigeon-hole for him. At first glance, he could have passed for Flying Officer Kite, sporting a choker in the mess plus a 'wizard prang' moustache. Then there was the Douglas Bader Oxford accent to go with it; or was he putting that on for our benefit? Packed solid with energetic animal magnetism, there was no doubting he was born to command.

His origins were well cloaked. He spoke a multitude of languages without trace of accent. His name, which might have afforded a clue, was Chris Giannou. He told us he was a Greek Canadian, educated in Algiers. I suppose we should have guessed.

In more ways than one, his operation, although much larger, was every bit as impeccable as that other ICRC showpiece we had seen with Markus Thonius at Mazar-e-Sharif. But here, by contrast, many hands had played a part. The Nangahar District Hospital was designed by the Russians, built by Indians with American money! The subsequent introduction of hygiene and all the surgical facilities was entirely due to ICRC supervision, upgrading and financing. But, even here, the latrines were being excavated, as if as an afterthought!

It was amazing what a lick of paint, electric fans, disinfectant and the considerate spacing of beds could do to a tawdry shell.

One is told that what matters most is morale. In these circumstances, Chris Giannou was undoubtedly the inspiration for all that we were to see here. The man had an amazing lust for life and massive energy. He commanded total respect. His hospital worked all day. This was a phenomenon we had not met before - notwithstanding the added inducement of extra pay. Here were we, in mid-afternoon, with all systems go. There were three ultra-clean, well-equipped, modern operating theatres, with good instrumentation for trauma surgery. We were to meet three general surgeons and some of the eighteen trainees, who gave their enthusiastic support.

But, as always, there was a snag. Nobody knew what was to become of the place, once the ICRC departed, come September 1993. That would be the moment when visiting surgeons from Orthopaedics Overseas and World Orthopaedic Concern would be more than welcome. This would make an ideal base for the relocation of all sorts of training schemes currently to be found in Peshawar; if and when the Pakistani push came to shove.

Jalalabad had many of the goods and services on offer in Peshawar. It also had the advantage of being the nearest accessible point from Pakistan. It was better endowed than anywhere else we had been in Afghanistan - if only by applying the yardstick of edible fruit and vegetables! Security was also less of a problem than in many another comparable place.

Chris Giannou took us on his ward round. There were piteous mine casualties. One boy, who had in fact been lucky to avoid the worst kind of multiple injuries, with only half of his right foot blown away, sat staring incessantly at what remained. Despite the evidence of adjacent sufferers, he refused to accept that he had got off lightly and could be heard moaning and, rarer still amongst Afghans, occasionally allowed himself to cry out loud, in protest at his spatchcocked member.

On the other hand, an amazing harlequinade figure, bedecked and bedizened with multi-coloured feather dusters and a beatific smile set in a magnificent head, was a silent inspiration to us all. With both legs amputated, one above the knee, the other below, his crotch and one hand and forearm blown away, he still managed to smile contentedly as we passed, only too happy to be alive. It was amazing, and humbling.

We had almost finished the round when we heard Chris up ahead, plainly losing his cool. For want of a bed in a ward, a patient had been set down in a passage. He wanted to know when he had been admitted and why he had not been told. Any answer was better than none to such an autocrat. Somebody mumbled 7.30 a.m. Chris then bellowed that the patient was in shock and that if not operated on in the next half-hour, he would surely die. Turning towards the two bearers who had brought the patient in, he told them that the operation would require the maximum blood available from donors. A lot of guilty scurrying about ensued, with sheepish nurses and trainee surgeons fussing around the patient.

As if on cue, the patient raised his head to emit a blood-curdling yell. As his body writhed with pain, his face grimaced. He bared his teeth and gums and momentarily resembled a horse more than a human. Positioned as I was, hunkered down at the foot of his stretcher bed, he had already taken on a death's-head mask.

Nevertheless, I promptly set off for the clearly signed blood bank, to make my contribution. I was professionally drained by one of the vampire ladies who had also been at lunch earlier. I then went and waited quietly outside the operating theatre where Chris and Peter, working side by side, were conducting the emergency operation.

After half-an-hour, which felt more like four, Chris came out of the theatre and to my alarm, straight up to me.

'Thank you for giving your blood. I'm afraid it wasn't enough to save the patient. Both bowels perforated with bullets.'

So symptomatic of Afghanistan, I thought of the modern Islamic saying, 'The microcosm is but a paradigm of the macrocosm.' More than likely, it had been some shabby domestic brawl, or land dispute, not worthy of a Corsican vendetta. Peter had not donated his blood. He had sweated it.

I could see beyond him to where one of the trainees had been set the task of patiently stitching together the corpse's abdomen, preparatory to decent entire Muslim burial.

Later that afternoon, we were in for a worse shock.

We had sent out an enquiry for our old friend Dr Abdul Satar Paktiss, who we were told had recently relocated the whole of his hospital from Hyatabad to Jalalabad. Since he had been so actively and prominently engaged with the Afghan Interim Government he should have had little difficulty with the authorisation or indeed, the documentation!

At a staging post between Torqam and the ultimate site chosen in Jalalabad, the ten Bedford trucks it had taken to transport the laboriously assembled hospital had been hijacked. A band of armed Mujahedeen had systematically looted the lot.

Dr Abdul Satar Paktiss stood accused of having lived the fat-cat life in Peshawar, whilst they had suffered and fought and won the war. Now it was their turn to enjoy the spoils of war. Every moveable object had been carted off to be sold in the bazaar for whatever it would fetch probably a pittance compared to its practical value.

There was no such thing any more as the national interest in Afghanistan. With aid drying up as aid fatigue set in, 'help yourself' would increasingly become the order of the day. This policy of cutting their nose to spite their face began, strangely enough, with the hospitals. The Mujahedeen were aleady saturated with weapons, so hospitals must have been the next high profile public utility to come to their attention.

On the appointed day, as for a public auction, every little tin pot commander had turned up to claim 'his' electric fan, 'his' gas cylinder, 'his' surgical instruments, 'his' bedpan, 'his' rubber gloves, syringes, etc., etc. In Dr Abdul Satar Paktiss' case every single item had vanished.

In other similar reported cases, the formula had been much the same. They would wait until the hospital was as nearly complete as possible. Only then could the vultures be certain of maximising their opportunity. According to their ideal, a cash-down payment would already have been extracted for 'setting up costs', before the looting could begin.

Of course, there was probably more to the story than we should ever hear or understand. It could have been a simple case of Abdul Satar Paktiss's face not fitting in with the new governor's regime. *Haji* Abdullah Qadir, who was the brother of Commander Abdul Haq, was a law unto himself. The very fact that the Rashid brothers enjoyed his protection spelled danger. But the whole tragedy could just as well have been the outcome of envy and greed. We would have to seek out our old friend back in Peshawar and give him our sympathy and support.

To an outsider, the greater tragedy was that there was no better Afghan or other surgeon to take over the running of the Nangalar District Hospital, when the ICRC was to pull out in September 1993. No doubt, this was the kind of role the Americans had in mind when they trained him up. If only these people could get on better together, without the stimulus of an outside threat! The threat within was much more serious. And, as for things - there was no end to more things ...

that damned inherent lure of loot.

Here was Dr Paktiss, a prophet, not without honour save in his own country and amongst his own people. What was to become of him now? Would it be his inexorable lot to drift off to take his turn amongst the 'great American dream' doctors of Miami?

As if to excuse what Doctor Abdul Satar Paktiss had suffered, we were taken off to see a more recently looted hospital. The looters had shown restraint by waiting until the roof was on before moving in. It had been an architect's geodesic dome standing on poplar props. In a final gesture after the contents had been removed, these had been taken out, so reuniting the concrete roof with the dirt floor. When called to account, they had cited God's wrath, manifested in an earthquake. Dust to dust, ashes to ashes. All their limited expectations were somehow built into the transience of those mud walls.

'Everything changes. Everything passes away.' The motto of Islam.

*

On the brighter side, and by now we needed cheering up, we called on the recently opened Eleanor Gall Clinic. This is housed within the Nangahar District Hospital complex, next door to the ICRC buildings. It was also adjacent to the Accident and Emergency reception, where our luckless 7.30 a.m. patient had been admitted.

The Eleanor Gall Clinic is purpose-fitted if not purpose-made. At the time of our visit it was administered by an enthusiastic Ethiopian named Thomas Bogale Berhane. With his wonderful sunny disposition, he brought a positive force to everything he touched, and this rubbed off on to the patients under his care, which was good physiotherapy.

We then wandered across to a most original bicycle therapy unit. Its full title was the Afghan Amputee Bicyclists for Rehabilitation and Recreation (AABRAR) but it was also billed as a 'DAP', which stood for Disabled Afghan Project. It was under UN aegis, but was the brainchild of a quiet, studious and very determined American, called Howard Williams. Half of his time was spent fundraising in the States. His Afghan opposite number was a vast bear of a man with a perpetual smile, called Basir, who managed to kid me he had an artificial limb, if not two.

Provided a patient had one remaining leg and one remaining arm, they had him riding a bicycle in next to no time. Not content with that achievement, they then concentrated on finding him a trade to go with his tailor-made bicycle. Knife grinding was a bit obvious, but diversity stretched to a banana milkshake operator. The symbol they had adopted was a poster of Albert Einstein, on a bicycle of course. Despite an office large enough to cycle in, most of their activity took place under the trees outside. It was an inspiration.

We had been offered accommodation by *Haji* Sadeqi Momand, the brother of Dr Momand whom I had met years before when he was running the only Obstetrics & Gynaecological Hospital to allow male western doctors to examine Afghan female patients. In those days it was based in Peshawar. It was he of the simple arithmetic funding figure of a thousand dollars a day for a year! Obviously, anticipating Pakistani pressure, he had been one of the first to make the move back to Jalalabad.

Before welcoming us to his brother's hospital, he took us off to see a luxury residence in a once smart neighbourhood. A guard ran to answer the call of the bell fast enough. We entered a pleasant garden, but on turning a corner, we were confronted with a totally wrecked villa. *Haji* Sadeqi explained that this was indeed the much-vaunted accommodation offered us by Dr Veggeberg, in his latest circular letter.

We both said it looked more like pure and simple vandalism than war damage. He agreed. It was vandalism, war vandalism. The result was the same. He was obviously hoping that Orthopaedics Overseas would take the property off his hands, restore it, afford a measure of protection, pay a modest rent and return it when the future was more settled.

Haji Sadeqi was obviously keen to promote the whole town as the one and only medical relocation centre. Next he took us to see what must once have been a stylish art deco hotel called the Spinghar. It was the selfsame hotel that "Scrubber" had visited with his group. There was an impressive approach through an avenue of chinar trees affording spaciousness which, in the hands of the Aga Khan's hotel chain, could match the charms of the Swat Serena. But any thoughts we might have had that the place could accommodate teams of visiting surgeons were shattered by *Haji* Sadeqi's dismissive comment about the manager on parting. We were not to believe a word he said, a most unreliable chap! So, why had he taken us there in the first place?

Finally he took us back to the family Obs & Gynae Hospital where we met up again with Hermione Youngs. She had been at the lunch at the ICRC and we had first met her at the American Club in Peshawar, where the offer of accommodation had originally been made. She in turn introduced us to her colleague, Julia McEwan.

Altogether, we were to spend two nights there of delightful hospitality in pristine surroundings - plus a woman's touch, which had been denied us for some time. The Afghan cooking was superb, with wonderful balanced meals and masses of good fruit, including mangoes. We insisted on contributing to the cost of all this, only to be told subsequently that half of our funding had gone to pay for fruit for the general staff.

On our second evening we were taken for an airing to see the Daruta Dam, some 10 kms out of town. This is one of those Russian showpieces, littered with concrete bollard breakwaters. These were only too reminiscent of the dogs' pissoir, erected in the name of modern art by the *dirigiste* French socialists as a blot on the glory of the Palais Royal. Was there no restraining these appalling politicians who seek immortality in signature buildings and so-called modern art? The only thing to be said for the Russian bollards was that they were functionally more acceptable than the Dieppe beach stones piled one on top of each other and then painted red white and blue in the Quai d'Orsay.

*

With all the wisdom of hindsight, we found ourselves saying that, we of all people should have known better. First we had stopped on the bridge to greet the bicycle programme director, Howard and Basir, and take a group photograph. Then, once we had reached the dam, two foreigners accompanying two foreign ladies with one Afghan minder. What could be more innocent?

As it happened, ours was the only vehicle in the car park. Gleaming white and clearly identified in both Arabic and Roman script as belonging to the Obstetrics & Gynaecological Hospital of Dr Momand.

Just as we got back to the vehicle, as if they had been lying in wait for us, there was a screeching of brakes, as a Toyota pick-up drew up in our midst. Inside were a driver and two ugly customers, suitably armed. Nobody got out. The nearest of the three leaned out of the nearside window and shouted at us in English 'Get this into your thickheads. We are going to kill you Inglestan doctors, every one. You defile our women. You are not wanted in Islam countries.'

I could believe my ears but not my eyes. We had heard much the same before, but perhaps it had never been quite so individual. What made it all so memorable, was that our abuser was wearing a Tommy Cooper fez, with the black tassle bobbing in time to the outburst!

To my amazement, good 'Dr' Stiles calmly asked him where he came from. It sounded like Bradford to me. The answer given was Arabistan. This is usually taken to mean anywhere from Morocco through to Iran. Then, as quicky as they had arrived, they departed, thankfully without further intimidation.

Haji Sadeqi was the most visibly shaken. We were his guests. He began bemoaning the fact that he had let us out at all. Least of all in the company of Hermione and Julia, both of whom remained totally unruffled. Taking a simple walk was a continual problem for them.

Haji Sadeqi's only recourse was to lodge a formal complaint with the Governor, *Haji* Abdullah Qadir - for all the good that would do. We couldn't even agree on the number plate! But from this moment on, *Haji* Sadeqi could not wait to be shot of us, and who can blame him? In Islam, there is little worse that can happen than that harm should befall a guest. So, he promptly organised that the hospital minibus should take us to Peshawar, first thing in the morning. He seemed genuinely upset. The threat may have been more serious than we had realised. My own view was that it had been a put-up job and was as good a piece of scare tactics as the 'look out for a mine' warning given to "Scrubber". I thought I detected the hand of *Haji* Ebrahim Rashid.

The trouble with "Scrubber" was that he was so damned upright and correct, and – above all – discreet, that you never quite knew to what he might have been referring. So, his confrontation with *Haji* Ebrahim Rashid had the added impact of possibly referring to any of one or more different causes for censure. "Scrubber" had called him dishonest and a thief, hardly adequate words for an arms for drugs trader. So, he could have been referring to the wholesale dismantling and hijacking of the Sadda hospital, which had now been brought piecemeal to Jalalabad. Once arrived, all the various constituents had been reassembled and set up against new-made bare mud walls and photographed to show off 'Out-Patients' Department', 'Surgery', 'Operating Theatre', etc., etc. The purpose of these photographs was to illustrate an appeal brochure for a new hospital, now ready for funding in Jalalabad. But they didn't work because - in true 'Potemkin' style - all the shadows gave the lie that they were stage sets. If that was the fate of Sadda, what on earth was to become of Chak?

No, the chances were that "Scrubber" was limiting his censure to the immediate bone of contention - vehicles. He had been charged for a journey that he had clearly understood was undertaken on behalf of a German Afghanistan Committee project in a GAC vehicle. It did not look right. His military background would have made him hyper-sensitive to most Mechanical Transport rackets; usually related to mileage. But there were plenty of other possibilities, like selling off vehicles that had been imported tax-free and had been, as often as not, donated by the manufacturers or others, then claiming they had been stolen inside Afghanistan, only to have them miraculously reappear under some other NGO banner! He may even, as the guest of the Rashid brothers in Jalalabad, have had a closer look at their vehicle registration book. A company had been set up especially between the German Afghanistan Committee, the Rashid brothers and a suitably senior Pakistani bureaucrat at the Commissionerate *(sic)* for Afghan Refugees. He would be responsible for fixing the cross-border passes, including the Tribal Areas. The company they established together was ARROS. The cars they rented out were all registered in the name of the German Afghanistan Committee. They were thought to have conveniently interchangeable Afghanistan/Pakistan number-plates. If necessary, 'part worn' vehicles could be used to buy the allegiance of local commanders.

However the business affairs of ARROS had not been all plain sailing. They had given a financial guarantee for the delivery of some food convoy, which had subsequently been hijacked by Hesbe-i-Islami. When the Rashid brothers had proved both unable to recover the food and unwilling to pay the guarantee, there had been a major falling out with the Pakistani bureaucrat. This had ended in a gun battle with bloodshed. The Afghan commander, hired to protect the Rashid brothers, had been killed and one of the brothers had had to flee to Germany. This could well have been the occasion of Khalid taking his revenge on Denny Hundeshagen's executive toys. The Pakistani in question was subsequently exiled to give 'expert' evidence in Germany (Hamburg) on behalf of the Commissionerate for Afghan Refugees and the Pakistan Government.

Whatever the case, the Rashid brothers had ample reason to want to see the back of us, and for the moment would contemplate anything just short of killing us. It might be as well not to tempt the fates. We learned by chance that the Rashid brothers did indeed own a large chicken farm outside Jalalabad and wondered if this had been one of the few of their joint-venture schemes ever to see the light of day. We also heard that they now owned most of the shops in Jalalabad. But all this greed had taken its toll.

Haji Ebrahim Rashid had had to go to Germany for emergency bypass heart surgery. It was rumoured that he was able to have this under a student health insurance scheme that had been taken out in his name early on by the German Afghanistan Committee.

His 'student' status had been established originally to avoid fiscal complications. By the time of his operation he would have made a remarkably mature student. Then there was an unfortunate delivery of arms to the wrong commander. Not long afterwards, somebody woke up to the fact that he might not be the most desirable Gast, let along Gast-arbeiter. His coveted German passport was forfeit.[1] Whoever took that decision must know a thing or two about this story. Who tipped the German authorities the wink? A pre-emptive strike by Kantel or Hundeshagen?

By now, DAK/GAC may well have decided on a sea change. They were certainly contemplating a name change. They could have already been making passport applications on behalf of deserving Angolans, Biafrans, Burmese, Ruandans, Somalis, Sudanese, Tibetans. What about giving dispossed Maoris a spin?

Sadly, there is many a true word said in jest!

*

Peter and I used the journey to the Khyber to analyse our trip and draft a report. It would be primarily for the Sandy Gall Afghanistan Appeal Organisation, but would also be handed in to the High Commission at Islamabad on our way out. Peter gave his *tour d'horizon* as follows.

'Orthopaedic services in Afghanistan were virtually non-existent. There were no trained surgeons to speak of, no equipment, no training scheme and precious few suitable hospitals. These deficiencies needed to be addressed urgently.

'Top priority should go to major investment in Mazar to provide an orthopaedic centre, plus support for the new Balkh Medical College. Peripheral clinics could then be established in Pul-e-Kumrhi and Taloqan. The latter will have to be serviced initially from Jalalabad, until the Mazar facilities allowed it to become the referral centre of the north.

'Both Orthopaedics Overseas and World Orthopaedic Concern should establish a collaborative programme of training at Jalalabad forthwith. This would provide clinical services and work with the Nangahar Medical College. The immediate appointment of an Afghan surgeon director, of the calibre of Doctor Abdul Satar Paktiss was of paramount importance.

'The new Eleanor Gall Clinic in Jalalabad was, for the present, the most suitable site for the expansion of SGAA activities within Afghanistan and a possible alternative location for the Hyatabad complex.

'For the foreseeable future, Kabul was too insecure for major ex-patriate participation. The logistics were against Mazar as much as its political uncertainty. For those UN and Non Government Organisations contemplating the move to Mazar, it could well turn out to be a case of jumping out of the Kabul frying pan into the Mazar fire.'

Much the greater problem was insoluble. The world had lost interest in Afghanistan. It had never had that much in the first place. Now the West, having allowed the Afghans to fight their poxy, proxy war for them, was content to leave the aftermath of the collapse of the Russian Empire to others to tend and to exploit. Nobody cares to be reminded of those who were in the vanguard. Eventually the West gave its aid. The Afghans gave their all. And the Russians weren't in any position to make reparations.

A debt of gold can be repaid. A debt of honour goes with you to the grave.

The common excuse is that the circus has moved on. Now there are other more pressing problems to concern mankind Bosnia, North Korea, Iraq, the Kurds, Algeria, South Africa, Haiti, Rwanda, Burundi and not least Mother Russia herself.

Who remembers Afghanistan? Who cares? It is like a voice crying in the wilderness, all over again.

Who can blame them if, in the absence of aid, they hit back with drug production and arms bazaar activities. They are simply reverting to type after one mammoth debilitating effort on behalf of us all.

Of course the other way out for the West was to hide behind the skirts of corruption. There was no point in handing out aid if it could not be monitored and accounted for properly. If we could witness sacks of seed corn for sale, still clearly labelled 'Gift of the European Community' as far afield as Taloqan, the mind boggles at the baksheesh paid along the length of that extended trail.

The only hope had to be to channel aid through to the peasant community at grass-roots level. Help restore irrigation, agriculture, introduce medical services, barefoot-doctoring and above all give every support to the de-mining programme. Ignore central government claims, or claims to central government, altogether.

We had by now just about exhausted ourselves, if not the subject, and had arrived, ironically, at the communist regime's model farms not far from the Pakistani border. Vast citrus groves and the most orderly olive trees were strangely reminiscent of the French mandate in Morocco. It was a model co-operative as yet untrammelled.

By contrast the Torkham border post was utterly run down - a depressing, shabby spot, affording no encouragement to travel in either direction. Glum officials still made the old communist regime's demand for a second document to get out of the country you had such difficulty getting into in the first place.

Those unfortunate enough to have no papers get beaten until they barter their possessions for their passage.

[1] It turns out later that he'd been given an American one instead!

42
Au revoir *Dr Paktiss - Hello Dr Erös!*

Each time I travel the Khyber, I find myself reminded of the same two observations. The first concerns the railway to Landi Kotal, an impressive piece of engineering which needs saving before it is beyond repair. Given time it could become a major tourist attraction.[1] The other concerns an Afridi tribal chieftain, who had the great good fortune to find a fresh water gusher in his garden, which was good enough to bottle for sale. He was also said to be an active drug trader, but nobody dared tell where his income derived.

Before leaving for Islamabad, Peter and I had two pressing social engagements to fulfil. Far and away the more important was to visit Dr Abdul Satar Paktiss and listen to his version of how his hospital came to be hijacked. We were also keen to beard Reinhard Erös or anybody at the German Afghanistan Committee.

When we reached Dean's Hotel we found we had been upgraded and given the Louis Dupree suite. We only hoped they would continue to respect his memory after we had gone.

We soon learned that Erös was not available. He had had to leave for Munich with his own very sick child. The good news was that Juliet's driver's brother had also been taken to Munich. There was also said to be a large envelope awaiting my collection from the GAC offices. It proved to be stuffed full of high definition colour satellite photographs of Afghanistan - the same set we had seen papering the walls of his office. It only went to show that Reinhard had friends in the right places - like, on this occasion, NASA. Of Schwittek, Müller or Joch there was no sign. We were told they had all gone their separate ways.

We were now free to give Dr Abdul Satar Paktiss our undivided attention. After first telephoning him, he insisted on coming to collect us at Dean's to take us to his home in Hyatabad. He had enjoyed considerable hospitality at Peter's home and also with John and Val Stoneham. I had made an effort with a high-powered lunch at The Athenaeum in London. So, a great deal of last minute preparations were in hand to make as much fuss as possible of our unexpected visit.

As we sat on the floor with him and his attractive children, one of whom was keen to study medicine in England, we commiserated with him over what had happened. To introduce a positive note, we said we would do our best to recommend him for some suitable post.

We even dared to mention the Nangahar District Hospital.

We shared a delightful last meal with him and tried our damnedest to remain positive and cheerful. The moment of our final parting was unforgettable. It was getting dark outside and he calmly took us out into his front yard. We thought it might be a signal for communal prayers. Not a bit of it; before our very eyes, without our realising at first what he was doing, he casually proceeded to attach all the barbed wire coils that topped his curtain wall to the mains electricity supply! We pretended not to notice.

But, after so many years of striving together towards an ideal, it was the final condemnation in his parting words that will remain with us for all time.

'There are no more Holy Warriors - only thieves!'

*

'It is the kaftan and the carpet which transform the peasant into a prince and the mud hut into a palace.'

Long before the Guildford Surgical Team learned that the Pakistan carpet industry was subsidised by the tiny nimble fingers of ten million slave children, one of their perennial recreations used to be to visit one or other of the many carpet emporia to be found in Peshawar. 'Carpet Palace' was a firm favourite among these. Most people were aware that comparable carpets were probably cheaper in Knightsbridge, but that was to miss the entertainment, which was a whole new shopping experience.

The sales pitch was accompanied with endless cups of 'free' green tea plus cardomom seeds. With such a large potential clientele, a third party would secure the entrance against the slightest outside distraction. The super carpet salesman could sense the least glimmer of interest shown by any one of a dozen team members, as each succeeding carpet was manhandled to be cast on the ever-growing pile at our feet. Selected items would be stacked on a second pile to be shown more deliberately. Half-a-dozen or so carpets would then be laid out in front of whoever had disclosed his interest. Nothing so offensive as price would be mentioned for ages yet, and many more cups of tea would have to be downed.

Abid Ali, the top salesman, was an amazing figure. In his girth, he resembled the ageing King Farouk. However, he had no problem sitting cross-legged on the floor, or in jacking himself upright when occasion demanded. Over the years, we learned that he had other establishments in Rawalpindi, Islamabad, Karachi and, believe it or not, Knightsbridge. He would cash a personal sterling cheque with the utmost alacrity. He told us he was on the point of buying a house in Queen's Gate, South Kensington. He also expected to send his two sons to Harrow, 'like Sir Winston and Pandit Nehru'. As John Stoneham, an Old Harrovian himself, remarked, it was strange he should have instanced Nehru.

Carpet Palace had genuine antiques as well as new-made old items for sale side by side. There was a lot of sales talk about vegetable and synthetic dyes.

Any day of the week, specimen carpets could be seen lying in the road, enduring the antiquing process, as the traffic thundered over them! They were notoriously hard wearing, so it took time. (A thief, in his haste, had once left one of ours out on the lawn. The grass had grown through it. It had recovered and may even have benefited from the addition of vegetable dyes! After all, they were intended for use on bare beaten earth or sand.)

The Carpet Palace game was to discover the real, rock-bottom price for any item. It was essential not to want anything too much, or you were sunk. Abid Ali would move in for the kill. Once he knew, he could close the sale in a trice. That would then be chalked up as a team casualty. A poker-faced total indifference had to be assumed from day to day, always returning to the fray and bargaining, whilst supposedly revealing nothing.

Anwar Chaudhri was far and away the most practised and hardened. He had been brought up in the thick of it in Lahore. It had been his daily bread. His philosophy, which he was only too ready to share, was to make absurdly low offers. These were combined with well-choreographed moves towards the door. He would only feel triumphant if the shopkeeper followed him down the street, pleading to embarrass him. Anwar could still manage a convincing disinterest.

Finally, on the eve of departure, there would be frantic telephone calls to Dean's. Anwar might appear to relent and offer a slightly increased, but still derisory sum.

Other smaller establishments concentrated on selling camel bags and prayer-mats as well as antique and not-so-antique jewellery. The genuinely older pieces 'spoke' sad stories of dowries realised to escape refugee privation. Anwar had spotted his fancy in one of these lesser establishments. He would have the money ready and if they were late, it was too bad. They'd just have to wait until next year. He said he knew these fellows, he knew their tricky ways. They would be there at 5 a.m., make no mistake, with both hands out for the money.

They were all rogues and vagabonds.

On reaching the British High Commission in Islamabad where we were due on the eve of our departure, there were two apparent changes to the rabble-proof concrete bunker. One was the brass nameplate at the entrance. When it had been taken down for a re-engraving, it was found to be a palimpsest, with the former 'High Commission' wording already incised on the reverse, awaiting timely restoration.

The other noteworthy return to the fold was the installation of a magnificent marble statue of the young Queen Victoria. Somehow, Sir Nicholas Barrington had managed to recover her from obscurity.

Once inside the siege-proof fortress, the High Commission is on the left-hand side and the residency is set back over to the right. Her Majesty indicates the way with her sceptre. Her face shines with all the expectation and self-confidence of her age.

Once we were admitted to the drawing-room, Peter Stiles had absorbed himself in Sir Nicholas's library of Afghan memorabilia. There were some fine messotints and one or two original drawings. Peter was particularly keen to see which books Sir Nicholas might have that were missing from his own extensive collection.

Sir Oliver Forster, Sir Nicholas's predecessor, had once told us that Sir Nicholas was quite brilliant at the social side of diplomacy and enjoyed nothing so much as good reason for a banquet, or a reception at least. As a young man he had mastered the inter-relationships of Pakistan's top two hundred families and could, with authority, astonish individuals by telling them of remote cousins of theirs whom he'd seen at a recent reception. But this facility can hardly have been what had prompted him to give a banquet in our honour two or three years beforehand.

The seating plan for dinner alone was worthy of a chess Grand Master. A matching body of relevant guests had been assembled from the Pathan and Pakistani medical fraternities, plus a few select editors and one or two other diplomats. Common interests had been juxtaposed, to ensure a lively evening. Quite unexpectedly, Sir Nicholas had given a polished address outlining the contribution made by the team over the years. To which Peter invited me to reply. At such short notice, I made a stumbling, obviously unprepared effort, altogether failing to mention the careful choice of fellow guests. But, it didn't seem to matter and everybody had a most enjoyable and totally unstuffy evening.

After dinner, we were led out on to a vast balcony. As observed at Bannu, Sir Nicholas is a very keen gardener. At a given signal, the *pièce de résistance* sprang to *lumière* if not *son* life. All the security perimeter floodlighting had been converted to discreet, indirect garden lighting. It was very subtle and went part way to transform that redoubtable prison wall into something almost sublime.

We were soon brought back to earth. There had been a 4 a.m. start the next morning and none of the usual hotels was available. They were booked out with a PLO conference. So, lodgings had been found for us in a Muslim-only establishment near the fire station. On this occasion, there were only the two of us left to tell our adventure to Sir Nicholas's deputy, Andrew Cale, over a mug of tea. Sir Nicholas was to look in on the meeting if he had a moment, which he did. He was always very gracious and genuinely interested in our travels. He was kind enough to place us in a long list of intrepid British adventurers in Afghanistan.

We intentionally forebore to say anything about our 'German' misgivings. It was all so shoddy and, anyway, we lacked proof. It would only sound churlish. European Community members were meant to be working together amicably. However, *en passant*, we did mention some of the more obvious 'fundamentalist' threats, if indeed that was what they were.

We both promised to file typed-up copies of our reports. Peter said that with so much report writing now required by the National Health Service, it had become second nature to him. His note-taking was always meticulous. We both used Chinese children's notebooks, with absurd plagiarized cartoon figures on the covers. We agreed that, given the opportunity, we would conduct a similar survey next year to cover Quetta, Qandahar and Herat. Sir Nicholas had a touching faith in Ismail Khan, who at least had got them mine-clearing and had put all the irregulars into the same militia uniform. We hoped he'd still be there, next year.

It was agreed that I should try and arrange a meeting with Colonel Colin Mitchell of HALO Trust, if only to thank him for safe haven and see if there were any grounds of common interest.

The final point on which we were both agreed was that, somehow, our full reports this year should emphasise the role played by women in the NGOs. Whereas the men came and went on an ephemeral basis, the women seemed to be the constant guiding factor. It was high time somebody gave them the credit they were due.

It was a long flight, sometimes stopping over at Dubai. With good timing and a window seat, you could look down and see most of Afghanistan from a great height. There was even a hint that the plane turned left at Taloqan.

It would be the weekend coming up in England, with a chance to catch up on sleep. The Guildford Surgical Team, however, will never quite live down the time they came back to find their wives and families had suffered far worse privations than they had. It was 1987, the year of the gales. There had been no water, no electricity, no heat, no light, no lifts. All the trees to cut and clear, plus all the gardening that hadn't been done. On such occasions it was as well once again to recall Robert Byron.

'His was the hyperactivity of the heroic depressive. He ferried himself past one vortex of melancholy after another by means of an astonishing spread of enthusiasm.'

[1] It was British built in the 1920s, presumably as a troop and munitions transporter, at the then enormous cost of £2 million. Over its 30 miles it climbs 3,600 feet (1,200 metres) through 34 tunnels and across 92 bridges. Spectacular views, bats in the tunnels. Women were advised not to travel alone.

Part 3
A Conspiracy of Silence

43

Lunch at The Athenaeum

Peter might be late. He not only had further to come, it wasn't always practicable to down tools in the middle of a hip replacement procedure. Social engagements were restricted to Wednesday evenings. Wednesday lunch had been a compromise.

One thing was for sure, Colin Mitchell would be bang on time, having paced out the rendezvous. For fear of being late myself, I had allowed an extra hour, to order my thoughts: 'The Lord is my shepherd and my thoughts are his sheep.'

We were obligated to HALO and it was time to thank the boss for the help they had given us, both at Pul-e-Kumrhi and Kabul and for facilitating Taloqan.

As I relished the tranquil atmosphere of the near deserted club, I cast my mind back as to how and when I had first come to know Colin Mitchell. It all seemed to be part of that strange, seemingly pre-ordained, pattern of Providence, especially when associated with public-spirited endeavour.

Of course, along with everybody else, I'd heard of him long ago, applauded him ever since he'd captured the public's imagination - together with the Heights of the Crater District, Aden - without casualties, in gym shoes, at night. It wasn't just that he'd managed to combine the heroics of Wolfe at Quebec with those of Nelson at Copenhagen. There had been no blind eye to turn. Nor any signal.

In an age of wasting Empire and world-weary abnegation of responsibility, here was a man who could, at least momentarily, turn the tables. His command had been one of the most glamorous in the British Army - the Argyll and Sutherland Highlanders. He then went on to be another kind of rarity amidst the lunatic Celtic fringe - a Conservative Member of Parliament for Scotland, where he was to further espouse the Argyll & Sutherland cause, amongst many another no doubt. Somehow he had come to epitomise the last of the Empire 'shorts and bayonet' brigade; except that in his case it had to be a kilt.

His election to the 'Best Club in the World' - the British Parliament - may have induced counter-productive convulsions, because he did not overstay his welcome. His scant respect for institutions may have begun earlier, but it was due to culminate in the United Nations Organisation in general and their mine-clearing activities in particular.[1]

It wasn't so much that he was an iconoclast. He is not. His is a massively positive force for nothing but good. It is more that he is wholly intolerant of the inefficient trappings of the 'aid industry'. He is one of those people whom one recognises, from the outset, as being intrinsically right. But they can be so uncompromising that the mass of mediocre moderates dismisses them with a 'utopian' label.

The 'no casualties' clue gives the clearest insight into the man. It puts him in the Wellington/Montgomery category of caring commanders. The gym shoes also suggested a light touch - like shooting snipe over bog or marshland, if not minefields. Finally, there was that degree of devotion that is only to be found amongst Moderators of the General Assembly of the Church of Scotland.

My original meeting with Colin had been through the 'old boy net', which can work wonders when it is for good rather than gain. Part of the reason is that it simply bypasses time-consuming red tape and its teeming tanglers.

With the perennial problem of Central London traffic jams, *pace* our glorious Mayor Ken Livingstone, and his congestion charge, more and more energetic people, with a need to clear their minds between meetings, have taken to walking again. The Royal Parks have thus become once more the setting for live encounters. It was in just this way that I ran into Sir Douglas Dodds-Parker. His office was in Grosvenor Place, not far from Hyde Park Corner. For the present he was striding, regulation 116 paces to the minute, across Green Park in the direction of St Margaret's, Westminster. As I fell in with him, he told me his social life now consisted of attending one memorial service after another, as, one by one, the old and the bold, the great and the good, toppled off their perches. He kept telling himself that it would be his turn next. However, he had to admit it did keep him in touch with his friends!

I reminded him that we had last met at Billy McLean's memorial service and reiterated how helpful Billy had been over matters Afghan.[2] Sir Douglas had rejoined instantly with the names of two people I should contact without delay. They were Colin Mitchell and Guy Willoughby, who were engaged in mine clearance and mine awareness programmes. He had deemed them 'A first-rate show, with the unlikely name of HALO - memorable, mind you.'

Sir Douglas is memorable too. He stands well over six foot of Queen's Company, Grenadier Guards height. He had experienced the most extraordinary of all wars, which was followed by a long stretch of parliamentary duties, which is when he is likely to have run across Colin Mitchell. His concern was always for others - never for himself, which, in turn, rendered him benign.

It may have been eighteen months or even as much as two years later that I found myself in that misaligned labyrinth of back alleys and lanes that run from Queen Anne's Gate through Westminster to Pimlico and, just before hitting the river, reputedly Europe's largest block of flats and incidentally HALO headquarters, Dolphin Square.

By coincidence, Colin and I shared the same ex-regimental tailor, halfway down this trail. I was headed there. Colin was coming away.

There was no mistaking the man. He is as short as Douglas Dodds-Parker is tall. He is spare to thin and wiry - what Private Eye used to refer to as perfectly formed. A cartoonist would exaggerate his fountain shock of shining white hair. His is the quizzically humorous face of the born optimist. His spiked and busy eyebrows accentuate the upward tilt of his irreverent smiling eyes. Above all, he is brisk and, if occasion demands, brusque. His pace is a kind of *bersaglieri* light infantry caper as if the paving stones were on fire. His turn-out is always impeccable. You have the impression that even his gardening clothes have just come back from the cleaners. The brogue boots would be polished to a mirror finish. The marl would never cake.

All of a sudden, his dapper figure was dead ahead, directly in my line of sight, steadily, rapidly approaching. In a flash he would have passed by, gone for ever. This was undoubtedly the moment Sir Douglas had ordained.

'Colin Mitchell. Sir Douglas Dodds-Parker suggested I should make myself known to you. Would you care to lunch one day at The Club, where we could discuss our common interest in Afghanistan?'

'I should like that very much.' We exchanged cards then and there. And, not to hesitate, set a date for the following week.

Once around the next bend, I took a closer look at his bookmark card. To my astonishment, it gave a Kabul fax number. That was serious.

In fact, the lunch was not an unqualified success. For reasons yet to be discovered, Colin managed to convince himself that I was a supplicant for his trust funds and that to prove my credentials I had brought along my taciturn 'bank manager'. This of course was Peter Stiles, whose purpose had been to endorse the relevance of orthopaedic surgery to mine injuries! Being a canny Scot, perhaps Colin had some difficulty in accepting the concept of a free lunch, but eventually we did communicate.

Once we had outlined the little we had achieved, what

our aspirations were inside Afghanistan, especially the training programme, Colin reciprocated by giving us an outline of his operations.

He emphasised that HALO had been at great pains to establish itself as a completely neutral 'straight bat' organisation. This was essential to its efficient operation. The teams of de-miners are drawn from a pool of voluntary professional staff, contracted on a short-term basis from ex-military sappers (engineers) and the medical profession, to undertake specific assignments, which are always clearly defined.

HALO's overall aim is to alleviate further human suffering in areas recently emerging from civil conflict - by making safe the debris of war - such as unexploded ordnance-bombs, shells and land-mines.

HALO Trust programmes to date had been mostly mines related, with medical support, and had been funded in Cambodia and Mozambique, as well as Afghanistan. The Trust's funds came from many sources, including: Her Majesty's Government, the EC, USA State Department, Bureau of Refugee Programs, UN, *Pro Victimis* Foundation (Sweden) and other private donations from the UK. Previous donors had included various other UN agencies and the Swedish Red Cross.

HALO had an on-going need for short-term (six months to one year) contract doctors to be in attendance on de-mining teams; likewise physiotherapists and nursing sisters. So, there were plenty of cross-referral points.

From inception, the Guildford Surgical Team had fulfilled a secondary synergistic role as a catalyst for all sorts of unrelated activities. For instance, Colin Mitchell was interested in the subject of vehicle selection and discount purchase possibilities. We had no vehicles of our own, but were confident that Sir Oliver Forster at AfghanAid would be prepared to help HALO secure the most advantageous terms by bulking up with their ambulance order. They were all Japanese or German anyway. In this we were wrong about Sir Oliver, but the thinking was right. There was to be no reconciling the rule-book civil servant with the 'rules are made to be broken' rebel. 'I am not to be dragged into this mine-clearing business, Rupert,' was Sir Oliver's constant protest whenever Colin's name was raised. In contrast, Colin saw himself and his teams as latter day Knights of St John of Jerusalem, keeping the 'way' open to the Holy City.

Part of the solution would have to be a limitation on manufacture of the so-called 'Italian' mine.[3] Another answer might be a long time coming, but there had to be a better way of detonating old mines than kids throwing stones in the air, or driving livestock over the land, or in the case of the Burmese, chain-gangs of prisoners. In this day and age there had to be a laser solution. If you could disintegrate kidney and gallstones with a laser, why not a landmine? In the end, it always came back to economics and laborious probing.

The purpose of The Athenaeum lunch was simply to thank Colin for the help HALO had afforded us and to try to reassure him that we were not intent on turning the operation into a bed and breakfast itinerary. There must be nothing to distract them from their main purpose, which was to get mines out of the ground. Colin had been kind enough to appreciate my written work as 'excellent - both witty and informative'. There was no doubting we shared the same sense of humour. I looked up at the clock. It was on the tick of 12.45 p.m. and, sure enough, there he was, sprightly as ever, bounding through the double doors, doffing his trilby hat. It was the kind that had been regulation and had a vulgar name when he had made his first reputation.

While waiting for Peter, we spoke of many things. How extraordinary it was that the Russians should have finally come up against two of the most spiritual nations on earth: the Pope's Polish battalions - the champions of Christianity since the XIIth century CE - and the Afghans.

Comparisons were made, ranging from their shared penchant for charging tanks with cavalry and other lesser similarities like terrible buses and abysmal maps.

I asked how much maps featured in mine clearance, expecting a positive response. The Russians supplied theirs.

The Mujahedeen tended not to keep records, which was what made the work doubly hazardous. There were cases of the same people laying mines over old areas; having forgotten they had been there before and blowing themselves up. Hekmatyar could be busy re-laying mines where HALO had just cleared. Massoud wanted his left in place, just in case.

I said I found it hard to credit that we could have NASA satellite photographs in glorious technicolor and no intermediate technology to produce adequate maps. In Afghanistan there had been no advance since the Durand line was determined.[4] Colin explained that the Afghan had no use for a map. He would distrust it anyway.

The work of mine-clearing was not only more dangerous because of the lack of record-keeping, the old concept of relying on the metal detectors didn't have the same relevance any more because there was precious little metal in modern mines to detect - other than the fragmentation mines generally placed above ground with tripwire. You could usually spot them. Most of the damage these days was done by blast alone.

I asked after the flail tanks we had seen in the parking lot at Pul-e-Kumrhi. Colin reminded me that they were a World War II phenomenon. There was always an 'acceptable' casualty rate associated with them, that is, acceptable in wartime. It was totally unacceptable in HALO's role. Colin said we may have heard that they had lost two of their best men (Tim Goggs, GM, and Julian Gregson). I said I had heard and that a German cameraman film-maker friend of mine, Dittmar Hack, had been out there shortly before to make a film about Tim's work and I had seen the footage. Dittmar had told me about the subsequent tragedy.

I asked Colin if he had ever considered using a remote dowser to locate mines. To make the notion appear less outlandish, I said I had recently noticed that the British Society of Dowsers, who met over the road at the Royal Academy, had no fewer than two sapper Major Generals on their council. They seemed to make a habit of appointing the Chief Sapper. Colin could remember sappers using dowsing for siting footings for bridge building and, of course, for finding water and locating drains, but nothing more. At present, he explained, casualties tended to be their most reliable indicator. They could have frightful problems with landslides, flooding, slippage and even earthquake. What was refreshing was that, provided dowsers could come up with mine locations that HALO did not know about and they turned out to be there, he would certainly listen. So, I felt sufficiently encouraged to touch on psychic dowsing. But it was never put to the test as, at that moment, Peter arrived and we went into lunch.

Colin told us how statistics on mine-clearance were notoriously unreliable. However, there was a new brochure on the subject, put out by the ICRC, which made it clear that there would be work for 'sawbones' for ever. It made the telling point that it was the negative effect of the denial of the agricultural land to the economy of the country which was crippling. Plus the fact that casualties were mainly from the civilian 'agricultural' population. This was true whether it was Cambodia, Mozambique or Afghanistan.

Peter asked had there been any response to Hekmatyar's offer to exchange Russian prisoners-of-war for Russian de-miners. Colin had heard of none.

Peter and I both made the point that HALO must be one of the only predominantly male NGOs left in the field. All the others we ran into seemed to be run by women. Colin's response was that HALO would collapse but for his wife Sue's devotion to the cause.

We had been thinking more of field workers. This led naturally, or so we hoped, to our next question. We wanted to know what Colin could remember of an Anglo-American nurse, Kate Straub, who was with HALO in Kabul and was a Farsi speaker. She had listed HALO on her c.v., along with her Fellowship of the Royal Geographical Society.

Colin said she had made a favourable impression as a no-nonsense operator, with plenty of guts. He then asked why.

We explained that Peter had recommended her for work in a hospital at Chak-e-Wardak. This was a German show and Kate had blown the whistle on them, because it seems they were not quite all they were cracked up to be. I added that I was on the point of departure to conduct further in-depth researches in Germany.

Colin warned me that I should have to watch my back there. If that was the case, I replied, then I knew of two people I could count on to recover the corpse.

On a lighter note Mitchell concluded by telling us the story of his Italian partisan liaison officer in Tuscany in the war. He had been a most remarkable young boy with fluent English. He had impressed them so much that they had made him an Honorary Argyll and Sutherland Highlander and even put him in a kilt. Then they couldn't get him out of it. It transpired that this prodigy's name was Franco Zeffirelli! [5]

[1] Colin Mitchell sadly died in 1996 .

[2] Dismissed by the SIS as 'a colourful romantic', Billy Mclean had served with Orde Wingate in Abyssinia and Tito in Yugoslavia. With political help from his old friend Julian Amery he was largely responsible for turning the Yemen tide against Nasser. See *The Perfect English Spy*, p.247. Mclean also served for many years as a Conservative Member of Parliament.

[3] The Italian arms industry is credited with the design of the blast as opposed to fragmentation anti-personnel mines. It is plastic not metal.

[4] An arbitrary map line drawn by British Indian Army cartographers to define the North West Frontier of India with Afghanistan in 1893. It has never been recognised as a final border by any Afghan government.

[5] See *'Tea with Mussolini'*

44

Dittmar Hack and Reinhard Erös

My first point of reference in any German context would be Dittmar Hack. We were friends of long standing. We shared many opinions and the same kind of humour. We had met originally through two Australian intermediaries. A friend of Dittmar's called Malcolm R. Olden and a friend of mine called Michael J.W. Young. The original rendezvous point had been the bar at Raffles Hotel, Singapore. Dittmar had seen service in the German army and Rhodesian special forces. He and Malcolm Olden had made joint trips inside Afghanistan. Dittmar was Bavarian so I was Munich bound.

Architecturally, Munich is for me the most exciting of airports. It reminds me of a fascinating exhibit I once saw at the Venice Biennale in the 1960s. It was an acrylic beehive, and is every bit as active. And yet, there is no feeling of delay, no shortfall in hostility spacing. What amazed me next was, just beyond the greeting area, on the very kerb next to the exit, were the public parking spots. Masses of space, none of that anxiety of hassling police; although Security was no doubt around the next corner. The Germans are so justifiably proud of this showpiece that they have built a kind of dry ski-slope hill from which the public can have a grandstand view of the beehive's activities.

Dittmar Hack had offered to meet me at Munich, and there was no mistaking his vehicle. As a trained mechanical engineer, he took great pride in his transport fleet. The showpiece, which had been brought to collect me, was a retired Post Office van. It was still the characteristic German bright yellow, but many modifications had been made under the bonnet. For more modest journeys he maintained three Post Office despatch rider's vintage motor-bicycles. They were all 1950s models. Two were in constant use. The third was dedicated to spare parts.

Dittmar lives a full hour's drive from the airport, along uncongested open country roads. We never seemed to go through a town. It was all picture-postcard villages in the middle distance, amidst vast stands of pine trees, and as we shot along, Dittmar explained that the Post Office van could get him to the Bosnian battlefront in less than seven hours.

I asked, wasn't it a trifle conspicuous? He said he only went as far as the first checkpoint, parked, took his camera equipment out of the back and walked on in. He billed it the first 'drive-in' war. There had been trouble with some of the types he had lifted out, but it wasn't going to be like Afghanistan.

As we got nearer to his home, he pointed out the teams of skin divers who, he assured me, were dredging the small lakes for what he described as disco-mafia victims. So far three bodies had been recovered in concrete Wellington boots. Now local diving groups had joined the police units in their search for long lists of missing junkies and pushers.

Whereas an Englishman might indulge himself in running electric trains around his attic, Dittmar had converted his into a museum. It was more what we might call a den, but he insists it is a 'museum to living history'. The point is, Dittmar is still living at the advanced age of forty, whereas most of his former war correspondent and photographer colleagues are dead and maybe buried. Over 1100 war correspondents have been killed between 1990 and 2004. This, then, was a museum to the living history that Dittmar had witnessed worldwide. There were the flags from both sides in the Nicaragua war; both boots that had taken him the length of the Jonas Svimbe trail in Angola - two thousand kilometers in four months; reckless, flak-less Afghan jackets, *pakool* and *shalwar kamees*. Other memorabilia came from Madagascar and Mozambique.

A few choice pre-Dittmar historical items had been admitted. There was a British carbine from the North West Frontier circa 1890, in mint condition. A weapon of great balance and beauty. Then in sequence there were even fresher sniper's rifles of German, Russian and British origin. This collection was all the more surprising for a man who had patently devoted his life to proving the news-camera to be mightier than the sword.

All his serviceable weapons and homemade ammunition gear were kept for active gun club use. He once told me he had suffered inordinate hassling from his own over-zealous police force. Germany is not a country renowned for civil liberties. Everything Dittmar kept was in apple-pie order, but nothing would stop the random police visits.

His film, tape, paper reference filing was perfectionist. He could lay his hands on whatever he was after instantly, as he was about to demonstrate. It goes without saying that he was deep into personal computers.

The only omission in the attic was any form of heating. There was a cheap Chinese kapok sleeping bag, rolled up vaguely in one corner. Was it an exhibit, or there for rigorous hardship training? This was unlikely. Frail looking at first glance, Dittmar was of that deceptively strong, wiry, stiffened-sinews breed of tiger.

As he put the showpiece weapons away, he asked if I knew that, in Germany, if you got caught driving over the alcohol limit, you didn't just lose your driving licence, you lost your gun licence too.

I asked him what he could remember of the German Afghanistan Committee. The weird thing was he couldn't remember ever meeting anybody belonging to it, either inside Afghanistan or in Peshawar. German Non-Governmental Organisations had been notorious for not getting along together. So he had given them a wide berth.

I then asked specifically about the Kunduz and Baghlan. Dittmar had heard nothing. I was particularly fascinated by this, because I knew he had covered the distance with Ahmed Shah Massoud and the subject would have been bound to come up simply because of the German connection.

He knew that the GAC had often bought his Afghan war film footage, in order to screen it on their fundraising lecture tours. But the only time he had met them was when they expressed interest in his Jonas Svimbe[1] material. They had wanted to buy all his footage. Dittmar gained the impression that they were attempting to hijack the Jonas Svimbe roadshow for their own ends. Dittmar had decided to stand well clear.

'History is full of nasty surprises!' was his comment. Other than that confrontation, most of what he had been able to assemble had come from newspaper and magazine files. Apart from the *Der Spiegel* article, reprinted in this volume, there were others in *Tageszeitung* and the *Westdeutsche Allgemeine Zeitung*.

So far as Dittmar had been able to discover, GAC began life as a minor, privately administered, charity sometime in 1982. It managed to muddle along on approximately DM 50,000 a year, apparently heads down, minding its own business; attracting very little attention to itself. Its funding was thought to have been generated by a well-placed, highly emotive poster advertising campaign. One such poster featured a TS4 tank above the slogan 'And what are you expecting for Christmas this year!' Another read 'Everybody talks about war. Here in Afghanistan we have it.'

The national banks seemed to suffer from none of the British belligerency inhibitions and were proud to give prominent display in their Christmas windows, no doubt endorsing GAC's credibility, as well as raking in subscriptions over their counters.

Again, as early as 1982, a laudable, if somewhat eccentric, but certainly brave Doctor Karl Victor Freigang set off for Afghanistan to see what deserving opportunities he could find for German humanitarian aid.

Massoud

For good measure, and to put war correspondents like Dittmar to shame if not out of work, Freigang took along his 8mm home movie camera. He returned with enough high-drama footage to take up a whole minute of Gerhard Löwenthal's *Zweites Deutsches Fernsehen* (Second German Television Station) television magazine. Dittmar had not been able to obtain a print. It had not been one of the Central Office of Information or United States Information Service offerings. Quality had not been a key factor, as it had guaranteed screening. The newscaster had also given the full name and address details for the German Afghanistan Committee, thus making donations vastly easier.

As Dittmar put it 'They hand you chicken shit and expect you to make a fairytale out of it. Sometimes even a blind chicken can stumble on a grain of corn.'

Not so surprisingly, when the Russian bear is grinning over the German garden fence, this appeal did, indeed, result in a deluge of donations. Suddenly, an organisation that had been jogging along on DM 50,000 a year, found itself with DM 5 million in the bank, with more coming in every day. Now they could afford to take a quantum leap in the dark!

Part and parcel of the problem of conducting any kind of research into charity fund administration in Germany, was that they suffer much the same system of regulation as in the United States. Perhaps they adopted the American law code books after the war? There is no requirement to account for all the monies received all the time. Just so long as an unspecified percentage of funds under management (even as little as 5% to 10%) is distributed within two years of the original date of receipt, the law is satisfied. What is more, unlike the British and other systems, all those involved can pay themselves handsomely, so long as the gravy-train lasts. Whatever happens to 90% of the donations, therefore, is very much the charity's own affair.

Usually, everything turns out to be cock-up, rather than conspiracy, but this time everything stank of conspiracy. The more we were confronted with the smoke and mirrors of Liechtenstein Stiftungs and Abteilungen, the more convinced we became that there was something worth hiding.

Other sources I accessed from amongst the German Non Governmental Organisation fraternity disclosed that Denny Hundeshagen, it will be recalled, the GAC bigwig who had been confronted by Kate Straub at Chak, had recently been able to buy a chemist shop in Bonn. And they don't come cheap in West Germany

- say, DM 1 million. He had also acquired a smart home in Bonn, a villa in Spain and a Lancia to get there. Dietrich Kantel was Hundeshagen's closest associate on the GAC. However, his known shopping-list was more modest and seemed to consist of a half-share (with a certain Kakojan Niazi) in a black 500SL Mercedes 2-seater sports car that cost DM 100,000 plus. The brothers Rashid found themselves able to afford a round dozen secondhand heavy duty Mercedes trucks.

Not content with this level of plunder, the GAC executives next elected to pay themselves handsomely on a regular monthly basis too. No doubt the Liechtenstein Stiftung came in handy here. There seems to have been a declared level for these salaries of around DM 7,000 a month each in the case of Kantel and Hundeshagen, plus a suspected hidden amount of as much as DM 18,000 each a month.

Officially, the Rashid brothers received DM 1,500 a month each paid into Grindlays Bank, Peshawar. One suspects their portion accrued from vehicle rentals, or that hidden payments were being made into a Swiss bank account.

Word was out, nothing succeeds like success, which may have been the thinking behind the US Aid people's decision that GAC were the right organisation to mastermind resettlement aid programmes inside Afghanistan. The thinking was valid enough; anything to counteract the 'pull' factor of the refugee camps in Pakistan, which were bursting to overflowing. Just as significant, if nobody stayed behind, there would be no resistance, because the vital guerilla infrastructure would have evaporated.

Projects were to be ambitiously established as far north, and as far away from the Pakistani border as possible. Chicken farms appear to have been flavour of the moment. Naturally, some of the money was to be dedicated to establishing barefoot doctor clinics, known as dispensaries. Initially, a minimum of twelve was envisaged.

A handsome budget for this was arbitrarily set at US$ 1.4 million. This was the sum rumoured to have been handed over, to vanish in the maw of the GAC creative accounting system.

Before long, the Rashid brothers had become the Pickfords of Afghanistan. They were pre-eminent. They could justly claim to know more than most, who was who, what was what, and where was where. How could the Americans check out anything inside Afghanistan, if they were not allowed to set foot in the country? It was, therefore, left to the Rashid brothers to determine where the resettlement activities would best locate and which communities would be most deserving of medical and other back-up. It would also fall to them to monitor progress.

As time went by, they were able to claim to have set up medical establishments, loosely defined as dispensaries, in almost any place you chose to name and quite a few besides.

By 1984/85, Ebrahim Rashid had taken to visiting Germany four or five times a year. He must have made it to Mecca too, because shortly thereafter he became accepted as *Haji* Ebrahim. It may not have been just a simple question of keeping a wary eye on his buddies and patrons. He was on the look out for new ones. By now he was believed to be working for German Intelligence, if not the CIA (or any one of the twelve other American agencies dealing with Intelligence matters) as well. He was the convenient possessor of a German passport and no longer needed to compromise himself with visits to Islamabad embassies or meetings at Dean's Hotel.

Then, like so many before and since, he went conspiciously absent on an extended visit to the United States. He must have been one of the few Afghans to have more good reason to return than stay on there. But, by now, he had sampled the usual range of fringe benefits that plastic money can buy. 'Like most men, about this time he fell in love with himself and flew around the world looking at pie in the sky projects, whilst things at home were in less than apple pie order.'[2]

By the time he got back, it must have come as a shock to find Lt. Col (Retired) Dr. med. Reinhard Erös installed as the new Field Director for the German Afghanistan Committee in Peshawar. It is also a measure of the conceit of the GAC directors at Base Camp One that they saw no danger to themselves in making such a sweeping change in their appointment. Or, was it possible that they received instructions from a higher authority?

Erös himself maintained at the time that he had resigned his commission to take on the challenge of the job. A family man with children, throwing security to the four winds? It didn't figure. Much more likely he was asked to 'sign off' (volunteer), firstly for the experience and, next, to give a well-endowed effort the muscle it deserved.

Fairly superficial enquiry in Germany will elicit that Erös is a member of the 500-plus parachute jump club elite. If you like to believe that people fulfil the promise inherent in their names, he does an adequate job with his. There are few places he hasn't been to in his time: all the obvious ones like Australia, Canada and the United States, and less obvious ones like Nicaragua, Guatemala, Cambodia, Bangladesh, Somalia, Namibia and, yet more surprising still, Siberia, twice. Also understated, prior to this appointment, he had made 'two or three previous trips' inside Afghanistan under the aegis of GAC. It is hard to believe that the Rashid brothers were not party to these. One visit came to a notorious conclusion. Some unidentified party had decided to blow away Erös's cover. It was either a fiendishly clever or crassly stupid move.

Normally, on his return from Afghanistan, Erös could expect to be greeted by half-a-dozen exclusively German journalists, eagerly hoping to pick up something about the Afghan war. On this particular occasion, he himself was the news story. He was faced with one hundred and nine journalists from the world's television and press. They had 'heard' that he was, in reality, a German army doctor on assignment from German Special Forces (GSG 9).

The authorities had over-reacted and were all for giving him an instant dishonourable discharge. That only served to confirm the connection.

The obliging German television public took this as a cue to send in millions more marks to swell the GAC coffers. Television stations, newspapers and magazines were at pains to ensure correct address details where donations might be sent and gratefully received, which suggests the hand of Hundeshagen. Justified German pride may also have played a part. The issue became a political tug-of-war, with all the usual background lobbying.

Face was only finally saved by the combination of a benign Minister of Defence, Werner Stoltenberg, and, as surprising, the *Frankfurter Allgemeine Zeitung*, which elected to publish its own New Year's Honours List. There were only four names, two women and two men, who were deemed to be the bravest and most noteworthy of 1984. Erös found himself paired off with Andrei Sakharov, the nuclear physicist and human rights campaigner.

It has been calculated that, overall, Erös went on personally to generate something of the order of DM 5.5 million in charitable subscriptions from television, press and periodical publications, combined with two lecture tours, amounting to some forty presentations.

All this publicity demonstrates how very different Erös was to his predecessors, or indeed his successor. He had other, valid, comparable third world experience. He knew what to expect, what to guard against, what to look out for. It seems amazing that GAC should have remained unaware of all this, unless he was the final seal of approval in their dealings with the CIA - i.e. he was imposed from the outside by *force majeure*.

Predictably, the first tour the new Field Director elected to

Dr Reinhard Erös on inspection tour.

make was to inspect his new empire: the much vaunted twelve - or was it fourteen? - 'in-country' clinics, beginning at the showpiece Sadda base camp. In all, his inspection audit lasted twelve weeks. Two sweeps of five weeks each with a fortnight in between to recover in the bosom of his family.

Inevitably, what he found on his travels was that those clinics which had premises, more often than not had no attendants and when he did meet up with barefoot doctors,[3] most of whom had received their training at Sadda, they were plaintively awaiting clinics!

If delayed by stories of sickness or absenteeism, he made a point of awaiting resolution. Likewise, if a clinic couldn't be reached by vehicle or horse, he would insist on continuing on foot. Such energy and zeal must have come as an unpleasant shock to his venal GAC masters in Bonn who were doubtless hoping that Erös would be content to do nothing apart from recline in Peshawar.

It is uncertain how far north Erös penetrated. Not far, because there would not have been sufficient time. However, the further he went the thinner became the evidence on the ground, until there was none. The facts failed to tally with the Rashid pay books, so the game was up.

Wisely, unlike "Scrubber" Stewart-Richardson, instead of remonstrating with a Rashid on his return, Erös bided his time. He waited until the next annual general meeting of the GAC. And this he took by storm. As if at a staff college briefing, he outlined precisely what he had and had not found on the ground. He culminated his tirade with the not unreasonable request that, in future, all financial responsibility was to be vested in him. His would be the only authorised signature. The motion put to the meeting was carried unanimously. That is to say, unanimously except for the vote of the chairman of the meeting, who on this occasion was Hundeshagen. Although it was constitutionally invalid as the chairman only had a casting vote, it was none the less interesting that Hundeshagen was prepared to stick his neck out to express support for the Rashid brothers. His sole dissenting vote was recorded.

At this stage it was still assumed that Afghanistan constituted the only hole in the GAC bucket. At no time did Erös or anybody else consider whether the rot may have begun in Bonn, the political heartland of Germany.

By now, 1985, Erös was on the crest of a wave and to celebrate, on his return to Peshawar, he it was who initiated the whole Chak-e-Wardak hospital project. He called the first *shoora* meeting to discuss the concept in his office in Peshawar. He and his team worked out a budget, which came to half a million Ecus. (US$ 770,000 in 1985 dollars.) This budget figure has remained constant ever since! Erös deserves the credit for this initiative.

More pertinently at the time, Erös could be seen to be in control of the purse strings and so caused the Rashid brothers untold loss of face. Either on their own initiative or in response to collusion from Bonn, they instituted a programme of intimidation, developing into persecution of Erös's family. Surely it must have been agreed at the top that it was time for Erös to go?

The war of nerves conducted against Annette Erös became unceasing. She and her family found themselves under virtual house arrest, herded around at the muzzles of Kalashnikov rifles. All the house locks were changed overnight. The minibus that was used to pick up the European Kindergarten children she taught each day had vanished. The guards were changed - and had to go on being changed - because none of them could cope with the family dog.

Ultimately a replacement Field Director was sent out. His name was Peter Schwittek.

Then a totally unconnected tragedy struck. One of the Erös children, a son, fell seriously ill. Reinhard dropped everything. Annette was able to farm out the other children amongst friends. She and Reinhard and their child were on the next flight to Munich, where he died in his father's arms on the steps of the hospital. The mercy flight which had saved Juliet's driver's brother and countless others, failed to spare their beloved youngest son. Some thirty-five brother officers, many high-ranking, were at the funeral to express their sympathy and solidarity. Kantel and Hundeshagen danced attendance too that day.

Within a week, Erös and his wife were back in Peshawar. Not long afterwards, in their inimitable way, the GAC chose to sue Erös for misappropriation of funds. He counter-petitioned for his back pay and out-of-pocket costs - notably the Kindergarten bus. The customary out-of-court settlement is thought to have been made, this time in Erös's favour for some DM 35,000. He seems to have been happy to call it a day and go peaceably about his normal business, which for him meant returning to the army.

It may not all have been so one-sided. There are conflicting allegations of Erös flogging off the GAC mechanical transport fleet to other unsuspecting NGOs. Unsuspecting that is, until it came to registering the ownership of the vehicles with the Pakistani authorities. This may have been what all the fuss had been about, requiring the presence in Hamburg of the senior Pakistani from the Social Services Department of the Commissionerate *(sic)* for Afghanistan Refugees.

Whatever the full facts of the matter, I like to believe that Erös was more than justified in showing the GAC and the Rashid brothers that he could beat them at their own game. And wherever the records and the bodies are buried, it was good and deep by now.

[1] Jonas Svimbe was the leader of the Angolan UNITA party in their civil war.

[2] Quote from Lady Joseph, wife of Sir Maxwell Joseph, deriding her son-in-law in court.

[3] Barefoot doctors are known as dispensers in Afghanistan.

45

Looting the Volunteers

Reinhard Erös's successor, Peter Schwittek, was a former mathematics lecturer at Kabul University in the 1970s. By the early 1980s, his name was listed along with Anne-Marie Schwittek as representing 'Fr. Kreis Afgh', which, translated from the German abbreviation, stands for 'Friendship Group for Afghanistan'.

It may have been under Schwittek's aegis that the first Chak-e-Wardak hospital funding appeared and disappeared, the self-same way as the US Aid refugee resettlement program monies. It is uncertain whether this was EC funded or not. Peter Schwittek was known to have his own dream, centred on building a hospital at Yatoqan in the Hazarajat.

By 1992, long after the Russian departure, the Chak *shoora* had become disenchanted with the endless promises of jam tomorrow. Khalid Rashid had fallen into arrears with basic pay and allowances. So many months of back pay were owing that the whole GAC set-up had become *persona non grata* at Chak; although Sadiq was still retained to drag out construction of the hospital buildings for as long as he could, because it was a sure-fire fundraiser. This had been the pivotal point witnessed by Kate Straub. Her threat to see the hospital closed down had caused total consternation, precisely because it struck at the very heart of GAC fundraising.

Of course, politically speaking the scam we are looking at here cannot compare with the malpractices under the European Commission's Common Agriculture Policy. Such sums do not even qualify for inclusion in the accounts for audit. However, surely it should be different when the sums have been subscribed voluntarily, when people have paid for something they particularly wanted to see happen in the non-government arena?

We all reconcile ourselves to the mismanagement of national budgets. Huge wasted defence programmes are accepted as the norm. But that is what happens to the money that is taxed away from us. Donations, as the word means, is money voluntarily given. Even then, a degree of mismanagement, inefficiency, is expected, built in, even tolerated. But not wholesale plunder. And who suffered? The poor Afghan, down the line, who gave his all in his war effort.

Dittmar agreed. Looking back we could only remember one journalist who had stuck his neck out far enough to say that life for the ordinary Afghan tribesman and his family would only get worse after the Russians had left. It was at an Afghan Support Committee meeting held at Oxford in 1985. His name was Simon Winchester and he was laughed to scorn. Half the people in the room would have packed him off to the Tower for treason.

I congratulated Dittmar on his scoop in filming the fall of the Berlin Wall from the side of the German Democratic Republic. As thin as a skeleton key, he was said to have slipped through some 'unlocked' emergency exit door in the underground railway system. If so, he wasn't telling. He simply grinned enigmatically and said that he personally was only too sorry to have missed out on all that clandestine 'peace' movement filming on offer at the time.

The eighties had been the golden age of freelance journalism. It had thrown up some giants and inflated not a few pygmies. The twilight had been signalled at the Battle of Jalalabad, which had been a fittingly chaotic climax to the hot 'cold' war.

Afghanistan had been, above all, a photographer's war. What had made Dittmar so different was, as Robert Capa counselled, he got closer. Dittmar never had the least misgivings about being killed by enemy fire in Afghanistan. He was far more likely to have been a casualty of friendly fire - amongst all those half-crazed, drug-doped 'poet' warriors.

Now he was pushing forty and he couldn't name a contemporary (with the same exposure) left alive to tell the tale. But falling sick through general debilitation, dehydration and disease, was the real killer. In Namibia, he had picked up some dreaded amoeba which could see him off within five years. His only consolation was that it wasn't Aids. He tended to blame the doctors for late diagnosis and wrong medication. He was being given massive doses of vitamin B12 to restore his nervous system. He spoke of spinal fluids.

He did not take kindly to my jests about the Prophets of the Old Testament suffering Vitamin B deficiency, and how he should now turn his talents to forecasting the news. And no wonder, because it transpired that what he was really suffering from was PTSS - 'Post Traumatic Stress Syndrome'. Then, in a more contrite moment, I remembered that Dittmar had had his sound man and buddy, Peter Berti known as 'Squeaky Wheel', killed beside him in Nicaragua. He had to carry the body back for miles and miles with his friend's brains spilling down his back.

The suppurating wounds, which were failing to heal after the lumber punctures he had to endure to extract the tainted spinal fluids, were nothing to the mental anguish Dittmar was suffering. In earlier wars it had been known as shell-shock. It gave added poignancy to the

dirge he could occasionally be heard to mutter
'Life's a bitch and then you die,
A harmless hack, a drudge, a butterfly!'
I pompously told him he could do better than that. In the old days Dittmar was cheerfuly given to writing off every minor mishap of daily life with, 'It must have been a deep-laid Communist plot!' What he needed was a good holiday, and I offered to do something about it. But he was not to be moved. The real clincher for him on the Afghan front had been the let-down he suffered at the hands of an Afghan friend. He had entrusted the man with DM 7,000 for some war-related purpose. The man had used the money instead to emigrate to Canada.

It was no good my pleading that I desperately needed his help as well as his moral support. He simply didn't care. It wasn't his affair. He had done his bit and he wanted no further involvement. It was nonsense to say I needed him as a linguist. Everybody spoke English these days. I said there were now more people with German as their first language in Europe, it was only when second languages were included that English came top. Anything to change the subject and take his mind off his health. I must have cast my mind back in some irrational way to Dr William Theodore Pennell. What would he have made of it all? Dittmar asked what he had got to do with anything.

Pennell's example, I explained, remained constant in an Afghan context. It made no earthly difference how much good you did preaching in the morning; there was no escaping your destiny of being stoned in the afternoon.

I am not sure whether Dittmar caught my drift. He may have even thought I meant stoned on hash. At this rate we would both end up weeping into our *alkoholfrei* beer. The fact of the matter was I now knew for certain that I would be travelling on alone.

As a talking point, I suggested it might be timely to look up Reinhard Erös, if he really was stationed in Munich. Dittmar said it shouldn't be too hard to find as his outfit was part of the largest military establishment in Europe. It was second in size only to the Pentagon. Provided I could get past the gate and find my way through a Minotaur's maze of seven kilometers of corridors with bomb-proof bogs, I'd be sure to find him. As a throwaway, he said it was the former Gestapo headquarters for Bavaria.

He asked me what was driving me on. I said it was curiosity. I felt compelled to find out what had happened to that Christmas present box of Winston Churchill cigars. I could not believe that Peter, John, Sarah, Frank and the rest of our team could have misread the man to such an extent. Surely, we could not all have been wrong?

Had it ever occurred to me, Dittmar asked, that there was possibly a much simpler explanation. I thought of the postman, but said nothing. In Germany that was unthinkable.

'Why shouldn't Kantel and Hundeshagen enjoy a good cigar? His notion was fit to point a moral or adorn a tale.

*

All there was now left for me was to go over with Dittmar what I was hoping to do next and invite him to punch holes in the plan. My objective was to get some proof for what evidence I had so far, which was little more than conjecture and hearsay.

The clues I had could be summarised as follows.

1. The *Der Spiegel* article, Nr 44, 1988. Dittmar supplied me with a less tattered copy, together with the name and Hamburg telephone number of the Overseas Editor.

2. The name of an English-speaking female executive inside GAC - Andrea Hörst, whose appointment was given as 'Project-Controlling' on a letter to Dr Kermit Veggeberg dated 16 July 1991. If she had become disaffected, she could prove my best lead.

3. The name of a senior Pakistani official from the Social Services section of the Commissionerate for Afghan Refugeees, who was known to have been called as an expert witness during a legal process at Hamburg, supposedly involving GAC or their personnel and the illegal sale of vehicles.

4. Last but not least, the fascinating, all-consuming English language prestige brochure on the 'Achievements of the German Afghanistan Committee', dated 1988.

I then outlined a three-pronged approach. I would call first on the Charities Register at Bonn to see what I could discover there. Dittmar, through one of his Rotarian friends, was able to give me the name of a Bonn lawyer whom he thought might be prepared to help a friend in need.

Next, I proposed to visit the University of Bonn to see what I could discover from the student register about Islamic fundamentalists and sympathisers in the mid-1970s. Would the known names tally with mine?

I should also, without fail, call early on the German Foreign Office and let them know why I was poking about in their backyard, before they heard for themselves. I had the name of their recently-returned-from-Islamabad expert on all the matters that interested me most. I was particularly keen to meet him. If he had a mind to, he could probably confirm or deny all my worst misgivings.

If all else failed, I could travel on to Hamburg and hope to resuscitate *Der Spiegel*'s interest in a long dead story.

I had the impression that Dittmar didn't rate my chances too highly and I was beginning to suffer grave misgivings myself. Then "Scrubber"'s admonition rang in my ears 'Whatever you do, don't quit.'

The next morning I put in a telephone call to Erös, but was told he was away in Hamburg for the week.

46
Kakojan Niazi

On the train journey from Augsburg to Bonn, the track runs for a good stretch along the banks of the Rhine. It is welded so smoothly that there is an illusion of being on a high-speed river cruise; especially if the Rhine is in spate. This feeling of luxury is heightened by the beautiful open-plan art deco design of the carriages. Out of the window, there is not only the active barge life to watch but also the famed castles and their neat supportive vineyards, each proudly proclaiming its name.

At Bonn I walked up to the Stern Hotel, which was next to the university and only a hundred yards from an underground station. I knew the German Foreign Office was so big and important it warranted its own station. The Charities Register would no doubt be buried deeper, and Karla Schefter had long ago warned me that it would serve no purpose to call on the offices of the German Afghanistan Committee or their successors, as only large doses of tight-lipped retribution would be on offer there.

The hotel had either been bombed or gutted and modernised. On each floor, there were tantalising photographs featuring the *fin-de-siècle* splendour of former times. The facelift had been confined to the facia alone. In common with all the other buildings in the square, except the cinema, it had been restored to create a remoulded town centre. There was an eighteenth-century obelisk in the centre of the square which was original - everything else was facsimile. But the workmanship was unrestrained.

Happily, the hotel, although ideally placed and comfortable in its semi-spartan way, was not extravagantly priced. As soon as I had checked in, I took a taxi to the offices of the lawyer, whom I was told I might come to need and could above all trust. He was an introduction of one of Dittmar's friends via Rotary. He proved extremely helpful over the Charities Register, cloaking my enquiries in respectable anonymity.

Amongst other things, he applauded my decision to call on the Foreign Office, and let them know my purpose. In truth my motivation was conditioned by the inherent belief, somewhat endorsed by Dittmar, that Germany was still a most authoritarian, highly self-disciplined near-police state, full of law-abiding citizens who never jay-walked. Also in my mind's eye, I could still not differentiate much between the uniforms of officialdom and those I had been taught to loathe instinctively as a child. It was that paranoid fear which had prompted me to call *ab initio* on the Auswartiges Amt and openly declare my purposes. I also hoped to learn a thing or two from them. I had the name of the most recently returned diplomat from their embassy in Islamabad, whom I knew was fully conversant with the background detail sought on the past and present activities of the German Afghanistan Committee and the German Afghanistan Foundation. At worst, he could only tell me it was none of my business.

From the Register, it appeared that the origins of the German Afghanistan Committee and its spin-off, the German Afghanistan Foundation, could be traced back to the Christian Democratic Youth Movement and their 'Peace Forum' of the 1970s. Known then as the Bonn Peace Forum, it had been established in knee-jerk response to Soviet 'Peace' initiatives.

The age bracket of the Bonn Youth Organisation Peace Forum had a threshold of sixteen, with a 'Club Med' style upper limit of thirty-five, with the exception of the federal chairman or political leader, who was allowed to continue in office to age thirty-eight. It all seemed horrendously reminiscent of earlier German youth movements, but my new lawyer friend told me not to attach undue importance to that - despite the same insistence on the issue of identity discs and arm bands for members!

So, it was no great surprise to find that the majority of those listed on the register gave their occupation as 'student'. It reminded me that I had read in *The Economist*, that before the Russian invasion of Afghanistan in 1979, the Bonn University campus had been a hotbed of Muslim fundamentalist activity.

There was no knowing from the register who had been the *primum mobile*. The Afghan contingent seemed the most likely - after all, they had the most to gain. The name which was to recur time and again was the most memorable of names to me. It was Kakojan Niazi. The other prominent name at the time was Nassery, Dr Toryalay Nassery, who had pioneered the first 'Help for Afghanistan' organisation VAF (*Verein Afghanistanischer Flüchtlingshilfe*, or Committee for Afghan Refugees Relief), shortly before the invasion.

It was Niazi who had been the vociferous spokesman (at that time on behalf of the German HELP organisation) at the Geneva conference in 1984, when he had declaimed the shortcomings of the German constitution in prohibiting cross-border activities inside Afghanistan. It was said that Niazi had nominated Nassery for the VAF post in Peshawar in the first place and that Nassery had returned the favour by having Niazi removed first from VAF and subsequently from HELP.

Nassery, who no doubt recognised a good thing when he saw it, also engineered the removal of the Rashid brothers, who were described at the time as 'young scions of a powerful political family', from the scene at the Peshawar end. So, what was more natural than that the disaffected parties should offer their combined talents elsewhere, where they would be better appreciated and made a lot more welcome.

The Bonn Peace Forum was the natural choice. They in turn were only too happy to take on board such a talented combination of fundraising expertise plus an enviable network of contacts inside Afghanistan. Out of a total of five, there were three other instantly recognisable names. If not exactly ideal youths, they were at least early recruits from the rank and file of the Bonn Christian Democratic Youth Movement. Kakojan Niazi soon trained them in the techniques of approaching donor companies and, subsequently, of how to loosen the purse-strings of the German general public.

Denny Hundeshagen and Khalid Rashid were thought to have had perpetual medical student status in common. Khalid had studied medicine at Kabul University for five years, but although Hundeshagen was now a qualified pharmacist there was no evidence of Khalid having, as yet, any qualification.

Dietrich Kantel was the son of a qualified lawyer (Willi Kantel) who seems to have experienced difficulty in passing his law exams. Any shortcomings in that direction however were to be more than adequately compensated for with political acumen. He it was who brought Michael Sagurna on board.[1] He may also have been responsible for spotting the loopholes in some of the laws appertaining to the administration of German charities.

The establishment of the actual Bonner Afghanisches Komitee can be dated from a protocol drawn up by Dietrich Kantel on 19 October 1984. Denny Hundeshagen's arrival can be established by a minute of 25 February 1985, which states that it was 'unanimously decided to co-opt Denny Hundeshagen to the executive committee with special responsibilities for medical personnel and computer programming.' (EDV, *Elektronische Daten Verarbeitung*; Electronic Data Processing). For the present Kantel was to have the humbler role of recording the minutes.

Surprisingly, it was decided at this same meeting that Afghans would be excluded from membership of the committee. The reason given was that political argument between Afghan factions should not be allowed to cloud issues. It would be simpler to exclude them. If the constitution required an open meeting for such a decision, then this was the moment to change the constitution!

Kakojan Niazi's position was not made clear. He has been labelled as apolitical, which must have been one of his strengths, but he was also invariably a late and short-term attendant at meetings. However, these cuckoo's nest activities could well have sewn the seeds of his alternative German Afghanistan Foundation.

The Bonn University campus is a sight to behold. I had difficulty calculating how many football pitches it could contain - I reckoned somewhere between eight and ten. The magnificent eighteenth-century university building itself was fully restored to pristine glory. At the time of my visit, the central courtyard was in use as an open-air cinema. There was a slight drizzle occasioning row upon row of Renoir umbrellas, with expectant students beneath, patiently awaiting the screening of *The Blue Angel*.

The student registry people were extremely willing, but unable to do much in under a week. Name and date of birth details were insufficient means for accessing their data bank, which was still, surprisingly, mainly manual. What was required were actual dates of attendance. These I did not have. Inspired guesswork produced nothing. Even at Stern Hotel prices, I was reluctant to give so much time, unless I were to go to Hamburg and back in the interim. I said I would call again if it became imperative. All I was working on was a wild hunch that Ebrahim Rashid and Denny Hundeshagen had been at Bonn University together. But, then, it equally occurred to me that they could have met on that campus without having any pretext. In fact, as things turned out, I could not have been more hilariously wrong.

So my next sortie led to the German Foreign Ministry. I telephoned to make an appointment with Leotard Bleifrei,[2] the German diplomat I knew to be recently returned from Islamabad, only to be told he was not available - not listed. I explained that I had come a long way to see him, although I was careful not to say Pakistan. My persistence paid off. I was put through to the chief of personnel postings, who asked me my business. I explained that it was a subject best discussed face to face, concerning Germans I had met in Peshawar and Afghanistan. This chief advised me that Leotard had left the Ministry; to which, half in jest, I hoped it was not in disgrace. On the contrary, he had been promoted to another ministry. When I asked for the telephone number of the new ministry, I was told that that would not be possible. I could only assume that he had been posted to some special operation, possibly related to the Maghreb where his fundamentalist experience would have added value. Consequently, I have masked his true identity. After a long pause, I asked if there was anybody else I could talk to in the same office, since I had taken the trouble to come so far. I was then given an internal telephone number and told to turn up at the gate.

I could hardly wait to take the underground to Auswartiges Amt, the Foreign Office Station. Buying the ticket was the hardest part. You had to have the exact change or risk being caught without a ticket. The fine was forty times the fare.

As I left the underpass, I couldn't help noticing that the lady exiting with me looked as if she might be an executive at the Foreign Office, so I asked the way. It wasn't quite as stupid or obvious a question as it may seem because, although their Foreign Office building is as big as our old Ministry of Defence and Air Ministry complex put together, it is well set back behind forbidding railings. The entrance itself is not full frontal, but is set very much to one side, tucked away down a back street.

The guard post was manned by what I subsequently took to be German special forces. Behind smoked glass windows, not shades, they studied my passport minutely, taking long looks at my Afghan visas, before telephoning the number I had been given to call. Whoever it was, was out to lunch, so I should call back later. A well-established formula was put to me. I should return along the way I had come from the underground station, but on the opposite side of the road. There, a quarter of a mile back, I should find a café-*cum*-restaurant. It was suggested I should go there and perhaps have a meal. In an hour or so's time, I should again telephone this same number, but this time using an outside prefix. When I had an answer I would no doubt be invited to return to the gate.

Although I felt I had been banished for life to the Café Adler (the rendezvous point for Check Point Charlie exchanges in Berlin), the delay afforded me valuable time to marshall my thoughts properly and everything thereafter went like clockwork.

A Frau Hoffmann invited me to return to the gate and ask for an escort to take me to her specified room number. Of course, they rang through first and removed my passport for safekeeping and, maybe, photocopying.

The most surprising aspect of the interior of the building was the lift system. It was open-plan on a continuous conveyor-belt. The right-hand side of two shafts went up. The left-hand side came down. But I couldn't work out what happened in order to side-step decapitation at the top. Perhaps only the uninvited ever ventured that far. With only minumum agility, passengers jumped on and off at whim. It looked alarming but fun and was soon casually mastered. It moved a lot slower than at first appeared.

Frau Hoffmann was most attractive, spoke excellent English and was a good listener. The room was on the small side, suggesting lowly status, but this impression may have been caused by the mass of papers piled in places from floor to ceiling. In contrast, the pins on the maps on the walls proclaimed she had responsibilities throughout the sub-continent. Visions passed before my eyes of Germans kidnapped in Kashmir.

I outlined to her what had brought me to Germany, and Bonn in particular. I mentioned the one or two leads and the host of suspicions I had about two specific German NGOs which had operated in Afghanistan for some time, one of which was now about to spread its wings. I tabled my slightly scuffed collection of exhibits - the only too-well-known article from *Der Spiegel*, one or two letters emanating from the German Afghanistan Committee's Bonn offices. I told Kate Straub's story and the suggestion that hers was not the only instance of female intimidation. I had been particularly keen to meet 'Leotard', because I felt sure he could have helped me in my researches.

To Frau Hoffmann's enquiry, I was able to tell her that I was not a journalist, but just engaged in writing a book about my experiences which happened to overlap with certain activities of the German Afghanistan Committee, both at Sadda and at Chak, and that I was eager to set the record straight. I would leave her the first draft of the material section, which was sure to be erroneous, but I had to begin somewhere!

She asked if she might take copies of my material and took the various bits and pieces off to the photocopier, leaving me to my thoughts. During this longish spell, I met her colleague, Frau Lange.

As Frau Hoffman took me to the lift to see me on my way, having as I suspected, told me very little, she astonished me on saying goodbye, by also wishing me good luck! This I had not expected and it was to be my encouragement ever afterwards.[3]

I returned to the hotel and began the search for Andrea Hörst's name in the Bonn telephone directory. Things looked promising. There was but one such name in the book and I put in a call directly and was brought back to earth with a bump. This Andrea Hörst spoke not a word of English, had never had anything to do with any organisation remotely connected with Afghanistan and sounded incapable of intimidation.

With my tail between my legs I decided to improve my German by going to the cinema in the square. Over the years, my German had deteriorated. It was a light American situation comedy and I failed to get the jokes. My only consolation was that there was little evidence of German mirth about either, although that could have been due to bad dubbing.

[1] Michael Sagurna - Hamburg journalist, German politician, Government speaker for Lower Saxonia.

[2] This is a pseudonym to protect this novice spy.

[3] It transpired later that my call had been timely as they were in the course of instituting enquiries along parallel lines.

47

'When the Fat Lady Sings'

On returning to the hotel, I was in for a pleasant surprise. My platter bore a scroll of faxes, which had arrived for me whilst I was out at the cinema. My initial reaction was that there must have been a mistake, because nobody knew my whereabouts. Then I remembered I had booked the hotel from Dittmar's house and, as a courtesy, I had left the hotel detail at the Auswartiges Amt. There was no cover sheet from Dittmar - just my name and 'Hotel guest' scrawled across the first sheet. There was no name of sender. The first few sheets were in English and they were startlingly clear as to purpose. Obviously the word was out that I was around.

The first items were letters in English from Kakojan Niazi to the Strategic Studies Institute of the US Army War College, Carlisle Barracks, Pennsylvania, and the second was to the Managing Direktor *(sic)* of Interarms, a British arms dealer in Manchester, United Kingdom.

Then, just in case anybody should have any doubts about their authenticity, there followed what looked like crumpled-up manuscript drafts for both letters in what had to be Mr Niazi's handwriting. On closer inspection, one of the drafts was for an earlier letter which was not available in typed form. The addressees were respectively Dr Alan Sabroski and Mr Hamilton Spence.

It looked very much like the work of a disaffected vengeful secretary, who had bided her time, judging by the dates of the two letters, for some nine odd years, not months, of maturation! The drafts could have been picked out of the waste-paper basket by anybody. The copy originals had come from the file.

What hit me like a sledgehammer was that the letter to America mentioned a name which had been familiar to me over twenty years ago - the Duke of Valderano. There was mention of a luncheon he hosted for Dr Alan Sabroski 'at White's Club, on Monday 6 January 1986 ... where particular matters relative to support for the Mujahedeen had been discussed.' If anybody ever wanted proof positive that the German Afghanistan Foundation was engaged in arms dealing, this was it!

The other papers were all in German and amounted to the protocol establishing the Foundation. There was also a two-page analysis of the early days of German aid for Afghanistan. This had been prepared by Kakojan Niazi on a strictly private and confidential basis exclusively for a certain Dr Jurgen Todenhofer.

From my point of view, there were more than enough damning points contained in these few pages, not the least of which was the overlap in signatories to the Foundation's formation from the original Committee ... notably Kantel and Lerch, as well, of course, as Kakojan Niazi himself. It was much too early yet for Dr Karl Victor Freigang to feature. I noticed that, for some reason, the protocol closed with reference to a briefing for Gerhard Löwenthal - described as the Moderator of ZDF Magazine - meaning anchorman for the documentary news programmes put out by *Zweites Deutsches Fernsehen*, the second German TV channel.

These were eleven of the most significant pieces of paper I had yet 'laid eyes on' in my quest. For one fleeting moment, I thought I detected a hint of hidden menace in the fact that the English letters pointed an accusing finger at Britain and the United States, as if to say 'put your own house in order, before presuming to sort us out!' But then I decided the sender had sent the English language material as the clearest possible signal of quality content. This was a clear-cut come-on. There was no 'beware of landmine' or latent Rashid threat inherent here.

Clearly, somebody had to be on my side. I put in a call to Dittmar. He denied all knowledge. Nobody had been asking after me. He suggested I trace the fax number of the sender. A bit obvious. It turned out to be a bright yellow German post office, just down the street.

Reception did confirm that a German lady had telephoned shortly before transmission. This set me wondering why my benefactor or benefactress couldn't afford to be seen in the hotel reception area, or posting an envelope in the hotel letter box. Then I remembered something that Kate Straub had said which was about all she could remember of Hundeshagen's other female victim. She had been significantly outsize, ample, generously proportioned. I had visions of a generous fat lady who had begun to sing for me. Perhaps she was a well-known Bonn personality?

Closer study of the documents, with the aid of my pocket dictionary, revealed that I had only seen the trailer. There were instructions of where I should go if I wanted more of the same.

I was set back a bit by the detail for the rendezvous. It was to be for three o'clock in the morning, in Hamburg - under conditions of total anonymity. I was told to come alone, or no deal. Hamburg seemed an appropriate setting. It was where *Der Spiegel* had their head office and a fortuitous reflection of the Pakistani bureaucrat's 'expert witness'. There was the remote chance that I might bump into Reinhard Erös, who was said to be there all week. Michael Sagurna, when he wasn't a Bonn student, passed as a Hamburg journalist.

Then I dimly remembered both Gerhard Löwenthal's and Dr Jungen Todenhofer's names from amongst those listed as belonging to a right-wing organisation called *Stahlhelm* (Steel Helmet) known to have CIA links, with a Hamburg focus if not headquarters.

I was so geared up, I was game for anything, but nevertheless, I took the precaution of posting what I had been so generously given, to Peter Stiles in England.

My imagination was doing overtime. I kept seeing an action-replay of the ancient George Raft gangster movie, *Some Like it Hot*. 'When the fat lady sings' had been the signal for machine-gun mayhem. I saw 'Spats', all expectant for the beautiful 'sing-a-gram' girl to spring out of the birthday cake ... instead there were just bullets. I wondered what was in store for me. If my benefactress's motive was revenge, I need fear no plot. I would have plenty of time to think it over between here and now and that rendezvous in Hamburg. I had visions of garish neon lights on the Reeperbahn. I hoped it would be somewhere more discreet!

48
The Secret Archives

Although the case had been quashed (it was even mooted to have been at the request of Gulbuddin Hekmatyar himself), being a German Court of Justice, all the paperwork had remained in place - on file somewhere. It was a collation of all these 'submissions of evidence' that I was being invited to view. Up until this moment, all I had to go on was hearsay, rumours, plus an over-active imagination to lead me astray, and some intuitive native cunning; precious little in the way of facts.

Exactly thirty hours later I pressed the appropriate answerphone, gave my name and was admitted to an old block of offices. A stair light came on and, since there was no lift, I began to climb the stairs. Two short flights up, a door stood invitingly ajar. There was total silence, but for the distant wail of police or ambulance sirens.

Inside, there was not one wellwisher but two. We shook hands without a word. No names. No pack drill.

I had the impression that the office had been lent for the occasion by one of the two to the other. It was certainly no ordinary repository for archives. It could have been the office of a long-established Greek or Turkish dried fig importer. There was a suggestion of Smyrna origins.

Although I felt, because of the nature of the mission, as if I were being given privileged admittance to some gloomy pre-war 'Hall of Remembrance', the parchment dry 'Rolls of Honour' were laid out for my inspection and I could take my pick. Except that, far from being leisurely and respectful, my pace was to be frenetic - more the just reflection of dishonour.

I concentrated on scanning the pages for personal and organisational names, which I knew by heart, and the sums of money which were quite new to me. My guardian angels may have suspected me of speed-reading the German. I was intent only on names and numbers and noting the page numbers of my 'finds'.

My minders were soon bored and I found myself left alone to my own devices.

Some of the papers looked to me as if they might have been the self-same ones that were supposedly either leaked or endorsed to *Der Spiegel* by von Rosen, Willi Brandt's press officer. The material facts were much the same as had appeared in the article. Otherwise it was all new.

The formerly large room had been sub-divided long ago with heavily frosted plate-glass partitioning. I wondered how it survived the air raids of World War II. Whenever I looked up, which wasn't often, I could see and hear a Punch & Judy show of animated profiles picked out on the translucent glass.

After what seemed like hours and probably was, they looked in to see how their mature student was getting on.

Ironically, my rusty German was to work to my advantage. Not only did I scan more bumph by not getting sucked into the text, but my new-found friends were to take pity on me. They allowed me to remove the 171 pages I had earmarked to photocopy them, so long as I returned them first thing in the morning - whatever that was meant to mean. It was now 6 a.m.!

Fortunately, Germany has more self-service photocopiers than beer halls. I doubt I have ever applied myself so diligently at 8 a.m. without breakfast. Everything was back in place, looking undisturbed in next to no time. And it would be a long time before anybody went rummaging through those old files again.

In case of any last-minute change of heart, I had made two complete sets of copies. I shipped one set to England and proposed to shuffle slowly out of Germany, tightly clutching the other.

I had one more call to make on the way. I had heard of an organisation in Berlin, whose sole purpose was corruption busting. Their executives spent most of their time in darkest Africa, concentrating on Third World countries. One of the senior executives had served with Robert McNamara at the World Bank, another had been with the Commonwealth Secretariat. If I wasn't much mistaken, I had something for them to do in their own backyard. They had an intriguing name - Transparency International.

With a good lawyer in Bonn and some World Bank class clout in Berlin, I should have begun to feel a little less worried about myself. But symptoms persisted in telling me otherwise. I needed to visit dentists for recurring abscesses, and also have my neck examined by a specialist. For reasons of stress or previous injury, I constantly felt as if my head were about to roll off my shoulders. The X-rays came back with a lengthy report, the only sentence of which I thought I understood said that there was a general degeneration of the 'neck bone' commensurate with, or ahead of my advancing years, or from previous injuries suffered in a punishing parachuting lifestyle! Again I packed the whole lot off to Peter Stiles for a second opinion, which I hoped would not cost half as much as the first! By return of post, back came the X-ray, plus the diagnosis. All it said was 'We didn't need a photograph to know you were degenerate!' signed Peter. When I put them up to the light, it looked to me as if my life hung on a very slender thread. But if Stiles saw no cause for alarm, then everybody else's life must hang by much the same narrow thread, or so I reasoned to myself.

THE ARCHIVES - GENESIS AND REVELATIONS
'Charity begins at home'

Although my high-speed scanning process had made a rather random selection of papers based on names I recognised, I had little difficulty in re-shuffling the pack back into date order.

The earliest document was still the two-page 'insight' prepared by Kakojan Niazi for the eyes of Dr Jürgen Todenhofer only. It traced the whole subject of aid for Afghanistan back to its earliest beginnings; to a time immediately prior to the Russian invasion, 24 December 1979.

There was no doubting a certain cavalier style had been set by Dr Nassery, which demonstrated just how wide open the possibilities were for plunder. However, the basis for the paper appeared to be a genuine desire to find a less rapacious conduit for the channelling of much-needed funds to what had become the world's largest-ever refugee community. This is likely to have been the prelude to the foundation of the German Afghanistan Committee. It seems as likely that such an astute politician as Todenhofer would have called for just such a paper, before making any commitment, either on behalf of himself or his political friends.

This 'review' therefore began properly by stating that VAF (Association for Afghan Refugees) was founded, presumably by Kakojan Niazi himself, amongst others, on 15 October 1979. It candidly stated that from day one there was to be an intelligence/information gathering role. The first appeals for donations began immediately after the Russian invasion.

In January 1980, Kakojan Niazi set up a meeting of ex-patriate Afghan doctors in Bonn. (Germany has a long, sometimes as much as seventy years, record of training Afghan doctors, policemen, royal guards, forestry workers etc.) The purpose of the meeting was to introduce Herr Neudeck of *Schiff für Vietnam* - 'Lifeboat for

Vietnam' - to the Afghan doctors. Herr Rupert Neudeck's charity was now eager to push the boat out on behalf of Afghan refugees. Their exodus, which had begun as a trickle in 1974, had now become a flood. Herr Neudeck was looking for a suitable Afghan doctor to skipper the 'ship' in Pakistan.

Dr Nassery had arrived from Japan, where he had met with a singular lack of support for a refugee relief scheme of his own and had been equally unsuccessful in finding his feet or employment in Germany. He was, therefore, selected as the man to skipper the *Schiff für Vietnam* into the stormy seas of the North-West Frontier. He left on 4 February 1980.

Later that month, Niazi flew to Pakistan to kit out the clinic for the team of doctors, who were to be funded by the former Vietnamese 'Lifeboat'. At the same time he established contact with the Pakistani Commissionerate for Afghan Refugees, as well as Afghan resistance 'commanders'.

The first press conference calling for donations on behalf of VAF took place on the evening of 5 March 1980 in 'Tulpenfeld' (The Tulip Field).[1] The conference was covered by the national broadcasting organisation's (ZDF) programme, *Heute* (Today). The plight of the Afghan refugees was featured and the appeal went public.

After obtaining the necessary authority from the Pakistani Ministry for Tribal Affairs, Niazi, arm-in-arm with Dr Nassery, founded the very first clinic for the exclusive use of Afghans in Peshawar. To consolidate this relationship, Dr Nassery became a fully-fledged member of VAF. At this time, donations amounted to DM 120,000.

On his return from Pakistan in April 1980, Niazi went to work to raise the wind to finance the project fully. In the course of this, he spoke several times to a Frau Fischer who, in turn, approached Herr Dr Todenhofer. In June 1980, Niazi was fortunate enough to meet Todenhofer in person in the *Bundeshaus*, the German Federal Parliament.

As a result of this meeting, Dr Todenhofer got in touch with Herr Gerhard Löwenthal, the well-known editor of the ZDF news programme, who on the basis of photographic material covering the refugee camps in VAF's care, produced an interview with Kakojan Niazi. There then followed the first appeal for donations for VAF to be broadcast on Gerhard Löwenthal's ZDF - Magazine documentary news programme.

In the month following, the volume of donations rose to over DM 1 million. This was more than enough to fund all the medical help required at the Peshawar clinic. At this time, Dr Nassery's co-operation could be counted on to the utmost limit of his loyalty. His only stipulation was that funds should be forwarded from Germany, as and when available, and whenever requested.

On 19 July 1980, Dr Jürgen Todenhofer, in the company of another right-wing politician, Herr Schultze-Vorberg, flew to Pakistan and from there they visited Afghanistan. On their return to Germany they made another appeal on Gerhard Löwenthal's television programme and in other media. As the result of this, a further DM 2 million poured into the VAF bank account.

VAF were now flush enough to charter a PIA plane-load of refugee aid material in December 1980. And in July 1981, at the request of Dr Nassery, Niazi visited Pakistan to inspect the various projects.

On the foundation day of the HELP organisation, VAF again chartered a PIA plane to ship twenty tonnes of medical and other goods to Dr Nassery.

However, during Niazi's stay in Pakistan this time, he could not fail to notice that Dr Nassery intended to break loose. He had, for instance, removed the words 'West Germany' from all public signs and notice boards. When Niazi took him to task for this, pointing out that all the help stemmed from Dr Todenhofer and Herr Löwenthal, his reply was that he did not consider himself beholden to the Germans. From this time on, relations between the VAF and Dr Nassery, and equally between Dr Nassery and Niazi, deteriorated.

Dr Nassery made constant threats by telephone and letter to the effect that he no longer wished to be any part of VAF. Simultaneously, he declaimed in the camps that the aid all came from his 'brothers in Germany'. Since VAF had no alternative candidate to replace him, they were obliged to maintain the *status quo*.

In October 1982, another plane-load (military, probably a Hercules), this time from the Bundeswehr, was sent. This had a mixed load (combi-configuration) of thirty tonnes of aid materials and fourteen journalists, including two television teams, from ARD (Arbeitsgemeinschaft der Rundfunkanstalten in Deutschland) and ZDF (Zweites Deutsches Fernsehen). The media circus had been assembled by ringmaster Gerhard Löwenthal himself. Whilst there, an Afghan Media/Research Centre was established - whose primary aim was to generate film material for his programme.

That same month, Dr Nassery had declared to the HELP organisation that he no longer wanted to work for VAF and that 'they' should find somebody else to release him. The next day he said he had changed his mind and would stay on after all.

Then, shortly before Niazi's departure for Germany, Dr Nassery announced that he no longer recognised VAF and that he again wanted out. It looked like a case of bad conscience.

Meanwhile, Niazi had discovered that Dr Nassery's expenditure on behalf of the refugees did not amount to one half of his monthly receipts of DM 130,000.

On Niazi's return he therefore made these facts known to his VAF executive commiteee and all further transfers of monies to Pakistan ceased.

In retrospect, the problem had been exacerbated by Dr Nassery's practice of spending half the year travelling abroad. He spent three months in Germany and a further three months in Japan, where he busied himself with and finally founded a new Non Government Organisation named 'Union Aid'. This afforded him the independent platform he craved; but from now on the refugees had no idea where the aid was coming from. All they were given to understand was that they had Dr Nassery 'and his old axis band of brothers' to thank.

Meanwhile, Dr Nassery used every means at his command to consolidate his independence. Not only did he promote himself as the personification of all this bounty, he made very sure that only his closest relatives were aboard the gravy train. VAF found that they could only expand their activities through this leech-like, blood-is-thicker-than-water network.

By March 1983, Dr Nassery had returned to the annual visit to Germany, but this time he complained everywhere he went that he was not being properly funded. In truth, he was sitting on more than DM 1.3 million at the bank in Peshawar!

By July 1983, on Dr Nassery's return to Peshawar, megalomania had set in. He dismissed thirty people who had taken exception to his cult of personality and blatant nepotism. Amongst other things, he had opened bank accounts for four of his nephews, whom he had entrusted with handling German donations.

From now on, anybody who opposed his views or even stood up to him, was branded a traitor, an enemy of Islamic Afghanistan, a bandit and a criminal.

Kakojan Niazi concludes his report with the plea that this is no way to build a proper organisation for German aid to Afghanistan. He expresses the sincere hope that there will shortly be the possibility of setting up other structures that will have nothing to do with Dr Nassery. The injunction that this paper is prepared exclusively for Dr Todenhofer is then repeated.

Interestingly enough, looking back at the notes I took of my own meeting with Dr Toryalai Nassery in Peshawar in 1982, which were incorporated into a report to Robert Cranborne, now the Marquess of Salisbury, at the Afghanistan Support Commiteee dated 12-28 November 1982, I found that Dr Toryalai Nassery had quite candidly disclosed that Union Aid was mainly funded by the Germans. The Dooley Foundation of New York and the Direct Relief Committee of Santa Barbara, California, were also mentioned. He also sought funds from Egypt and Japan. He said he undertook joint-ventures with Secretary General Britz of the German Help organisation, who was his main sponsor. Some well-meaning containers of German gifts were costing as much as DM 150,000 to air freight. A mixed blessing; on two subsequent occasions they were air-lifted free by Lufthansa.

Dr Nassery had gone on to claim that, thanks to German support, Union Aid was second only in size to the UN High Commission for Refugees amongst the voluntary agencies. He said at the time the annual budget amounted to DM 1.5 million, excluding gifts in kind.

'Union Aid is the only group providing medicines and food to the Mujahedeen.' He continued, 'If the civilian population leave Afghanistan the Mujahedeen will have nowhere to fight. The fish must have somewhere to swim.'

He then gratuitously added 'The German Embassy in Islamabad know nothing of this and they must NOT know!' He went on 'The Society of Afghanistan Doctors outside Afghanistan is a money-making organisation. Union Aid is not. Union Aid does no publicity and all its activities are low profile. However, some publicity is undertaken in Germany and Japan to raise funds.'

Dr Nassery then stated, 'I am not interested in the cult of the personality. I do not want to rule Afghanistan. I just want to get on with the fight against communism.

'Our good name has been blackened by both the main political groups based in the Refugee camps. Perhaps we can only count on the Babrak Kamal (Kabul) regime to recognise what we really do! The Russians are the real savages. You used to think we were barbarians. I tell you the Russian ambassador here attacks the Pakistanis for giving the refugees a blanket and 5 rupees a day each. How would he like the same treatment I wonder?'

And he wasn't above hurling the occasional insult in my own direction.

'You may be wondering why that chap won't sit next to you. It is probably since homosexuality has been made legal in Britain, we can no longer be too sure of you British!

'The French doctors are not popular because they make too much propaganda. The Russians then go out to capture them dead or alive. They are also too young and inexperienced to be much use.

'What we desperately need is specialist surgeons, one orthopaedic surgeon and one neuro-surgeon to open a hospital dedicated to treating Mujahedeen.'

There is some chance the airfreight container loads could account for some of the 200-300 tons of old clothes collected around Germany that went missing at the time.

Dr Jürgen Todenhofer was part hero and part peacock. He had defied his own government's official diktat that he should on no account go to Afghanistan. This was presumably for fear of his being captured by the Russians, brainwashed and paraded for general media exploitation.

Obviously, to judge from Niazi's paper, Dr Todenhofer could make himself extremely useful through his media connections, not the least of whom was Gerhard Löwenthal. Between them they had hatched a nice little double act, which had first come to light in the name of VAF, whereby they had already generated some DM 3.3 million.

Todenhofer's peacock label refers to his Afghanistan visit where his appearance was well-staged and the costume worthy of Ali-Baba, down to his 'presentation' silver-plated pistol. His preferred weapon in action however was said to be the more realistic 9mm Makerov.

Yet more relevant still to Niazi, once[2] the German Afghanistan Committee had been formed, was the fact that from his Federal Government position, Dr Todenhofer could make a 'public donation call'. What this amounted to was the placing of government monies directly into a suitable charitable fund, for them to handle as they saw fit; simply because the government had no alternative 'competent organisation'. This was directly in line with Niazi's outcry at the Geneva conference of NGOs in 1984. The German government was proscribed from furthering any hostile act in a foreign country. It had to be an invisible, indirect transaction and consequently became known as the 'by-pass operation'. It was to become the official way of how not to violate the German constitution. However, some unscrupulous politicians, not content with being the best paid in Europe, now saw the means of further lining their pockets in a positively Oriental manner.

A call is made for government monies to be paid into some anodyne charitable institution, with minimum accountability, allowing the perpetrators to make liberal plunderings of a help-yourself slush fund.

Under the system, government donations were made to charity status NGOs engaged in supposedly humanitarian work. At best, these turned out to be intelligence gathering tools, with genuine medical cover. At worst, they were guns for drugs for rockets for *sub rosa* terrorist training organisations run and robbed by hand-picked crooks, whose silence was assured and whose immunity has so far proved bullet-proof.

When summonsed to attend court, Dr Todenhofer found excuses not to take the witness stand on no fewer than four occasions - by pleading special parliamentary duties etc. When he did finally appear, quite a lot of water had flowed under the bridge. For instance, his able Christian Democratic Youth Movement assistant, Herr Egon Weimar, had already disclosed in evidence that during the course of one fortnight's TV promotion alone, GAC had received over DM 2.35 million. This figure had been extracted, by way of an example, from the regular weekly reports Weimar had supplied to Todenhofer; rather like adding up the returns from a unit trust or football pools advertising campaign.

Not only was Todenhofer unaware that Weimar had preceded him in the witness box, he obviously had no idea what he might have disclosed. Because, when it was his turn to give an account of what the returns might have been, he came up with the derisory notion of having an overall figure in his head of roughly DM 2 million. Damningly, he went on to add that that had anyway to be discounted to allow for the 50% handling fee charged by GAC!

It transpired that Dr Todenhofer, dissatisfied with this unacceptable level of commission, had gone on to found yet another spin-off organisation, where he might receive a larger slice of the cake. Even then he was to prove greedy for more, and always more than his agreed share.

In all of these transactions there was another element. The ultimate beneficiaries of 'genuine' humanitarian organisations usually only received the money donated after the money had been spent and against full docket/receipt documentation. Obviously, the pump needed priming. However, in the German case, receipts were tax deductible, which must have constituted a whole new dimension.

Dr Todenhofer, when asked, said that he had given his personal endorsement to Engineer Hekmatyar's Hesbe-i-Islami organisation because nobody else at the time would give him elbow room, on account of his 'fundamentalism'. He thought the time had come to give the other fellow a chance.

There is no doubting that prior to Todenhofer's patronage, Hesbe-i-Islami suffered the lowest level of German respect and support. Just one news conference with Dr Todenhofer caused the level of donations to jump from the lowest to the highest. This happened because Engineer Gulbuddin Hekmatyar's Mujahedeen party was now perceived to be the most efficient in the field. It also reflected the Pakistani and American view. However, until Dr Todenhofer's intervention, Hekmatyar was said to be suspicious of all NGOs. Feelings of mistrust were certainly mutual.

What also becomes apparent from this paper is the fact that the Gerhard Löwenthal - ZDF - TV programme formula for recycling donations had its inception much earlier than the *Der Spiegel* article supposed - in 1980, not 1985.

The ingenuity of it all seems to have been that his authoritative high moral ground stance on national television appealed to an equally highly-responsive and motivitated audience. A well-disciplined race, used to being told what to do and think, is invited to participate in a practised formula, telling it of another chance to send tax-deductible DMs to help with the war, to such and such a bank giro number (specially created in the 4433 series[3]). Part of these subscribed funds are then earmarked for funding freelance journalists to cover the war, whose film footage is then screened to trigger yet more donations ... *ad infinitum.*

To think, without this leg up, the GAC might never have taken off. The patronage of Gerhard Löwenthal could mean 'make or break'. Over one Christmas period alone (1985), his programme was to generate DM 1.5 million - all from large numbers of small individual donors - over 100,000 generous people.They naturally had no means of checking how their money was spent.

[1] This was a common venue for Bonn political press conferences.

[2] At this stage the organisation was still Bonn Afghanistan Committee.

[3] '4433' - *Deutsche Banken Verband bei allen banken und Sparkassen* - German Bankers Association - agreed all member banks would allocate '4433' as classification for charitable funds. Then, all donors had to do was name their charity payee and the system would see to the rest.

49

'Smoke & Mirrors' - Nominee Front Organisations

Next in my date-order pile of papers came an item which had been the first amongst equals to catch my eye. It concerned the fascinating 'front' organisation which the GAC had set up especially not to compromise themselves in the transfer of large sums of money to Hesbe-i-Islami. For some inexplicable reason, unless it be an inherent quirk - like calling your top-secret radar 'Wotan' - they had elected to call it *Frauen helfen Afghanistan* (Women help Afghanistan).

As a concept, it was undeniably laudable. Perhaps the name was conceived as a fund-raising ploy, which could well have succeeded; or it may, more simply, have been a 'shelf' company, held in reserve, to keep the GAC wives busy and happy, one day. Be that as it may, it was never going to pass a 'low profile' identity parade.

The beneficiaries of all this bounty, Hesbe-i-Islami, the party of Engineer Gulbuddin Hekmatyar, not to be outdone, had also elected to interpose their own nominee company for the transfer of these same funds. It was to be called *Solidaritëtskomitee für Afghanistan* (Solidarity Committee for Afghanistan). Doubtless, for equally valid 'by-pass' reasons, it had been bespoke in Germany.

Michael Josef Adolf Maria Sagurna, born on 2 September 1955, one of the original student founder members of the Bonn - later German - Afghanistan Committee, was chairing this particular meeting, and laying down the correct procedures for the transfer of such an important sum of money. Possibly, also for reasons of anonymity, he seems to have decided that the 'Bonn' or 'German' prefix should be dropped from the name. Like Dr Toryalai Nassery, he had gone bashful over the 'West German' label. The doctored diktat read

'It should, therefore, be clearly stated that the "Afghanistan Committee" hereby transfers the agreed sum of "not less than DM 750,000" to the account of *Frauen helfen Afghanistan*, via the office of solicitor Göschenberg of Bad Godesberg. It will then be the sole responsibility of *Frauen helfen Afghanistan* to arrange the subsequent transfer to *Solidaritëtskomitee für Afghanistan*. Since the money is now going to be paid over in Germany and not Pakistan, the operation will need careful planning to avoid any risk of a fiscal cock-up, with such a large sum of money. Herr Thomas Gaida was charged to clarify this with the Tax Office on Friday.'

In the light of what was to follow, it is perhaps important to note that the minute is signed and dated by Michael Sagurna on 25 February 1985. On 11 May 1985, he left for a fortnight's trip to Pakistan and Afghanistan. Whilst in Peshawar, he was able to indulge his political ambitions to the full, seeing all the right people. The ones of special interest to me were the representatives (unnamed) of the 'Children's mercie friend USA' [1] *(sic)*, Freedom Medicine (USA) and the American consul in Peshawar. There may well have been a seed or two cast on less than stony ground, here.

In the same minutes as the big money transfer disclosure, there followed a fascinating 'cameo' insight of Dr Karl Viktor Freigang and his views.

'Dr Freigang suggests that GAC should endow a professorship at a university. The purpose of this would be to enable GAC candidate doctors for Afghanistan to be screened as to their suitability by other experienced university professors. Dr Freigang points out that character is as important as medical competence in the harsh unrelenting conditions of Afghanistan. In support of his argument he cites the French precedent.' (Presumably *Médecins Sans Frontières*.)

At the same time as this proposal, Dr Freigang (described here respectfully as the Chairman of the Advisory Group), tabled a working paper on some more down-to-earth recommendations. Such mundane matters as minimum wage levels and the need for the clothing allowance to reflect current catalogue prices are inevitably featured. Herr Hundeshagen is charged with preparing a list and making bulk purchases of sleeping bags, mosquito nets, knife fork and spoon sets etc. All of which would have cost a lot less in Peshawar.

We then read three statements

'Aid workers should be discouraged from taking useless items with them, as it only adds to transport costs!'

Next, Herr Thomas Gaida is charged 'to procure arm bands and dog tags (identity discs).'

'Each aid worker will be issued with an English/German letter of protection.' It might have been more use in Farsi, Pashtu, even Arabic.

Lastly, the committee promised to provide Street Maps, presumably of Peshawar, and Herr Gaida was also charged to procure two walkie-talkies.

At this point Kakojan Niazi disconcertingly popped up, like the devil incarnate, to point out, once again, that he had it 'on very reliable authority', that the Russians were searching high and low for

Dr Freigang 'with a magnifying glass'. Since Dr Freigang's contract of employment was currently before the Committee for endorsement, and Michael Sagurna was looking into the possibilities of insuring the doctor's life and Herr Gaida was conferring with his tax consultant, Freigang agreed, for once, to let discretion be the better part of valour and said he would return to Pakistan if he sensed the slightest danger or found himself subjected to persistent bombing. The Russians paid a bounty of US $7,000 for any western medics captured or killed. This was for an Afghan the equivalent of a lifetime's total earnings.

Dr Freigang left for Afghanistan on 10 March. A month later he was to be joined by Frau Dr Klockner, Frau Müller (both now members of the same Advisory Group to the Committee, of which Dr Freigang was Chairman) and possibly two more German doctors in Nangahar. As soon as they were established, Dr Freigang proposed to travel on, possibly accompanied by one of the two newly-arrived doctors, to Bamiyan.

It was emphasised that all these 'critical path' arrangements would need to be cleared as soon as possible with Ebrahim Rashid - preferably *not* on the telephone.

American Aid Organisations for Afghanistan

It is hard to determine absolutely which path led the German Afghanistan Committee to the Department of State in Washington. It could have been any one of a dozen different routings. It might well have been set up by the politically astute Michael Sagurna on his two-week tour, visiting the right people in Peshawar. Alternatively, the idea could have arisen as the result of discussions held during the briefings and de-briefings of all Western NGO representatives held weekly (on Tuesdays) in Peshawar, and known familiarly as the 'White House prayer-meetings'. At these, revelations were freely exchanged between NGOs and the diplomatic representatives of the various Western powers, alternating on availability.

My own feeling, which is based purely on hunch and one sentence in the 'up-coming' report, is that a Ms Anne Hurd, listed as the Mercy Fund's Humanitarian News service representative in Peshawar, and whose job description was given as 'Assists journalists', probably made the strongest recommendation that GAC should be singled out for special attention. Part of my assessment is that Ms Hurd had a friend, Kurt von Loabeck. Both of them had devoted themselves to the subject of Afghanistan. Herr von Loabeck had been into Afghanistan several times where he took video films, which he then sold to American TV companies. It would not have been a chauvinist prejudice for him to have sung the praises of Dr Freigang and his dedicated team of doctors and nurses. They were undeniably among the best and certainly the bravest in the field. It might then be part of Anne Hurd's responsibilities to draw the phenomenon to the attention of her superiors.

But who was it who paid the first visit to the State Department in July 1985 on behalf of the German Afghanistan Committee? I have deduced that it must have been Herr Thomas Gaida, who features attending subsequent GAC meetings, especially on 15 September 1985 as a guest. During the course of this meeting Herr Gaida reported on affairs in Peshawar with a 'not binding financial balance'. There then followed discussion about which project should be checked out and supervised by whom. At this juncture Herr Thomas Gaida referred to conversations he had had in the United States. These could have taken place two months earlier (*i.e.* in July 1985). What is significant is that Herr Gaida next produces draft letter texts to Institutions in the United States. This would dovetail neatly with the intention expressed by the writer of the first visit report to make contact by letter with the Afghan Relief Commiteee in the next few weeks. The address is given in the 'enclosure', as are the conversation reports referred to.

For his pains, Herr Gaida is next told in no uncertain terms that in future all contacts with American Organisations will be the sole concern of executive officers of GAC. This would explain Dietrich Kantel being sent out for the second meeting with the State Department in Washington, on 4 November 1985.

As a matter of pure conjecture, Jennifer Taylor-Gaida, the translator of the German Afghanistan Committee prestige brochure into English, sounds like an American wife to me, which would help to explain the opening 'holiday in USA' comment which follows. Anyway, what is certain is that the first visit took place in July 1985 and begins nonchalantly enough.

'During the course of my holiday in the USA, I visited the State Department and various American Aid Organisations.

'The objective of my journey was to establish contact with Americans who, on account of their great wealth, are likely to cause an inflation spiral in Peshawar, and ruin our wage structure.'

As an opening caveat, Thomas Gaida, if indeed it is he, is at great pains to declare at all times, in all places, and on all occasions that the German Afghanistan Committee was determined, above all else, to remain independent of all other German, Pakistani, or Afghan organisations, and by inference, American ones too.

During the course of this planned visit, he was able to answer a number of pertinent questions put to him by other organisations intending to start up in Peshawar and/or Afghanistan, or which had already done so.

He outlined the German Afghanistan Commiteee's two-tier structure, or rather, he exposed two of the four facets he wanted them to know about. Contacts about day-to-day operating matters were to be addressed to Peshawar. The Bonn office should be reserved for long-term planning and co-operation matters. Wherever finance was involved, the most rigid controls should be put in place.

His first meeting was to be with a Ms Phyllis E. Oakley,[2] who was the Country Officer responsible for Afghanistan at the Department of State.

Thomas Gaida, if it is he, disarmingly begins by comparing her most unfavourably to her German Foreign Office counterpart, Frau Hoffmann. 'Like our Foreign Office civil servants, she only seems to have the most superficial knowledge of the situation in Pakistan and Afghanistan.'

Ms Oakley told him that either the money, which had been voted by Congress for Afghanistan, had not been applied for, or, since they had such negative, disappointing experiences, funding had often been refused. They had found that too many of the NGO organisations in Peshawar had not come up to their expectations for reliability or efficiency. Alternatively, those whom they had entrusted with funds had proved to be dishonest.

Not so surprisingly, Dr Toryalai Nassery's organisation, 'Union Aid' for Afghan Refugees, came top in that category and it was even suggested that the list be extended to include the august Swedish Committee, which had not been above playing a double game, putting in for funding of medicines that had already been paid for by other Western donor sources. There had been too many NGOs created expressly for the Afghan crisis. The whole history of the relief programme in Pakistan was plagued with corruption.

First encounters mattered most and Thomas Gaida (our GAC representative) must have made a very favourable impression indeed. Either that or he had been oversold already by Anne Hurd, because Phyllis Oakley next gave him to understand that the State Department was 'actively seeking suitable new partners'!

The criteria had changed. They were no longer so interested in funding the refugee camps in Pakistan, as these were now adequately catered for. What the State Department now sought was cross-border participation to stem the refugee exodus - counter the 'pull factor'. However, the State Department did not fund directly. They had special conduits for this purpose.

Such funding was to be achieved through a large number of different organisations on a 'horses for courses' basis. For instance, both the Committee for a Free Afghanistan, whose initial funding came from the Heritage Foundation, and the International Medical Corps, would be likely to be sponsoring bodies where GAC was concerned. However, for those who accepted such funding, there was to be one overriding Catch 22 clause ... on no account could any American citizen engaged be sent to Afghanistan.

A list of other relevant funding bodies contained the following:- Direct Relief International; National Endowment for Democracy; The Council for Intercontinental Development; World Anti-Communist League; US Council for World Freedom.

In summary, Gaida advised that the Committee should keep in close touch with Ms Oakley. She had indicated that money was available from Congress; and she had agreed to bring to bear what influence she could to persuade other American organisations to contact Ebrahim Rashid in Peshawar, before determining wage scales and needlessly rocking the inflation boat.

There was also a distinct possibility that she could put in a good word for special funding or press for GAC to be considered for Congressional money, via one or other of the authorised channels.

One of the aspects of the Swedish Committee's work, however, which was outstanding in many respects, was that they had a reputation for going in-country and checking out that the aid had got through to those for whom it was intended. The other mitigating factor was that the Swedish Government multiplied all donations from the private sector fourfold (aggregating to fivefold) and were said to be the biggest per capita spenders in the aid business worldwide. The Swedes were also deemed to be more acceptable to the Russians as a neutral Nordic state.

The diffidence of Thomas Gaida, our GAC hero, returns as he moves on to his afternoon appointment where 'he was unfortunately unable to meet the Secretary of the Committee for a Free Afghanistan, since the Chairman, Major General J. Milner Roberts, had insisted on interviewing him himself.' There then follows an all-revealing passage. 'Anne Hurd had described General Roberts to him as reliable and trustworthy! He was retired and seemed to expend all his energy on the affairs of the Committee. He was interested in both past operations and future plans. He seemed to be altogether very taken with GAC ideas.

'The General, for his part, outlined his various activities on behalf of the Afghan cause. His committee saw itself as a significant lobbying force on behalf of the Afghans. It was also an embryo aid organisation, yet to be properly funded, which was co-operating closely with the equally newly set up International Medical Corps. The General also tended to take Afghan refugees, based in the USA, under his wing. The CFFA staff complement was not given, nor was overhead detail. However, there was evidence of extensive PR expenditure, on such items as T-shirts, car stickers, and lapel badges.'

Two significant observations were made about the meeting. Firstly, 'there was no doubting the General had outstanding contacts with Congress.'

Next, 'it was a basic fact of American aid organisation life that they all cried poor. This general lack of funds was attributed to the fact that in America, donations to charity were not tax deductible. However, all was not doom and gloom, as General Roberts was shortly expecting to obtain funds from the State Department. Since his committee had no intention of operating even in Pakistan, let alone Afghanistan, funding would be channelled through to the International Medical Corps.'

The only note to sour the meeting came from the wash-up session which followed afterwards with Anne Hurd.

'She seemed to know all there was to know about both the Committee for a Free Afghanistan and the International Medical Corps. She took a dim view of both organisations. She felt they could have done more to obtain funding from sources other than the State Department.

'Since she was on her way to Pakistan and Afghanistan, Gaida asked her to be sure to make contact with Michael Sagurna and the GAC team of doctors (which suggests Gaida initiated the contact).'

In closing, Gaida exhorted the German Afghanistan Committee to 'stay in close contact with Ms Anne Hurd, since in this way we can discover details about other organisations. Moreover, we might be able to obtain video films from her and Herr von Loabeck, which would enable us to put together a new promotional film on Afghanistan.'

If the GAC were seriously intending to use some of Kurt von Loabeck's clips, they would need to be extra careful. With an inexpert eye, they could come to rue their plagiarism. Whatever his origins, von Loabeck had gained a reputation for faking material for CBS (Columbia Broadcasting System).

It happened a lot. Such were the pressures to perform!

*

Although we could take General Roberts's trustworthiness and reliability as read, there has to be more to the General than met either Gaida's eye or Ms Hurd's caustic tongue. I sensed the 'infuriating, maniacal, irresistible Yankee guts'[3] of the man who had other far-reaching ideas to contribute to the war effort. The first of these was 'Project - Boots'.

Having doled out direct aid to some hand-picked Mujahedeen commanders, communications and medical equipment were soon to follow suit. In the search for 'low intensity, non-combatant items', clothing came next. After that, boots would spring naturally to the General's well-trained mind. What is staggering is the scale. The concept was so grandiose that it required a co-sponsor, the United States Council for World Freedom, no less.

The objective was to provide a quarter of a million pairs of work boots for 'freedom fighters' in Nicaragua and Afghanistan. Whatever the facts behind the scheme, even the Afghan half-share would have been enough to give every man in the Russian army of occupation a spare pair each. As for the numberless Afghan host, I only hope the General hadn't deluded himself that once he'd got them in boots it would be a simple matter to have them marching in step! In justice to the project, for an Afghan, boots were a highly desirable status symbol. And, come the winter, would stand between him and frostbite. At an optimistic pinch they might even extend the fighting season. However, conjecture did not end there. With the Nicaraguan joint-venture, they would need to be a mixed bag of boots. Dittmar could vouch for plenty of canvas jungle boot drops by the CIA in Nicaragua, but they would be useless in Afghanistan. There was a big sluice hole in the sole, to let the water out! There was ample evidence of cheap shoes, but neither of us ever saw a pair of regulation issue boots, other than Russian. Dittmar even took the trouble to scan his film library without turning up anything.

One can only wonder where all the boots went. No doubt the self-same way of so much other war materiel destined for the Afghans. The Pakistani army got its look in first. It was part of the rent for harbouring their brothers-in-Islam.

The Children's Mercy Fund

Before Gaida had quit Ms Hurd's office, they were joined, as if casually, by a Mr Antony L. Campaigne, the President of the Children's

Mercy Fund. Mr Campaigne explained that he had been fund-raising for his charity since its inception two years ago in 1983. He handed Gaida a brochure describing the work of the fund.[4] Mr Campaigne said that he would now like to raise some more money for Ms Hurd to administer in Afghanistan. Furthermore, Ms Hurd had had such a powerful influence on his thinking that he had decided it would be ill-advised to place his funds with any American organisation and so he was now looking for a 'more effective and successful operation'.

Entirely as a result of the favourable impression the GAC had made on Ms Hurd and her subsequent unqualified endorsement, Mr Campaigne felt encouraged to make an offer.

1. He has a mailing list of about a million subscribers at his disposal. He proposes to place all the money which he can raise on behalf of the Afghan cause, with GAC.

2. There is no need for GAC to render accounts for this 'contribution'. All they have to do is furnish a fortnightly report of what has been done with the money.

3. Armed with this information, which will need to be supported with plenty of photographs, log books, etc, he will proceed to raise more money.

At this point, the vision of the gold brick proved too unreal for Gaida and he replayed the worn old record about the German Afghanistan Committee having no intention of working with any other organisation, especially one that might want to impose conditions at a later date.

Not only was this meeting too brief and hurried to discuss any plans or strategy properly, Gaida let it be known that he was not empowered so to do. He therefore suggested that Mr Campaigne and/or Ms Hurd come to Germany for discussions in depth. That should prove very interesting for GAC; not least to familiarise themselves with the principles of fund-raising.

However, Gaida did have to promise to supply Mr Campaigne with a report of all GAC activities in English. (Could this have been what prompted the GAC prestige brochure?)

In Herr Kantel's view, Mr Campaigne's offer was not without interest. However he proposed that a thorough investigation should be instituted into the man and his organisation. Gaida's abiding impression was that Campaigne was looking ultimately to infiltrate each of the various ventures he intended funding, so it seems all the more surprising that Campaigne did not do likewise with the GAC in Bonn.

During discussions the idea was floated of setting up an

autonomous organisation in Pakistan, which would run individual clinics and mobile units. The whole organisation and its management would be under GAC supervision. Part of the effort and purpose should be geared towards promotion and publicity which Americans term 'Advocacy', with all that that entails. For the cognoscenti, for whom the Children's Mercy Fund came to be known as the Murky Fund, as opposed to Michael Sagurna's interpretation as the 'Mercie friend', the telling of this tale would remind them all of Little Red Riding Hood, with interchangeable roles.

Mr Campaigne obtained his money from the Department of State in half-million dollar dollops.

International Medical Corps

Whilst in America, Gaida devoted more of his time to this organisation than to any other. He was impressed with its founding Chairman, Dr Robert R. Simon, who was a professor of accident surgery at UCLA, Los Angeles. As Dr Simon's Executive Director, Michael Utter, expressed it, 'Dr Simon had a great dedication to work and worked himself into his present position by creating the International Medical Corps from the bottom up.'

(Dr Simon's name was one of those that had leapt off the page for me as it had long been coupled with that of Dr Veggeberg as co-authors of articles on war surgery in the Orthopaedics Overseas house magazine.)

More than any other medical faculty in America, Dr Simon was attempting to analyse and prepare for the long-term health-care future of Afghanistan and Pakistan; and in the profoundest way. Fortunately he had the charisma to go with the job and had attracted about him an outstanding team of specialists and technicians. It included professors from the Mayo Clinic, American Government specialists in the public health department and there was even a former Afghan Minister of Health. They were all gearing up for a medical/surgical training programme to be established in Peshawar. Gaida was vastly impressed with the whole undertaking. The only problem was the usual one of funding.

As stated above, Dr Simon had an Executive Director to assist him. This was Michael Utter, who explained that excellent relations were enjoyed with Congress through the good offices of the Committee for a Free Afghanistan. It was Mr Utter's prime responsibility to maintain this relationship, across the continent. He also confided some 'backgrounder' information on Afghanistan to Gaida, who was enjoined not to write it down.

Not to be written down, nor vaunted, was the fact that the dynamic Dr Simon had done a stint of five weeks field surgery in the Kunar Valley in 1984.[5]

Although the International Medical Corps looked well-heeled, with impressive headquarters in Los Angeles, it essentially had no money. It was working towards an agreement with the State Department due for consummation in the very month of Gaida's visit, and expected shortly to receive US $650,000 to set up the said training camp in Peshawar. But the price they had to pay was that they were not to allow any American to go to Afghanistan.

Dr Simon and those other doctors who have been to the North West Frontier, usually at their own expense, were understandably as mad as hell at this imposition. It was reckoned that IMC had available on its books some 200 American doctors, many of them Vietnam veterans, who were more than prepared to go to Afghanistan, whilst serving with the IMC. Where there's a will, there's often a way round, and it was mooted that they might serve under a GAC flag of convenience.

Mention was also made of Australian and British doctors, which may have been the original seed corn of Veggeberg's approach to Anwar Chaudhri.

Gaida could only indicate that he had no authority to take such a decision.

There then followed much the usual imprecation that GAC personnel should at all times keep in close contact with Dr Simon and IMC. At the same time, Dr Simon promised that his organisation, once established in Peshawar, would keep in close touch with Ebrahim Rashid, especially before coming to any Afghan wages agreement. That objective looked as if it might be achieved.

Then, very much as an afterthought and buried amongst a plethora of detail on standardisation of medicines, their packaging and transportation, there is the following afterword. 'IMC advised that any GAC requirement for medicines could be met by them, quickly, without red-tape or indeed charge in Pakistan.'

Kakojan Niazi had kindly supplied the address detail for Direct Relief International. This worldwide organisation was similar in purpose and structure to ASME in Germany.[6] They had recently made a substantial delivery of aid to Dr Toryalai Nassery's 'Union Aid'. From this, Gaida assumed that free medicines and other aid materials might be forthcoming from that quarter. They should therefore be kept fully informed of GAC's activities.

From now on the GAC was to be privy to the Special Country Reports of the Department of State.

They belonged.

However, and significantly for the future, there had been no time to go back to New York, to meet the Afghan Relief Committee[7] on the introduction of Direct Relief International. In hindsight, it may have been just as well, in the interests of both posterity and probity.

[1] 'mercie friend' was how Michael Sagurna idiosyncratically chose to log the Mercy Fund - replete with Freudian slip.

[2] She is married to retired Ambassador Robert B. Oakley, U.S. Ambassador to Pakistan from August 1988.

[3] Attributed to a Sam Wannamaker obituary.

[4] Mercy Fund also listed by USIS/Under Council for International Development/Mercy Fund. Antony L. Campaigne, 2812 Woodland Drive N.W., Washington DC 20009. T/F(202) 628 1000.

[5] Nonetheless, this exposure is in fact described in detail in American Medical News 27 (4)): 21/11/1984 and later referred to in Contemporary Orthopaedics August 1987, vol 15 No.2 pp.53/54. This latter article is one that links Dr Simon's name with Dr Veggeberg, and could account for our subsequent involvement.

[6] ASME: ASME-HUMANITAS e. V. Humanitäre Gesellschaft für soziale und medizinische Hilfe, an organisation especially set up to deal with natural and war catastrophes both in Europe and Africa.

[7] It is the reference to the Afghan Relief Committee which identifies Gaida as the author of the report on the first visit to the State Department since he states the intention of making contact with them 'by letter in the next few weeks'. Four to six weeks later, Thomas Gaida tabled his draft letters to American institutions at the DAK/GAC meeting of 15 September 1985.

50
The Dollars Begin to Flow

Some four months later, on Monday, 4 November 1985, there was to be a follow-up meeting arranged with the State Department and the International Medical Corps.

That afternoon, Dietrich Kantel (there is no shadow of a doubt this time) was to meet with a Mrs Millikan, the next State Department Country Officer for Afghanistan. Presumably, Mrs Millikan had replaced Ms Phyllis E. Oakley, as she opened by admitting to Kantel that she had only been in her post since the summer. The previous GAC visit by Herr Gaida had been in July. Mrs Millikan explained that she was not fully up-to-speed yet on all aspects of her field of responsibility and had, for instance, no knowledge of the German Afghanistan Committee, or its work.

After Kantel had tabled papers covering the full range of GAC activities, Mrs Millikan expressed more than polite interest. She was enthusiastic, but insisted that, to qualify for serious consideration, the whole story would first have to be presented in English! This then was the second mention of the need for an English language GAC prestige Manual.

Mrs Millikan then proceeded to indicate which projects would be likely to attract American backing and which would not. Cash for food, for example, was already catered for.

She then gave Kantel the tip that all the other 'in-country projects', which she did find interesting, should be described in the fullest possible detail in the English text, in order to attract sponsorship. This again would explain the detailed description of each and every sub-station in the GAC Manual which we saw.

What had happened to effect this policy about-face was best explained by the following extract, taken from an all-revealing, freedom-of-information inspired article in *Third World Quarterly*, issue of January 1990, pp. 62-85, contributed by Ms Helga Baitmann.

'A key aspect of the Soviet Kabul Government's strategy for defeating the resistance was to deny them the means for treating the wounded, the sick and the starving. Thus medicine-based NGOs were to be actively sought out to counteract this Kabul regime strategy of depopulation.'

It was to be a long haul. In Autumn 1988 a Co-ordination of Medical Committees 'had concluded that the provision of health-care throughout the region was wholly uneven - with many areas having none at all.'

To summarise these new criteria. The first requirement was to be non-American, *i.e.* foreign. The second was to be actively engaged in the medical field. The third was to operate primarily, or at least substantially cross-border. And the last requirement was to be media-wise ... actively committed to advocacy, or propaganda, as we British know it. Everything was to be geared to that overriding preoccupation with winning the 'living-room' war.

Once more, every known device - wired pictures, fax and, above, all video and normal film - were to wing their way to feed the lions and the lambs of the TV, cinema, newspaper and magazine parts of the media circus. All the wiles of both hidden and open persuaders must be engaged to influence friendly foreign governments, government institutions, domestic and world public opinion and, not least, the US government itself. All was fair in love and war. At all costs, the hardy annual UN vote of Russian censure had to be kept in place and absolute. Style might have preceded content at times. The media remained the message.

The routine crack of the ringmaster's whip was heard calling the NGOs to order - as for previous performances in Nicaragua, El Salvador, Guatemala, Angola or indeed Poland, 'whereby the chosen NGOs were encouraged to apply for US government funds.' In recompense, these "suitable" NGOs would be expected to co-ordinate their efforts with US government policy.

In line with this policy, the US Embassy in Islamabad had advised the Department of State to continue working through international organisations, since a higher US profile would damage the credibility of the Afghan resistance as an indigenous freedom struggle and compromise the currently independent position of American afiliated voluntary agencies .

This policy also fitted the facts on the ground, since there were many more European NGOs than American in the first place, and secondly, very few of the American NGOs, if any, operated cross-border. They were, after all, banned; although this failed to inhibit many an individual effort - Kermit Veggeberg, Mary Macmakin, Jane Orlando, Kate Straub, Jill Hoffman, etc., etc.

In summary then, GAC qualified for special consideration on all four counts. No doubt Ms Oakley had marked their card accordingly; although it had somehow become buried by the time of Mrs Millikan's arrival. Or, more likely, she wanted to hear the whole story again, from the beginning, for herself. The delay did not matter, because everything was ready, in place, when the time came to throw money at it - or to make it go away!

GAC were advised that their funding would need to be channelled through a Mr Crandel at the American Embassy in Islamabad.

As a last request Mrs Millikan said she would be most happy to receive any appropriate information on GAC activities from journalists inside Afghanistan, with supporting photographs. For no apparent reason, Hörst Walpuski was mentioned by name. Unless Mrs Millikan was deliberately feeding Dietrich Kantel with this journalist's name as a suitable recorder and 'advocate' of GAC cross-border activities. Who knows, he may have been another of Ann Hurd's candidates.

One was left wondering how the American administration ever expected to monitor all this expenditure on cross-border programmes, if they were not prepared to send in anybody of their own. Were they seriously going to rely on the chance reports of journalists? Or were they counting instead on the long-established inspection-audit capabilities of the Rashid brothers?

Or had SATINT (Satellite Intelligence) finally left the HUMINT (on the ground human intelligence) ploughman plodding forlornly behind?

One of the more endearing qualities of the American 'cousins' is their abiding faith in man's goodness. Whilst GAC were busy checking out the Mercy Fund and Mr Campaigne, you would have thought somebody might have returned the compliment in Bonn. Instead, they appear to have swallowed the integrity inherent in the German Afghanistan Committee name - hook, line and sinker. They were not to be the first or the last to get caught.

All GAC now had to do was prepare the boldest, biggest, most boastful English language prestige brochure possible and hold out the begging bowl and wait. It also helped to explain how it came to be quite so aggressively written. 'We are the biggest and best in the West!' it said. Now we knew why. They had no need to write it in German to convince themselves. Although Reinhard Erös had pressed it on us, it was hardly fit for Anglo-Saxon consumption. A parental guidance certification would have been *de rigueur* for any francophone NGO. *Médecins Sans Frontières* (MSF) would not have taken kindly to its extravagant claims.

No, the whole style and presentation could only have been conceived in response to the thrice-stated American request. This then was how GAC thought to impress the Department of State, the Committee for a Free Afghanistan and The Mercy Fund.

It was to be an investment in the future. They should think of it as the 'ante' to get to play in Uncle Sam's big crap game.

*

Dietrich Kantel next met with Dr Robert R. Simon at 3.30 on Saturday, 9 November 1985 - West Coast time. Whatever shortcomings there may have been, about the State Department's ignorance of GAC's work, was more than made up for by the International Medical Corps. They knew 'all about GAC's operations' and were keen to co-operate. It was agreed to co-ordinate the work of both organisations expecially at grass-roots level.

GAC would also support a think-tank in Peshawar, along with two French NGOs *Médecins Sans Frontières* and *Aide Medicale Internationale*. Dr Simon and his team made no bones about the difficulties they had in getting on with the French, but, happily, the differences were said to be only skin deep.

However, the greatest concern remained two hundred or so American, British and Australian doctors unable to visit Afghanistan under the aegis of IMC. If only they could serve under the GAC flag of convenience, Dr Simon believed that financial support would be forthcoming from IMC to GAC. This speculation could account for Dr Kermit Veggeberg's interest in Chak and in turn be the initial reason for our referral to the GAC. In almost the same breath Dr Simon asked that any barefoot doctors, surplus to GAC's requirements should be sent on to join his IMC teaching programme in Peshawar.

Dietrich Kantel made his usual offer of the Rashid Brothers (ARROS) transport fleet in Peshawar, but with the GAC label. Later, Dr Simon was able to advise that he saw a distinct possibility of obtaining financial support for the GAC hospital 'joint-venture' in Quetta, through a donor organisation in California.[1]

---

[1] Yet to be identified, but quite possibly that same Direct Relief Committee, Santa Barbara, California body that had proved so munificent to Nassery's Union Aid.

51

Origins of The German Afghanistan Foundation

What had prompted Kakojan Niazi to go his own way to found the German Afghanistan Foundation had yet to be revealed. First thoughts were that it might have been triggered by the GAC's 'No Afghans need apply' membership exclusion clause, but that is too simplistic, because Niazi, after all, had been a founding member of the original Bonn Afghanistan Committee.[1] Then, as precise details of the setting up of the 'Foundation' came to light, it became apparent that there had been some collusion with the old GAC guard. It was as if they had jointly decided to enter a new brand name into the charitable funds pool, so as to increase their market share. Was it even possible they were responding to a public relations-cum-marketing organisation's proposal? The colluded name similarity, *ab initio*, was surely a piggy-back link. For European financial whizzkids, the very word *Stiftung* (Foundation) has other connotations; for instance, a Liechtenstein *Stiftung* generally denotes an 'off-shore' device for operations. The late Robert Maxwell was an adept.

Another reason for the splinter could well have been a difference of opinion over arms dealing. From his various public statements, Kakojan Niazi gives the appearance of a patriot who, having had enough of subterfuge, decided to go all-out for the main chance. Kantel and Hundeshagen, happy with the flow of funds as they were, may have pushed him to go and do his own thing.

Whatever the reasoning, the decision not to admit Afghan members to the GAC was taken on 17 August 1985 and Kakojan Niazi officially announced his intention to found the German Afghanistan Foundation by letter[2] to the GAC Committee, less than a month later, on 5 September 1985.

The timing could not have been more auspicious. As the direct result of two radio interviews featuring Nursing Sister Maria Müller with Franz Alt, another public newscaster of the highest integrity, there had been a massive upturn in public donations. Over DM 120,000 had been subscribed. Patently from now on, the market could sustain two similar brand names.

The ensuing euphoria sparked off a sustained burst of man-management gestures, of which the following was to coincide with Ebrahim Rashid's next visit to Bonn. It was unanimously agreed to offer him the blessings of German Health Insurance! However, to effect this as economically as possible, he needed to be registered as yet another 'student' attending a German university. Only thus would all the tedious problems of employment legislation be circumvented. The secretary to the Committee (Herr Norbert Huther) was charged to make the necessary arrangements with the Overseas Student Department at Bonn University.

I had guessed that Ebrahim Rashid fitted in to the Bonn University student mould somewhere, but once again I had been looking in the wrong filing cabinets. At much the same time, he became due for a very different, more divine unction - meaning the blessings to be derived from a visit to the Holy Shrine (Ka'bah) at Mecca. Henceforth he would be entitled to be called *Haji* Ebrahim.

After such open-handedness, there was sure to be a tight-fisted reaction. Having opted for a 'no Afghan need apply' exclusion clause, the Committee next elected not to allow any new German members either! Could this have been caused by the fear that too many crooks increase the risk of exposure? Rolf Erich Lerch, a co-founder, was instructed to prepare all the necessary changes to the constitution, which would then be put to the members in general meeting as a *fait accompli*!

No sooner had Kakojan Niazi been cast adrift, than the usurpers elected to close ranks. There was a paramount need to keep the party as small as possible. They reduced to the ideal primitive hunting band number, twelve.

Two damning items of ongoing accord are next recorded in the minutes. Kakojan Niazi reports on his negotiations with Pakistan International Airlines (PIA) for bargain flights and the free carriage of medicines, on the back-haul. Obviously, it made sense for the two 'sister' organisations to pool their bargaining power. Presumably, Niazi was to PIA, what Kantel and Hundeshagen were to Lufthansa and the Bundeswehr.

Another item concerned the protection of the 'brand name' before last. The Secretary, Norbert Huther, was ordered to establish copyright protection for the Bonn Afghanistan Committee name with the Bonn Court of Justice. Either they were worried that Kakojan Niazi was going to sequester it and plunder all their old mailing lists, or - more likely - it may simply have been to secure the valued emotive logo of a Mujahedeen holding a sick child in his arms.

There then followed some more predictable items relating to GAC accounting practice It was hoped that in a month or two's time, in October 1985 there would be an extended trial balance for the first six months of the year to 30 June 1985. If this proved 'satisfactory', the accounts for 1984 would be rejigged to conform with the new 1985 accounting practice. This was always provided the books from the Peshawar end were ready and available in time!

Also planned was a consolidated budget, in a fit state to submit to the Committee for 1986.

As mentioned before, there was a staggering figure of DM 27,000 for computer costs for the year. But for a subscription list of anything between 30,000 and 100,000 people it seemed a bit steep.

Next, for no given reason, both the US dollar and the Pakistani rupee bank accounts in the name of Rashid, were to be closed in Peshawar. Were they moving their account to Switzerland?

And finally, the currant in the bun, withheld till last. The ethical pharmaceutical firm of JU Rottenburg, based in Rottenburg, had 'volunteered' to collect medicines from the pharmaceutical industry as a whole, for donation to GAC. A local pharmacist volunteered to sort and pack all the various items. Ultimately they were to succeed in marshalling DM 1.5 millions' worth of medicines. A highly laudable effort which needs, perforce, to be followed through to its conclusion. Significantly, all the supplicant letters to the manufacturers were written and signed by none other than Dr Todenhofer.

*

Next, a motion was put to the meeting by Herr Thomas Gaida, who had initiated contact with the US State Department, that Dr Karl Viktor Freigang, GAC's outstanding field doctor in Afghanistan, should be sacked forthwith, without notice! The reason stated was that he had entered into contractual obligations in Pakistan without authority; to wit, the purchase of vehicles.

After lengthy debate, it was resolved that Dietrich Kantel and Denny Hundeshagen should point out to Dr Freigang his waywardness and demand an explanation. They were then to give him a severe reprimand and insist that he refrain from unilateral action in the future. As Dr Freigang's behaviour was deemed to be so unacceptable, there could be no question of offering him further employment with GAC. The second stipulation was positively demonic - from henceforth, he was to be ostracised,, unceremoniously dumped, banished by his fellow members.

But they bided their time. They stayed their hand. They had little option, because there was much more to come than appeared on the surface. When he did finally go, however, Dr Freigang was able to quit on his own terms, with his integrity intact.

Meanwhile, there were two major projects shaping up in Peshawar. The first was the setting up of the German Afghanistan Committee's headquarters at 26c Park Avenue, University Town. Maria Müller and Frank Paulin were in charge of this and *Haji* Ebrahim Rashid was 'required to conduct his activities within this overall establishment budget'. With his bank accounts closed, he cannot have taken kindly to this new stricture, if genuine stricture it was. What was more, it was to be presented as a *fait accompli*.

Kantel and Hundeshagen would break the news in person in Peshawar. It was also likely that they would bump into Dr Freigang. If a suitable opportunity were to present itself, the sheepish pair were 'to administer a rocket to Dr Freigang about his irresponsible excursions into Afghanistan and generally profligate behaviour.' However, 'since journalists were likely to be present, it might not be the best moment to dress him down!' That let them off the hook. The 'bullshit' brochure made the point that part of the purpose of the University Town, Peshawar, premises was to provide 'free' accommodation for 'suitable' German journalists, for the sake of advocacy.

The other event requiring the simultaneous presence of Hundeshagen and Kantel was the ceremonial opening of the Sadda Clinic and School.

And the last minuted item formally states that 'on their return from Afghanistan and Pakistan, there will need to be a *closed* meeting, to be called before the year's end'. One can only speculate as to what needed to be concealed in such already close company.

On the morning of 7 November 1985, Dietrich Kantel met with General Roberts again, together with other members of his Committee for a Free Afghanistan (CFFA). Since Roberts was the Chairman, conversation touched on their varied activities, the exchange of information, and the cultivation of mutual contacts.

Next they switched to the wider subject of advocacy and public relations, which appeared to be the General's major preoccupation. He cited a topical case in point. Two wounded Afghan boys were receiving special medical attention. In the General's opinion it was the case of these two boys which had alerted the Senate to the whole topic of Afghanistan. Once their attention had been consolidated, the opening of the flood gates of funding for his Committee for a Free Afghanistan had quickly followed. This, in turn, would shortly trigger aid action inside Afghanistan. Only low-intensity non-combatant items such as his 'Project Boots' or similar non-belligerent items were to be countenanced.

As a friendly gesture, with no strings attached, Dietrich Kantel offered the services of the Rashid Brothers ARROS transport fleet for the 'safe delivery of all these goods'. Should the General feel the need at any time, he had only to contact their Peshawar office ...

For the next two days Dietrich Kantel concentrated on trying to persuade pop groups to give concerts in Germany to raise funds for GAC. After seeing a number of promoters, notably the 'Fuck the Russians' group, he gave it up as a lost cause.

The all-seeing eye of the General no doubt registered the monitoring potential implicit in such an arrangement, but what was a lot more certain was that there was no end to the General's bountiful connections. In all probability wearing his World Anti-Communist League hat, he arranged for GAC to meet Peter Sager, director of the Swiss Ost (East) Institute. This set-up has been described elsewhere[3] as 'that exemplary private organisation which has been active in the realm of international politics for thirty years.'

Based in Switzerland, the Swiss East Institute controlled large amounts of 'donations', but lacked any 'presence' in Afghanistan. Other than the International Committee of the Red Cross, the only other Swiss involvement Peter and I knowingly encountered was a fascinating field trial to harden high-altitude varieties of foxglove, *digitalis,* for heart disease patients. The dream was that the strain would then translate to Switzerland, where this improved variety was yet to be introduced.

*

Following General Roberts' valuable introduction to the Swiss East Institute and after some initial haggling by Hundeshagen, it was agreed that 'provided the GAC took on board a minimum of four Swiss national doctors and introduced them to the Afghanistan theatre during the course of 1986, GAC could count on an irrevocable subsidy of DM 2,000,000 with, all being well, a further DM 2,000,000, under the same terms for 1987; by which time many more candidate doctors would be lined up.'

The names of those already assigned for 1986 included our old long-lost friend, Dr Michael Müller, last seen vanishing in a cloud of 'Chak' dust! It was good to see his name in print again. For the immediate present, the other names listed, meant very little - Frau Dr Tamara Czierny and Nurse Frau Ruth Buser. The former was a dentist mentioned in despatches in the GAC prestige Manual, and the latter was to be linked by Hundeshagen with Dr Freigang as a scapegoat.[4]

'With total conviction, Herr Denny Hundeshagen was able to report that, during the latter part of 1985, GAC had been able to conclude a number of other very pleasing and advantageous co-operation agreements with other European NGOs, such as the *international Gesellschaft für Menschenrechte,* or International Society for Human Rights. He was happy to report that this organisation anticipated that an appeal to its members would raise a sum in excess of DM 150,000.'[5]

In closing the meeting, Hundeshagen stated that during the coming year (1986) further, even larger, sums were anticipated from yet other organisations in Luxembourg, Holland and, most especially, the United States.

Then, with great pride he announced that the GAC was the only German organisation to have been nominated for the prestigious board of *Co-ordination Humanitaire Européenne pour l'Afghanistane.*

Dr Karl Victor Freigang was to represent GAC, which, among other things, must have obliged Hundeshagen to stay his hand.

Seen in retrospect, the establishment of the GAC local headquarters compound in University Town, Peshawar, came at just the right psychological moment and not a moment too soon. Caught in the same searchlight sweep as the Sadda Clinic and School, it demonstrated a clear commitment to Pakistan by an NGO renowned for its cross-border preference. The Pakistanis looked favourably on appropriate expenditures in their economy.

The other determining factor, supposedly on an American initiative, was that the Pakistani Government were proposing from now on, to channel all aid through their painfully patched-together coalition of the seven main Afghan political parties - known as the Afghanistan Interim Government (AIG). But the ploy was fraught with half-hobbled horses, since it was those very 'renegade' cross-border NGOs who had first pointed up that practical power was no longer vested in the political parties in Peshawar, but in the local 'commanders' in the field.

Either the Americans weren't harkening to their own listening posts, or, for the time being, it suited them not to. In fairness, they had introduced some exquisite weasel words into the agreement, which out-manoeuvred even the highly manipulative Pakistanis. Effectively, there was a claw-back clause, making final distributions only possible, subject to the wishes of local commanders; or words to that effect!

Not so surprisingly, GAC saw the word and the World rather differently. They were being invited to let some outside entity tuck into 'their' cake. This was a vile interference up with which the generous German 'donors' (or, more likely, their 'nominees') would not put! The posturings which ensued included the hollow threat to shut up shop and remove to Iran.

'Outside interference of any kind was *not* to be tolerated.' One of the oft-repeated claims made by GAC was that what made them so exceptional was that nothing stood between 'their' donors and 'their' ultimate beneficiaries - except, of course, themselves!

The unequivocal view of the Bonn High Command was that any switch of emphasis in favour of the Afghan Government in Exile, could well lead to the end of private aid to Afghanistan from Pakistani territory.

[1] Originally constituted as the Bonner Afghanistanische Komitee - Bonn Afghanistan Committee, it soon became fairly naturally and universally known, certainly in Pakistan, as the 'German' Afghanistan Committee. This happened by force majeur long before the legal wrangle described later.

[2] The letter asked for DM 30,000. Possibly to cloak a backhander, DAK/GAC only `publicly' conceded the minimum amount to enable him to register with the authorities (DM 10,000). Subject to good behaviour, there was a promise of further support of DM 2,000 a month for four months. At which time DAK/GAC would decide whether or not to continue payment. It was all the subject of a precise contractual agreement - in order to secure an unspecified interest-free loan believed to be (DM 30,000). At first glance, the terms may have looked unduly harsh, but the overall impression is one of a fair-wind launch.

[3] Drs Hans and Karl Daniels' submission to Bonn Court of Justice 4 vi 1986. (Where Swiss East Institute is so described). See also Third World Quarterly 12(i) January 1990/ISSN 0143-6597/90. $1.25; Helga Baitenmann 'NGOs and the Afghan War: The politicisation of humanitarian aid. This points up General Roberts GAC and Peter Sager connection. Finally, Swiss Ost Institute was also reputed to have a secondary (undisclosed) role of analysing Hind helicopter armour-plating and bullet-proof glass.

[4] Hundeshagen linked Frau Ruth Buser to Dr Freigang as two people responsible for introducing/ recommending Ahmed Jan to DAK/GAC. This was in line with his habitual practice of turning everything on its head by making gross reverse of truth allegations.

[5]In fact, this was to become Herr Kantel's baby. It is known that he did pass on some monies to the *soi-disant* 'Gucci-muj' commanders in the Qandahar area. In the event, it was well wasted, which may have been partly what prompted him to pass on less and less, as the years went by!

52
Musical Chairs in Committee

By the end of November 1985, either in the interests of a fresh look, ringing the changes, or adjustment for a power struggle, a meeting was convened to endorse a GAC Board re-shuffle. The hardcore band of twelve were all present and correct. Apologies for absence were received from Frau Kantel and Frau Hundeshagen, who, it was explained, could be called upon to vote, if necessary, by telephone. Seven 'others' were in attendance, and their alterity, what defined them as being others, derived solely from their denuded voting rights.

The meeting began with the announcement of three interesting resignations, without explanation. First, Kakojan Niazi, which was to be anticipated. Next came Herr & Frau Rolf Lerch. As co-founder members there had to be a good reason for their quitting, whether the resignations were related or not. Otherwise, what followed was merely a musical comedy. The Lerchs' 'resignation' may have been a condition exacted for their appointment to the new Peshawar local headquarters. It could be argued, in any event, that they would be unable to attend regular meetings.

The next item came as a big surprise. It had been decided to appoint 'independent' auditors and publish financial results for the year! It sounded too good to be true, until it was revealed that the 'independent' auditors to the annual report and accounts, were to be none other than Dietrich Kantel's father, Herr Willi Kantel, and another member of the Executive Committee, to be determined later!

As previously revealed in a letter from Andrea Hörst to Dr Veggeberg - one of the very few communications ever received from GAC by the Royal Surrey County Hospital, Guildford - it was now Denny Hundeshagen's turn to be President - First Class. Once firmly at the helm, there were to be a number of sparkling innovations.

In future, foreign funding would only be acceptable, so long as it did not come to dominate any single project. Expressed otherwise, all project-related aid would always remain the sole responsibility of the Committee. As if further proclamation were necessary, it was here stated yet again. No outside interference would be countenanced.

As anticipated, a number of new restrictive clauses were introduced to eliminate the chances of any aspiring new German members - let alone Afghans!

Whilst making membership appear eligible to all Germans,

any applicant had first to make a written 'declaration' that he/she shared the unstated aims and objects of the Committee and offered his/her services to it unconditionally. If this hurdle was cleared, there then followed an 'adoption agreement'. If this was negotiated satisfactorily, the Executive Committee would next put the names of proposed candidates forward to the not-so-general general meeting. The final 'Catch 22' obstacle resembled the conditions of a self-liquidating premium offer on a packet of groceries: the applicant must not be related in any way to the organisers and the decision of the judge was final! Anyway, candidates required a two-thirds majority for election.

As disclosed in documentary evidence later, all voting members conveniently belonged to the same two families and/or student fraternity/sorority clique. Mad Hatter's tea-party or not, the clique had everything stitched up. From the onset of the new year - 1986 - GAC were in a dilemma, however. The papers are full of contradictions, the only likely explanation for which must stem from that long-ago leak, that Kantel and Hundeshagen did not always see eye-to-eye or, indeed, share the same objectives.

1986 was their apocalyptic year.

On 15 March, Dietrich Kantel went on record with his projection that 'everything was rosy in the garden'. GAC advanced into the new year with a financial cushion of DM 1.5 million. When the anticipated high level of donations was added to this, including one single 'private' donation of DM 1.2 million, there could be little doubt that a much more extensive, more comprehensive programme, could be 'planned' if not 'executed'. For 'top security' reasons, precise details would have to remain 'under wraps'. The 'private' donation almost certainly referred to an American institution (perhaps the Children's Mercy Fund).

However, there was one news item on which he was only too happy to go public. Either at the instigation of Todenhofer or possibly Michael Sagurna, the final accolade of respectability and recognition was to be accorded them. GAC had been invited to address the Bundestag, the West German Federal Parliament.

53

A Ruse by any other Name

Nursing Sister and associate German Afghanistan Committee member - actually, she was a member of an advisory group only - Maria Müller was invited to address the German Parliament on the subject of humanitarian aid for Afghanistan. The date set was for 18-19 March 1986, perhaps in an overnight sitting? Her address was to be based on her two nursing visits. GAC were already well-versed in public address techniques, for they had by now made over a thousand presentations nationwide. Also the Christian Democratic Union political party's public relations consultants may have extended a helping hand.

Yet here ended the rosy, upbeat view of the future.

In stark contrast, despite all the other 'European' organisations (e.g. the Swiss Ost Institute) falling over each other to fund GAC, the overhead expenses had grown to such proportions that the organisation could no longer be supported solely by voluntary contributions. It was spending at the rate of anything between DM 1.8 and DM 2.4 million p.a., against an income 'best guesstimate' of DM 1.5 millon p.a. It was eating its head off. The need to co-operate with other outside funding organisations had become paramount.

Another reason cited was that the German public donations market had been spoiled by the bad reputation gained by 'other' German charitable institutions for 'sloppy accounting'.

Of equal interest as this statement of affairs was the apparent need to make the standard panic-stricken cry for no sell out. Nothing must bring about any diminution of voting control, or loss of autonomy, or - in particular - a closer look at the books. All of this was of little or no concern to the Americans, who would, in any event, have preferred to keep the party small, for their own good reasons.

One month to the day after Maria Müller had addressed Parliament, the committee moved that the time had come to change the name officially to German Afghanistan Committee, whilst retaining their original Bonn label as an historical sub-heading. For ease of following the argument I have so far referred to the German Afghanistan Committee - GAC - throughout, but it should be noted that for the first few years of its life it was known as the Bonn Afghanistan Committee. After the name change it was known in Germany as the Deutsches Afghanistan Komitee (DAK). Make no mistake though, the same bunch were running all permutations of these sets of initials in both English and German!

A number of convincing arguments were made, mostly related to the size and widespread acceptability of the assumed name already. These were all contained in a submission to the Bonn Court of Justice, dated 4 June 1986. The arguments put forward are interesting because they show the committee putting its best foot forward. Here again, it looked very much as if a professional firm of public relations consultants was involved, as well as the inevitable lawyers. From the language, it could have been the preamble for a prospectus to potential shareholders. But, first, before going to such lengths, American participation would have to be assured.

The constitution was to be changed yet again to accommodate 'honorary members' and 'sponsoring members'. They were to be afforded a 'sense of belonging'; although they were to be categorically denied any voting rights. The pinnacle of recognition and 'belonging' was to be accorded by the public ceremonial presentation of a certificate of honour; preferably by the head of state!

Denny Hundeshagen reported that Ms Anne Hurd and Mr Antony L. Campaigne of the Children's Mercy Fund were due to visit Bonn on 23 April 1986, for wide-ranging discussions. He wanted it put on record that, generally speaking, GAC's relations with the American Department of State, the Committee for a Free Afghanistan and indeed the Mercy Fund itself, were very good. They were 'co-operative'. This patronising remark related to the earlier State Department stipulation that contact had to be maintained both at the American Embassy in Islamabad as well as in Bonn. It was therefore GAC who co-operated.

Hundeshagen went on to say that the US$ 400,000 announced by the State Department had now been 'authorised' in the budget and was due to arrive any day.

In answer to a direct question from one of the 'other' members, Herr von Renese,[1] Hundeshagen insisted that this money would be paid directly into GAC's bank accounts, of which there were six. This move was apparently necessary 'in the interests of ensuring orderly accounting procedures'.

However, there was other highly satisfactory news, with the DM 1.5 million worth of JU Rottenburg medicines, to look forward to. This 'donation' would require 'especially creative soft pencil accounting techniques and must not, on any account, appear in the Pakistani books'![2]

Press & Public Relations

To coincide with Maria Müller's parliamentary address, a major public relations campaign had been launched. Copious press release material was supplied to some 950 publishing houses. Between them these just about leaflet-bombed the whole of the German Federal Republic. Of this total, some 110 serious publishing houses were asked to concentrate on the parliamentary hearing given to Frau Maria Müller. A new advertisement was launched, featuring Maria Müller.

Incredibly, Dr Karl Victor Freigang was wheeled out again to appear on a simultaneous chat show. There was now little doubting the nationwide recognition accorded GAC.

At the same time their house needed to appear squeaky-clean and concurrently, on 18 April 1986, one month after the hearing and conveniently five days before the Mercy Fund visit, a summary of finances was tabled.

There was DM 100,000 on current account.

There was DM 1.4 million on deposit account. This sum was said to be the residue of the lump sum receipts from Herr Gerhard Löwenthal's broadcast made fifteen months earlier, in December 1984. One is left speculating what the original sum must have been - most likely it was DM 3 to DM 5 million. The main reason it was disclosed at all at this stage was because it had to be justified as a carried forward item.

Generally speaking, distribution of charitable funds needed to be made within two years of receipt. Withholding distribution could be justified in this case only because the organisation had outgrown itself and this was now the sum required to underwrite the overhead expenses for the coming year.

*

There is another illustration of the turning of the tide, contained in a paradoxical report made by Dietrich Kantel and Denny Hundeshagen and covering conversations they had with their old ally, the Parliamentary Deputy, Dr Jürgen Todenhofer.

They had met to discuss the growing issue of 'Fundamentalism'. As both Dr Todenhofer, and to a lesser extend Gerhard Löwenthal, preferred to lend their support to the fundamentalists - notably Engineer Gulbuddin Hekmatyar and his party faction of Hesbe-i-

Islami - Dr Todenhofer now reiterated the basis for his personal support. It was almost as if he preferred to side with the underdog out of a sense of cussedness. However, he did have the grace to say that, 'when the going got tough, he preferred to entrust the task to GAC, because he knew the matter would then be "in safe hands".'

This, as minuted, comment could have been a euphemism to cover official US policy preferences or the tricky matter of ensuring donations were paid into the right bank accounts. What follows would support such a conclusion.

Dietrich Kantel gave it as his opinion that 'Dr Todenhofer would shortly be withdrawing his support from Afghanistan. It would be a mistake to count on him in future, least of all for appeals.' He had no doubt found a better row to hoe in a more fertile field.

Frau Maria Müller rose, as if on cue. She reported that after the *Zweites Deutsches Fernsehen* TV news report on the Bundestag (Parliamentary) hearing on Afghanistan, in which she had played such a prominent part, she had been astonished to find that the subsequent appeal went out in the joint-names of *Verein für Flüchtlingshilfe* (VAF) and HELP. She telephoned Gerhard Löwenthal immediately to demand an explanation. He promised to ring back. He had yet to do so!

Notwithstanding this marked change of allegiance, Kantel and Hundeshagen remained convinced that the work of the German Afghanistan Committee was held in such high esteem by both the West German Radio as well as *Arbeitsgemeinschaft der Rundfunkanstalten in Deutschland,* the equivalent of the BBC, that there was no cause for alarm. However, whilst whistling up their courage, they were both equally sceptical of any future co-operation from Dr Todenhofer; just as they would consider it unwise to place any further dependence on 'the impartial reporting of Herr Gerhard Löwenthal'. As his Parthian shot, Todenhofer said how much it had grieved him to find that the co-operation between the two organisations - GAC and VAF - was so small.

In riposte, Kantel and Hundeshagen stated that the German Afghanistan Committee's well-balanced strategy had borne fruit and was the correct policy to pursue in future. It looked more like sour grapes!

Amidst all this gloom, the first lorry transport had arrived in Peshawar - undamaged (this was not the story Andrea Hörst gave Kermit Veggeberg in her 'report') and the new GAC representative's house was open and working well. This must be where Rolf and Anke Lerch were destined to reside. The medical warehouse was to be built in the garden and would be manned for at least two years by a conscientious objector, who was due to arrive at the end of June 1986. This must have been the 'student type' (whose name was listed as Jan Rietz) whom we had met on Reinhard Erös's terrace, as we awaited his arrival, all those years ago.

[1] Herr von Renese was the second 'other' independent auditor appointed, together with Dietrich Kantel's father, Willi Kantel. This could well have been his valiant attempt to see fair play.

[2] This is taken directly from DAK/GAC minute book. They would be free to 'buy in' medicines donated and shipped; alternatively they could sell on anything surplus to requirement.

54
Situation Report 1986

The following overview of the BAK/DAK/GAC (Bonn/ Deutsches/German Afghanistan Committee) operations in 1986 was recorded very much in line and tone with the prestige brochure Reinhard Erös had handed out to us. No doubt it had something to do with the authorship of Denny Hundeshagen and Thomas Gaida.

'In 1986, there were no fewer than fifteen European medics going into Afghanistan, under the aegis of GAC. So as to achieve as much pan-Afghanistan coverage as possible, they would be divided up into variably-sized teams, according to location, distance to be covered and terrain. The basic concept was for 'mobile units' which came in two varieties, with optional extras. Teams destined for the southern provinces would be equipped with either two or three vehicles. Those headed for the less accessible mountain regions would have horses and/or mules.'

Although GAC were 'far and away the largest humanitarian aid organisation operating inside Afghanistan', and with no limit in sight to the numbers of European doctors and nurses volunteering for this work, the hard facts of the matter were that no more personnel could be engaged - simply due to lack of funds. Saturation had been reached, at least for 1986.

Dietrich Kantel chipped in his halfpence worth here, 'to emphasise that the taking on of European medics was only ever intended as support for Afghan doctors.

'The European personnel did have a secondary objective, which was to identify suitable long-term locations for medical centres i.e. hospitals.

'In answer to some direct questions put by members in open meeting, as to the current status of hospitals and clinics inside Afghanistan, Herr Kantel replied that it was impossible to give precise details since the situation was so insecure. Any news would have to await the return of the mobile units. As a general rule, Kantel begs those present not to make precise statements about the location of clinics, for fear of reprisal, jeopardising the personal safety of doctors and nurses.'

More general discussion follows.

'Herr von Renese reported on his recent visit to Afghanistan. *Haji* Ebrahim Rashid had told him categorically that there were now five clinics in place and fully operational, inside Afghanistan.

A further seven were planned during 1986, making a grand total of twelve by year's end.

'Herr Kantel again stalled by repeating that precise details would only be revealed on the return of the mobile units. Only then would it be possible to determine the number and size of the clinics established.' This was in marked contrast to the heavyweight `statistical' storyline supplied to the Bonn Court of Justice in support of the change of name, where, it will be noted, it was claimed there were no fewer than seventeen fixed hospital locations already inside Afghanistan!

The other point raised by Herr von Renese was the old chestnut of 'the Pakistani Government continuing in its attempts to exercise control through one designated Afghanistan Interim Government (AIG) central clearing house for the distribution of aid to Afghanistan. Kantel reiterated that any question of centralised control would be strongly resisted by GAC and its donors as irresponsible. However sound the original concept may have been, and, after all, the Americans had initiated it, the fact remained that any notion that the seven political parties could act in concert in the distribution of anything like money had, not surprisingly, proved impracticable.

'He went on to say that if such a centralised aid distribution system had been instituted, there would have been no reason for the United States Department of State funding of US$ 400,000 to come their way!

'Whereupon the general meeting expressed the wholehearted conviction that any question of the central pooling of German donations, outside German control, would be an irresponsible act and was to be firmly resisted - at all costs.

'Dietrich Kantel then took advantage of the mood of the moment to announce with heavy emphasis that the GAC was now held in such universal high esteem, that it would be reasonable to assume that its reputation accorded it a political influence out of all proportion to its size.

'As to the precise number and size of clinics, Hundeshagen pointed out that the "domestic budget" for 1986 had allowed *Haji* Ebrahim Rashid to plan for no fewer than eight clinics. These were, of course, those that existed already, as leftovers from 1985. Naturally, there would be additions, but they could only be confirmed once the financial picture became clearer.

'Herr von Renese went on to describe his visit to Sadda Hospital. He considered the project well-led and he had noticed no fewer than six doctors, "some of whom were actively treating patients whilst he was there!" For the time being relations in Pakistan were smooth and work progressed satisfactorily.

'Hundeshagen and Kantel between them proposed the following new members:

Herr Eckhart Ritter, Herr Christian Schlottfeld, Herr Doctor Ludger Bernd and last but by no means least, Frau Andrea Hundeshagen. All were unanimously elected.'

At this stage my eyes were popping out of my head as I speculated whether, by any chance, Frau Hundeshagen had once had the maiden name of Hörst. There had been another candidate for election, a Herr Doctor Farhang, but for some undisclosed reason he was ineligible under the constitution, so he was to be offered 'honorary' status instead.

The name of Bonn Afghanistan Committee was to be retained as a sub-title, come hell or high water.

Relations with other German Organisations (NGOs)

As promised earlier on, there was a need to answer allegations of poor relations experienced with other German organisations. In particular, this referred to Dr Toryalai Nassery's VAF, the Association for help to Afghan Refugees, as also alleged by Dr Jürgen Todenhofer, but also latterly, the HELP organisation. The subject could not be allowed to go away and, this time, Herr von Renese had chosen to ventriloquise on behalf of a certain Herr von Psyborowsky.

As if in answer to a tabled written question, Hundeshagen and Kantel issued the following joint statement.

'Notwithstanding the on-going personal differences between members of the executive commiteee and their opposite numbers in the two other named organisations, GAC has no objection to the general discussion of certain forms of co-operation.

'Such discussions with other kindred organisations could indeed make sense, where the question of aid for Afghanistan is concerned. However, it must be made abundantly plain that only matters of principle may be discussed, long before the consideration of any concrete plans for co-operation can be laid.

'The chief purpose behind any such conciliatory move, would be to establish GAC as a suitable conduit for German Government funding, along with HELP, for instance, which has wide experience of this form of subsidy.

'This kind of German Government backing has yet to come

the way of GAC; although, it must be stated, nor has it ever been requested. Your committee is confident that a most positive outcome can be anticipated to any such forthcoming discussions.'

Name Change and Letter of Justification to Bonn Court of Justice
Submitted 4 June 1986

The reason why this whole matter of change in name is so important, is that the organisation was required to justify itself and its claims in writing. In studying the submission we can therefore see very clearly how it saw itself at a pivotal moment in its development. A previous attempt had been made and had failed. There was now considerable cause to puff itself up and try again, this time with greater arrogance and yet more extravagant claims.

The peroration consequently began:

'In answer to any misgivings the Bonn Court of Justice may suffer on account of the limited membership of the BAK/DAK/GAC, the rationale put forward in justification of the Pan-German name is that, whereas it cannot boast the following of, say, the German Red Cross or our Automobile Association, it would nevertheless be wrong to classify it any longer as purely provincial to Bonn. Sheer weight of numbers are not the whole story. The consultative medical board is pan-national, as indeed are the sponsors and some 100,000 donors. Furthermore, the reputation of BAK/DAK/GAC is by now, truly international.

'During the past two years (1985, 1986) alone, the organisation has delivered over a thousand lectures on its activities throughout the German Federal Republic.

'These lectures have often been given in concert with such august bodies as Amnesty International and the German Red Cross, as well as "Lions" and numerous political groupings. A number of well-known Bundestag deputies' [five are mentioned by name] 'have given their support to the Committee, as have five of the leading lending banks. The German Foreign Office has been unstinting in its aid and support for the work of the Committee.

'Frau Maria Müller' [described here erroneously as a "member of the Committee"] 'was invited to address the Federal Parliament at a special hearing on the 18, 19, March 1986, on her experiences of the administration of humanitarian aid inside Afghanistan. This was a reflection that BAK/DAK/GAC was/is not only the largest German organisation to operate in-country to this extent, but also the largest European operation so to do. The balance sheet for 1985/86 is a true reflection of this position of strength. Frau Maria Müller has also subsequently been invited to address the Danish Parliament.'

Active co-operation with Amnesty International and the German Red Cross in the field, is given as the next good reason, together with ASME (mentioned earlier as an association devoted to medical assistance in crisis areas - mostly in Europe and Africa). Membership of a string of 'international' organisations and consortia is then cited to add credence to the claim: Peace Village - Oberhausen, International Association for Human Rights - *Internationale Gesellschaft für Menschenrechte, Co-operation Humanitaire Européene pour L'Afghanistane*, which represents all non-state-funded organisations in the business of delivering aid to Afghanistan.

The significance of the latter is that Doctor Karl Viktor Freigang is named as the BAK/DAK/GAC representative on the executive committee.

He is also given star billing as the Chairman of the BAK/DAK/GAC Medical Advisory Council. In his capacity as a member of the *Cooperation Humanitaire* Executive Commiteee, it is 'on the record' here, that Dr Freigang was 'invited to attend a conference of Commonwealth Countries' experts in London.' Sadly, there is no record as to whether he went or not. It was surely recognition enough to have been invited!

Moving on into the international stratosphere, big billing is now given to the Swiss Ost Institute - 'that exemplary "private" organisation which has been pre-eminent in the realms of "international politics" for over 30 years.' 'These good people not only dole out large sums (exact amounts of US dollars not disclosed), but have sufficient faith in the German organisation to delegate their doctors and nurses to work under their aegis inside Afghanistan. What better proof could there be of size and integrity, with such an intensive degree of co-operation existing between two such organisations?'

The submission, which was drafted by Doctors Hans and Karl Daniels (the latter was Mayor of Bonn) then continues with a *fait accompli* claim, which was well-founded:

`Throughout Pakistan and Afghanistan BAK/DAK/GAC is already known and accepted as the German Afghanistan Committee.'

However what then follows, may be harder to substantiate either then or now!

'At the present time, the German Afghanistan Committee *(sic)* maintains seventeen clinics in Afghanistan. These are at fixed locations, manned by doctors and nurses. The carefully documented GAC workload has increased by three hundred per centum (300%) over the last year. The precise extent of activities in the bordering country of Pakistan can be easily assessed from the balance sheet attached.'

As a clincher, in the summary, it is disclosed that 'the Bonner Afghanistan Committee (BAK) has been using the name German Afghanistan Committee (GAC) for some time as a subordinate (subsidiary) title. It is contended most forcibly that the work of the subsidiary now justifies the same switch.'

If that were not enough to sway the authorities, who no doubt still had grave misgivings about such a tightly-held close company operation, the case of intensive media coverage of the 'German Afghanistan Committee' was given as the final *coup de grace*. Everybody now knew it to be the case.

The submission was signed Hundeshagen (President - First Rate), Kantel (Vice-President) and Huther (Secretary).

Herr Norbert Huther, at the same time as submitting the application, requested that all former reservations expressed would be expunged from the official records.

So, as from 19 August 1986, the name was formally changed to German Afghanistan Committee - GAC.

In amongst these pages, which I obtained in Hamburg, there is a rogue page 6. It is the last page of a six-page document, but it is not part of any of the other exhibits. It has a different typeface. What it has to say makes one wonder what must be contained in the preceding five pages! Whatever was said must have been sufficiently damning for them to have been removed from the file, but why leave page 6?

Another explanation could be that it was part of an earlier draft, which was bowdlerised, leaving only page 6 intact. In which case it must have been meant as an addendum to the Bonn Court of Justice - name change submission. The message indeed suggests this:

'Not only are the activities of BAK/DAK/GAC well-known throughout Europe, but also particularly in America. For instance, US Aid (a Department of State Organisation) sponsored the work of the BAK/DAK/GAC to the extent of US$ 1 million during 1986. The German Afghanistan Committee is the only German organisation to receive such sponsorship from the US Government.

'There also exists another "co-operation agreement" with a "private" American aid organisation, called the Children's Mercy Fund/Afghan Mercy. This organisation raises charitable subscriptions on behalf of the German Afghanistan Committee throughout the length and breadth of the United States of America. These regular donors amount to some 2.5 million American citizens.'

In fact, Antony Campaigne only ever said that he had around a million subscribers. Nor is any mention made of the Children's Mercy Fund's alternative and even more reliable and regular source of finance, Uncle Sam.

55

1986 - A peak year seen in retrospect

It is worth taking a second retrospective look at this pivotal year, 1986, as seen through the eyes of the German Afghanistan Committee's Executive Committee report which paid particular attention to the controversial Resettlement Programme for refugees.

During the year some 30,000 German donors had come to aid an estimated 150,000 Afghan medical patients, through the good offices of the German Afghanistan Committee. This is the only German organisation to send doctors into Afghanistan, operating from fixed medical stations in-country. Tight control is kept on donors' funds right through to the ultimate beneficiary. (i.e. There is no intervening Afghan political party creaming off funds.)

The German Afghanistan Committee is actively engaged in Resettlement Projects (note the plural) inside Afghanistan. The GAC also helps out in disaster areas inside Afghanistan, trains nursing staff and distributes aid to refugees both inside Afghanistan and in the camps in Pakistan. The long-term objective is to lay the foundation stone for rebuilding the country after the war.

Over the past year, a total of twelve German or Swiss doctors, made up into seven "mobile units" toured Afghanistan. In this way, some of the doctors covered their tracks several times.

Notably, German Dr Karl Victor Freigang, accompanied by Swiss Nurse Frau Ruth Buser, brought succour to the suffering civilian population, under the most trying circumstances in two of the southern-most provinces - Qandahar and Helmund, where there was severe fighting. They were able to conduct a most successful operation from a motorised "mobile clinic". On their second summer and autumn tour of duty, they were accompanied by another German doctor, Gunther Ermert.

Other European "mobile medical units" travelled by horse, or on foot. Dr Paulin, Dr Kley and the dentist Dr Czierny and Nurse Winifried Grundel served in the province of Ghazni.

The Swiss doctor Michael Müller and his German colleague Dr Hertel, travelled to the far north of Afghanistan, a journey which took them almost four months. After weeks of riding, and stopping to treat hundreds of patients along the way, they reached the province of Baghlan. Once arrived, they set up their clinic where they put in two months' solid work.

It was during this time that Dr Reinhard Erös took leave from his post as Senior Field Doctor of the German Army (Bundeswehr) in order to work with the German Afghanistan Committee in the province of Nangahar.

Where there were no roads - for instance in the north-east province of Kunar - GAC personnel were obliged to travel on foot. Dr Ruckl of Munich covered vast distances this way to set up the three Kunar clinics; each of which required an arduous mountain journey.

All these doctors were witness to the genocide in Afghanistan and can testify to the facts.'

German Clinics Establishment in Afghanistan

The DAK/GAC report continues by stating that

there are now thirteen fixed medical centres in Afghanistan. They are to be found in the provinces of Samangan, Baghlan, Paktia, Nangahar, Kunar, Wardak, Logar, Kabul and Ghazni.

The permanent staff employed include: 13 Afghan doctors, 12 nurses and 51 medical orderlies. This is the heart of GAC's medical work. At the end of hostilities, it is intended that these units will serve as the basis for a regional health-care system. Housed in the simplest of traditional buildings or, during bombardments, in caves hewed out of the rockface by GAC's own teams. In this way, these various clinics are able to provide basic medical attention to meet the needs of Afghanistan's suffering people. A ton a week of medical supplies was shipped into Afghanistan.

This confirms the statistic given above of fifty tons a year.

During the course of the year, all the clinics were visited at least once to be inspected by one or other of the Committee's European doctors.

From our Base Camp One in Peshawar, co-ordinators liaise with the GAC's own distribution network inside Afghanistan. Contracted doctors man each of the GAC medical centres in-country. GAC is fortunate indeed to be able to rely on its "own" transport system, made up of lorries and mules. Thus, in stark contrast with other aid organisations, GAC's input does not suffer the predations of party political intermediaries. Furthermore, we have come to rely on accurate feed-back to enable us to boost supplies where the need is acute.

Refugee Resettlement

In the spring of 1986, GAC started up the first ever resettlement project inside Afghanistan. A total of 362 families (approximately 3,000 souls) who had been obliged to flee their villages in other war-stricken areas, either as the result of bombing or ground troups, were able to find refuge in this new GAC settlement. Each family was supplied with the basic necessities of life:

food, seed, materials for clothes and tentage. During the year, most families have managed to convert their homes into the traditional solid mud houses. However, the village, by no means self-sufficient, has to be constantly supplied. This has involved 15 people full-time with no fewer than 45 mules to transport an estimated 36 tonnes of aid materials to date. Most of this material has to come from Pakistan, over routes that take weeks if not months to negotiate. The long-term hope was that the infrastructure being put in place would eventually render the village independent of all outside help.

Thus 40 families are equipped with 40 sewing-machines with which to produce tents, blankets, clothes etc. Another 120 families have been allocated sheep and goats as breeding stock (numbers unspecified). Yet others were to engage in spinning, weaving, carpet knotting and beaten brass-ware.

And, as if the Utopian dream were incomplete, there was a handy coalmine on the site to help engender winter warmth - the ultimate in self-sufficiency. The earlier prestige handbook reported the site chosen at Talabafak valley also enjoyed a year-round water-supply.

The ideal conditions of this project will undoubtedly encourage these people to remain in their homeland under conditions of human dignity, instead of making themselves an additional burden to the international aid organisations and the Pakistan Government', as the GAC report says. It adds, however, that 'None of this would have been possible without the generous grant from the American Foreign Aid Programme.'

Die Tageszeitung - literally Daily Newspaper of 24 October 1988 confirmed the arrival in Germany of this US Aid specifically earmarked for refugee resettlement programme inside Afghanistan.

'Under the guise of emergency aid, the German Embassy in Islamabad added a donation of DM 20,000 in order to fund medicines specifically for the Baghlan medical centre in Baghlan', on the site of a pre-war German cotton mill.

'On a pan-Afghanistan scale, some 150,000 patients were attended by GAC "German" doctors during 1986. The most frequent cases were infectious, malaria, and parasitic diseases as well as war wounds.'

'In the treatment of these patients, some 44 truck-loads of medicines were shipped in carrying some 26 tonnes. A further 14 tonnes of aid materials, not readily available in Pakistan were brought in from Germany.'

Sadda Modern Clinic & Training School

The GAC Report also gives a rundown on the activities of this model clinic at Sadda. Mention is made of the fifteen barefoot 'dispensers' undergoing training, who will then

take their knowledge back to their clinics inside Afghanistan. Then after practical experience in the field, they would return to Sadda for refresher courses. There was ample evidence of Dr Paulin's excellent handbook being used by students to retain the valuable lessons learned on the course.

As well as the resettlement programme in Baghlan, GAC was engaged in setting up a second "New Camp" at Sadda. This will be home to some 800 families. These refugees had as yet been unable to register with the Pakistani authorities, and so were ineligible for aid.

The basic needs of these people were therefore underwritten by GAC to improve their chances of survival. This covered all aspects of aid materials. For instance, in October the Committee was a conduit for two (ship) container loads of winter clothes donated by the *Bundeswehr* (German Military) and the *Bundesdeutscher Zivilschutz* (Civil Defence). Again in December, the German Government made a special grant for the purchase of 200 tents for families with nothing between them and the bare ground. Austrian schoolchildren collected enough money to buy blankets to be given out with these tents. The dream for future years was to be able to hand out foodstuffs too.

The long-term objective was to establish GAC medical centres throughout the length and breadth of the land, as focal points around which village communities could be rebuilt, once peace returned to the provinces. The regeneration of agricultural activity around these "nodal points" would, it was anticipated guarantee a viable agricultural economy in the post-war era. Joint ventures were planned with the UK AfghanAid, who were to supply the specialist agronomists, plus the "seedcorn".[1]

'In the meantime, GAC had three full-time construction teams engaged in excavating cave-shelters, digging roads, repairing damaged irrigation channels and, in two notable cases, the running of an hydro-electric power station (presumably Chak) and in Baghlan the working of a coalmine for the Resettlement Programme.'

*

Dr Freigang Speaks Up

Sure enough, by 1987, the general picture was by no means as rosy as the '1986 Retrospective' would make its readers believe. On

20 May 1987, Dr Freigang felt compelled to put his opinion in writing. He opened his formal letter of complaint by saying 'that it had become self-evident more than a year ago that there was diminishing mutual trust between himself and the committee.' Indeed, the committee had in fact minuted its decision 'not to re-engage his services', some eighteen months previously (5 September 1985), although he did not know this.

Dr Freigang had recognised, *ab initio*, that there would be friction between himself and the committee. Differences of approach, as between his "experience" and the "impetuosity of youth", were but a reflection of the gap in generations. He had, however, been prepared to overlook such disparity in the overall interest of helping the Afghan cause. He hoped that his acquiescence might generate a beneficial rub-off effect on the younger generation - both socially and politically. In this he had been much mistaken.

In the first few years all had gone well, but the organisation proved incapable of following up its initial success. The committee lacked follow-through and found it expedient to make him their multi-purpose scapegoat; blaming him for their shortcomings both in Afghanistan and Pakistan. This peaked when Herr Hundeshagen and Herr Gaida made the astonishing claim that they had had to rectify the many things Dr Freigang had botched up in Pakistan. This was particularly rich, coming from two people who knew neither the region and its difficulties nor the political intrigues of the people living there. Nevertheless, in the interests of the shared objective, he had chosen to ignore these small-minded criticisms. The internal squabbles of the GAC/DAK were not his concern. His only interest was to serve the Afghan cause.

However, by the spring of 1986, confrontation was inevitable. Dr Freigang was made aware that he was powerless to influence the very medical advisory committee of which he was the nominal chairman. Herr Hundeshagen had interposed himself as the medical director, with Herr Paulin as his chief medical adviser. Dr Freigang was even accused of being power-hungry, if not power-mad.

With the interests of Dr Freigang and those of the executive committee no longer in harmony, Dr Freigang was only soldiering on in the interests of the overall aim of serving the Afghan people, but without any trust. He had even become apathetic about returning to Afghanistan and considered throwing in the towel. But he was swayed by the overriding problems of the Afghans. Instead, Freigang turned his attentions to the business of fund-raising and publicity for DAK/ GAC both of which activities he undertook with remarkable success.

However, the committee responded by passing a resolution (4 March 1987, topic No 2) banning him from all their deliberations.

The committee then pursued a policy of engaging doctors themselves, without seeking qualified advice, or, indeed, bothering to obtain any subsequent confirmation of "suitable" candidates by accredited medical personnel.

If this were not irresponsible enough, in the case of the joint-venture with Humanitärer Information Dienst (HID)[2] in their Quetta office, there had been a distinct lack of political acumen. Dr Freigang had objected to the engagement of Herr Andrea Goetz, also known as Ahmed Jan - the German Muslim Mujahedeen, from the outset, but the high-handed manner in which the committee prevented Freigang from returning to Afghanistan "in the interests of his personal safety" was most undignified. It led him to believe that DAK/GAC was more concerned with the cult of their own personalities and their personal advancement and had suppressed the original stated aims of helping the people of Afghanistan.

He would remind them that the original intention had been to build an organisation to help these people and not just run a CIA office to provide "jobs for the boys!"

His criticisms therefore were the following:

1. There was a distinct lack of trust between the various German organisations working for the Afghan cause. There was less than no trust between himself and the DAK/GAC.

2. As for the organisation of the Committee in Germany, there was no clear dividing line between the committee and the executive. The committee interfered constantly in the day to day workings of the executive.

3. There was no proper medical advisory body, which resulted in the committee rejecting the medical budget out of hand.

4. There was scarcely any co-operation with other NGOs.

5. The engagement of the German Muslim Ahmed Jan was made without proper prior consultation.

6. There was a total lack of professional exploitation of government funding, with special reference to the financial support available from various government ministries.

[There is a major and obvious discrepancy here in that the GAC/DAK Manual maintains that the Committee received grants (both in 1986 and 1987) from the Ministries *(sic)* of Development Aid of the German Federal Republic . Alternatively, and perhaps more plausibly, Dr Freigang was being kept in the dark.

As the minutes of concurrent meetings reveal, the committee

seem to have adopted a semi-ostrich approach to both the Freigang and the Ahmed Jan problems, so that by the 14 August 1987, Dr Freigang was obliged to send in his final, second salvo, letter of resignation. In this, he expressed his views in even stronger terms.

His reasons for resignation were both professional and personal. On the professional score, the original objective of providing humanitarian aid to the Afghans had been superseded by the committee's preoccupation with the organisation itself. Any idea of aid for Afghanistan was to be diverted for the advancement and development of the organisation, which would in turn enhance the profiles of a few select members of the committee.]

Dr Freigang reiterated how 'the organisation suffered from faulty structure in that there was no clear division of responsibility, or competence, between the committee and the executive.

'The salary level of the chairman of the committee was wholly unjustified. The committee was a self-perpetuating oligarchy with unlimited power. Because of its small size, limited membership and structure, dissolution was virtually impossible. Over two-thirds of the members belonged to the same group of interests - either the same extended family, or student association.'

Freigang then cites the misappropriation of funds donated by the German general public.

'These had been syphoned off to futher the purpose of other "front" organisations not directly engaged in humanitarian aid. Here he re-iterated his objections to one group, whose chairman was clearly identifiable as a GAC committee member.'

In the Bonn Charities Register, both Hundeshagen and Kantel are named as directors, together with a certain Frau Ute Dorothea Lundberg.

Dr Freigang's professional qualms 'were concentrated especially on the unwarranted engagement of the "German Muslim Mujahedeen" Ahmed Jan. This decision had occasioned the (unwise and unnecessary[3]) politicisation of DAK/GAC, with negative and possibly life-threatening consequences for all the medical personnel working inside Afghanistan.

'Although Freigang was personally all in favour of active and open support for the Mujahedeen freedom fighters in Afghanistan, he was not in favour of any closer linking of politics and humanitarian aid, because it led on to negative reactions from political opponents and the inevitable associations of CIA links.'

He next cited 'the total lack of qualified medical personnel on the committee, despite the fact that the DAK/GAC was supposedly engaged exclusively in the pursuit of medical activities.'

Dr Freigang's personal reasons for resignation were centred on an 'abusive, slanderous and stupid' letter, emanating from Michael Sagurna and Herr Norbert Hutter, the DAK/GAC company secretary. (This may have been in response to his first salvo but I found no copy on file.) In reply, Dr Freigang states how 'he can provide any number of letters of thanks from grateful Afghans for his healing work performed inside Afghanistan - where letter-writing is a rarity in itself! He finally sets a time limit of fourteen days for an apology. If no such apology is forthcoming, then he and the committee will have no alternative but to communicate through lawyers.'

His next complaint, under the personal heading, concerns another letter altogether, from a lady, which occasioned a bitter breakdown between himself and the committee.

The name of the lady was Rosanne Klass, and for a long time I assumed she was German. Then one day I found her listed as an 'Overseas Expert' in an old Peshawar 'directory' with the tell-tale American middle initial, in this case a 'T'. At one stage she was working for Freedom House in New York, which may also have housed the Committee for a Free Afghanistan and the Afghanistan Information Centre. Freedom House is known as an American Government think-tank that monitors freedom round the world. Whilst on secondment in Peshawar, Rosanne Klass had written a 'Strictly Private & Confidential' letter to Dr Freigang, care of DAK/GAC, Peshawar. Presumably it had been necessary to write the letter because Dr Freigang was busily engaged treating Afghans inside Afghanistan. The letter may have even been marked to await his return. For all I know, the contents could well have given Dr Freigang a clearer indication of the true nature of the Mercy Fund (Murky Fund), or a clearer insight into the activities of HID. In Dr Freigang's absence this letter had been forwarded to headquarters in Bonn, where it had been opened 'by the committee'.

By the time Dr Freigang caught up with his letter in Bonn, it lacked its envelope and a photocopy had been forwarded to the Mercy Fund, thus compromising Rosanne Klass. Not only was this a breach of trust in the highest degree, it was crass stupidity, but it surely showed where the loyalties of the committee lay. They were beholden to the Mercy Fund. Rosanne Klass subsequently asked Dr Freigang not to take the matter any further.

For all these reasons, Dr Freigang considered the time had come when DAK/GAC should be dissolved and somehow re-formed with more independent-minded and representative members.

At about the same time there were rumours that the German Red Cross had labelled DAK/GAC as arms for drugs traffickers. Whether this allegation was restricted to the Rashid/Chak operation, or reached as far as the Bonn headquarters itself has never been established, but Dr Freigang makes no mention of it. One gets the impression that he would have done.

[1] The GAC August 1989 summary sheet also mentions the opening of a new clinic in Achin, Nangahar - a joint project with AfghanAid, UK. Reinhard Erös was dedicated to Nangahar - see above.

[2] Also known, in Pakistan, as German Humanitarian Service, possibly to differentiate it from Ms Anne Hurd's Humanitarian News Service under Mercy Fund aegis.

[3] 'unwise and unnecessary' are in original German letter.

56
The Rot Sets In

According to the secret and suppressed archives which I had been able to access, 27 June 1987 was the date of a significant meeting reported in the most meticulous of minutes. As a German friend of mine has frequently pointed out to me, the more heinous the crime, the more constrained the German psyche seems to feel to make the most accurate of reports. The Holocaust remains the prime example.

To begin with, on this occasion the necessary quorum consisted of twelve members out of a possible total of seventeen. This gives us an exact idea of just how small the party was. Short notice apologies for absence were received, due to the pressures of other business, from Michael Sagurna, the sometime Chairman, and Herr von Renese, the Treasurer.

'Dietrich Kantel promptly proposed in the absence of the Treasurer, and in view of the unaudited state of the accounts, that financial matters should therefore be dropped from the agenda.' There was also a far more pressing matter requiring urgent attention ... mass defections.

'Dr Freigang and Rolf and Anke Lerch, two other founder members of the original *Bonner Afghanistan Komitee*, who currently represented DAK/GAC in Peshawar. So it was agreed to discuss this subject instead under the milder heading of "Resignation of old members and adoption of new members".

But before this could happen, there was general complaint about the unsatisfactory circumstances covering the minutes of the last meeting held on 7 March 1987. Many questions had been raised and corrections made during endless discussion. A unanimous request was made that in future minutes should be dispatched not later than four weeks after any meeting.

Dietrich Kantel responded to an enquiry that had been made about what was being done to track down the defecting Bundeswehr doctors.[1] The somewhat lame reply came from the Chairman Hundeshagen and Secretary Hutter that nothing was being done, as this was a matter for the Medical Advisory Board which had not met on account of the resignation of its chairman Dr Freigang. However, purposeful steps would now be taken to find out the reasons which lay behind these desertions.

Members, however thin on the ground, were not to be deflected and a further general complaint followed that they were being kept in the dark. There had been no newsletter for months and there was a near total lack of information. The committee was asked to communicate at least once every three months on the progress of DAK/GAC work.

The newly joined Doctor Bernd made a similar complaint on the medical front. To date he had yet to receive any of the agreed doctors' reports or summaries of medical findings. The chairman attempted to justify this on the grounds of the confidential nature of the contents of the reports. However, the members chose to support Doctor Bernd in his belief that such cautious behaviour was not always justified. In future, all such medical reports would be made available for members to examine at the offices at any time and suitable extracts would be circulated to the medically qualified.

Herr Gerhard Löwenthal's name cropped up again, although there was not much new to report about his negative attitude towards DAK/GAC. During a live interview, he had reiterated and insisted that their name and bank giro detail should not be broadcast; although he had not hesitated to sponsor others such as Dr Ermat. Clearly DAK/GAC had failed to look after him as he would have wished, and it was noted with relief that Gerhard Löwenthal was due to be replaced that year (1987) by Herr Hauser.

There followed a loose comment that although *Solidaritätskreis* was originally thought to be synonymous with *Hesbe-i-Islami* interests, this was no longer necessarily the case. The inference here being that even if the missing money had ever got that far, it would have gone missing anyway!

Herr Schlottfeld complained that members still had not been allowed to see Rolf Lerch's letter of resignation from Peshawar; although it had been acknowledged that changes would have to be made in line with his expressed misgivings.

After covering one or two other items, which were matters arising from the previous meetings, plus the need to take on a second secretary because the work of the committee had almost doubled in 1986, it was disclosed that a complete break had been made with Herr and Frau Lerch. The reason given was their disloyalty, since these two former colleagues and co-founder members had mounted a concerted takeover bid for the Peshawar end of DAK/GAC, to include the Rashid brothers and ARROS. Instant dismissal was modified to a mutual agreement to sever relations.

The Lerchs therefore no longer had any links with the committee and had resigned from their membership of "our respective organisations" - plural, suggesting more than one board of directorships.

This in turn brought to light the laudable role played by *Haji* Ebrahim Rashid. This time he had excelled himself in his loyalty to the committee. It was he who had felt compelled to inform the committee of Herr Lerch's plans to sequester the operation at the Peshawar end. At his own request and in recognition of his loyal service, a new post was to be created for him as Special Adviser, with responsibility for all projects. As an additional reward, *Haji* Ebrahim Rashid sought freedom to undertake political activity which could only serve DAK/GAC's best interests. (This could well be a euphemism for some other CIA-related activity.) He further proposed that his post as director of clinic programmes be taken over by his brother Khalid Rashid, whose five years of medical studies at Kabul University would help to forge yet closer links to the committee. It was almost as if he were offering him as a hostage.

This was deemed to be the trigger to itemise the whole range of projects currently being undertaken. The emphasis and contradictions are of particular interest here. It was stated that:

1. At present there were fourteen medical stations, as well as the two dispensaries at Sadda and New Camp, managed in conjunction with the German Red Cross. (This joint-venture could have prompted that 'gun running, drugs for arms deals' allegation, since the sites were well placed for such activities.)

2. The Baghlan Resettlement Project. This was continuing thanks to a large contribution of US Aid. (This cryptic sentence seems on the short side for year two of a US $400,000 investment.)

3. The Paulin Book project was proceeding according to plan and is due to be completed in 1988.

4. The committee's views on the German Humanitarian Service (GHS) - also known as Humanitarian Information Service (HID) joint-venture project in Quetta - will be given at a later date.

5. The "Mobile Units" of European doctors. Dr Michael Müller and Dr Hertel were reported to be on their way to Bamian and Baghlan. This time they are accompanied by Herr Hesse and Herr Bialek, who will be making a film. So, the lessons of 1986 will bear fruit in far-reaching improvements in 1987.

6. There would, of course be the need to replace Herr Lerch at Peshawar. Hundeshagen and Kantel (who may already have had Reinhard Erös in mind as Lerch's replacement) explained that the committee had decided to advertise the post. Somebody should be found from outside the DAK/GAC sphere of influence. There was

speculation that the Rashid brothers might get the wrong signals from the Lerch resignations. Kantel explained that there were always tensions between the German representative and the Afghans. However, it had been made clear to the Rashid brothers that the German representative in Peshawar was not at their disposal. The newcomer, Dr Bernd, expressed his surprise at the outcome to this dispute. He had understood in March that it was considered to be an over-reaction which was not beyond repair. The point was again raised whether the committee had taken account of the factual core of the Lerch criticism.

Dietrich Kantel broached the possibility of his own resignation from the committee on account of his close, life-long, friendship with the Lerchs. He particularly wished to know whether there had been any hint of misappropriation of funds by the Lerchs and was mollified to learn there had been none.

However, as the direct result of the Lerchs' departure, the much vaunted US Aid programme "had been temporarily suspended".

Dr Bernd expressed the disappointment of the floor by stating that it was most unfortunate, since the dispute could have been avoided and, whatever happened, the lesson must be learned before the appointment of the next Peshawar representative.

Having dealt with the Lerchs, the "altercations" with Dr Freigang were then expressed in the following guarded way: "Personal disagreements arose between Dr Freigang and the committee, which it would serve no purpose to repeat here." The committee said these differences related to their desire to prevent him exposing himself to the unnecessary dangers of travelling deep inside Afghanistan. The committee had received clear indications of danger from well-informed sources in-country.

Dr Freigang's reaction had been to approach other rival organisations to sponsor his next trip which, it transpired, the German Afghanistan Foundation , had been delighted to do.

According to them, Dr Freigang was currently in Afghanistan on their behalf. Consequently, his links with DAK/GAC were, for the most part, dissolved. (This can only refer to Dr Freigang's letter of 20 May 1987, although no mention is made of it since the actual letter of resignation was not sent until 14 August 1987.)

'Dr Freigang's contract with DAK/GAC had been terminated and his company car sold, albeit at a loss. Ever since his departure, Freigang had done his utmost to blacken DAK/GAC's good name amongst other non-government organisations.' Not surprisingly, Freigang saw things rather differently.

*

If the convolutions of the committee in their dealings with Dr Freigang are surprising, they seem as nothing compared to the somersaults performed on behalf of their association with the 'German Muslim Mujahedeen' Ahmed Jan (also known as Ahmed Shan and Adrea Görtz).

Precisely one month and one week after Dr Freigang's deposition, the committee were ready to turn the whole 'HID' proposition on its head - representing it as a Freigang-sponsored misfortune. In those same minutes dated 27 June 1987 there was an item which stated that, 'in response to a long-drawn-out discussion concerning the appointment of Herr Goertz - or as he preferred to be known by his Muslim name, Ahmed Jan - to run a joint-venture office in Quetta, the Committee (no individual names recorded) had explained that Freigang had 'co-opted Ahmed Jan in his activities to an extent that was entirely unknown to them'.

Ahmed Jan had indeed visited the committee at their offices in Bonn on the introduction and recommendation of Dr Freigang and Frau Buser who was on secondment from Swiss East Institute. He had offered to work with DAK/GAC and set up a base at Quetta. The committee had seen this as an opportunity to establish medical clinics in Southern Afghanistan, which had, up to that time, suffered unfortunate neglect.

By April, *Haji* Ebrahim Rashid and Anke Lerch, at that time still on the strength of GAC, came to hear of the plan which both recognised as a lessening of their authority.

Partly to placate the Rashids, it was decided that the Quetta operation would henceforth fly the "HID" flag of convenience. Cross directorships predominated and were held on behalf of DAK/GAC by Sagurna, Kantel and Hundeshagen. HID was known to have been funded by DAK/GAC "amongst other major donors'.[2]

This eleventh-hour disclosure occasioned some sharp questioning from the floor of the meeting. Herr Lottmann, a recently joined member who found himself "unanimously elected" chairman/king for the day, wanted to know, for instance, why members had not been advised earlier of "yet another front organisation". Herr Lottmann feared Herr Görtz, with his querulous nature and active political involvement in the internecine Afghan affairs plus the fact that "his origins were well-known to insiders",[3] would only too soon come to be identified with DAK/GAC and so compromise its humanitarian charter.'

The inside story that went the rounds was that Goertz's speciality had been as a hit man whom the CIA used for 'wet jobs' to liquidate Russian opponents in East Germany. They were even said to have 'sprung' him from an East German prison to take on the challenge of his new tailor-made Muslim role.

Kantel justified the cloaking of the Ahmed Jan activities under the HID umbrella on the grounds that it was necessary to do everything possible to dampen disquiet in the Rashid quarter. The consensus of the members was that, however expiatory the deeds of Herr Goertz might be in Afghanistan, they could never entirely compensate for his lurid past.

But Ahmed Jan was not without champions. Frau Maria Müller emphasised the need to make aid available at Quetta - whatever the negative factors might be. Hundeshagen also sprang to his defence, saying that on his recent visit, he had been impressed by the level-headed and competent impression made by Ahmed Jan. What was beyond dispute was the value of his activities on behalf of the Mujahedeen inside Afghanistan. Nobody could gainsay that.

Clinics

The persistent Dr Bernd demanded to know "how many clinics existed at any one time in Afghanistan and, furthermore, why the figures varied so much. Hundeshagen answered that, in the 1987 budget, fourteen clinics had been planned. However, how many existed at any one time was a matter for conjecture, since DAK/GAC had subjected their clinics to constant quality-control checks. Often as the result of war damage, they had to relocate and sometimes start again from scratch. Such news could take weeks, even months to reach Pakistan, and Bonn would hear it later still.

Auditor's Report

Since the auditor's report was still not available, approval to the accounts could not be given. The report could therefore only be approved minus the financial content, which would have to be deferred to a later date, like, say, 14 or possibly 15 October. Members agreed to the suggestion put by the committee that this meeting should coincide with a gathering of "The 1987 Afghanistan travellers".

Somewhat surprisingly, the meeting now moved on to the welcome and adoption of new members. Hundeshagen was pleased to propose Frau Martina Müller and Herr Michael Commes, both of JU

Rottenburg (also of the place name - Rottenburg) for membership of the DAK/GAC "on account of their great devotion in amassing DM 1.5 million worth of medical supplies". The members voted unanimously for their adoption.

Dietrich Kantel then spoke movingly on behalf of Dr Reinhard Erös, who had originally only left the organisation on account of other pressing obligations, namely to the Bundeswehr. Dr Erös had not only made a written request to be re-admitted to membership of the DAK/ GAC, he had also made a personal approach to Dietrich Kantel. It was unanimously agreed that Dr Erös be re-admitted in recognition of the great services that he had rendered in times past as one of the outstanding DAK/GAC doctors in Afghanistan.

The date was 27 June 1987, precisely nine months before his appointment as Field Director in Peshawar in March 1988. Perhaps he had been earmarked all along as the 'independent outsider' mooted by Hundeshagen. (It was a strange choice when coupled with Kantel's comments on defecting Bundeswehr doctors.)

Such 'foresight' would surely come to be regretted. However, Dr Freigang posed a more immediate disintegration threat to the committee, constituting, as he did, one of their brightest earliest stars, his revolt and departure amounted to a death blow to the main core of the organisation.

Three courses of action presented themselves to Herr Lottmann, as chairman of the meeting.

1. Despite the divorce, the committee could retain him as a member - so as to avoid any further repercussions.

2. It could perhaps be diplomatically suggested to Dr Freigang that he resign voluntarily, especially since his new allegiance (DAS/GAF) could only lead to confusion in the minds of the German donating public.

3. Dr Freigang should be expelled from the organisation forthwith, with fanfares. His work for a rival establishment was not consistent with continued membership. (The chairman surely cannot have been aware of the committee's decision "not to re-engage his - Dr Freigang's - services" eighteen months earlier.)

'It was agreed by all that Dr Freigang had caused the DAK/ GAC considerable damage through his behaviour and the detrimental nature of his public statements. Damage limitation was to be the order of the day. There was no denying the great services rendered to the DAK/GAC by Dr Freigang in the past. The basis of the present discord was represented to them as his unreasonable demands over his immediate deployment in Afghanistan.

'After a vote was taken, eight members were for expulsion, two for forced resignation.' (Strange to relate, the numbers add up to more people than were stated to be present at the meeting, unless the chairman added his invalid, non-casting vote.)

'As if anticipating attack from several quarters at once, it was emphasised that everything should be done to avoid litigation.'

In the light of this diktat, it is strange that Sagurna and Huther should have subsequently indulged in their slanderous and absurd letter to Dr Freigang.

'However, the chairman determined that the members in general meeting were of the unanimous opinion that as the result of Dr Freigang's promotion of a rival organisation, his membership should be terminated forthwith. It was also recorded that the majority desired expulsion.'

Unfortunately, on this occasion the figures for the 1987 budget had been sent out in advance and so the chairman proposed to forego a run through. However, some highlights were touched upon, and I was therefore able to get some idea of the scale of DAK/GAC operations.

It was also charged that the committee was not doing enough in the way of press and public relations. Other aid organisations were much more prevalent in the media. It was not enough to rely on attracting donations from address lists. Hundeshagen admitted that private donations had decreased. This was a general trend, linked to general aid-fatigue and not peculiar to DAK/GAC. Media attitude was of paramount importance. DAK/GAC had also adopted a policy of not displaying photographs of the wounded or maimed children. They had an urgent need for prominent spokesmen. Appeals via address lists should not be underestimated, since they produced a higher level of return than public appeals. Furthermore, DAK/GAC always had the advantage, amongst others, of falling back on help from Switzerland and Austria.

Kantel added that the press was not the only yardstick for publicity work. Dozens of promotional events had been organised by the committee. Important groundwork had been done on countless occasions by Dr Freigang, Dr Erös and Frau Müller. Also, on public relations, the committee explained that nothing had been set up yet, but something was due to be done in the coming year. It was a matter of staff capacity.

Returning to the budget, Dr Bernd expressed surprise that the cost of adminstration soared whilst the expenditure on operations declined. The reply of the executive committee was that in the light of experience the figure given for public donations was a cautious estimate. Clearly, it was to be hoped that a higher figure would be achieved.

Admission was also made that the "book figure" for the cost of acquisition of materials for 1987 had been set artificially low, since purchases made in 1986 were still being used.

It was asked if it were permissable in charity law to accumulate and carry forward a "reserve" of the magnitude of DM 1.7 million. Treasurer Huther answered that a "safety reserve" of four months operating costs was in no way exceptional in the light of uncertain revenues and the high level of outgoings and obligations.

However, a sum of not less than DM 400,000 would need to be budgeted for the purpose of medicines in Pakistan. As a general rule it was cheaper to buy medicines in Pakistan than in Germany, especially when transport costs were taken into consideration. This explained the high estimate. Any medicines from Germany should preferably be in the form of donations. As for donated German medicines, the exceptional JU Rottenburg donation, amounting to some DM 1.5 million worth, seems to have escaped the equation. But then, it was never intended that it should appear in the Pakistani books, which only appeared spasmodically, anyway.

'The meeting approved the budget proposals subject to the discussion and amendments.'

Thus, the budgeted figure of DM 1.7 million for four months tends to confirm an annual guesstimate total of around DM 5 million.

Changes in Constitution

Kantel - who by this stage had evidently decided not to resign after all - made an abortive bid to "broaden" the aims and objects under the constitution. It is uncertain what his purpose was, but it may have been to enable a lucrative switch of sights to fresh fields of exploitation, such as Angola, Ethiopia, etc. ... Whatever the motive, the move confirms Dr Freigang's contention that the organisation had become an end in itself. Either as a sop or a blind, a subordinate proposal was injected to 'increase the executive committee to make it more professional and at the same time the honorary advisory body could be seen as a means of attracting prominent spokesmen.'

Herr Lottmann quashed this idea. There was insufficient time to discuss such an important matter properly. Furthermore, any change in aims would require the votes of all members, and it was a proposal unlikely to merit his support.

Kantel tried to backtrack by contradicting the chairman, explaining that the changes proposed were not intended to change the aims themselves so much as the means of achieving the aims, but the members decided that it was out of order to discuss this topic at this meeting.

Some concessions were made, however. The most notable of these were that the joint chief executives of the commiteee (Hundeshagen and Kantel) should have "elevated" positions. It was also agreed, in the light of the exceptionally heavy workload, that they should work from now on as full-time paid executives. This was subject to further ratification. In addition to the President and Vice President, the Treasurer and Press Officer were also to be full-time salaried posts, as all executive committee members were eligible under the new ruling.

[1] Documentation reveals Erös and a second name 'Troy', but there must have been others ...

[2] For 'other major donors' read American (CIA) money.

[3] CIA.

57
The New Director

The thread of the story now leads back to Dr Erös at the time of his stint as Field Director for DAK/GAC at Peshawar - at the time when the Guildford team were on his horizon.

Like Dr Freigang, he had been engaged in a fund-raising 'dog & pony show' of no fewer than forty lectures throughout West Germany in December 1988 and again in March 1989. These generated in excess of DM 5 million, but, increasingly, he found himself at question time in the firing line of 'the Freigang flak'. This referred to questions from the floor about the adverse publicity in the *Der Spiegel* article of October 1988.

Close examination of that article suggests the information was indeed supplied by Dr Freigang. He would certainly have had access to the supporting documentation, nor, indeed, has he ever denied supplying either written or verbal information to *Der Spiegel*. There was only one other, politically motivated conspiracy theory involving Willi Brandt's press officer. But it could have been any one of seventeen people with access to the minutes and an axe to grind, for instance Kakojan Niazi on behalf of Dr Freigang, or von Rosen simply endorsing Dr Freigang.

Relations between the various German charities personnel based in Peshawar were markedly better than the behaviour pattern of the basketful of 'rotten fruit' back home in Germany.

Erös deserves the credit for this. With the exception of the German Afghanistan Foundation, where Freigang and Niazi no doubt had their reasons for keeping their distance, good relations were established with HELP, NOTHILFE and indirectly with *Gesellschaft für technische Zusammenarbeit*, the Overseas Technical Co-Operation Organisation, or German trade organisation, which played such a strongly supportive role whenever required to do so.

However, the German Afghanistan Foundation, not content with keeping itself aloof, determined to fan the flames of dissent by distributing the article from *Der Spiegel* in Peshawar. This included the main Afghan political parties, foreign embassies in Islamabad, as well as all other non-government organisations. Where thought appropriate, English and/or French texts were supplied.

Three independent recipients were able to identify the German Afghanistan Foundation as the source of all this material. It was a short step from identifying Dr Freigang as the 'author' of the article, with too many mentions of his name, to the suspicion that he alone could have supplied so many confidential internal documents, to the conclusion that he alone had most to gain from publication and distribution in Pakistan. It was an action that was to have far-reaching consequences for Reinhard Erös; although he was himself entirely blameless.

Obviously Dr Freigang was no longer in the mood to bury the hatchet in the name of the cause. All attempts by Erös to involve GAS/GAF in joint operations were met with abuse, attempts at domination, and such off-hand behaviour that further rational discussion was rendered impossible.

However, other joint operations were not impeded.

One such example was the joint action taken by Dr Reinhard Erös of DAK/GAC and Dr Lorenz Göser of HELP and Dr von Mallinckrodt of *Nothilfe* to co-ordinate a highly effective all-German cross-border operation.

This is an example of German efficiency at its best.

'Afghan contacts of HELP identified a cholera epidemic at Khost. Thanks to DAK/GAC mechanical and mule transport, Dr Hakenberg of *Nothilfe* and Sister Barbara of DAK/GAC were on the spot within forty-eight hours and succeeded in bringing the epidemic under timely control.'

On the perfidy score, if Erös wanted any further proof he did not have long to wait. He was approached by an English-speaking young Afghan informer, bearing an English language version of the *Der Spiegel* article, which he claimed had been given him by the German Afghanistan Foundation. He was loath 'for security reasons' to divulge any more detailed information - certainly no names.

Not long afterwards, Erös was again visited, by another personable young Afghan of about twenty-five, who this time spoke impeccable German. In a most friendly manner he showed Erös the selfsame article from *Der Spiegel* (presumably in German this time).

He said he would like to suggest that, in the light of certain statements made by Dr Freigang and the comments contained in the article, the DAK/GAC could only be considered forthwith as an enemy of Hesbe-i-Islami. He had therefore called by to suggest that, for personal safety reasons, the DAK/GAC might prefer to shut up shop (i.e. terminate its activities), pack its bags and return to Germany. He specifically meant Dr Erös, his wife and their four small children.

Then in equally gracious fashion, he took his leave.

Erös claimed subsequently to have been so stunned by the visit that he neither noted the man's name nor his provenance. This does not equate well with Erös's military background (GSG9), nor his well-known preoccupation with security, whereby, in common with most other non-government establishments in Peshawar, all visitors were required to identify themselves and sign a visitors' book both on arrival and departure at the *chowkidar*'s checkpoint.

Be that as it may, after consulting his wife Annette and the Bonn office of DAK/GAC, he advised the German Embassy at Islamabad of the incident. Nothing more was heard for the time being, although he continued to feel under threat. What he had failed to identify was the correct quarter from which the threat emanated.

It proved to be the enemy within.

58

Dr Erös under severe Attack

Within three months of Dr Reinhard Erös's appointment as the Field Director (March 1988), Hundeshagen paid an unscheduled visit to Peshawar (June 1988). From that moment on Erös could be in no doubt that 'Denny-boy' was conspiring his downfall with the Rashid brothers. The longer he remained *en poste*, the more monetary irregularities he uncovered. Although most of these could be attributed to the Rashid brothers, some undoubtedly led straight back to Bonn.

In August 1989, he and his family suffered a death blow when their young son died. The family raced to Germany, in an effort to save him, but in vain. On his return to Peshawar, after just one week, Erös succeeded in wrestling financial control of operations from the Rashid brothers. This he achieved in the spring of 1990. From that time on the pressures became seriously heavy.

The executive committee, in the persons of Hundeshagen and Kantel, called Erös back to Bonn for consultations. They then confronted him with accusations of fraud, whilst summarily docking his pay.

Meanwhile, Erös's family had been subjected to severe harassment in Peshawar. Frau Erös and her children were threatened by Mujahedeen brandishing Kalashnikovs! If there was the slightest protest or hint of opposing the orders of the new head of DAK/GAC mission, they were threatened with kidnapping!

The new Field Director was to be none other than Peter Schwitteck, the selfsame 'jolly good fellow' brought to our attention in correspondence by the ever optimistic Dr Veggeberg. It rather looked as if he was nothing more than the henchman of the Rashid brothers, and was busy undoing all Erös's good work and putting control back in the hands of the Afghans.

Life was no longer safe for Annette Erös and her family and on Reinhard's return in June 1990 they had no alternative but to leave for Germany. But with Kantel's habitual litigation to contend with, Erös had to go to court to recover his salary and the loss of his car, a mini-bus engaged primarily for the Kindergarten school run by Annette. Erös obtained financial settlement and clearance of his good name from the false accusations levelled at him. As usual, settlement was out of court.

Nor did the Rashids have everything their own way.

For some time they had enjoyed a very close business relationship with a Pakistani Government official, high up in the Social Welfare Commissionerate for Afghan Refugees: Askar Azam Sahibzada, who was heading up *Gesellschaft für Technische Zusammenarbeit* operations in Peshawar (1996). It was with him that the ARROS transport company had been established to exploit the German donated DAK/GAC fleet of vehicles. He presumably facilitated vehicle registration and eased any problems with tribal areas passes. He is also the most likely candidate to have been called to give 'expert witness' at the Hamburg 'missing vehicles' trial.

The vehicles that were rented out were in a special category, because they had either been purchased tax-import duty free or donated. Whatever the case, what they all had in common was that they were registered in the name of DAK/GAC, with the Pakistani authorities.

No doubt this was the detail that "Scrubber" Stewart-Richardson's eagle eye had lighted on when Ebrahim Rashid had invited him to pay his unwarranted travel bill. It was an enviable little racket. No doubt if Ebrahim Rashid had presented us with a modest invoice for shipping all that Cuban Miami Doctors Medical Team Inc. junk to Chak, we should have been happy enough to settle up and re-invoice Dr Veggeberg. But Ebrahim either knew better or had more sense.

Now and again, the Pakistani official, who came from a well-heeled background stretching back to the days of the Raj, was no doubt able to introduce new business to the ARROS Transport company. It was one such contract that was to blow up in their faces.

Amongst their own, by now out-of-control Hesbe-i-Islami ranks, a renegade band elected to hijack a convoy of ARROS lorries, transporting foodstuffs.

Unfortunately, the Rashid brothers had given their Pakistani protector a financial guarantee against good delivery. In the event they were unable to recover the food, which had been eaten. When put under pressure for a financial settlement in lieu, an unholy row ensued. This escalated into an exchange of 'High Noon' gunfire, during which the 'commander' gunslinger, hired to protect the Rashid brothers, was killed.

At this, one of the Rashid brothers fled to Germany to seek asylum. Could this have been when Khalid decided to get even with Hundeshagen by stealing a kit-bag full of his bright yellow executive toys?

The shoot-out must have curtailed ARROS' activities for a

while. No doubt their Pakistani partner would be keen to come to an accommodation. He would not have wished to see such a lucrative source of income dwindle. No doubt there were other minions for whom the merest trickle would suffice, so long as it did not fail altogether.

As for the help-yourself 'lucky dip' pecking order, you would be hard put to determine which made the bigger hole in the bucket as between Bonn and Peshawar.

After allowing for the funds that never left Germany in the first place, the next glaring anomaly had to be the large throughput of donated medicines. During our visit to the DAK/GAC container warehouse in Peshawar, we were given a figure of fifty tonnes throughput a year. It was perfectly possible therefore that all those medicines so meticulously and generously shipped from Hamburg by Messrs J U Rottenburg, found their way, through several cycles of creative accounting, until they finally settled into the Peshawar and Afghan markets at the retail prices then ruling.

Or simpler still, they would be bought 'locally' in Peshawar with the DM 400,000 earmarked for that purpose. And even when delivered to final point of distribution in Afghanistan, who is to know that they weren't subject to further resale, unless, by chance, there were a rigorous German doctor present to supervise prescription.

A key informant in all this would be the accountant/storekeeper Jan P. Rietz, whom we met fleetingly as our guide. He had been assigned to serve out his Civil (National) Service in this capacity. He could no doubt shed some useful light on this aspect, since he certainly had a firm grip on the throughput figures at the time at the Peshawar end. He was also known to have scant respect for his compatriot bosses and even less for the Afghan 'leaders'.

Any leads he might be able to give to shed light on the Baghlan Refugee Resettlement Programme could only be too helpful and revealing. However, his co-operation was thought to be unlikely. He was known to have been subjected to heavy *Muerta* - a Mafia-style vow of silence - pressure at the time and probably ever since. But truth, happily, will out.

59
Women Help Afghanistan - Indeed!

'Women Help Afghanistan' was just another phoney front organisation which was probably originally conceived to give the GAC/DAK wives something to do, to keep the women busy, happy and interested. It was the *Der Spiegel* article which had exposed its ultimate purpose. It had proved to be just another device for syphoning off funds in whatever direction required whilst masking the true identity of the manipulator.

I had seized the closing down minutes of this, but more as an afterthought, in the hope of slaying the dragon with satire!

Formal notice convening the meeting was sent out in good time to all seven members entitled to attend.

However, at the appointed hour, only the chairperson, Annette Kantel (wife of Dietrich Kantel), and Frau Schlottfeld showed up.

Frau Kantel, realising that she had not got a quorum (of at least three members), deferred the meeting for an hour. In that hour, as luck would have it, she was able to co-opt Denny Hundeshagen to attend "as a guest". By mutual agreement, the meeting proceeded with Frau Kantel in the chair and guest Hundeshagen recording the minutes.

The chairperson having agreed to take the agenda as circulated, attempted to explain the activities and financial report of the committee.

First, mention was made of the misappropriation of some DM 350,000 by the Bad Godesberg lawyer Gotschenberg. This accident occurred when Michael Sagurna had stipulated in his minute of 25 February 1985 that not less than US $750,000 should be transferred to Women Help Afghanistan through the good offices of lawyer Gotschenberg. However, according to Frau Kantel, all was not lost, since the DAK/GAC lawyer Lenke had miraculously "recovered the money." (No mention is made of what he did with it.)

Anyway, there was a major shortfall between the DM 350,000 recovered and the original sum of not less than US$ 750,000 to be accounted for. The chairperson referred to this as 'the transfer of money intended by notary's contract for the benefit of the Solidarity Group for the Rights of Islamic Afghan People.' It looks more like a case of little fleas on bigger fleas.

Until the attempt to discredit it, in the minutes of the meeting of 27 June 1987, two months before this meeting, "Solidarity" was the equivalent tailor-made anonymous conduit set up by Engineer Gulbuddin Hekmatyar to receive the funds dedicated for his use by the Americans, who, in their wisdom, had chosen to channel it via DAK/GAC. It is as if someone felt the need to sound an alarm bell that, after all Michael Sagurna's precautions and admonishments contained in his procedural minute of 25 February 1985, and Thomas Gaida's visit to the Tax Office that week, the money had got no further than the office of some seemingly dodgy solicitor.

The chairperson summarised what had happened to that missing money as follows:

1. Part of the money - DM 200,000 - has yet to be correctly accounted for.

2. Another amount of - DM 100,000 - is not accounted for at all. As was revealed by a tour of inspection of the Afghan border region, the relevant projects never existed.

3. These irregularities prompted the demand for the repayment of DM 350,000 via the lawyers - Lenke and Partners.

4. On 22 July 1987 - less than a month before this meeting - this Women Help Afghanistan Association entered into a contract with DAK/GAC whereby it was agreed that DAK/GAC take over all the rights and obligations of this Women's Association *vis-à-vis* the Solidarity Group for the Rights of Islamic Afghan People; so that the matter could be pursued by their appointed lawyers.

5. It was emphasised that it was of paramount importance that this matter be resolved *out of court* (which tends to suggest that perhaps the money never left Germany?).

The minutes continue: 'After this report, the committee received open unanimous approval!' (From all three of them!)

If that was not enough, on arrival at topic number 4, Any other business, it was minuted:

"It was stated that further matters should not be cleared up before the dissolution of the association."

For the purpose of the dissolution of the association, it was unanimously decided:

a. In accordance with section twelve of the constitution, the chairperson will appoint herself as liquidator. She is free to avail herself of legal help to ensure a correct dissolution of the association. (In the event, she opted for her father-in-law, Willi Kantel.)

b. The benevolent sister association *Humanitarer Informations Dienst* of Bonn, should receive an appropriate sum, in lieu of rent for the use of its office facilities, to be applied to its medical and humanitarian projects in South Afghanistan. (This, of course, was Ahmed Jan's HID.) The amount of this "allowance" is only to be limited by the amount of interest accrued from the funds of the Women's Association and, naturally, after deducting all costs of the latter's liquidation.

"Afterwards" (this may mean "Whatever remains"), under section two, clause nine, of the constitution, the funds of the Women's Association will be transferred to the DAK EV/GAC (EV, *Eingetragener Verein* denotes registered charity status), which will use it for its humanitarian aid.

'The chairperson stated that the above resolutions concerning the dissolution, having received the necessary four-fifths majority according to section ten of the constitution, she hereby declared the association dissolved.' With three members present out of a possible total of seven, this makes for some more original arithmetic. 'She went on to thank those present for their kind attendance and declared the meeting closed at 20.30 hours.' It had taken just half an hour, plus the hour arranging Denny Hundeshagen's 'guest appearance'.

The signatories were
Chairperson and president, Annette Kantel
Minutes, Denny Hundeshagen

The date was 17 August 1987 at Bonn.
This was three days after Dr Freigang's second salvo and final letter of resignation.

*

That, then, just about concludes the exposure of the court papers retrieved so far by me, as a first stab in the dark, as it were. As for proof, what constitutes proof? There is no analysis, there have been no findings. There has been no summary, no final judgement. There probably never was, nor ever will be.

It looked to me very much as if all these papers were assembled and submitted for some civil action, which after it had proceeded for a few days, possibly even a week or two, petered out and was finally settled out of court.

I still had no idea who had brought the action. It could have been any of so many disaffected parties. Or, perhaps, for once they all acted in concert. Whoever it was, was after their fair share of the cake.

If, as contended in the papers, DAK/GAC had been levying a management fee of as much as 50% on all 'outside' funds entrusted to their care, one can't help wondering what the percentage level might have been on monies they raised themselves. It wouldn't have taken much to induce feelings of resentment.

What seems likely to have happened, by as late as 1988, is that the various warring parties would have come to the realisation that any public airing of all this dirty linen could well lead to the demise of the golden goose, which had already begun to lay smaller and smaller eggs.

Once they realised the only way to keep the pump primed and the funds flowing was to shut up and pocket their differences, they must have reconciled themselves, amidst church bazaar and souk smiles, to a concerted German-Afghanistan conspiracy of silence.

As for whatever I thought I could or should do next, I contemplated packing all the papers off to the German Public Prosecutor, but suspected that, with the passage of time, they would only go to join other piles of similar plaintive files in yet deeper dust than I had found them.

Then for some reason my mind cast back to those unacceptably bellicose words contained in Osman Streeter's brilliant advertisement for the Afghan Support Committee, which had had to be suppressed all those years ago, for fear of affecting its charitable status:

'Afghans tend to do horrible things to people who try to steal their country. And you can take it from us that they wouldn't be any kindlier disposed to anyone who purloined funds intended to buy food for their starving children.'

It conjured up Michelangelo's Last Judgement, Sistine visions of ritual mutilation, with Hundeshagen and Kantel carrying their freshly flayed skins over their arms.

In the next fifty years or so, when water may well be more precious than oil or gold, the hordes of Central Asia will be on the move again.

Once more, Afghanistan will feature as the place people pass through on their way to somewhere else. In their train, if not in the vanguard, will be Afghans, who will catch up with the likes of Hundeshagen and Kantel, the Sagurnas and the Todenhofers of this world and mete out to them their just desserts. That is, so long as some of those Afghans already resident in Germany haven't saved them the trouble.

Or, just as much on their doorstep, perhaps some or other amongst those large numbers of individual small German donors, ever mindful of their own post-war sufferings and enraged by the misappropriation of their donations, will rise up and seek retribution from these Kriegsgewinnlers (war swindlers).

No quarter will be given. No time to turn the problem on its head or indulge their hackneyed formula of deceit, distortion, delay and denial, which will only serve to more readily condemn them.

60

A prophet is not without honour save ... in own country and amongst his own people

There was one last avenue left for me to pursue. I was loath to go down it, but I knew it had to be followed to its conclusion. It was the Valderano link. The reason I was so hesitant was because I felt I could anticipate the outcome already. It did not augur well for British complacency.

My mood had been induced partly by a wicked cartoon from the New Yorker. It was a brilliant drawing, instantly recognisable as an aging James Bond (the original Sean Connery version). He was shuffling away in dressing-gown and slippers, with the aid of a Zimmer-frame. There was a redoubtable middle-aged female nurse in attendance in starched uniform - unmistakably Miss Moneypenny. The caption read:

'No, Commander, we are not going to Islamabad, we are going to the bathroom.'

I suppose it is nothing more than the update of an old joke. Every dog must have his day. The 18th Duke of Valderano's day had been long, long ago. It had to be all of twenty years since Michael Ivens had suggested introducing us.

So far as I could remember, Valderano had gained his formidable reputation for insight into terror, insurgency and guerilla warfare alongside the partisans in the north of Italy towards the end of the Second World War. This was before he had assumed his many Italian and Sicilian titles, as they would have been unlikely to cut much ice with the mostly communist *partigiani*. His more prosaic name was Ronnie Waring.

He had gone on to valiant deeds in the early, tense days of the Cold War. This, in turn, had led to his appointment as an instructor at the NATO War College near Lisbon. With the 1974 revolution in Portugal, he was moved on to lectureships in Rome and London, as well as the United States and Brazil. Other countries of special interest to him were Angola, the Congo, Mozambique and Zimbabwe.

At much the same time, mid-1970s, he set up a Research Foundation for the Study of Terrorism. One of my special interests as a consultant to the Boeing Company at that time had been the subject of the hijacking of civil aircraft and that was to have been our common ground. Valderano's Research Foundation was to attract any number of august names but, unfortunately, a lesser enthusiasm for funding.

He had the satisfaction of being chairman of a board, which included Senator 'Little John' John Tower, Sam Cummings, Paul Channon, Nathan Adams and the Archduke Otto von Habsburg, amongst many others from Europe, Latin America, the Far East, Asia and even Africa.

From what I could gather, none of these good people felt the urge sufficiently to put in their own money.

So far as our story is concerned, the next significant milestone came when Sir John Biggs-Davison, M.P., was invited by a 'German Foundation' to attend an Afghan Conference in Munich in order to meet Afghan leaders. Sir John had asked his old friend Valderano to stand in for him.

In the event, he was not much taken with the 'wild and woolly' leaders presented to him. However, he appears to have taken a shine to Kakojan Niazi, who may just have been organising the whole show in the name of the German Afghanistan Foundation, and whom I believed, from the evidence collected in Germany, to have been associated with certain elements of the German fund-raising campaigns.

As to the subject of the conference, Valderano's lecture to Kakojan Niazi had been along the lines of a highly perceptive priorities appreciation.

There was no point in attempting to kill every Russian. They would only send more to fill the live training-ground gaps. Anti-tank weapons weren't going to do the job either. Any tanks knocked out would get replaced with later models. No, their Achilles heel was helicopter gun-ships and, more particularly, their crews. What was needed was ground-to-air missiles, the American-manufactured Stinger and/or the less predictable British Blowpipe. These would tip the scales by reducing Russian air dominance. All this must have been music to Kakojan Niazi's ears. He found that Valderano was not only the answer to the maiden's prayer, but that he was also about to have his prayers answered.

In fairness to Valderano, Kakojan Niazi was already well played in. He was highly experienced. After studying Dr Nassery at close quarters, he had moved on to HELP, followed by his German Afghanistan Committee exposure. He had been around for a long time and had become a familiar figure at conferences ever since 1984 at Geneva.

In all probability, in such a forum, he could have been

introduced to Valderano by somebody of the calibre of a former British ambassador at Kabul, who, as an aside, could well have added his own personal endorsement, to the effect that, in the vituperative Afghan snake-pit, Kakojan Niazi was refreshingly apolitical and had been involved at the sharp end from the very beginning.

Kakojan Niazi would have missed no opportunity to insinuate the names of common acquaintances met at other conferences held in Geneva, London, New York or elsewhere.

Whatever the facts, his credentials were deemed to be beyond reproach. With such a prestigious name and the national flag of Germany flying on the visiting card, who indeed would have the temerity to question them? Let alone make so bold as to ask to meet a fellow German member of the Foundation? Furthermore, Kakojan Niazi spoke excellent German and the Bonn address can only have added to the good impression. He was reading German law and may even have worn a western-style suit, as opposed to the more alarming Afghan garb.

The man filled the need. He was just the type of operator for whom the Anglo-American 'cousins' were on the look out. At the time, he must have been part of an Afghan *élite*, not to be labelled as a political hothead. His sobriety would have stood out amongst all those 'wild and woolly' leaders.

The upshot was that Valderano was sufficiently taken with Kakojan Niazi to invite him to visit him in London. There he would have been wined and dined to death like Pocohontas, by all the right 'OK' people from both Houses of Parliament and, who knows, White's Club itself.

What is certain is that after first introducing him to Sir John Biggs-Davison, Valderano saw fit to introduce him to all and sundry in both Houses of Parliament; he did likewise amongst his extensive connections in the American House of Representatives and the Senate. Then he wrote a letter of introduction to Professor Alan Sabroski, the Director of Strategic Studies at the American Army War College at Carlisle, Pennsylvania.

Since Valderano's purpose was without any doubt to do everything possible to help the Afghans in their efforts to expel the Soviets from Afghanistan, a specific introduction was given for Niazi to meet Senator John Tower. His relevance was as Secretary of Defense, Senate Armed Forces Committee, Washington, D.C.

None of us cares to be told we may have been hoodwinked; and certainly not for eight years by the wily Pathan. The larger the ego, the harder it falls. It was going to need very careful attention.

"Scrubber" Stewart-Richardson was a long-standing member of White's, so I asked him first if he knew Valderano. He did not, but kindly volunteered to look him up in his members' list. He came back to say he thought he might have found him. This could have meant a listing under Waring. Anyway, I gave up on that route and decided on the most direct approach of all - a telephone call. Valderano sounded disarmingly charming. He was sorry to be unable to see me right away. He was just off to Portugal for a couple of months. If there were any papers I wanted him to see, his daughter would be sure to forward them. He would be only too happy to help if he could.

I put together some selected photo-stats of what I thought would be the most interesting prime source material and wrote a covering letter to say I should welcome an introduction to Kakojan Niazi. I could hardly be more direct than that.

I then walked the package round to the address he had given me in Knightsbridge.

As luck would have it (and in these matters, luck matters), the packet was too big for the letterbox, so I rang the bell. Nothing happened for a while. As I was about to try another flat, a voice answered. I stated my business, which was simply to leave an envelope on the hall table. But it was not to be as simple as that.

The Valderano flat was at the very top of the building with no lift. By the time I reached the top, I must have looked ready for a glass of water, but found myself invited to lunch instead by his daughter and Portuguese son-in-law.

Three months later, Valderano invited me to meet him for tea at White's. On arrival, on time, I gave the Ducal title and once I saw it was recognised, my own unadorned name. By now I had some idea what to expect. After all, I had visited his home, indeed met his daughter. Somebody had told me he affected a monocle. I need not have worried for one moment about failing to recognise him in a crowd. We had the whole place to ourselves. Perhaps he knew that this would be the case at such an hour. My impression was of a very tall figure with pebbly black eyes, and no sign of a monocle. He seemed to me to have stepped straight out of an Osbert Lancaster 'Maudie Littlehampton' cartoon, or possibly even earlier, Robert Benchley. His turnout was impeccable and he enunciated very distinctly but rather quietly.

Once he had established my interest in all this, he told me that in all his dealings with Kakojan Niazi, over eight or nine years, he had always found him to be totally honest and reliable. He was a patriot, and, to spell it out, in case it was a word unfamiliar to me, he said he was a man entirely motivated by a desire to help his country.

Latterly, however, he had become so disgusted with the feuding between the various political parties, the corruption and the inability to get the Afghans to work together, that he had given up all his political activities and wanted to have nothing more to do with them. In future, he would concentrate his energies on becoming a businessman, pure and simple.

Valderano found it difficult to believe that Niazi could have benefited in any way from funds destined for the Afghan Resistance. Although he may well have had his extensive travel bills paid, he was by no means flush.

For the record, he believed Kakojan Niazi to be responsible for sending considerable amounts of medical and other supplies to Afghanistan. However, he had told Valderano that a good deal of this was stolen in transit through Pakistan.

In Valderano's judgement, therefore, Kakojan Niazi was an honest and honourable man who did his best under well nigh impossible circumstances. He certainly was able to get some military aid as well as humanitarian aid to the Afghan Resistance.

In closing, Valderano said he was not in the least surprised that some German politicians and perhaps others in Germany and Afghanistan should have helped themselves to relief funds contributed to the Foundation. As he personally had long been convinced of the venality of most politicians, it would have been much more surprising had it been found that nobody had had their hands in the till! Valderano made the gratuitous point that he had had nothing to do with fund-raising himself. Plainly, Valderano was not to be budged in his loyalty to Kakojan Niazi.

I opened up on three initiatives, known to me, which I now supposed embraced Niazi's current field of business activity. The first was a hotel project in Herat, with his 'cousin' Ishmail Khan. I personally regarded this enterprise as unlikely to succeed. The other two were more grandiose still and had been touted round to the British and the Americans. The first was an airfield and, as off-set, there was a promise to discourage the growth of poppies, plus the offer of surveillance facilities to monitor Iran. The other was a dam to control the water supply there. I did add that I had always understood the waters disappeared into the sand anyway on the border!

To this, Valderano said he could see how Niazi could have been duped by German colleagues. He was to some extent naive in business - not being a professional business man, but having had only some training as a lawyer.

As for himself, he told me he had to confess that he was not

Duke of Valderano, Incognito - Viva Zapata!

enormously interested. He was now too old, too ill and too tired to care.

It hardly seemed the time or the place to go on to discuss the German Afghanistan Foundation special fund which had supposedly raised four million Deutschmarks for the stray dogs of Herat. Then there were the tons and tons of old clothes which had been collected all over Germany and were still not accounted for. And the maltreated 'equines' too would have to wait for other, more sympathetic ears.

Valderano was kind enough to say he had enjoyed meeting me and looked forward to reading my book. I asked if he had ever considered writing his memoirs, to which he replied that, since he was neither a seedy politician, nor a pop-star, nor a mass-murderer, nobody would be in the slightest bit interested in publishing them [They were subsequently published as "The Owl and the Pussycat".]

Furthermore he had spent a lifetime cultivating anonymity.

The silence that followed this statement somehow signalled the interview was over. I was left wondering about the purpose of the dukedom. I said nothing, but spotted the blank in his experience. He did not seem to know the Muslim world.

*

Conclusion

In their determination to humiliate the Russians in the manner of Vietnam, the grand irony was that however unwittingly western agencies, (supposedly dedicated to the study and eradication of terrorism) had in identifying and exploiting the Mujahadeen Jihad, opportunity aded and abetted funded and equipped a whole new breed of terrorists. Afghanistan and its foster-child 'Arabistan' spawned all those bombings which have now become such a feature of our daily lives – from Aden to Algiers, Chechnya to Madrid via Luxor, Nairobi, Dar-es-Salaam, all the way to New York.

One man's freedom fighter is the next man's terrorist

In intelligence circles they have a name for it: BLOWBACK.

As ye sow, so also shall ye reap.

My father chastised you with rods, but I shall chastise you with scorpions.

The evil that men do lives after them, the good lies oft interred with their bones.

Fact: 194 US Stinger missiles are still in the hands of radical Islamic militias, once supported by the CIA in its proxy war against the Kremlin, and now America's bitter foes.

Sunday Times August 1, 2004

Fact: only 32 tons of Afghan opium poppies have been seized or destroyed in the past two years from a total harvest of 8000 tons. Police chiefs accuse the government of allowing Afghan heroin to flood Britain

Sunday Times August 1, 2004

Fact: after the murder of one of its volunteers, *Médecins sans Frontières* announced it was pulling out of Afghanistan , claiming that today's context is rendering independent humanitarian aid for the Afghan people all but impossible

The Times August 5, 2004

Appendix

Reprinted from **Der Spiegel**, *Nr 44, 1988*

Purely a Clique

One of the largest aid organizations for Afghanistan, with millions in donations at its disposal, resorts to the law to collect money – from Afghans.

In the remote wastes of the Hindu Kush, commanders of Afghan resistance groups have fixed on a new object of attack. The target in their sights is an aid organization based in Bonn: the German Afghanistan Committee *(Deutsches Afghanistan-Komitee e.V.)* or DAK.

In a three-page letter, the irregular fighters – who for nine years have been resisting the Soviet occupation – threatened that the Committee's supporters could soon be faced with "unforeseeable consequences". This organization, which claimed to be dedicated to humanitarian aid, was (the letter said) interfering increasingly in politics. The DAK was therefore gradually coming to be seen no longer as a friend but as an enemy.

The document was passed to western diplomats and secret services. Its originators – leaders of four different guerrilla groups – maintained that the Committee was promoting one Afghan party only: the Rashid brothers and their political friends, who stand for restoration of the monarchy in the Asiatic country.

The Bonn group that has come under fire is viewed as one of the most significant among more than 20 German associations that work to provide support for Afghanistan. The DAK is alleged to have 30,000 donors behind it and is backed by the American State Department and the German Foreign Ministry. It has an annual budget of between three and five million marks. As much as 1.7 million has been deposited in blocked accounts. A DAK man described this as a "safety device".

Like other Afghanistan organizations, the DAK cares for refugees and resistance fighters; it finances the building of medical centres, delivers medical and pharmacuetical supplies, and works for the resettlement of refugees in Afghanistan itself.

Now the DAK is being talked about in this country too, on account of some dubious transactions and political sleaze.

–A Bonn lawyer appropriated 350,000 marks from donations accumulated in an account earmarked for Afghanistan. The sum has since been returned.

–To camouflage the flow of financial assets, a money-laundering scheme was set up.

–The organization is conducting a legal battle with Afghans over the restitution of at least 300,000 marks. Jürgen Todenhöfer, a member of parliament for the Christian Democrats, is implicated in the affair.

The Rhineland doctor Karl Freigang sees here "self-advancement and the mixing of politics with humanitarian work". Freigang, who has been caring for the wounded in the war zone for four years and belongs to international bodies involved in the region, considers these happenings "outrageous".

While other aid associations welcome all newcomers, the members of this one in Bonn are carefully vetted like those of a golf club for the super-rich. Anyone joining the DAK has to be approved by a two-thirds majority at a members' meeting.

When the Committee was founded in November 1984, it had ten members. Four years later the figure is only just doubled. Some of these comrades-in-arms are interrelated by blood or marriage. The organization, said a Committee man, has "admittedly rather less members than the ADAC" *[Germany's AA, which numbered 8.7 million at the time]*.

Afghans above all are unwelcome in this organization for Afghanistan. Following an amendment to the statutes in 1985, foreigners may not belong to the Committee. The reason? There would otherwise be "in-fighting between political groups".

The exclusive club is headed by two well-paid full-time executives: Denny Hundeshagen who is in the pharmaceutical trade, and the Bonn businessman Norbert Hüther. Insiders maintain that this has made the work "more professional".

The critical Freigang, himself a non-voting board member of the DAK since 1987, sees this as "a means of self-serving". He considers the organization a "purely self-interested clique of friendly families who help each other into cushy positions in other institutions too". Hundeshagen, on the other hand, insists that in reality the disputes are "only about money" and that Afghan support groups fight against each other like the parties in Afghanistan itself.

What is clear is that the DAK is intertwined with a growing network of subsidiary groups with a handful of officials sitting at the controls. Among them are the Bonn-based "Society for the Promotion of Civic Education", which according to Hundeshagen has set itself the task of "fundraising", and the Bonn Peace Forum which is close to the CDU. In 1987 the clique members set up an additional body, the "Foundation for Help in Distress".

The chairman of the last-mentioned body is the Bonn jurist Dietrich Kantel, ex-director of the Peace Forum and founding member of the DAK; he is also on the board of the "Civic Education" society. As sponsor, he picked up the bill for the cost of setting up the Foundation. The post of manager was assumed by DAK Chairman Hundeshagen himself. Five of the nine original members of "Help in Distress" had been present at the launching of the DAK, which naturally supplies the Foundation with money.

To donors, the institutional labyrinth is barely intelligible. Only the notary is in the picture, and *he* sits in the office of Hans Daniels, Mayor of Bonn and a CDU member of parliament.

Other Christian Democrats too, such as Jürgen Todenhöfer (another Bundestag member), play a part in this impenetrable web of organizations. The Federal Minister for Economic Co-operation, Hans Klein of the CSU, has praised the "Help in Distress" foundation for its "face-to-face human initiatives which deserve our support". These initiatives take place especially in Angola, where the Foundation operates in the territory of the Unita guerrillas – the movement which fights against the left-wing government in Luanda, with support from South Africa's apartheid regime amongst others.

When Unita leader Jonas Savimbi visited West Germany in July, the political and other preparations were the work of "Help in Distress". Thus for example it was the Foundation that arranged for Savimbi to see the Chancellor.

Most of the protagonists who wish to support anti-Communists the world over are Christian Democrat Party members or sympathizers. They maintain links with the Nicaragua Society – which sides with the Contras – and the El Salvador Society which backs the government in its fight against the guerrillas.

Many of the DAK's activities are irritating even to its own members. Thus, half way through last year, there were internal disputes about 27-year-old Andreas Goertz – the former GDR detainee who, after the Federal government had purchased his release, returned to the inter-German border to vandalize East German boundary posts with his own hands.

Goertz had gone off to Afghanistan in 1984 under the name of Ahmadjan and fought against the reds for two years with kalashnikov in hand. "I'm a German *Mujahedin* fighter," he said.

In 1986 in Quetta, Pakistan, the DAK appointed him head of the branch of "Help in Distress" which operates there under the name of the "German Humanitarian Service". The DAK managers were too squeamish to set up Goertz officially as their own representative.

To some of them, however, this camouflage device seemed just too transparent. The Committee member Jürgen Lottmann criticized it on the grounds that with a man like that, "the humanitarian character of the DAK will be called into question." Freigang comments: "No one should be surprised then, when political opponents talk of CIA activities."

For a long time now, adherents of the Bonn group have needed to combat the suspicion of being the paid stooges of American interests. One of the DAK's most important supporters is the retired US Major General J.Milnor Roberts. He is chairman of the "Committee for a Free Afghanistan" and president of the "Americans for a High Frontier" society, which pressed for the space armaments programme. It is thanks to Roberts's help that state funding from Washington flows into the DAK coffers – 837,000 dollars during this year alone.

The *Internationale Gesellschaft für Menschenrechte* or IGFM ("International Society for Human Rights") and the far-right Swiss Eastern Institute have also concluded deals for co-operation with the DAK and are paying handsomely. The IGFM counts among its members such such prominent right-wingers as Gerhard Löwenthal who was once in charge of a television current affairs programme. It was Löwenthal and Todenhöfer who unintentionally brought a severe crisis on the DAK.

At the beginning of 1985 the television presenter had repeatedly appealed for donations to the German Afghanistan Committee. The immediate occasion was a visit to the war zone undertaken by Todenhöfer amidst a great deal of PR hype.

Though described by the DAK as a patron, Todenhöfer is not a member of the organization. According to one of his staff, he was "unaware of this patronage until after it had been reported in the press", and then "out of loyalty he didn't reject the role."

Todenhöfer says that as far as he can recall, he approached the DAK with a request that the donations resulting from the television appeal should be shared with the group led by Gulbuddin Hekmatjar, a *Hisbi-i-islami* chief. It was these Hisbis, a fundamentalist group, who had arranged Todenhöfer's visit and were to ensure his safety at the battlefront; one guerrilla lost his life in the process.

In truth the DAK was averse to supporting the Hisbis, as it was sending its donations to the Rashid clan. According to a DAK lawyer, "there was virtually no co-operation between the Hisbis and us, and we wish if possible to have nothing to do with them in future."

Todenhöfer, however, insisted on making the

agreement, since the group was being supported by no one else and "they are close to my heart." For political reasons, however (the DAK lawyer explains), he wished the payments to the fundamentalists to be kept secret. He therefore brought in a laundering service in the shape of "Women for Afghanistan", an association formed for this specific purpose. Its chair was the wife of the multiple office-holder Dietrich Kantel, and members were recruited from the circle of acquaintances of Kantel and Hundedshagen. The ostensible foundation date, 7 January 1985, preceded the real one.

In the presence of a lawyer, the donation strategists agreed that the women's association should pay "at least 750,000 marks for purposes of medical and humanitarian aid" to a "Solidarity Circle for the Rights of the Muslim-Afghan People" – which was close to the Hisbis. The deal was concluded with an Afghan exile who had been living in Bonn for many years. After handing over 300,000 marks, however, the Bonn group refused to pay out any more.

The reason given for this refusal was that evidence of how the money had been used was deficient. The accounting did not "conform to the criteria customary in Germany". Documents furnished later were also queried.

Since then, the parties to the deal have been in bitter conflict. A representative of the Bonn group reported that the DAK in Pakistan had been visited by an Afghan "in the company of a man armed with a Russian automatic kalashnikov. He declared that in future he expected 'payment without any complications'. If the DAK 'made things difficult', it might 'turn out very badly for those responsible for the delay'. With that he pointed to the armed man."

This the Afghans deny. "A cock-and-bull story", says a representative of the Solidarity Circle; the meeting did indeed take place but was "very amicable".

Since the beginning of November, the DAK's fund-allocating practices have been a matter for the courts. The Committee, to which the "Women for Afghanistan" society has bequeathed all its claims, is suing the Solidarity Circle in the Bonn District Court for restitution of the 300,000 marks. The

Afghans have retaliated with a counter-claim for payment of 450,000 marks, and have called CDU deputy Todenhöfer as a witness.

Meanwhile the Afghanistan Committee is clearly perturbed by the affair. Weeks before the case opened, it offered the Hisbi supporters an extra 100,000 marks with "no requirement for accounting or proof of use".

And the association at the centre of the case has ceased to exist: the "Women for Afghanistan" have disbanded themselves. The services of liquidator were performed by one of the DAK family, Willy Kantel, a solicitor from Hagen and father of DAK member Dietrich.

Index

D

E

F

G

Gardez 165, 172, 173, 237, 239
German Afghan Committee 187, 196, 198, 201, 209, 211, 216, 220,
    221, 223-7, 230, 231, 258-61, 323, 325, 328, 346, 348-56, 359,
    379-446, 459-65
Ghazni 233, 251, 261, 418, 419
Giannou, Chris 316, 317
Gorbachev, Mikhail 38, 254, 256
Green's Hotel 63, 72, 74, 76, 95, 96, 257
Guildford 31-3, 40, 43, 45, 47, 49, 55, 56, 60, 65, 69, 77, 80, 81, 88, 100,
    101, 108, 110, 121, 133, 139, 201-3, 207, 211, 271, 329, 333, 340,
    404, 437

H

Hack, Dittmar 36, 153, 185, 342, 344
HALO *see* Hazardous Areas Logistical Organisation
Haq, Fazli 108, 109
Haqquani, Jalaluddin 128-30, 140, 167
Hazardous Areas Logistical Organisation 215, 254, 262, 280, 288-92,
    305-8, 311, 332, 337-43
Hekmatyar, Engineer Gulbuddin 81, 86, 116, 119, 148, 150, 173, 209,
    214, 233, 237, 261, 294, 307-10, 314, 341, 371, 380, 381, 408, 444
HELP *see* Verein Afghanistanischer Flüchtlingshilfe
Herbert, Peter 278, 287
Hesbe-i-Islami 81, 86, 116-9, 122, 172, 173, 213, 214, 235, 236, 241,
    266, 307, 309, 324, 379, 380, 381, 408, 428, 438, 441
Hoffmann, Frau, civil servant 365, 366, 385
Hoffman, Jill 394
Hörst, Andrea 359, 366, 395, 404, 409, 413
Hörstel, Christopher 185
Housaini, Dr Mohammed Nabi 200, 244, 249
Hundeshagen, Denny 216, 218, 258-62, 325, 348, 349, 351, 353, 354,
    359, 363, 364, 382, 397-446, 461
Hurd, Anne 383, 385, 386, 387, 389, 407
Hussein, Dr Sayed Iftikhar, 81, 82, 102-5, 200
Hyder, Dr 296, 297

I

Ibn Sina Balkh Hospital 88, 122, 152
ICRC *see* International Committee of the Red Cross / Red Crescent
International Committee of the Red Cross / Red Crescent 44, 56, 78,
    87, 100, 105, 280, 281, 283, 316-21, 342
Iqbal, 'Doctor' 33, 193, 195, 216, 261
Islamabad 27, 47, 49, 65, 66, 69, 84, 95, 96, 108, 142, 200, 325, 328,
    329, 331, 350, 359, 362, 364, 377, 394, 395, 407, 420, 437, 439,
    448

M

McEwan, Julia 321
McLean, Billy 338
McLeod, Geoff 48, 78, 97, 304
Macmakin, Mary 265, 266, 292, 296-9, 394
Maddoo 246
Mahmood 53, 111, 249
Majrooh 37
Malang, interpreter 125-8, 132, 138, 143, 146, 150, 156, 157, 160, 161, 163, 170-2, 176-8
Manual, GAC 77, 189, 220, 229, 233, 259, 393, 401, 423
Massoud, Ahmad Shah 291, 297, 309
Mazar-e-Sharif 264-281, 289, 294, 297, 298, 300, 316, 325, 326
Médecins Sans Frontières 148, 382, 395, 396, 457
Millikan, Ms 393, 395
Miram Shah 66, 125, 138-42, 145, 146, 148, 154, 170, 173, 175-8, 224
Mitchell, Colonel Colin 215, 253, 288, 291, 332, 337-40, 343
Mohammed Ali 72
Mohammed Anwar 148, 154, 176
Mohammed Jaffar 220
Mohammed Mansur 247
Mohammed Nadir 247
Mohammed Nabi Houssaini 200, 210, 245, 249
Mohammed Shafique 277, 284
Mohammed Youssuf 74
Mojadidi, Dr Najibullah 200, 202
Momand, Dr 46, 90,
Momand, Sadeqi 321, 322
Morrell, William Sydney 36, 37, 39, 66
Moynihan, David Patrick 35
Mujahedeen 31, 34, 38, 83, 103, 104, 116, 126, 147, 152, 153, 159, 162, 165, 166, 168, 173, 178, 188, 199, 200, 209, 213, 219, 229, 230, 233, 236, 237, 239, 249, 251-3, 255, 258, 259, 291, 314, 319, 341, 368, 377, 378, 380, 388, 398, 423, 424, 431, 432, 440
Müller, Maria 383, 397, 401, 406, 408, 409, 414, 415, 432, 434
Müller, Michael 188, 207, 208, 228, 244, 328, 401, 418, 429

N

Nangahar 224, 231, 317, 320, 325, 329, 383, 419, 426
Narmgui, Dr. 290
Nassery, Dr Totyalay 362, 363, 373-7, 381, 449
Niazi, Kakojan 225, 349, 361-63, 368, 369, 373-6, 378, 382, 391, 397, 398, 404, 437, 449-52

For Exemplary Humanitarian Service

We proudly acknowledge

Rupert Chetwynd

for your sacrificial efforts to provide healing and with that hope, to those men, women and children suffering through "the worst medical situation in the world" in Afghanistan.

Presented March 26, 1988
on behalf of the City of Houston
and State of Texas

Kathy Whitmire
Mayor Kathy Whitmire

Charles Wilson
Congressman Charles Wilson

Sponsored by Town & Country Mall and Horizon Galleries

CPSIA information can be obtained at www.ICGtesting.com
Printed in the USA
LVOW10s0759061213

364159LV00001B/12/A